The Nation's Cause

The Nation's Cause

French, English and German poetry of
the First World War

Elizabeth A. Marsland

London and New York

First published 1991
by Routledge
11 New Fetter Lane, London EC4P 4EE

Simultaneously published in the USA and Canada
by Routledge
a division of Routledge, Chapman & Hall, Inc.
29 West 35th Street, New York, NY 10001

Typeset by Ponting–Green Publishing Services, London

Printed in Great Britain by T. J. Press (Padstow) Ltd,
Padstow, Cornwall

British Library Cataloguing in Publication Data
Marsland, Elizabeth A.,
    The nation's cause : French, English and German poetry of the First
World War.
1. Poetry in European languages – critical studies
I. Title
809

Library of Congress Cataloging in Publication Data
Marsland, Elizabeth, A.
    The nation's cause : French, English and German poetry of the First
World War / Elizabeth A. Marsland.
    p.   cm.
Includes bibliographical references.
1. War poetry–History and criticism.   2. War poetry, English–History.
and criticism.   3. War poetry, French–History and criticism.   4. War poetry,
German–History and criticism.   5. World War, 1914–1918–Literature and
War.   I. Title.
PN1083W37M37 1991   809.1'9358–dc20 90–32947

ISBN 0 415 05460 5

Jacket illustration: *Europe, 1916. 'Am I not yet sufficiently civilised?'* Repro-
duced by permission of the Mary Evans Picture Library.

For Tony, with thanks

Contents

Preface   ix

Acknowledgements   xi

1   They all write poetry: the poems and their context   1

2   Heilig Vaterland: nationalism and national image   33

3   We serve you best: the promoting of mass heroism   70

4   Cruel thy sword: the war against words   104

5   Laissez-les donc dormir: protest against the heroic ethic   133

6   A few alone: readers, non-readers and protest   156

7   Men would gather sense: non-propagandist poetry of combatants   191

8   Relics for the present: poems and history   219

Notes   241

Bibliography   261

General index   272

Index of poems   277

Preface

Unlike most previous studies of First World War poetry, which deal with the verse of a single language and which focus, for the most part, on a few select poets, the present undertaking is concerned with the poetry as an international corpus. It is an attempt to describe the characteristics of the poetry as a whole, to explain its existence, and to indicate how the ideas and feelings that inspired the poems are linked to the attitudes that determined the conduct of the war. Because the poetry is viewed as a social as well as a literary phenomenon, value-judgement has been set aside almost totally. The study is based on the reading of a very large quantity of verse in three languages, English, French and German. Ideally an international study of the war poetry would encompass works from all the combatant countries, but because minor poems are rarely translated, and because the context of publication is an important factor, I have limited the scope to the languages with which I am closely familiar. English translations of all French and German quotations from poems are provided in brackets in the text, in such a way that readers unfamiliar with the other languages may simply omit the original. Prose quotations are in English, with the original version in a note.

The study resulted from many years of research. In addition to my predecessors in the field, without whose work First World War poetry might have disappeared completely, I wish to thank the numerous friends and colleagues who have taken an interest in my project. They include, amongst many others at different times and in various places, Peter Schubert, Edith Gruber, Barry Mills, Alison Scott Prelorenzos, Isobel Mailloux, M.V. Dimic, E.D. Blodgett, Colin Veitch, Muriel Whitaker, Mark Salopek and Keith Wikeley. Catherine Reilly has given me the benefit of her extensive knowledge about minor war poets, and Dr G.A.E. Parfitt read an early version of the manuscript and made very helpful comments. My friend 'Clarkus' kindly provided accommodation in London, and the Rickard family in Birmingham. The assistance is appreciated of the staff of the Imperial War Museum

Reading Room, of the Language and Literature Department in the Birmingham Public Libraries, especially the head of the department, Nesta Jenkins, and of the University of Alberta libraries. Above all, I thank Paul A. Robberecht for his constant encouragement and judgement since the project was first conceived many years ago.

I would also like to take this opportunity to express my gratitude to my family: my mother, whose choice of bedtime stories included 'The Battle of Blenheim' and 'The Burial of Sir John Moore at Corunna'; my father, who likes to question the accepted view; my children, who have become pleasant and reasonable adults despite their mother's preoccupation with First World War poetry throughout much of their childhood; and my husband, who has helped and supported me in innumerable ways – not least by persuading the computer to behave properly. Without their encouragement, this project would not have been completed.

Acknowledgements

Extracts from poems by Siegfried Sassoon are reprinted with the permission of Mr George Sassoon, and a letter from Elsie Mewis is quoted with approval of the language and literature Department, Birmingham Public Libraries.

They all write poetry
The poems and their context

'They all write poetry, and recite it with gusto to any three hours' old acquaintance. We all write poetry too, in England, but we write it on the bedroom washstand and lock the bedroom door and disclaim it vehemently in public.'[1] Charles Sorley's purpose when he wrote those words in June of 1914 was to emphasise difference – to contrast the friendly confidence of his German associates at the University of Jena (a confidence which, despite his slightly mocking tone, he admired) with the characteristic reserve of the English. But his comment also serves as an indicator of a major similarity: a shared taste amongst young people for writing verse. When war broke out later in the summer, though it disrupted many aspects of social life (including the walking tour on which Sorley had by then embarked in the Moselle valley), it did not apparently disturb the flow of poetry. On the contrary, not only did the kind of people to whom his 'all' refers continue to write, but they were joined by many more who became poets for the occasion. Nor was the output confined to the young and well-educated, or to England and Germany; and in this moment of crisis even the English admitted to their secret vice and offered their work for publication. The result is an international literary corpus of uncommonly large proportions, marked by sometimes astonishing cross-cultural homogeneity; a corpus, moreover, which is tied so unusually closely to the period of its origin that the poetry is rarely mentioned without the epithet 'First World War' or 'Great War', even when the reference is to a single poet. Although, as Michael Hamburger maintains in *The Truth of Poetry*, it is often difficult in the modern age to distinguish war poems from any other kind, 'since peace has become a sequence of limited wars, either political or military', the Great War poetry is so thoroughly impregnated with the spirit of its period, so totally 'possessed by war' (to borrow from Simone Weil's description of the *Iliad*), that it is for the most part quite distinctive.[2]

In the three languages with which I am concerned, English, French and German, the number of published volumes far exceeded the output of the prewar years, despite the poetic 'renaissance' from about 1910 onwards that is reflected in Sorley's remark. The 1921 catalogue of a war-poetry collection donated to the Birmingham Public Libraries lists 1,200 different titles of anthologies and individual volumes in English and over 200 in French; Jean Vic's bibliography (1927) of wartime publications in French includes about 250 poetry titles, of which only half overlap with the Birmingham collection; and Julius Bab's bibliography of German poetry of the World War (1920) lists some 450 individual works, but leaves out many others, as well as the numerous anthologies, broadsheets, and newspaper and magazine poems. The German book trade catalogue for the years 1915–19 has well over 1,000 entries in the category 'World War: Poems', including, amazingly enough, six collections of 'Inscriptions on Railway-Carriages, Dug-Outs, and the Like' – graffiti, no less.[3] None of these lists takes into account material that may have been written during the war but published later than, say, 1920, but a recent bibliography of First World War poetry in English compiled by Catherine Reilly includes the names of over 2,000 writers. The Birmingham library also holds several large scrapbook volumes of war poems clipped from newspapers and magazines, many of them never reprinted. Julius Bab, who set out in August 1914 to compile an anthology of the best German poems that the war had inspired so far, calculated that 1,5000,00 were written in that month.[4] He probably overestimated, but even so his claim to have received 'as the relatively harmless editor of an anthology of war poems' an average of forty submissions a day, indicates that a very large amount of poetry was being produced.[5] (An anonymous poet replied in verse, regretting his lack of skill, because otherwise, he said, he would write 'Nummer / Einmillion-fünfhunderttausendeins'–Number 1,500,001.)[6]

By its very existence this enormous body of texts begs a multitude of questions. Why, in the first place, did so very many people throughout Europe feel a need to write about the war, whether to voice their patriotic fervour, to protest their country's involvement, or to express publicly their grief or longing? And why was verse such a popular medium, not only with writers but also with publishers and, one must assume, the reading public? The role of newspapers in circulating the poetry is an intriguing topic in its own right; it is hard to imagine popular newspapers at present assuming that their readers would appreciate a new poem every day. As one begins to look at individual poems from a wide range of sources, especially when the perspective is international, their homogeneity within categories is remarkable. That the response of English and German combatants describing the conditions of their life at the Front might have a common dimension is perhaps not surprising, in view of the physical proximity of the opposing forces; but how does one account for the even more striking international similarity amongst poems by civilians, in circumstances where influence across national boundaries was minimal? Equally fascinating, how can one explain some startling anomalies, such as that which distinguishes most Belgian patriotic poetry from any other, including French, or the overwhelmingly English preference for anti-heroic deaths? And behind all these lie the questions raised by the poetry's unavoidable historicity: the many and complex links between the texts and their period of origin, the implications of this relation-ship in terms of literary theory and methodology, and the potential value of the poems as evidence of social attitudes in general.

All literary works are a product of their age, if only in the sense that the language and literary conventions they employ are engaged at a specific moment of development, a moment that, in turn, is given a degree of permanence by the work in question. Many writers seek to escape their historical bond (and on occasion the importunity of civilian or military authorities) by addressing their contemporary concerns obliquely, through a classical or archetypal subject. Others, however, choose to deal in a direct way with contemporary events or the social situation, locating their work deliberately and firmly in its own period. The most obvious examples lie in the realm of narrative fiction, though drama, too, especially comedy, is often concerned with immediate social realities. Lyric poetry, on the other hand, with its tendency to focus on the self rather than on society and on private rather than public topics, has the reputation of being the least socially-committed of modern genres. Yet this perception is not verified by literary history, for many well-known writers in the past have used their verse to comment on contemporary affairs – Bertran de Born and Walther von der Vogelweide in the Middle Ages, Dante and Petrarch, German poets of the Thirty Years' War such as Andreas Gryphius and Johannes Rist, Pope and Coleridge in England, and Whitman in the United States, to select arbitrarily from amongst many possibilities. There is also a strong tradition of social and political verse at the popular level. Nevertheless, although much of this writing is concerned with war or extreme political strife, nowhere before 1914 does one find such a large and international body of poetry so firmly implanted in a specific historical context as that which the Great War inspired.

That moment in history prevails in poems by combatants, through descriptions of the extraordinary world of reality that they encoun-tered, and through the recurrence of technical terms like 'whizz-bang' and 'salient'. The awareness that the poems relate to actual experience – to the suffering, boredom, and occasional amusing interludes in the writer's life at the Front – is often an important factor in determining the reader's response. History prevails, too, in civilian verse replete with names such as Louvain and Emden, Kitchener and Cavell, which may signify little now, but which obviously carried a considerable weight of meaning to contemporary readers, and it is evident also in the special vocabulary of archaic expressions familiar to an audience well-versed in nineteenth-century medievalism. A modern reader might be forgiven for assuming that the phrase 'You have lost your spurs!' conveys a piece of helpful (though possibly unusual) information; the poet's contemporaries undoubtedly recognised it as an accusation of dishonour. Similarly, those earlier readers apparently saw nothing incongruous in the picture evoked when words like 'Wir tragen den Kaiser auf ehernem Schild' (We are carrying the Kaiser on a bronze shield), or 'Knight of the tarnished mail' are applied to a modern personage (in this case, the German emperor). The accommodation to a contemporary audience is also evident in the propagandist nature of much of the writing, whether the poet's inclination was for or against involvement in the war, and many of the poems cannot be appreciated now without making allowance for the political and social situation that prevailed at the time.

Form, too, reflects to an unusually large degree the historical moment. The war coincided with a point in the development of poetry where old conventions were being challenged seriously by extreme technical innovation, most notably the abandoning of traditional rhyme, metre and normal (though poetic) syntax. The Imagistes in England, including Ezra Pound, Richard Aldington, and T. E. Hulme, had been active from at least 1910; the various Expressionist groups in Germany began to publish about the same time; and in France, where *vers libre* was already several decades old, Apollinaire's Futurism nevertheless found ways of being revolutionary. For poets such as these, and for readers similarly interested in formal experimentation, the war may have seemed to offer proof of the inadequacy of traditional technique in dealing with modern reality, while the writers' radically new experience undoubtedly encouraged their concern with technical innovation. The verse of August Stramm, for instance, is indisputably a product of what has become known as Modernism. The opening of 'Haidekampf' (Battle on the heath) is typical:

Sonne Halde stampfen keuche Bange
Sonne Halde glimmt stumpfe Wut
Sonne Halde sprenkeln irre Stahle
Sonne Halde flirrt faches Blut.[7]

(Sun slope stamp gasping fears Sun slope gleams dull rage Sun slope speckle stray swords Sun slope flickers many-fold blood.)

The scene here is not necessarily modern, for this picture of a bloody hillside in the relentless sun calls to mind a representation of a battle in the American West – Custer's troops at the Little Big Horn, perhaps – rather than the more usual image of the First World War with its mud and shell-holes. At first glance the format, too, may appear traditional, since the opening quatrain evinces a regular pattern in both rhyme and metre. What makes these lines distinctively modern is Stramm's adaptation or disregard of the normal rules of syntax, so that, for instance, the adjective 'bange' (fearful) becomes a noun, and is in turn personified, while the verb 'keuchen' (cough or gasp) takes on the role of an adjective. The effect of this revision of the language is a unique merging of sensory impression and emotional response. It is hard to imagine any earlier conflict producing a poem like this, or even like Georges Sabiron's more readily comprehensible 'Haï-Kaï' (Haiku):

Trous d'obus où cinq cadavres
Unis par les pieds rayonnent,
Lugubre étoile de mer.[8]

(A shell-hole where five corpses, their feet together, form a macabre starfish.)

The special character of Sabiron's poetic response to the war lies in neither compassion nor realism, the two features most commonly identified with the poetry of First World War combatants, but in a sense of detachment and impersonality, of a predominant concern with precision of poetic form and image. This concern is the essence of the new literary movement, especially in English and French, and Sabiron's poem is fully in keeping with the principles of Imagisme outlined by Pound and F.S. Flint.

On the whole, however, experimental writing was not common, and by far the majority of war poets adhered to conventional rhyme, metre, and poetic syntax. Such an inclination towards the traditional should not necessarily be considered significant – as evidence, for example, of the withdrawal into conservatism that tends to accompany national crises; one should rather bear in mind that most of the poets, amateurs as they were, were unfamiliar with experimental techniques. Nor should one assume that the division between traditional and innovative forms is concomitant with acceptance or rejection of the Establishment position *vis-à-vis* the war itself. In fact, much of the highly experimental verse, like 'Haï-Kaï', is not explicitly propagandist, while conversely many protest poets use entirely

traditional techniques. Yet there is little doubt that the conflict between
pro-war and anti-war factions hastened the demise of nineteenth-
century poetic conventions, when it disestablished amongst the young
literati after the war the social attitudes that traditional verse had
expressed *pro patria*. Indeed, even the relatively modern Symbolist
poets in France were to be rejected, as Philippe Audoin explains with
reference to the Surrealists:

> The majority of the writers whom these young people [the Surrealists]
> had admired in their adolescence had more or less lent their pen to
> the service of 'the war effort'. . . . The future Surrealists had no
> intention of prolonging a movement of which the most prominent
> representatives had compromised themselves so seriously through
> their dedication to war.[9]

Although such tension between traditional and modern conventions
is undoubtedly more evident with hindsight, it nevertheless marks
the war poetry, for modern readers at least, as a product of its age.

The link between poetry and period is emphasised by the close
association between individual poems and the context in which they
were published. Under normal circumstances, readers of literary texts
are hardly conscious of the format of publication. They may perhaps
notice the cover-design of a novel, or occasionally become irritated by
the quality of print; or they may associate a short story with the
magazine in which they first read it, or link a poem with a favourite
anthology. On the whole, however, the reader tends to assume that
the text exists regardless of the precise context in which it is
encountered, and to regard the format of publication as irrelevant.
(Publishers, of course, are well aware of the importance of context.) In
this respect, too, the First World War poetry is unusual, for the
context had and still has a significant effect on the reader's expecta-
tions and response. Thousands of the poems were first published in
popular daily newspapers, where they reflected or reiterated the
paper's political stance – rampantly chauvinistic in the *Daily Mail* or
the *Tägliche Rundschau*, for example, and perhaps a little more subdued
in *The Times* or the *Frankfurter Zeitung*. Others appeared in news-
papers and magazines with an anti-war leaning – and consequently
with a much more limited circulation – while a small number were
apparently refused publication altogether by censorship boards until
after the war. Even when poems are reprinted in later anthologies,
with the result that the modern reader no longer encounters them in a
wartime format, the location and date of earlier publication are often
supplied by the editor. And if one comes upon a First World War
poem for the first time in, say, an anthology called *Poems of War
Resistance* (a product of the period of the Vietnam War, published in

the United States in 1968), one's response is largely predetermined – one reads it as a poem of protest. But less obvious editorial 'asides' remain similarly important. All except the most text-centred reader must have difficulty in ignoring such comments as 'Died 1 July, 1916' or 'Drei Tage vor seinem Tode geschrieben' (Written three days before his death), or the sadly recurrent black-framed announcements, in the pages of the magazine *Die Aktion*, of the death of yet another talented young contributor. In reading through Vera Brittain's *Poems of a V.A.D.* one senses, not so much in the poems themselves as behind them, the despair of this young woman hearing about the deaths, one after the other, of the young men who were her contemporaries, including her fiancé and her brother. What Joy Cave says in connection with her research into an incident involving a Newfoundland regiment during the war – that the tears intervene in one's attempt to be objective – is equally applicable to the war poetry.[10]

In addition to their role as contexts, the books in which the poetry was published still have considerable appeal as historical artifacts. With the exception of a few anthologies, they are mostly small, thin volumes, often soft-covered, many in pocket-sized editions for use by 'the troops'. Some are clearly the inexpert and inexpensive work of amateur printers, while others are elaborately laid out, a few even gold-edged, with every poem set in an ornate border. Illustrations range from sturdy, sword-wielding Britannias to Expressionist woodcuts of ruined towns, droopy art nouveau ladies taking leave of their knights, and apocalyptic representations of War or Death, after the manner of Dürer. Collections of poems by combatants are often illustrated with a photograph of the author in uniform. Many covers are embellished with epigraphs or lengthy subtitles; *A Crown of Amaranth*, for example, has both, printed in silver on a blue ground. Its splendid subtitle reads, 'Being a Collection of Noble Poems to the Memory of the Brave and Gallant Gentlemen Who Have Given Their Lives for Great and Greater Britain, MCMXVII'. (Roman numerals are clearly more dignified than Arabic.) The subtitle of *Deutschland, Deutschland über alles* is scarcely less imposing: 'Ein vaterländisches Hausbuch für jung und alt zur Verherrlichung deutscher Heldenkraft und Herzensgüte, deutscher Kultur und Wesensart' (A Patriotic Book for the Family, for Young and Old, in Celebration of German Heroic Strength and Goodness, German Culture and Way of Life). A small Australian work called *My Friend, Remember! Lines Written on Reading Lissauer's Chant of Hate* was designed as a Christmas card, though the words 'Season's Greetings' on the cover hardly seem commensurate with the malevolence of the contents – a translation of Ernst Lissauer's notorious 'Haßgesang gegen England' (Song of Hate against

England) and an equally belligerent poem in response. Many volumes of patriotic verse advertise that proceeds will go to a particular worthy cause, including the Red Cross, which, ironically enough, is supported by the sale of adamantly chauvinistic books from both sides.

From the point of view of context, there is also an unexpected bonus in the special interest of individual volumes. Dated inscriptions abound, and authors' signatures are no rarity, though probably few writers went so far as to send an inscribed copy to the President of the United States, as a French soldier-poet, Alfred Droin, did. (One wonders how President Wilson responded; admittedly the book, now housed in the Library of Congress, does not look well-thumbed.) The University of Alberta's first edition copy of *Cinquante-Quatre*, a collection of verse about the exploits of the 54th Squadron, Air Force Corps, contains the signatures of nineteen squadron members; in a newspaper clipping pasted inside the front cover two of those men are listed as missing. Was the original owner perhaps a member of the squadron, and the clipping a memorial to his friends? Mudstains on a copy of the German anthology *Heil, Kaiser, Dir!* held by the Imperial War Museum in London raise similar speculation about the book's history. Was it, as one is tempted to assume, found in the trenches? And if so, what became of the German soldier who had owned it? (The book came to the library as a private donation after the Second World War.) The typescript of a single poem called 'The Mother's Son', in the same museum, is a sociological document in its own right. By most critical standards the poem would be dismissed as completely worthless, yet the fact that it was typed up and submitted to the museum implies that it was treasured by the writer (an army private) or his family, suggesting, perhaps, that literacy was a relatively new phenomenon amongst them. The context is indeed, as Jon Silkin asserts, 'an inescapable impingement' when the printed text arouses such an extraordinary affinity not only with the writer but with specific earlier readers.[11]

In general, poetry reading is a 'timeless' occupation, in the sense that, in Virginia Woolf's words, 'The poet is always our contemporary'. In view of the many bonds that tie Great War poetry to its historical period, one might be tempted to question its worth to a modern audience. Yet contrary to the prognostication of Sir Henry Newbolt, who observed in 1924. 'I don't think these shell-shocked war poems will move our grandchildren greatly', succeeding generations have obviously found something of value in the work of poets such as Wilfred Owen, Siegfried Sassoon, Isaac Rosenberg, René Arcos and August Stramm.[12] Possibly their appeal lies in the continuing importance of their message about war in a world where the threat of an ultimate conflict has been omnipresent, and where still, as Franz Pfemfert observed in 1914, 'Chauvinism is humanity's lasting danger', or perhaps it rests in the fact that

> Whatever mourns when many leave these shores;
> Whatever shares
> The eternal reciprocity of tears,

is, as Wilfred Owen's lines suggest, a constant.[13] But no matter what the reason, a small number of First World War poems, especially in English and German, are established as part of the literary canon of the respective languages. The rest reveal varying degrees of artistic talent, though even amongst minor works one often encounters a line or phrase of verse that can still speak to readers no longer attuned to the conventions and facts of history. Furthermore, many war poems of considerable literary merit are now very little known – amongst them Arnold Ulitz's 'Gasangriff' (Gas Attack), Marc Larreguy de Civrieux's 'Debout les Morts!' (Let the Dead Arise), Margaret Sackville's 'Quo vaditis?' and Ludwig Bäumer's more difficult 'Dämmerung im Graben' (Dusk in the Trenches). Recent anthologies like Brian Gardner's *Up the Line to Death* (1964), Jon Silkin's *The Penguin Book of First World War Poetry* (1979, 1981), Thomas Anz and Joseph Vogl's *Die Dichter und der Krieg: Deutsche Lyrik, 1914 bis 1918* (1982), and Catherine Reilly's *Scars upon my Heart* (1981), or earlier collections such as *Les Poètes contre la guerre* (1920), Bertram Lloyd's *The Paths of Glory* (1919) and *Poems Written during the Great War* (1918), and Franz Pfemfert's *1914–1916* (1916) all contain a substantial amount of poetry that deserves to be kept alive, for both its technical adeptness and the importance of its collective message.

The willingness to read First World War poetry assumes a mind prepared to stray beyond the confines of so-called 'great' writing, for amongst the writers who are at present most commonly designated as the major poets of the time in the languages in question – Yeats, Rilke, Eliot, Trakl, Valéry, Claudel and Apollinaire – only the last two contributed significantly to the field. Although Trakl is by reputation a poet of the First World War, the connection is mainly biographical, for he composed only three poems between the beginning of the war and his death in November 1914. While one can appreciate why Dominic Hibberd and John Onions suggest that Eliot's 'The Waste Land' should be considered a First World War poem, it is much more essentially a product of the postwar period – inspired by the after-effects of war, rather than by the war itself. Rilke's contribution to the category is limited to his 'Fünf Gesänge, August 1914', and Valéry's wartime poetry seems to have been quite untouched by contemporary events. Although Yeats declined in verse the invitation to write a war poem, preferring, he said, to leave war to the politicians, he actually produced several that may be considered a response to some aspect of the conflict, including the highly political 'Easter 1916'. Nevertheless, in the context of a study devoted to First World War poetry, few of these writers are likely to receive more than passing attention.

Fortunately, not all literary scholars are dedicated to the exclusive pursuit of famous names, and over the past three decades some authors known primarily for their poetry about the war have become accepted in all but the most fastidious critical circles. In English, at least, a number of these poets have received considerable attention. After about 1920, interest in most of the English war poetry faded rapidly, and remained at an ebb for several years. A minor revival in the 1930s, coinciding with a strong resurgence of other kinds of war literature, produced at least two new anthologies, Frederick Brereton's *An Anthology of War Poems* (1930) and Frederic Ziv's *The Valiant Muse* (1936), as well as more complete editions of the work of Wilfred Owen, Edmund Blunden, Isaac Rosenberg and Siegfried Sassoon, some of the most respected English war poets. The more recent revival in critical interest dates from the mid 1960s, though with two notable predecessors. D.S.R. Welland's work throughout the 1950s, culminating in *Wilfred Owen: A Critical Study* (1960), was invaluable in breaking trail, but unfortunately Welland's suggestion that poetic response to the war falls into three categories, not merely the 'pro-war' and 'anti-war' positions one might expect, was not taken up immediately. The first general study, Edmund Blunden's 1958 British Council booklets *War Poets, 1914–18*, set the dichotomy pattern that most critics have followed until recently.

Since the mid 1960s, many biographical and critical studies of individual poets have emerged, as well as several full-length works of criticism dealing with the poetry in general. J.H. Johnston's deliberately provocative *English Poetry of the First World War* appeared in 1964, and still rouses a desire to defend the poetry against the critic's attacks. Bernard Bergonzi's *Heroes' Twilight*, which discusses prose writers as well as poets, was published in 1965, and Jon Silkin's politically committed *Out of Battle* in 1972. Paul Fussell's 'Inquiry into the Curious Literariness of Real Life', *The Great War and Modern Memory*, published in 1975, deals with the poetry *inter alia*, and offers an interesting and radically different perspective. In addition to new editions of the work of individual poets, including Ivor Gurney and Charles Sorley as well as the more established figures, there are several modern anthologies. I.M. Parsons' *Men Who March Away* (1965) and Brian Gardner's *Up the Line to Death* (1964), in both of which the poems are grouped thematically, aim to convey the story of the poets' changing attitudes, while Jon Silkin in *The Penguin Book of First World*

War Poetry concentrates on the work of a few outstanding writers. Observing that a substantial number of war poets were women, yet that almost none are represented in modern anthologies or mentioned in criticism, Catherine Reilly compiled a selection of women's poems of the Great War, published in 1981 under the title *Scars upon my Heart*.[14] More recently, Dominic Hibberd and John Onions have edited an anthology, *Poetry of the Great War*, that represents more fully than earlier works (except perhaps Reilly's) the wide range of poems available to wartime readers. Because Hibberd and Onions have adopted a broader perspective, and have concerned themselves closely with the dates of writing and original publication, they have called into question several of the tenets upon which the English criticism has until recently been based.

In France, where the tendency for literary scholars to adhere to the accepted canon of major writers is extremely strong, the war poetry appears to have been ignored almost totally by critics, apart from a few magazine articles written before about 1920. Only that by people known for their earlier or later work has received more than passing reference, and even in the case of famous writers their war poetry is usually dismissed as unimportant, with the single exception of Apollinaire. There were a few postwar anthologies, such as the five-volume *Anthologie des écrivains morts à la guerre* (1924) and *Les Poètes contre la guerre* (1920), but very little of the poetry has been reprinted, and some of it, including part of Pierre-Jean Jouve's wartime writing, was actually suppressed by the author. The only indication of modern interest in the French war poetry, beyond the few poems that have appeared in international anthologies, lies in the reissuing of Jules Romains' *Europe* (1960) and Marcel Martinet's Les *Temps maudits* (1975), and in the fact that the *Unanimistes* – a group of writers associated with Romains, including the war poets Georges Duhamel, René Arcos, Charles Vildrac and Georges Chennevière – have attracted some scholarly interest.[15]

With regard to the German poetry, a revival is now apparently under way, after many years of neglect. During and immediately after the war the poetry received some critical attention, instigated to a large degree by Julius Bab and the journal *Das literarische Echo*. Bab edited a series of twelve anthologies, all under the title *1914: Der deutsche Krieg im deutschen Gedicht*, between September 1914 and 1919. His intention was to offer reprints of poems already published in newspapers and magazines, but he was soon the unwilling recipient of many original contributions. He also wrote critical articles for *Das literarische Echo*, and compiled a bibliography, *Die deutsche Kriegslyrik, 1914–1918*. The latter was published in 1920, augmented with reprints of the articles and short chapters on the work of individual poets.

Interest in the German war poetry was revived in the 1930s, partly from the stimulus of recently-published novels like Remarque's *Im Westen nichts Neues* (well known in English as *All Quiet on the Western Front*), but also through the influence of National Socialism. Rather surprisingly, the period immediately before the Second World War reveals a concern with the work not only of the German poets, but also of those in France and other countries. Ernst Hardt translated a selection of 'Gedichte von gefallenen Franzosen aus dem Weltkrieg' (Poems of French soldiers who died in the World War), printed in *Neue Rundschau* in 1939, and the same year saw the publication of W.J. Hartmann's book *Sie alle fielen: Gedichte europäischer Soldaten* (They all died in battle: Poems of European soldiers), consisting of translations into German of First World War poems by writers from seven countries. Although *Sie alle fielen* contains no anti-war poems, it is also lacking in the most fervently patriotic type – and that, in the Germany of 1939, was perhaps a protest in itself, at least as far as the German contributions are concerned. The absence of anti-war poems is felt more strongly in Ernst Volkmann's *Deutsche Dichtung im Weltkrieg*, published in 1934 in the political section of the Reclam series 'Deutsche Literatur . . . in Entwicklungsreihen'. 'Poetry by the opponents of war' was excluded as a matter of explicit policy from this otherwise very perceptive and carefully annotated anthology.[16] Herbert Cysarz was apparently more impartial in the paragraphs devoted to poets in *Zur Geistesgeschichte des Weltkriegs* (1931, reissued in 1976), perhaps because the banning and burning of books was not yet such a popular occupation. The protest poetry is also discussed briefly, but with some interesting observations, by Ronald Peacock in his paper 'The Great War in German Lyrical Poetry', published in England in 1934. Unlike most critics of the English poetry, Cysarz and Peacock are concerned with 'tendencies' (the term is Peacock's) in the poetry at large, rather than with the work of a few individual authors.

Relatively little of the poetry reprinted in Julius Bab's wartime anthologies was taken from the magazines associated with Expressionism, the new literary movement of the immediate pre war years, although some of these periodicals – most notably *Die Aktion* and *Die weissen Blätter* – continued to publish experimental verse throughout the war. *Die Aktion* in particular was very much conscious of its soldier-poets, and the editor, Franz Pfemfert, introduced a column of 'Verse vom Schlachtfeld', poems from the battlefield (or, as Patrick Bridgwater points out, 'field of slaughter'), in October 1914. An anthology of these poems, *1914–1916*, appeared in 1916. Most of the Expressionist writing was omitted from war-poetry anthologies of the earlier revival, but some of it has been kept alive by scholarly interest in that literary and artistic movement. In the last two decades, both the war poetry and the war motif have attracted specific attention. Uwe Wandrey in *Das Motif des Krieges in der expressionistischen Lyrik* (1972) and Hermann Korte in *Der Krieg in der Lyrik des Expressionismus* (1981) explore the recurrence of the war motif in poetry of the period from 1910 to, respectively, 1920 and 1923. Anz and Vogl's 1982 war anthology consists mainly of Expressionist poems but offers a small sampling of others. More recently Patrick Bridgwater, who was responsible for some earlier translations and articles, has published *The German Poets of the First World War*, which offers English prose translations of the poems, as well as much valuable biographical information and textual analysis. There is also evidence of renewed interest in individuals whose reputation was made by their war poetry – Wilhelm Klemm, for instance, the subject of a 1979 monograph by Hanns-Josef Ortheil, and (although not Expressionists) the worker-poets, including Heinrich Lersch and Karl Brïger.

At least two modern critics have given consideration to the war poetry as an international phenomenon. C.M. Bowra's 1961 Taylorian Lecture *Poetry and the First World War*, published as a thirty-five page monograph, is necessarily only an overview, and is unfortunately marred by minor inaccuracies, which leave one slightly uncomfortable about accepting other facts.[17] However, Bowra also deals with the war poetry in the chapter 'Prophets and Seers' in *Poetry and Politics* (1966), an interesting study of 'public' poetry in the period from 1900 to 1960. Michael Hamburger devotes a chapter of *The Truth of Poetry* (1969) to 'Internationalism and War'. In it he places the Modernist war poetry in the context of other poetic developments in the early years of the century, and draws its link with the political verse of the 1930s and the poetry of the Second World War. It is interesting to note that both Bowra and Hamburger perceive in the poetry a fundamental division between 'public' or propagandist writing on the one hand and that which they identify as 'personal' or 'private' on the other. This particular binary distinction has apparently not been recognised by scholars concerned only with the war poetry of a single language; there, the more striking dichotomy evidently lies in the poet's attitude towards the war, so that pro-war and anti-war poems are viewed as opposites, instead of being considered as two forms of propaganda that together form a contrast with the non-propagandist or 'personal' writing. While Hamburger and Bowra observe similarities from one country to another in the poetry, an earlier international critic, Harvey C. Grumbine, was anxious to prove differences. Grumbine's *Humanity or Hate – Which?*, published in 1917, was intentional propaganda aimed at convincing the author's fellow-Americans that their country was right in joining the war on the French side. In spite of the book's obviously biased title, Grumbine's preface is a thoughtful study of the religious attitudes revealed in French and German patriotic poetry of the war, and he provides translations of a selection of patriotic poems from each language.

Although the war poetry in English has received considerably more attention than that in the other two languages, it has not been covered so widely as the greater number of critical works might suggest. Almost all book-length studies of the poetry follow the same format. They begin (perhaps after some introductory remarks about the war or about literary antecedents) with a description of the initial poetic response, which is discussed in general terms and usually exemplified in the work of Rupert Brooke. Then follows a series of chapters each devoted to a combatant poet of high repute, whose work differs markedly from the early response – though the implication prevails that most of these individuals passed through a stage similar to that represented by Brooke. The names that occur most frequently are Wilfred Owen, Siegfried Sassoon, Isaac Rosenberg, David Jones (the author of an epic poem, *In Parenthesis*, published in 1936) and Edmund Blunden, together with some lesser figures – in the sense that they rarely merit a full chapter – such as Charles Sorley, Robert Graves, Ivor Gurney, Edward Thomas and Herbert Read. In each case the critic correlates features in the poetry with events in the poet's life and his attitude as evinced by letters and other contemporary documents, while offering interpretations of a few poems, or parts of them, with special emphasis on literary influences or parallels. Some of the names are challenged occasionally, and in a rare case a new one may be added, but none of the critics ventures so far from the accepted path as to analyse the work of a woman poet, and few pay more than passing attention to the war poetry of any non-combatant male, except perhaps Thomas Hardy. Although little rationale is offered in the criticism for the choice of poets, apart from Brooke, who, it is claimed, represents the early response, the names that recur are the same as those in Jon Silkin's anthology, which were selected on the basis of 'excellence'. Yet because the discussion of the early poetry aims to give a representative picture, one tends to assume that the same is true for the rest – clearly an erroneous assumption if the poets, far from being representative, were chosen because they were outstanding. (Patrick Bridgwater, on the other hand, states quite clearly the criteria on which his selection of German poets is based.) The format of the English studies, together with the exclusive focusing on a consensual group of no more than ten or twelve writers, has produced a decidedly warped image of the English First World War poetry in general, and especially of the protest writing.

In the image that the criticism promotes, a typical English First World War poet was a combatant, usually a junior officer, apolitical,

who, if he lived long enough, was converted by his war experience
from a patriotic idealist to a disillusioned realist, and who then used
his poetry as a tool of protest. Fundamental to this view is the belief
that one can trace in the poetry a straightforward history of change in
attitude, as a consequence of personal experience. Because Britain had
been involved in no major conflict in the previous hundred years, so
the argument runs, there was universal enthusiasm when war was
declared in August 1914, and young men volunteered full of heroic
idealism and patriotic dedication. At least a fraction of the enthusiasm
and idealism of the early days is said to have remained throughout
the first two years of the war, but after about mid-1916, when the
combatants recognised the full horror of modern warfare, a sense of
angry disillusionment prevailed, magnified by its contrast with the
hopeful idealism that had preceded it. From this disillusionment, the
critics maintain, came protest poetry, an attempt to convey the newly-
discovered truth to the people at home through realistic description,
with Siegfried Sassoon leading the way and serving as an inspiration
to other writers. The change in war poetry, from that which upholds
to that which denies the value of war, is thus considered to be
primarily a consequence of the altered nature of warfare itself, though
what Michael Hamburger terms the 'essentially civilian' outlook of
the majority of poets is seen as a contributory factor.

This picture of the evolution of protest poetry in English is disconcert-
ingly different from that in the other two languages, where much of the
better-known work was a product of the first half of the war. Marcel
Martinet's 'Tu vas te battre' (You are going to fight), in which the
speaker tries to persuade the workers of Europe that they have more
worthy goals than to kill each other, is dated 30 July 1914, and the entire
collection of the poet's *Les Temps maudits*, as it appeared in the original
edition, was written between 1914 and 1916. Jules Romains' *Europe*, a
lament for what the poet had hoped would be a unified continent, was
published in 1916, while Pierre-Jean Jouve's *Vous êtes les hommes*, which
appeared in 1915, was available to English readers in the same year,
through a translation by the pacifist Roger Fry. And already in December
1914, Robert de Sousa made the juxtaposition of heroism and 'the facts'
that is characteristic of the combatant protest poetry in English:

L'espérance nous emportait
Comme une brise porte la flamme;
'La guerre est gloire', disait l'ancêtre,
'En sacrifice pour la justice.'
Mais toute la brise est tombée,
Toute la jeunesse est là qui gît.
La guerre n'est que deuil et que boue.[18]

(Hope bore us along as a breeze carries flames; 'War is glory', said our forefathers, 'in sacrifice for justice.' But the breeze has dropped, the whole of youth lies dead. War is nothing but mourning and mud.)

Amongst the earlier protest poems in German were Franz Werfel's 'Krieg' (War), dated 4 August, 1914, and 'Die Wortemacher des Krieges' (The wordmakers of the war), a bitter attack on the numerous propagandists the war had already generated. Like Werfel's poems, Erwin Piscator's 'Denk an seine Bleisoldaten' (Remember his lead soldiers) originated within the first month of the conflict, though it would be easy to believe that this image of 'heroes' dropping dead in a row, like so many toy soldiers, was inspired by the experience of a First World War attack. The war poems of Alfred Lichtenstein similarly make a mockery of heroism, and they, too, are a product of the beginning of the war; Lichtenstein was nearing the end of a year's military service in August 1914, and this unwilling combatant was dead by the end of September. Georg Trakl's three war poems, 'Im Osten' (In the East), 'Klage' (Lament), and 'Grodek', all lacking in grand ideals, were written in the late summer of 1914. As early as October of that year the magazine *Die Aktion* introduced its regular column of verse from the Front, with realistic description its speciality, and the 1916 anthology of these poems was advertised as 'eine Antikriegs-Anthologie'. It is clear that by mid-1916 the two languages had produced a substantial body of protest verse by both combatants and civilians.

If the pattern promoted in the English criticism were valid, one would have to assume either that English poets *en masse* were decidedly less perceptive than their counterparts in France and Germany, in their failure to recognise the implications of the war, or that as a nation the English, despite a reputation for individualism, were in fact more unanimous in their response to the conflict than even the supposedly ultra-conformist Germans. Yet a letter to *The Nation* in December 1914 suggests quite the reverse: 'I do not suppose there is any equivalent to the *Nation* published in Germany – at all events just now, and if there were, the average German would think the present no time to write letters to it'.[19] (One is reminded sadly of Erwin Piscator's recollection of reading *Die Aktion* at the Front, and wishing he could give it to the English and Canadian soldiers in the trenches opposite, with the comment, 'Look, there's this, too – a different Germany!'[20]) The traditional English pride in individualism had not, in fact, been abandoned, and contemporary newspapers and magazines provide adequate evidence that poets in Britain were neither more nor less perceptive than those on the Continent. The assumption that one can trace so simply a story of changing attitudes through the poetry is, as Hibberd and Onions claim in the introduction to their anthology, a myth – and one from which, in their tactful phrase, 'Much misrepresentation results'.[21]

Yet the prevalence of the belief that there was a major shift in attitude in the poetry about mid-1916 is easy to explain in terms of historical events, for July of that year saw the start of the Somme offensive, an ill-conceived attack that, like most other attempted advances in this war, gained almost nothing. On 1 July 1916, between 7.30 in the morning, when the first attackers left the shelter of the trenches, and late evening, by which time it was abundantly clear that the attack had not gone according to plan, almost 20,000 British soldiers were killed. (The defending Germans are believed to have lost a comparable number.) Yet despite this initial disaster, the same largely futile strategy was followed for two more weeks before the attack was finally abandoned. It seems logical, therefore, that amongst the men who survived into the second half of the war, patriotic and heroic ideals would be replaced by disillusionment – that, in Brian Gardner's words, 'After the Somme, it was never the same'.[22] Furthermore, the view of the war as a journey from innocence and idealism to experience and disillusionment is promoted widely in retrospectives by combatants, not least some of the poets themselves. The two decades after 1918, and especially the second, saw the publication of numerous novels and memoirs about the war, and of prose works in which fact and fiction are consciously merged, like Robert Graves' *Goodbye to All That*. A recurrent theme was the recognition that the horrifying ugliness of the battlefields of the Great War had destroyed for ever the possibility of idealism like that of 1914 and before. These texts were highly influential in establishing the modern perception of the war, both through their description of the reality of the Front and through the contrast they drew between the combatants' initial naive optimism and their subsequent cynicism and disillusionment. Since the English war-poetry criticism is much concerned with the connection between the poems and the individual writer's war experience, it is not surprising that the poets' recollections should be taken as a true picture of the events of the past. In the contemporary response represented by the poetry itself, however, the polarities that have become such an important part of 'modern memory' of the war are far less distinct than this retrospective view suggests. While what Paul Fussell calls 'dichotomising' is highly characteristic of the poetry in general, whether of individual poems or the phenomenon as a whole, its pattern is much more complex than the simple parallel oppositions of innocence and experience, civilian and combatant, before and after the Somme, that are taken for granted in most of the English criticism.

By broadening one's perspective to look beyond a small and select group of writers, one sees readily the inaccuracy of the image that has been promoted. It becomes clear immediately, for instance, that a typical English First World War poet was not a combatant but a civilian. In Catherine Reilly's bibliography less than one fifth of all the names listed belong to writers who were on active service, whereas women poets, who (as Reilly points out) have been almost completely ignored in the criticism, make up nearly a quarter of the total – a biased picture indeed. Even if one restricts one's scope to the protest writing the widely-promoted image is inappropriate, for a substantial amount of English protest verse came from civilians, including women. The notion that the English protest, unlike its Continental counterparts, was apolitical is easily dispelled by a glance at the poems in wartime issues of the major socialist newspaper, *The Herald*, or at Bertram Lloyd's two anthologies. The automatic linking of idealism with patriotic fervour, and of protest with realism, proves to be unwarranted, since many protest poets are clearly idealistic (albeit in a different cause), and conversely, the use of realistic description as a protest device is surprisingly limited. Above all, it becomes evident that the connection between the protest and the massive destructiveness of the war is by no means so direct as critics have liked to maintain, for in English, too, anti-war poetry appeared long before the Somme.

The earliest protest poem of the war to be published in England was probably Cale Young Rice's 'The Greater Crime', which appeared in the *Daily Herald* on 5 August 1914, and like many others it has an uncomfortably familiar ring for modern readers (though 'ships and armies' would now read 'nuclear weapons'):

You have built ships and armies with the bread
That should have driven hunger from the land.

Amongst the more prolific protest poets of the early part of the war were Margaret Sackville, a Scottish pacifist, and J.C. Squire, literary editor of the *New Statesman* (and later its general editor), a fervent protester against hypocrisy, but not a pacifist; W.N. Ewer, a left-wing journalist, two of whose protest poems, '1814–1914: On Reading *The Dynasts*' and 'Five Souls', were highly regarded in the socialist community and beyond; and George Russell, an Irish Theosophist who was a friend of W.B. Yeats. The main outlet for protest poetry – though not necessarily for the work of these poets – was the *Herald*, edited by George Lansbury, a socialist and pacifist who objected to war on both political and religious grounds, and who, still a pacifist, was leader of the Labour party in the early 1930s. The paper became a weekly in October 1914, when the threatening shortage of newsprint, and consequent high prices, affected the small-circulation press in general, but it maintained its dissenting position throughout the war, and continued to publish protest poetry. (After the war Siegfried Sassoon, by then well known for his own protest, became its literary editor.)

Some early protest poems also appeared in *The Nation*, a magazine associated with the progressive branch of the Liberal party, and a few in the *New Statesman*, a journal founded in 1913 (with Bertrand Russell a major contributor) and devoted to 'the world movement towards collectivism'. Small magazines like *The Ploughshare* ('Organ of the Quaker Socialist Society') and *The Worker's Dreadnought* (from the Worker's Suffrage Federation) offered occasional examples, and some of George Russell's verse was published in *The Times*, under the pseudonym 'A.E'. In the last eighteen months of the war *The Nation* adopted a more central role in the publication of protest poetry, especially by combatants. Shortly after the Armistice the magazine printed an anonymous poem that immediately became famous, 'Any Soldier to His Son'. The poem begins by rephrasing the question that was asked on a well-known recruiting poster from 1914: 'What did you do in the Great War, Daddy?' – to which the soldier in the poem replies, 'I learned to peel potatoes and to scrub the barrack floor.'[23] The ending, however, is on a darker note, for after describing some of the effects of a battle, the speaker closes with the plea:

> Before the things that were that day should ever more befall,
> May God, in common pity, destroy us one and all.

'Any Soldier', whose author was later identified as George Willis, prompted numerous letters to the editor of *The Nation*, mostly of acclaim. Although Willis' poem seems an obvious choice to include in the war-poetry studies, to balance against Brooke's 'The Soldier' or Hardy's 'Men Who March Away' as a popular statement of current opinion at the end of the war, it has been generally ignored, presumably because the format of the studies necessarily excludes the work of minor poets of protest.

The inaccuracy of the accepted picture, however, is not confined to the misleading characterisation of a typical First World War poet or to the false impression that there was no protest poetry before 1916. It is evident also in a widely-held premise about historical precedents, whether in literature or in warfare. Although Patrick Bridgwater's concern is the German poetry, he subscribes largely to the same belief as most of the English critics concerning the effect of modern weaponry on the poetic response to war, and his opening paragraph exemplifies a common perception:

> So long as war remained essentially a matter of hand-to-hand combat, man versus man, it could be seen in a chivalrous and

heroic light, and was in fact still seen in such a light in the initial period of euphoria in 1914.[24]

Since the word 'still' suggests a continuum, Bridgwater implies (though perhaps unintentionally) that until 1914 warfare had been mainly hand-to-hand combat, which granted the opportunity for personal heroism and chivalrous conduct, and thus allowed war to be viewed favourably. This perception is refuted by military history, where 'unchivalrous' weapons are found in abundance, from burning arrows and crossbows to cannons and rifles. Nor is one justified in assuming that before 1914 people were so blind to reality as to believe that modern warfare was 'chivalrous and heroic', since even the evidence of recent poetry contradicts that assumption. As Jon Silkin has pointed out, both Kipling and Hardy promoted in general an unheroic picture of warfare, and the latter's 'Channel Firing', which condemns the foolishness of the nations preparing to make 'Red war yet redder', is dated April 1914. Even Sir Henry Newbolt's 'Vitaï Lampada', often quoted to demonstrate prewar attitudes (and famous for the line 'Play up, play up, and play the game!'), depicts a relatively modern and bloody form of combat, rather than a chivalrous man-to-man battle: the desert sand is 'Red with the wreck of a square that broke' and 'the Gatling's jammed'. (It is worth noting too, in passing, that neither 'England' nor 'honour' is capable of inspiring the dejected combatants in Newbolt's poem.) But because the history of First World War poetry that the criticism tells is a story of changing values, where the devastation brought about by modern weapons creates a new attitude to war and a new kind of war poetry, it is logical to assume that, until this time, both warfare and the poetry it inspired had been in the 'chivalrous and heroic' mode. Examples of earlier verse that contradict this premise, if they are not ignored completely, are usually either treated as exceptions or excused on the grounds that they are not totally unheroic. Instead, critics are inclined to accept at face value the view promoted by the patriotic poets of 1914, whose interest was best served by suggesting, regardless of the evidence of either history or literature, that war had always been perceived as a glorious adventure, and that the nation's heroes who went gladly to sacrificial death were following in a noble and ancient tradition. Bridgwater is right in maintaining that war was 'seen in a chivalrous and heroic light' in August 1914, but if this judgement is assumed to come from the population at large, 'for the first time' would be more appropriate than 'still'.

Yet however limited its validity, the account of chronological progression from pro-war to anti-war poetry has served a useful purpose, not least by furnishing a convenient link between the genre and its broader social and historical context. The change from tradi-tional to modern poetic technique as a result of war experience – the progression from Brooke to Owen – has been presented (perhaps appropriately) as a symptom of the major transition in literature during the second decade of the century; and the corresponding change in attitude has been widely used, not only by literary scholars, to epitomise a transformation in society at large: from the orderly, innocent and tradition-filled world of the past, which culminated in the idyllic 'summer of 1914', to the chaos, discord and cynicism that have prevailed in the modern age. The premise that the war effected such a transformation is central to the poetry studies, while the studies in turn are a valuable source of evidence to sustain the premise. Unfortunately, just as the simple chronological account of the poetry can no longer be upheld in the face of contradictory evidence, so the corresponding picture of sudden social transition has been largely discredited. In the view of many historians the idyllic world that Brooke supposedly represented is little more than a myth, while the image of the Great War as an absolute borderline between two modes of existence is recognised as a major and usually inappro-priate oversimplification. Dramatic changes in European society during the nineteenth century had destroyed the old political and social order long before 1914, as the spread of industry gave rise not only to urbanisation and geographical mobility, but also to general education, almost universal adult male suffrage, and a redistribution of wealth and power. Rather than initiating change, the war served to confirm the validity of the new form of society that had already evolved in the course of the previous century – the modern nation. Meanwhile, many of the traditions that in retrospect lend an aura of peaceful continuity to pre-war social life – tennis on the lawn and folk-dancing on the village square, for example – were in fact recent inventions or revivals, no more than two or three decades old when war broke out.[25] And their function, for the most part, was not to perpetuate the ancient and established order but to strengthen new group identity within a completely restructured society, or to increase the sense of devotion to the nation itself.

The First World War, with its massive armies and industrialised weaponry, is clearly a product of the modern world; but the assump-tion has prevailed that the popular response to war in August 1914 derived unaltered from the patriotic and heroic ethic of earlier centuries. It is certainly taken for granted in literary–critical circles that, while the post-Somme protest marks the beginning of a new kind of war poetry, the patriotic verse that gave expression to the initial war-enthusiasm follows well-used but no longer appropriate paths. On the surface this belief seems to be justified, since these archaic-sounding declarations of patriotic loyalty owe much to the poetic conventions of the past and little, apparently, to the reality of modern life; and if the First World War inspired a substantially larger number of such poems than earlier conflicts, the explanation may appear to lie in the increase in general literacy. Yet this very disparity raises doubts about the assumption that Great War patriotic-heroic poetry marks the end of an established tradition – doubts that are reinforced by the difficulty in finding more than a handful of well-known lyric poems of this kind, in the languages in question, from before the nineteenth century. Furthermore, the intense and apparently spontaneous homogeneity of the patriotic verse of 1914, and especially its similarity across national boundaries, suggests a vigorous poetic form perfectly suited for its historical role; and an analysis of its widely-shared characteristics confirms that this poetry is indeed a modern phenomenon, the voice *par excellence* of the new sense of nationhood that came to fruition with the onset of war. To regard Great War patriotic poetry as a new and distinct genre, rather than as the dying remnant of tradition, is to reverse the accepted view, and as a consequence of this altered perspective one perceives the war poetry as a whole – the protest poetry no less than the patriotic verse – in a significantly different way. Some major characteristics lose their prominence, while others that were previously disregarded assume new importance; some of the established assumptions are discredited and others validated by the new context; and well-known poems take on a new appearence against the unfamiliar background. This new perception offers an account of the war poetry commensurate with the revised social history of the period, and it contributes, at least in small measure, to the understanding of wartime social attitudes. But it can be justified only if one abandons the critical method that has predominated in earlier studies, and adopts an approach much more deliberately concerned with the interconnection between literature and the society in which it originated and functioned.

Most of the misrepresentation associated with the English war poetry results from the attempt to reconcile the demands of a historical study with the requirements of textual analysis, the approved method in English and American poetry scholarship in recent decades. Textual close reading or interpretation is dedicated to the task of establishing the significance of the poem to an ideally perceptive modern reader; and although it acknowledges the poetic conventions that prevailed when the poem was written, it focuses on the special features that account for the work's unique and enduring aesthetic appeal – that is to say, on the poem's value for the present. The emphasis on uniqueness militates against the discussion of shared characteristics and historical 'tendencies', except in the work of a single poet, while the importance attached to aesthetic worth and value-judgement precludes the deliberate selecting of minor or popular poems representative of historical attitudes. Not only is the method therefore essentially ahistorical, but it has led in the case of the war poetry to the canonisation of a very small number of writers, whose work, in the absence of truly representative figures, has been used to exemplify (and misrepresent) the genre as a whole.

Ideally, the 'close reading' method considers each poem as a so-called 'autonomous text' free of any social or biographical context, but that ideal is rarely achieved. In the existing war-poetry criticism individual works are almost invariably discussed in the context of the poet's biography, with particular attention to situations and events that are assumed to have inspired the poems. The focus on the poet's life may appear to be a useful means of countering the ahistorical inclination of textual criticism, since the biographical approach locates the work firmly in its period of origin. But perhaps because its primary aim is to offer an interpretation of the poem, biographical criticism tends to limit discussion of the historical dimension to a single aspect – the connection between the text and the writer's individual experience. This narrow focus, with its concentration on the creative process, ignores almost totally the social function of the poetry; and it augments the misrepresentation by equating the protest poets' image of the wartime situation with historical 'truth', on the basis of assumptions that make little allowance for the complexity of the relationship between words and reality.

The principle that underlies biographical criticism at its least soph-isticated is a relatively recent convention identifying the 'lyric I', the traditional first-person speaker in lyric poetry, with the poet as a person. The inference follows that poems are autobiographical, and that what the poet says through his or her 'I' voice is true in an empirical sense. Yet this assumption, customary since Romanticism on the part of readers, has not necessarily been shared by poets. William Wordsworth amongst others had no compunction about presenting as personal experience, through the use of an 'I' voice, incidents that had happened to other people. The song of the 'solitary reaper', for example, was overheard by a friend, Thomas Wilkinson, while the scene with the famous daffodils was first described by Dorothy Wordsworth in her journal. Clearly the conventions of lyric poetry, unlike those of memoirs or news reports, do not include the requirement that the writer's statement should be capable of being 'guaranteed by empirical reality or substantiated by concrete truths.'[26] Although it is possible, and even probable, that many combatant war poems were inspired directly by the writer's experience, the 'facts' were necessarily subjected to the demands of the poetic medium. At the very least, empirical truth may have been sacrificed to allow the poet to comply with a rhyme scheme or metric pattern, or to match the conventional poetic usage of the moment; and it was almost certainly subordinated to the requirements of symbolic effect and to the principles of concentration and refinement that dictated the writer's choice of representational details. Nor is there any doubt that some 'personal' experiences were invented or appropriated to serve the writer's needs, for poets, as Aristotle pointed out, are not concerned with 'what has happened', but with 'the kind of thing that *can* happen.'[27] Minimising the importance of biographical parallels does not detract from one's appreciation of the poems, nor should it raise the question of sincerity. Once the choice of subject ceases to be viewed as an accident of circumstance or the direct consequence of an overwhelming experience, one must look elsewhere for the poet's purpose in writing; paradoxically, therefore, removing the emphasis from the autobiographical component may help one to understand the working of the mind that created the poem.

The emphasis on biography and textual analysis has focused the attention of critics and other readers upon the role of the war poems as a vehicle for self-expression. But poetry is not only a means of formulating a personal response to a situation; it is also a mode of communication, a way of conveying that response to other people. All written communication is produced with a reader in mind; and however indefinite this 'implied reader' or (since poetry often gives the impression of being spoken rather than written) 'implied listener' may be, the communicative or social function of the poem is reflected in textual devices – the euphemism 'the Dead' instead of 'corpses', for instance, or the choice of free verse instead of a regular metric pattern. Much of the war poetry is propagandist in intent, whether for or against the nation's involvement, and the implied reader or listener in the text represents an actual and sometimes very specific audience whom the poet wishes to contact and influence. Critics have tended to accept the propaganda of protest poets without question as a picture of reality, regardless of the fact that propaganda and truth are notoriously divergent; and most have assumed, because writers of patriotic verse depict loyal dedication in terms of the archaic values of heroism and chivalry, that those values prevailed in society through the ages, until the Great War destroyed them. In neither case has the propagandist function of the poems, the desire to communicate with a particular audience, received adequate attention. In assessing the value of written documents as evidence of historical events or attitudes, one must always balance the accuracy of the account against the purpose of the communication, no matter whether the documents are letters, news reports, official government papers – or poems.

One must bear in mind, too, that poems exist not only as texts – a series of words joined together in unvarying order (and the subject of analytical close reading) – but also as commodities, printed objects that circulate in society and are bought and sold. They are part of what is termed the 'literary system', and are subject to the network of controls that decides which poems are to be published and circulated (and very little unpublished poetry survives), that gives to some the stamp of critical approval, and that exerts indirect influence on what is written, as well as determining very directly the type of material that is available to be read. In turn, the literary system functions within a larger social system (or a section of it), where it both echoes and helps to create the attitudes that govern the conduct of the social group as a whole. First World War patriotic poetry, where textual devices and mode of publication are ideally suited for the role of reinforcing government policy throughout the nation, exemplifies particularly well this pattern of concentric circles. Provided one remains aware of the power of the literary Establishment to control what is circulated, the war poems as commodities can offer very valuable evidence of popular taste and official acceptability (including a surprisingly lenient attitude towards protest poets) during and after the war. But as far as the content of the poems is concerned, it is important to remember that their role as objects of trade affects both the kind of truth they tell and the way it is told.

Bernard Bergonzi observes in the 1980 preface to the second edition of *Heroes' Twilight* that his book seems to him in retrospect 'remarkably simple, even naïve, in the way in which it combines bits of proper history, literary history and biography with close analysis of poems and prose passages'.[28] In comparison with the past, he maintains, 'The problems of relating the texts of literature and the texts of history now loom larger and more dauntingly.' The change that Bergonzi recognises has occurred largely because developments in literary theory have brought an increased awareness of subtleties in the relationship between literary texts and the world of reality, including the challenge to the assumption that poems are primarily self-expression. But the difficulty in understanding the link between words and their referent (that is, the reality to which they refer) is not confined to literature. When Lewis Carroll's Humpty Dumpty first declared autocratically, 'When *I* use a word, it means just what I choose it to mean – neither more nor less', his statement may have seemed nothing more than an amusing and absurd reversal, in a looking-glass land, of the accepted belief that meaning is fixed, since words were generally taken to be unassailably linked to an objective reality. (The author himself, of course, did not share that delusion.) But with the rapid growth of mass communication – and perhaps with the help of some lessons from George Orwell – more people now recognise that individuals with power, whether political or financial, can indeed establish new words and distort the meaning of old ones almost arbitrarily. At the same time, linguistic philosophy has raised many doubts about the accepted link between word and referent, not least by denying the validity of the notion that words are primarily a means of naming 'the one and only real world' (as Nelson Goodman calls it in *Ways of Worldmaking*, in rejecting the concept). Language, it is claimed, is not so much a response to a perceived reality as an aid to perception. According to this view, perception rests on conventions – those usually unofficial and largely arbitrary agreements that govern most human social activities, including verbal communication – rather than on how the world 'actually *is*', and it varies in accordance with the conventions of different cultures. That is to say, how one sees reality is inseparable from the traditions one's culture has provided. This recognition has important repercussions for history (amongst other fields), and historians increasingly acknowledge that historical fact is not 'what was there' but the sum of many perceptions of the event. Thus both meaning and facts have become relative, and linguistics and history have joined other disciplines in robbing modern Western civilisation of its certainties.

In view of this acknowledgement of the complexity in the relationship between language and reality, whether in literary or in non-literary discourse, it is not surprising that the problems of relating literature and history now 'loom larger and more dauntingly' than in the past. Nor is it surprising that Bergonzi's observation appears in the same context as a reprint of his review of Paul Fussell's *The Great War and Modern Memory*, since Fussell's analysis of the way literary conventions dictated how writers perceived the war may indeed make other descriptions of the relationship between texts and so-called facts seems 'simple, even naïve'. Rather than treating poems and other writings about the war as the response of individuals to a real situation, the book examines 'the simultaneous and reciprocal process by which life feeds materials to literature while literature returns the favour by conferring forms on life'.[29] Focusing on 'places and situations where literary tradition and life notably transect', Fussell suggests that the perception of the war amongst English writers of diaries, letters, memoirs and poems was conditioned to a considerable degree by their literary education, including the enormously influential *Oxford Book of English Verse*. He observes, for instance, that 'It would be a mistake to imagine that the poppies in Great War writings get there just because they are actually there in

the French and Belgian fields'. In reality, he says, 'Flanders fields are .
. . as dramatically profuse in bright blue cornflowers as in scarlet
poppies'; but cornflowers, unlike poppies, 'have no connection with
English pastoral elegaic tradition' in poetry, and they go unnoticed by
most writers.[30] Ultimately, he suggests, these perceptions through
literature became the image of the war that has formed an important
part of twentieth-century consciousness.

While the issue of whether blue flowers are as visually striking as
red ones is perhaps open to debate (quite apart from the fact that the
red of the poppies is so obviously convenient as a symbol for blood),
Fussell's argument about the impact of literary experience upon percep-
tion is both convincing and relevant. Applied to the poetry as an
international phenomenon, it sheds interesting light on some of the
anomalies amongst poems of the different languages. German involve-
ment on the Eastern Front, where the deployment of cavalry remained
possible for longer than in the west, might seem to explain the
relatively greater occurrence of poems about riding in the poetry of
that language, even when the riding is metaphorical. At the same
time it is worth noting that popular poetry of the late nineteenth
century, such as that of Detlev von Liliencron, as well as a large
number of folksongs devoted to riding and cavalry warfare, offered
German examples of riding poems to be followed. In English on the
other hand, even so enthusiastic a horseman as Siegfried Sassoon was
apparently not inspired, either before or during the war, to write
poems that celebrate riding, presumably because such verse was not a
part of his immediate poetic inheritance. A similar 'transection' of
facts and literary tradition may explain the far more frequent references
to snow in the German war poetry; undoubtedly the reality of winter
on the Eastern Front played its part, but one should also remember
the strong position of poems about winter in the German literary
tradition, evident, for instance, in Goethe's 'Harzreise im Winter' and
Müller's 'Winterreise' cycles (the latter made especially well-known
through Schubert's setting). Accordingly, one must not assume that
German poems describing the winter landscape in the war come from
the Eastern Front, simply because Western Front poets in the other
languages mention snow far less frequently. As for Fussell's observa-
tions about the preference of English poets for poppies, larks and
nightingales, it is noticeable that German and French poets shared
precisely the same predilection, and undoubtedly for much the same
reason as their English counterparts – namely, that some birds and
flowers are a part of their poetic tradition (presumably inherited from
the same classical sources), and others are not.

No doubt many readers of *The Great War and Modern Memory* have
found points on which Fussell's study is incomplete, inaccurate or

even, in Desmond Graham's term, 'infuriating'. Jon Stallworthy notes the lack of reference to the intensive classical education that the public schools offered. Another notable absence is that of Francis Palgrave's highly popular *Golden Treasury of Songs and Lyrics*, which must surely have been as influential as the relatively new *Oxford Book*, particularly since the updated and inexpensive World Classics edition of Palgrave ran to seven reprintings in the course of the war. (There is considerable overlap between the two anthologies.) Such points are minor in comparison with the richness of *The Great War and Modern Memory*, but they underline a perhaps unavoidable difficulty in so wide-ranging a study – an apparent arbitrariness in the choice of examples. A more serious problem lies in Fussell's failure to apply in his own study his theory about the relationship between reality and perception. The theory throws doubt upon the supposedly factual basis of the 'modern memory' of the war, but the author perpetuates as if on factual grounds the very tenets that his method invites one to challenge, most notably the concept of the 'innocence' of the pre-war years. Meanwhile, his contention that the binary thinking of the modern age is a consequence of the total alignment situation of trench warfare is belied not only by the social divisiveness in the previous century (as Bergonzi points out in his review), but also by both the patriotic and the protest poetry of the early part of the war, character- ised in each case by a 'remorselessly binary' outlook. If binary thinking is indeed characteristically modern, surely it is the consequence of a more profound and far-reaching social change – perhaps the competi- tiveness that industrial capitalism encourages, or the 'us' versus 'them' of socialism, but more probably the intensive boundary-drawing that occurs when the world is perceived in terms of nations.

It is conceivable that any study of the war poetry that leaves the well-travelled paths of biographical and text-analytical criticism to venture into a large and scarcely-explored field must proceed on the basis of arbitrary choices, especially when, as in the present case, an already wide boundary is extended to encompass the relevant work in three languages. My primary aim has been to present a picture of the poetry in general, and rather than attempting an exhaustive empirical study that could never hope to encompass all the surviving material, I have drawn up generalisations on the basis of a very wide reading of poems from many sources. From these, and taking into account both the texts and their context of publication, I have developed a series of hypotheses about the functioning of the poetry in its contemporary society. The texts on which the study is based – and of which only a fraction are listed in the bibliography – were chosen by a process combining random and deliberate selection. Anthologies, which represent not only what was written but also an editor's assessment of public taste, were an obvious starting-point. Individual collections – that is, volumes comprising the work of a single author – were selected almost by chance, apart from the relatively few by poets whose names occur in contemporary or later criticism, and whose poetry I sought out particularly. (Only in this respect did value judgement affect the choice.) In addition, some volumes were included because the title suggested a typical outlook – Pierre d'Arcangues' *Les Lauriers sur les tombes* (Laurels on the tombs), for instance – and others because the poet's response promised to be unusual, such as Pastor H.A.F. Tech's *Kampfreime eines Friedfertigen aus dem Kriegsjahr 1914* (Battle-rhymes of a man ready for peace, from the war year 1914). I also consulted many wartime newspapers and magazines, which are invaluable as a source of poems, since the context gives an indication of the type of reader who is likely to have encountered the work.

The study is confined to verse that most readers would readily include under the rubric 'First World War poetry' – a consensus based primarily on subject-matter, but influenced also by biographical considerations and the context of publication. Although it might be argued that all poems from the war years should be taken into account, I have disregarded civilian poetry that is linked to the conflict in no direct way, such as Eliot's *Prufrock and other Observations* and Valéry's *La Jeune parque*. (Some of Hugh Lofting's Doctor Doolittle stories for children, written in the trenches, have a strong claim to be considered a product of the war, though it is doubtful whether any critic would feel impelled to include them in a study of Great War fiction.) Nevertheless, the limits of the field are not firmly set. While few casual readers are likely to identify 'Lament of the Frontier Guard' or 'Song of the Bowmen of Shu', from Ezra Pound's *Cathay*, as First World War verse (their ostensible subject is ancient China rather than modern Belgium), the critic Hugh Kenner describes them as 'among the most durable of all poetic responses to World War I', and a combatant friend to whom Pound sent the manuscript in the autumn of 1914, the sculptor Henri Gaudier-Brzeska, observed, 'They depict our situation in a wonderful way.'[31] To define the term 'First World War poetry' in such a way as to accommodate poems like these, but possibly to exclude others, would serve little purpose, since the characteristics of the genre can be described without an exact definition.

The geographical boundaries of the field are similarly indeterminate. Since most of the books and journals that provided the material for my study were published in England, France or Germany, the verse on the whole is from the geographical centre in each case, and comments about nationalism *per se* are confined almost exclusively to those three countries. At the same time, I did not deliberately avoid examples that originated elsewhere; for instance, poems from Ireland, Scotland and the British Empire are included if they happened to be published in 'central' anthologies. Interestingly enough I found little to distinguish the majority of Empire poems from others of the same kind in English; the sense of independent nationhood that developed in Australia, Canada and New Zealand as a result of the war seems to have had little effect on the patriotic verse from those countries. Nor in the texts I have read is there much trace of a distinctive Scottish identity. Accordingly, while recognising that a detailed comparison would probably reveal unique national characteristics, I have chosen to treat the poems I encountered – amongst others 'In Flanders Field' by the Canadian John McCrae – as simply 'English'. American poetry on the other hand is excluded almost totally, on the grounds that, because of the country's official neutrality, the social functioning of the verse was often significantly different from that of Britain or the colonies. (For example, Isabelle Howe Fiske's *Sonnets of Protest* are not anti-war poems, but a protest against the failure of the American government to declare war on Germany.) For similar reasons most poems that refer to Irish independence are omitted, though the Irish poetry as a whole, with its questions of conscience and its two distinct forms of nationalistic propaganda, would make a fascinating study in its own right. With regard to the German poetry, although the majority of examples are from Germany itself, I have followed the lead of Austrian writers like Richard Schaukal, who, although they may refer to their homeland by name, use the adjective 'deutsch' to encompass the whole Germanic culture. While Austrian and German patriotic poems are therefore largely indistinguishable, the same is not true of those of France and Belgium. Not only do Belgian patriotic poets devote their loyalty specifically to the culture of Belgium or Flanders, but the verse as a whole has a distinctive character.

The war poetry falls naturally into three categories, regardless of national and linguistic boundaries. The most striking in both size and homogeneity is that which voices dedication to the cause of the homeland. Although the poetry in itself probably appeals little to modern readers, as a historical phenomenon it provides fruitful ground for an exploration of nationalism, as well as offering an unusually clear example of the interrelated working of the literary and social systems. The basis of my discussion of nationalism is Ernest Gellner's theory, propounded mainly in *Nations and Nationalism*, which explains very cogently the link between industrialism and mass education, and the connection between both of these and the new type of society that developed in the course of the nineteenth century. In the two chapters devoted to the patriotic verse of the war I have shown how the poetry reflects a new sense of individual identification with the nation's cause, and I have examined the themes and textual devices that characterise this celebration of nationhood. Surprisingly enough, nationalism is also an important factor in determining the character of the verse in the second of the three categories, that of protest. To a very large extent the latter is a condemnation, not of the war *per se* but of the flood of propaganda promoting the nation's initial or continuing involvement; the three chapters dealing with the protest poetry explore some of the recurring themes in this counter-propaganda, to show how they represent a repudiation of the new creed or of the way it is promoted. While in many respects protest poetry and patriotic verse are antithetical, they share the same primary goal: to persuade. The recognition of a common propagandist intent in these two distinct kinds of poetry invites an examination of the textual features that account for their effectiveness as propaganda. The result is a reversal of some widely-held assumptions about the functioning of the protest poetry, and an insight into how this minority propaganda reaches out to its intended audience. Because the character-istics of propaganda are lacking in the majority of poems by com-batants, I have suggested (as D.S.R. Welland did) that they belong, not to the second category, the poetry of protest, but to a third group, comprising non-propagandist writing. The focus of my study as a whole is the propaganda poetry but I have devoted one chapter to the soldier-poets, arguing that although they and their poetry have been used by others for propaganda purposes, their writing served a personal rather than a propagandist function. The last chapter touches very briefly on some personal war-poems by civilians (another area worthy of much fuller exploration) before discussing a few inter-national differences in the poetry in general, and finally returning to the problem of the use of poems as historical evidence.

The study, therefore, is not a work of poetry criticism in the conven-tional sense, since textual analysis and value judgement play little part. Biographical detail is similarly lacking, in part because, approp-riately in a war where the nation's heroes are represented by a symbolic 'unknown soldier', most of the poetry comes from 'unknown' writers. (The phrase 'autonomous text' assumes new meaning when one is confronted with a poem by an author identified only through initials, on an undated newspaper clipping from an unnamed source.) Nor, if the term 'history' implies chronological sequence, is this a literary history, since the three categories evolve simultaneously, and since, without extra-textual evidence, it is surprisingly difficult to distinguish between early-war and late-war poems. And although theoretical considerations have an important place in the study, it cannot be termed a work of literary theory. Rather it is an attempt to explain the existence and the nature of an unusual literary phenomenon – a phenomenon consisting of poems in three languages, and by authors of a wide range of abilities – by taking account not only of the literary dimension but also of the social function of the poetry, in the historical context to which it is inextricably bound.

2

Heilig Vaterland
Nationalism and national image

Heilig Vaterland
Heb zur Stunde
Kühn dein Angesicht
In die Runde.
Sieh uns all entbrannt,
Sohn bei Söhnen stehn:
Du sollst bleiben, Land!
Wir vergehn.

Rudolf Alexander Schröder, 'Heilig Vaterland'[1]

Of the 'inescapable' historical facts concerning the war, two are of particular significance for the poetry – the vast size of the armies involved and the siege-like situation of trench warfare. It is usual to describe the conflict of 1914–18 as the first modern war (although the military historian Basil Liddell Hart gives that title to the American Civil War instead).[2] Modern warfare, however, is characterised by large-scale mobility, whereas the First World War, in spite of new mobile weapons such as submarines, aircraft and tanks, was essentially immobile, especially on the Western Front. Nevertheless, it was mainly as a consequence of the capability of both sides to move large numbers of troops quickly by rail that the armies in Belgium and northern France were deadlocked from November 1914 until mid-1918.[3] Both sides established strong defences, mostly in the form of trenches, which also provided access routes and temporary living accommodation in 'dug-outs'. Life in the trenches offered few comforts and sometimes little shelter, and in addition to the hazards of rifle-fire and shells the soldiers had to accustom themselves to the close proximity of other people, the cold, rain and mud, the presence of rats, sometimes the smell of corpses, and an invisible enemy similarly entrenched, perhaps only a hundred yards away, at the other side of the so-called 'No-Man's-Land'. As Tony Ashworth points out in *Trench Warfare, 1914–1918*, boredom was a major feature of trench living, though under ideal conditions one might expect to be able to withdraw for a few days to the relative comfort and safety of a billet behind the lines, after a tour of duty in the trenches. Since the only hope for breaking the deadlock that held the opposing armies almost immobile was to advance, the military authorities periodically assembled troops to stage an attack. As a prelude to the advance (and at other times) the enemy position was bombarded with heavy-artillery fire for several hours – a terrifying experience for the recipients, since there was no alternative but to shelter as safely as possible and wait for the bombardment to end. Unfortunately for the attackers, the bombardment rarely achieved its intended purpose of destroying the enemy's defences, so when the troops advanced they were usually met by severe artillery, machine-gun and rifle fire. Consequently, most attempted advances produced a very large number of casualties for only a small gain.[4]

The condition that not only brought about the deadlock situation but also allowed the war to continue despite the heavy losses was the size of the military forces involved. The mass armies resulted from a relatively new principle of recruitment, under which every young man in the country was considered eligible for military service. In 1870, at the start of the Franco-Prussian War, the rival powers each had less than half a million soldiers and reservists. In August 1914, by contrast, Germany's military strength was more than five million, eight per cent of the population, while France's force, though somewhat smaller, consisted of more than ten per cent of the population. (By the end of September France had already lost almost as many men as comprised its whole army in the earlier war – over 300,000.) Although Britain's military strength in 1914 was only 700,000, since military service was not compulsory, an army of comparable size was easily raised, mostly through volunteers. The fact that young men in Britain went so willingly to war underlines the appropriateness of the laws that made their counterparts on the Continent eligible for peacetime military training. As nineteenth-century industrialisation increasingly offered the possibility of mass-produced armaments and large, powerful weapons, it had became clear, especially to the Germans, that the defence of the homeland could no longer be perceived as a matter for a small professional army and navy, augmented when the need arose. At the same time a concept of nationhood was evolving under which the task was considered to be a collective responsibility, assigned in practice to all men of combatant age. Germany and France had granted formal approval to a principle that the British accepted as a matter of course when war came (though the attempt to give that acceptance the legal status of conscription in 1916 still aroused considerable unease). Unfortunately, the existence of the massive armies that resulted from the new policy called for innovative military strategies, while the military leaders responsible for making major decisions continued to fight the kind of war with which they were familiar – and which, one might add, the public expected; largely as a result of this incompatibility, more than eight million people died in battle, most of them young men.[5]

The reason for the outbreak of war is still debated, but a generally-accepted expert opinion maintains that 'it was a system of alliances and the changing balance of military power in Europe that converted a Balkan dispute into a world war in 1914'.[6] The incident that caused the Balkan dispute to flare up – the assassination of the Archduke Franz Ferdinand of Austria-Hungary and his wife in Bosnia by a Serb nationalist – led within a few weeks to threats and counterthreats from one country to another, and a chain-reaction of mobilisation. The 'system of alliances' involving Russia and France posed a sufficiently strong threat to the other group of allies, Germany and the Austro-Hungarian Empire, to prompt a German decision to take the offensive. In accordance with military plans drawn up long before-hand, the 'Schlieffen Plan', the chosen victim was France, by way of Belgium. The attack upon that small neutral country brought Britain into the fray, rather to the surprise, it seems, of the population at large, for the British press at the end of July 1914 was largely occupied with the forthcoming parliamentary debate on 'the Irish question'. The introduction to a recent symposium on the subject of war aims and policies in the Great War states that modern research 'has largely destroyed the fallacy that most of the powers declared war in 1914 without any clear perception of why and to what ultimate end'.[7] Yet although the purpose of the war may now be clear to historians, laymen are still likely to echo Old Kasper's comment in Robert Southey's poem about the Battle of Blenheim: 'But what they kill'd each other for, / I could not well make out'.[8]

At the time, however, no explanation was necessary, at least on the evidence of the war poetry: the cause, the 'ultimate end', was the homeland itself. Literally thousands of Great War poems abound with the names of countries or with terms like 'fatherland' and 'mother-land': 'O mein Vaterland, heiliges Heimatland' (O my Fatherland, blessed homeland), 'Deutschland muß leben, und wenn wir sterben müssen' (Germany must live, even if we must die), 'Fürs Vaterland und deutsches Blut' (For the Fatherland and the German race), 'La France appelle ses soldats' (France calls to her soldiers), 'O France, tant que tu voudras' (O France, whatever you wish), 'Pays natal! O terre entre toutes bénie' (Land of my birth! O country blessed above all others), 'Happy is England now, as never yet', 'England mourns for her dead across the sea', 'Who dies if England live?' to quote from only a few of the more famous, by such well-known writers as

Gerhart Hauptmann, Paul Claudel and Rudyard Kipling.[9] As these quotations indicate, the country's name and the various words for *patria* are not synonymous with the physical terrain, since obviously a geographical entity cannot call to its soldiers or feel happy or, as in the poem by Rudolf Alexander Schröder that I quoted as an epigraph, raise its head and gaze around. Nor does the name represent the people of the land, for there is an implication that the country's life can be guaranteed only by the death of its inhabitants. Rather, the commitment that these poems proclaim is to a nation, which is something more than either the physical terrain or the people and their culture. 'The nation' as the poets perceive it (perhaps unconsciously) is an abstraction, a concept to which a particular name is attached – 'la France', 'das Vaterland' – but to which, in turn, the poets assign human characteristics and feelings, so that the abstraction becomes a single individual.

In his study of the German Great War poetry, Ronald Peacock describes how the concept of a nation develops out of the desire to protect one's physical surroundings. When home and native land are threatened, he suggests, the 'material heritage', 'the land on which one has lived', assumes 'a mantle of holiness'.[10] As national consciousness is awakened by the threat, people become aware that 'the freedom, the integrity, the independence of the nation must be preserved', and ultimately 'that material and spiritual possession, the nation', is 'raised to a principle'. With the discovery of patriotic love, Peacock concludes, comes an understanding of the relationship of the individual and the state, and of the duty implicit in it. The arousing of national sentiment in 1914, however, was both simpler and more complex than this explanation suggests. There is no reason to believe that mankind has by nature an attachment to its 'native land', since the biological 'territorial imperative' in humans, if it exists at all, is no more than vestigial. With regard to Peacock's 'mantle of holiness', it is worth recalling that, for most inhabitants of Europe through many centuries, the land on which they lived was owned by someone else, whose best interest might or might not be served by engendering a sense of possessiveness in his (or, more rarely, her) tenants. If 'material heritage' is the basis of patriotic commitment, it seems logical that the people with most possessions will fight most determinedly to protect their country, while others, if they have the choice, will not. This suggestion is borne out (in Europe at least) by the evidence of all but the more recent history, for major armies have usually been inspired, not by a spirit of nationhood, but by the threat of punishment or the promise of spoils or other payment. Yet at the outbreak of the First World War, commitment to the Fatherland was apparently almost universal, regardless of wealth and social status.

Such an attitude can be explained only by recognising that national sentiment is acquired through a sustained process of social conditioning, and that, when individuals perceive a threat to their country as a threat to themselves, their loyalty is evidence of the effectiveness of the lesson to which they have been subjected. Once a commitment to the nation has been learnt, along with the various devices that are associated with the name of the homeland, an appropriate response is easily evoked by such stimuli as a speech or poem, the tune of a particular song, the sight of an emblem or flag – or the recognition that the country's territory or prestige is under attack. Because such a response is emotional rather than rational, it was unnecessary for the German people to become aware, as Peacock suggests, that the 'integrity' of the nation must be preserved, or to be conscious of their position within the relationship of individual and state, before volunteering their enthusiastic support when their country was believed to be threatened. The poet Rudolf Herzog describes the stimulus-response situation much more accurately when he writes,

Zwei Worte – Feind und Vaterland –
Und alles ist gesprochen.[11]

(Just two words – enemy and Fatherland – and all is said.)

One might tend to assume, with Peacock, that 'the spirit which is the nation' is 'the growth of centuries' and that 'the patriotic ideals of freedom, honour and justice . . . have spurred nations on since nations were' – in other words, that national consciousness comparable to that of August 1914 was a typical response to war throughout history. Sociologists and historians agree, however, that apart from possibly a few isolated examples like the states of ancient Greece, the concept of nationhood that prompted this response is a modern phenomenon. Unlike patriotism, which it encompasses, and which denotes a sense of loyalty or attachment to any country or region (and presumably its inhabitants), nationalism implies a commitment to a specific kind of society – 'a new form of social organisation', to use Ernest Gellner's phrase – called a nation.[12] There are innumerable theories about the nature and development of nationalism in nineteenth-century Europe, but rather than wandering inexpertly through this large and controversial field, I have chosen to focus on a particular hypothesis that explains in almost every detail the character and functioning of Great War patriotic verse. Ernest Gellner in *Nations and Nationalism* (1983) and *Culture, Identity and Politics* (1987) propounds a theory which, while not unique in postulating a link between nationalism and industrialism, is unusual both in the explanation it offers for the intensive boundary-drawing that accompanied the spread of industry, and in its conclusion that, contrary to the Marxist view, nationalistic industrial society is potentially (and intrinsically) egalitarian. Whether the theory is applicable to the 'new regional nationalisms' is, Gellner admits, 'an open question', but there is no doubt that it accommodates the nationalistic creed that evolved in the three major countries whose poetry forms the basis of my discussion, England, France and Germany.[13]

Industrialism, Gellner maintains, has its roots in the new world vision presented by seventeenth- and eighteenth-century philosophy – a world totally subject to Descartes' *esprit d'analyse*, 'the separation of all separables', offering 'endless possibilities of new combinations of means with no prior expectations or limits'.[14] The result is a wholehearted commitment to the ideal of progress and to 'sustained and perpetual growth' and change, and a form of society significantly different in structure from its predecessors. An agrarian society, Gellner observes, usually involves a number of small, stable, sometimes almost autonomous communities governed collectively by a small and powerful ruling class, which is rigidly separated from the peasants of the producing communities and strongly stratified within itself. Literacy is the privilege of the upper classes, most notably the clerisy. The inward-turning nature of the communities encourages cultural difference from one to another and, as Gellner says, 'The state is interested in extracting taxes, maintaining the peace, and not much else, and has no interest in promoting lateral communication between its subject communities.'[15] Consequently, the major principle of nationalism – the demand that political and cultural boundaries should coincide – is irrelevant, if not antithetical, to such a society. An industrial society, on the other hand, with its incessant demand for growth and change, requires above all a diverse and mobile workforce, 'perpetually, and often rapidly, changing', composed of individuals who are able to communicate with others throughout the area of the society's jurisdiction, and who are capable of moving into positions of authority. The necessary mobility and the required single code of communication are dependent upon general literacy. As a consequence, a homogeneous, standardised education system evolves, the basis of which is a single 'high' culture (as distinct from a variety of folk-cultures), with 'a school-mediated, academy-supervised idiom, codified for the requirement of reasonably precise bureaucratic and technological communication.'[16] The provision of education and the protection of the culture become major functions of the state, which also strives to make the limits of the culture congruent with the country's political boundaries, whether by imposing the culture throughout the territory or by seeking to extend the borders to encompass all who might be considered to belong. With increasing education and the possibility of upward mobility, the earlier internal stratification – often based on hereditary status, and rigidly separating the rulers of various degree from each other and from the ruled – is replaced by 'merely fluid, continuous and temporary inequalities' – a 'seamless society' called a nation.[17] And because, as Gellner observes, 'the high (literate) culture in which they have been educated is, for most men, their most precious investment, the core of their identity, their insurance, and their security', national boundaries assume special significance, both as the limit of employability and as the border between one's own and an alien culture, and ultimately 'a situation arises in which well-defined educationally-sanctioned and unified cultures constitute very nearly the only kind of unit with which men willingly and often ardently identify'.[18] (Since Gellner's remarks appear to be equally applicable to women, it is probably safe to assume that his use of the word 'men' is for the most part generic rather than gender-related: that is, for 'men' read 'people'.)

As the commitment to endless discovery and perpetual change increasingly calls into question the tenets of traditional religion, Gellner claims, direct worship of the culture takes its place. Although the evidence of the patriotic poetry suggests that the new religion merges with, rather than totally replaces, the old, there is no doubt about the affinity between the two, nor that the Fatherland becomes 'the Sacred'. 'Ich glaub an Deutschland wie an Gott' (I believe in Germany as I believe in God), the poet Heinrich Lersch writes, and his credo is echoed in a poem about a priest whose perspective has been altered by the war, and who now declares, 'Notre Dieu, c'est la France!' (France is our God).[19] Like Protestantism, the worship of the Fatherland is (in Gellner's term) 'unmediated', for each individual has direct access to the unifying concept that is the nation. And like all religions it involves the whole mind – the will, the intellect, the imagination and the emotions – as C.J.H. Hayes observes in his study of the affinity between religion and nationalism.[20] Further, just as the deities representing the various conceptions of the Supreme Being are given human attributes, so the abstraction known as the nation is personified and endowed with the ability to live, think, feel, die, and call for sacrifice. While mythic figures like Britannia, Germania and France's Marianne, or cartoon images such as John Bull and 'der deutsche Michel', may sometimes have served as patriotic symbols in the past, in the First World War poetry it is the nation itself that is personified – and so all-pervasively that one soon finds oneself taking the usage as much for granted as the poets obviously did.

Central to Gellner's account of the development of a nationalistic society is the role of education, which serves not only to generate a versatile workforce and to open the way for social equality, but also to produce in each individual a strong commitment to the culture in which he or she has been educated. It is, moreover, closely integrated with enfranchisement: literate people demand, and are more willingly granted, their part in the electoral process, while the possibility of wider voting rights encourages the spread of schooling, in order to guarantee an educated electorate. Gladstone's rationale in promoting the enfranchisement of skilled workers (who were granted suffrage under the 1867 Reform Bill) was that these men were taking full advantage of educational opportunities to improve themselves;[21] and a well-known parliamentary speech in response to the passage of the bill advocated more schooling: 'I believe it will be absolutely necessary that you prevail on our future masters to learn their letters.'[22] (The Education Act initiating compulsory schooling in England followed in 1870.) Until the end of the eighteenth century, schooling in the countries in question was mainly in the hands of the churches or independent charities, but as early as 1794 Prussia formally recognised education as a function of the state. From the 1820s its church school-boards were replaced by provincial ones, and an 1840 law made elementary education compulsory. There was general literacy in Prussia by 1830.[23] In the unified Germany of 1872, secondary education in fee-paying *Mittelschulen* was added to the state's mandate, and fears of excessive secularisation were quieted by encouraging both these and the elementary *Volksschulen* to teach religion in accordance with the community's wishes. In France, too, the concept of state education and the recognition of its potential came early, with the Revolution; church schools were closed, and a 1795 law established primary schools in the large cities. Although many measures taken by the revolutionary governments were rescinded after the Restoration in 1815, the move towards general education continued, and 1833 saw the passing of a more comprehensive primary education law. Defeat in the Franco-Prussian War of 1870 brought the recognition that education in France was far behind that in Germany, especially in practical areas, and a new determination arose to correct the situation by implementing a complete national system. This was eventually approved in 1886, with emphasis on improving scientific and technical schooling (and its image *vis-à-vis* the long-standing classical tradition), and providing access for all regions and classes.

In England the progress towards universal education may be seen, especially in contrast with the systematic Prussian approach, as a matter of characteristic compromise or 'muddling through'. A combination of church day-schools, Sunday schools, dame schools and charities initially provided some primary education for children of the lower classes, while the wealthy received their early instruction at home. From 1833, when a bill proposing state education was rejected, the government helped fund voluntary schools, establishing in 1839 a Committee of Council for Education to oversee and administer the funding. In 1861, when there was still no state system, a parliamentary commission reported that 97 percent of the children of poorer classes were receiving some elementary education. The 1870 Education Act called for continued financial support of the charity and church schools, but required the establishing of board schools where they were needed to supplement the existing system. Fee-paying secondary education, in both wholly private (called 'public') and partially-funded schools, also proliferated in the course of the century, as the middle class grew in size and affluence. The government, or at least the local education authorities, became more closely involved in the supervision of funded schools not directly under their jurisdiction, but resistance to a uniform national system remained (and has remained) strong, and the tradition of two types of schooling, private and state, has prevailed.

In other respects, too, the three countries followed different paths to full national awareness, though the result, if one may judge by majority attitudes in the First World War, was ultimately the same. A sense of national distinctiveness began to emerge in all three cases in the eighteenth century, a countercurrent to the cosmopolitan tendency of the aristocracy and the Enlightenment. Although Herder's writings about Germanic culture are considered seminal, and though France is often assumed to be the original home of nationalism, a convincing argument has been made (by Gerald Newman in *The Rise of English Nationalism, 1750 to 1830*) that the prototype is to be found in eighteenth-century England, where national sentiment developed as middle-class radicals challenged the upper classes' belief in the superiority of French culture. Certainly industrialisation (which appears to go hand in hand with nationalism) progressed very swiftly in Britain in the early stages, possibly because some of the conditions of 'modern society' already existed – a relatively mobile populace in both a geographical and a social sense, with a middle class comprising at least thirty percent of the population by about 1750, and literacy extending to craftsmen and artisans.[24] In France, nationalism manifested itself vociferously in the Revolution, when (nominally at least) 'the people' replaced the monarchy and the church as the decisive social force, and the *tricolore* was adopted as a symbol of the nation. Germany became a single nation only in 1871, but long before that time there was a widespread feeling for German national identity (beginning, as in England, with a questioning of the value of French influence), and the *Zollverein* (Customs Union) established in 1833 enhanced the awareness of belonging to a single culture. A sense of nationhood was apparently not difficult to engender after unification, despite the determined resistance to Prussian influence in some parts of the country.

The last three decades of the nineteenth century witnessed a burgeoning of national awareness throughout Europe. Eric Hobsbawm in the essay 'Mass-Producing Traditions' tells of the large-scale 'invention' of traditions between 1870 and 1914, including many that were apparently designed to foster a spirit of nationhood.[25] Bastille Day in France was 'invented' in 1880, for instance, and in Germany a 'mass of masonry and statuary' affirmed the validity of the new empire, and gave an aura of history to recent events in its brief common past. In Britain the Golden Jubilee of Queen Victoria's accession (1887) marked the beginning of a tradition of royal ceremonial and of respect for the monarchy – a tradition which, as David Cannadine points out, is now usually assumed to be ancient.[26] Not surprisingly, an important vehicle for promoting the sense of nationhood was the schoolroom; there, according to Kaiser Wilhelm II, one might hope to 'lay the foundation for a healthy conception of political and social relations, through the cultivation of God and love of country'.[27] The Kaiser maintained that history instruction should focus on the Germanic past, and should be designed 'primarily to prepare the pupils for heroic and historic greatness'. 'Love of country' was a strong element in literary studies, too; the author of a series of instruction manuals for teachers in *Volksschulen*, published in 1902, provided a list of patriotic poems to be studied, but noted that it was unnecessary to print complete texts, 'since they are already included in most sets of readers'.[28] A similarly patriotic mood governed the curriculum in English schools of the same period, though the goal preached in an 1890 history text – of 'helping to keep our beloved old England in honour and safety' – tended to merge with that of serving (and preserving) the Empire, of 'handing on unimpaired to our descendants the treasures of freedom and dominion which our ancestors acquired and entrusted to us'.[29] (This way of describing the Empire was of course another recently invented tradition.) And as in Germany, the texts selected for poetry study were not uncommonly 'inspired by that spirit or influence which prepares for and conduces to true patriotism in the youth of any great nation or people', like those in a 1912 textbook *Poems of Loyalty by British and Canadian Authors*.[30] In France, in the years following the débâcle of 1870, patriotism played an important part in the revitalising of the education system. According to Mona Ozouf in her study *L'École, l'Église et la République, 1871–1914*, even learning to read was promoted as a patriotic activity, and with the role of religion in the state system diminishing, patriotism took its place as the element providing unity in the curriculum.[31] A textbook called *Tour de la France par deux enfants*, first published in 1877 and rife with 'la

France' and 'la Patrie', is described by Jean Lestocquoy as 'the book *par excellence* of the French people from 1880 to 1914'; its 409th edition, incidentally, appeared in 1964.[32] Lestocquoy observes of *Tour de la France* that 'everyone in it speaks a kind of French that is grammatically perfect, pure as mineral water' – this, presumably, is exactly what Gellner means by the 'school-mediated, academy-supervised idiom' of a high culture.[33]

That German nationhood might need deliberate fostering in the period after 1870 is logical, since unification was not universally welcomed; and political turmoil in France at various times during the century may seem to justify the teaching of patriotic commitment and the introduction of unifying 'traditions' in that country, too. Yet the fact that Britain was engaged in similar activities suggests that the specific historical situation may have been less important than a concern that was common to all. And almost certainly that problem was the increasing political self-awareness amongst the members of the working class. The urban proletariat grew substantially in the second half of the century, both in numbers – through migration from the land and an increased birth and survival rate – and in political strength, with the coming of extensive adult male suffrage (at least at the national level) in the 1870s and '80s, and with the development of a sense of class unity. The International Workingmen's Association, the First International, was formed in the 1860s, and was especially active in France; and in the 1877 elections for the German Reichstag one of every seven votes cast favoured the Social Democratic Party.[34] As Hobsbawm observes, 'from the 1870s onwards it became increasingly obvious that the masses were becoming involved in politics and could not be relied upon to follow their masters'.[35] Not surprisingly, therefore, there was a move to manipulate opinion and to counter the leaning towards socialism, whether by stressing the commitment to a particular national ideal through pageantry and statuary, or by deliberately striving, in the words of Kaiser Wilhelm, 'to give our youth the impression that the teachings of Social Democracy not only contradict the divine commandments and Christian morals, but that they are in reality impossible of achievement and, in their consequences, dangerous to the individual and society'.[36] Yet it would be a mistake to over-emphasise the part played by propaganda in the new wave of nationalism, whatever the politicians may have intended. Valerie Chancellor, in her study of nineteenth-century English history textbooks, finds relatively little evidence of a deliberate attempt to convert the children of the poor into good citizens of the state, except to the extent of preaching a moral code which is distinctly that of the established middle class. (It is worth noting, too, that the same books tended to be used in private and state schools.) Hobsbawm similarly cautions against overestimating the role of manipulation: the invented nationalistic traditions of the period flourished, he suggests, not because they were vigorously promoted, but 'in proportion to [their] success in broadcasting on a wavelength to which the public was ready to tune in'.[37] A century earlier the members of the growing middle class throughout Europe, recognising that their individual importance was linked to their role in the society of their own country, rather than to the pan-European culture of the aristocracy, had accepted with alacrity the 'invention' of national literary tradition and cultural history; now, it appears, members of the working class, literate and (for many males, at least) enfranchised, joined with enthusiasm in the celebration of their country's – and therefore their own – unique national identity.

General education, so crucial in the evolution of this sense of nationhood, influenced the output of patriotic poetry in the war in a variety of ways, quite apart from its effect in engendering national commitment. In the first place it had imbued students, for most of whom school was the main source of literary influence, with a taste for a restricted canon of verse, including the nation's treasury of patriotic and heroic poems. Second, it was a vital factor in determining the size of the poetic response: by its very existence, the greatly-expanded reading public encouraged the production of printed material, and the possibility of publication undoubtedly increased the number of poems being written. And most significantly, general literacy led to a proliferation of newspapers and magazines, which in turn provided the war poets with their single most important outlet. Benedict Anderson, who defines nations as 'imagined communities' of a particular kind, points to the role of newspapers in the development of a sense of nationhood. A community is imagined, he maintains, if the connection amongst its members is not the consequence of face-to-face contact, but depends rather on each person's confidence in the existence and the 'steady, anonymous, simultaneous activity' of all the others.[38] Newspapers, through the assumptions they imply about calendrical coincidence and about the reader's relation to other readers and to the material presented, both represent and contribute significantly to the 'imagining' of the communities known as nations.[39] Their part in giving the Great War patriotic poets access to a wide audience undoubtedly helped to reinforce the messages of nationalism, and it had many implications for the character of the poetry. For instance, it is possible that, because the earliest poems to be published were mainly by established writers, who worked in the accepted tradition of the moment, and because newspapers circulated their poems with unusual speed, the standard for an appropriate patriotic poem was very quickly set. Such poems were part of the daily news and, reciprocally, the news was part of the poems. Michael Hamburger writes that the 'most characteristic' poetry of the First World War arose because this conflict brought about the first major encounter between warfare and 'sensibilities essentially civilian'.[40] He refers, of course, to combatant poets, and specifically those whose work is of high quality. If, however, the criterion for 'most characteristic' were quantity, one would have to reverse Hamburger's intended meaning: the sensibility of the majority of poets was indeed civilian, but, rather than the poets going to the battlefield, the war was brought to them at home by means of the daily news. To a retrospective reader the news of the war that the popular newspapers printed may appear selective and inaccurate, but contemporaries were probably no more sceptical than the vast majority of American viewers of television newscasts during the early years of the Vietnam War. Because of the news reports (even if their origin was actually rumour or imagination) the reading public felt truly informed about the facts, and therefore in a position not only to comment but, later in the war, to claim sometimes that combatants' reports which contradicted what the papers said were false.

In July and early August of 1914 the most important news that the papers carried was about threats of invasion and measures taken to counter the threats in various countries throughout Europe. When nationalism has become an established *modus vivendi*, as it had in Europe by that time, borders between nations are both distinct (Gellner compares the modern map to a painting by Mondrian) and sacrosanct, and animosity strengthens the intensity of the dividing lines. Not surprisingly, therefore, once the invasion became a reality it generated an unprecedented outcry – a clamour of protest and indignation from the one side, and an equally fervent outpouring of angry and bitter justification from the other. It is not difficult to understand why poetry was a popular medium amongst the contributors to this verbal defence of the homeland. Prose writings of comparable length for public consumption, such as letters to newspapers, editorial comment, or short magazine articles, were likely to be printed only if the author could offer new information or unusual insights. Poems, on the other hand, are self-justifying; as works of art they are free from a referential constraint, and, however over-used their theme, almost any variation meets the demand for novelty of expression that validates the act of writing and publication. At the beginning of the war the outraged citizens of each country, as readers of the nation's newspapers, had access to a common pool of information, and all were potentially familiar with the same canon of poetic texts, which might serve as models. All, therefore, were equally well equipped for the poetic defence of the beleaguered homeland. The possibility that the writing of verse demanded unusual talent seems not to have been raised, and even the factors that normally discourage amateur poets, or at least confine their efforts to the privacy of the bedroom washstand – the aesthetic judgement of editors and publishers, and their preference for writers whose work is likely to sell – appear to have been temporarily suspended. Poetry, for the moment, was an ideal medium for nationalistic expression, the more so because the publishing of the poems converted them from a personal declaration of loyalty into a work of propaganda. Since the poetry that protested the violation of borders gave enduring form to the indignation that greeted the war, it helped sustain the initial sense of outrage and injustice, and thus served as a useful tool in strengthening and maintaining public animosity towards the enemy.

The poetic onslaught began with a scattering of newspaper offerings in the first few days of August, increased rapidly until there were daily poems in some papers, and continued in full strength for many months as old poems were reissued on broadsheets and in anthologies, and new ones were published. French and Belgian poets were in the best position to express indignation about the transgression of borders, since the German infringement upon their territory was a fact and not a mere possibility. Nicolas Beauduin states with unusual calmness the French justification for fighting, when he says in 'Collecte',

> Nous ne désirons rien que ce qui est à nous, . . .
> Nous luttons simplement pour défendre nos villes,
> Nos fermes, nos enclos fleuris, nos champs de blé'.[41]

(We wish for nothing except that which is our own. We are fighting only to defend our towns, our farms, our flowery meadows, our fields of corn.)

Much more typically, the German attack is greeted with cries of outrage, protesting the intrusion upon French ground by 'le torrent ravageur' (the ravaging torrent) and deprecating the destruction caused by the invaders – 'Les villages fumants, les fermes acroulées, / Tout broyé, tout rasé comme par l'ouragan' (Smouldering villages, ruined farms, everything scorched and razed as if by a storm).[42] Both the scale of this poetic outburst against German aggression and the manner in which the anger was expressed bear witness to the effectiveness of national and nationalistic education. The awareness of geographical unity, deliberately fostered by the use of school-books like *Tour de la France par deux enfants*, was an important contributory in generating a sense of nationhood, and reciprocally, the sense of nationhood endowed the physical unit – no longer a series of regions but a single entity – with a new 'mantle of holiness' (to borrow Peacock's term). The difference between the conceptualised homeland and the physical terrain becomes clear if one extends the comparison raised by two of the poets I have quoted here (and many others), in their use of the 'flood' or 'storm' metaphor. When natural disaster occurs, the people directly affected are identified by their compatriots as a distinct group – 'they' are the victims, while 'we', who have fortunately escaped harm, are in a position to express sympathy and offer assistance. Any attempt on the part of the second group to claim a share in the hardship would be viewed with contempt. In the war poems, however, the farms and meadows ruined by the metaphorical storm are not 'theirs' but 'ours', and one finds surprisingly little compassion for the actual victims. The despoiling of the countryside is regarded as an injury to the entire people, to 'all of us', for the invasion is a violation of a sacred domain, 'la France', and it is an affront to the pride and dignity both of the nation as a whole and of each individual member. In such a conceptualisation, one's link with 'the land on which one has lived' is actually of relatively little importance – hence the readiness of men from the colonies to come to the support of a British 'homeland' most had never seen, and the title of an American publication supporting Germany – simply 'The Fatherland'; and hence also – more significantly in the present context – the fact that a similar invasion in 1870, before nationalistic education had achieved its full effect, produced only a weak foreshadowing in France of the poetic outcry of 1914.

Nevertheless the threat to the terrain was ultimately the reason for fighting, and for the French poets in particular, physical destruction served as a symbol for the attack upon the nation as a whole. Although the devastation of the countryside is widely condemned, and of ancient Belgian towns like Liège, Louvain and Ypres, most acrimony in the French poetry is reserved for the destruction of churches, convents and cathedrals – Verdun, Arras, Reims, and not uncommonly all of them together – for these ruined shrines of the old religion have become the sacred sites of the new. Accordingly one finds, in addition to indignation, a glorying in martyrdom; in Raymond de la Tailhède's 'Hymne pour la France', for instance, the country is a saint whose adornments are made from the ruined cathedrals:

Dans la pierre de Reims sculpte ton diadème,
Arras ensanglante soit aussi ton emblème,
Taille pour ton manteau la pourpre de Verdun.[43]

(In the stone of Reims carve your diadem; take Arras, bleeding, for your emblem, too; fashion your cloak from the purple of Verdun.)

Reims in particular serves as a focal point for protest, almost as if a statement about the destruction of this cathedral were a passport to respectability amongst French patriotic poets. Most follow a similar pattern: a rhetorical invocation ('O sainte basilique, auguste cathé-drale'),[44] a description of the building's former splendour and some reference to the manner of its destruction, followed by a vociferous condemnation of the enemy, an expression of righteous determination, and a call for revenge. Contrary to what one might expect, no attempt is made to describe the scene of devastation. According to Cate Haste in *Keep the Home Fires Burning* the story was overstated by the authorities for propaganda purposes, and in fact only a small part of the cathedral was badly damaged; but it is unlikely that a concern for the truth was the reason for the poets' reticence. More probably they felt that too close a focus might impede the revelling in destruction and the righteous indignation that the destruction justified, and there is no doubt that the tone of the poetry lent itself more readily to recollected beauty than to unpleasant reality. Even amongst the pictures of past glory, however, few are memorable. A notable exception is Émile Verhaeren's 'Reims', which opens with a striking image:

> Depuis le matin clair jusqu'au tomber du jour
> Elle avançait et s'approchait
> De celui qui marchait;
> Et sitôt qu'il sentait l'ombre des grandes tours
> Qui barraient la contrée
> Le gagner à leur tour,
> Il entrait dans la pierre
> Creusée immensement et pénétrée
> Par mille ans de beauté et mille ans de prière.[45]

(All day long, from morning until evening, it advanced, approaching the person who was walking towards it; and as soon as he felt the shadow of the great towers that barred the countryside catching up with him in turn, he entered into the immense hollowed rock, which had been penetrated by a thousand years of beauty and a thousand years of prayer.)

Verhaeren resorts ultimately to rhetoric and invective, but unlike most of the Reims poets, who indiscriminately mingle concrete and abstract, oratory and description, he focuses first on the object and establishes its reality. His image of the massive cathedral seeming to move towards the traveller across the plain, of the cool shade, and of the ancient stones that have absorbed the beauty and prayer of centuries, leaves the reader with no doubt that the loss of this ancient treasure is a tragedy. This effect is unusual,however, for the primary concern of the poets is to give voice to their feelings of outrage, and the specific material object that serves as the focus of their protest is important mainly because its destruction justifies the act of writing.

Although history, following in the steps of contemporary opinion in France and Britain, has judged Germany as the aggressor in the war, the German patriotic poets were quite as much concerned as their French counterparts about the violation of national boundaries. The departing soldier in Heinrich Lersch's 'Soldaten-Abschied', one of the most popular German poems of the war, states his purpose and that of his fellows simply: 'Denn wir gehen, das Vaterland zu schützen' (For we are going to protect the Fatherland).[46] Karl Bröger shows how the need for defence justifies what seems to be an act of aggression:

Daß kein fremder Fuß betrete den heimischen Grund,
Stirbt ein Bruder in Polen, liegt einer in Flandern wund.

(So that no foreigner's foot may tread on the soil of home, a brother dies in Poland, another lies wounded in Flanders.)[47]

Bröger's attitude is easily understood in light of the frequency with which German poets refer to the sense of being surrounded by enemies, and of belonging to a country standing alone against three strong forces. (Relatively few poems distinguish Austria's involvement from that of Germany.) Cäsar Flaischlen's 'Deutscher Weltkrieg' is typical:

Sie haben seit Jahren uns umstellt
An allen Ecken und Kanten,
Verträge und Klauseln ausgeheckt
Und einander Schmiere gestanden.
[. . .]
Nun geht ein Kesseltreiben los
Rundum, uns fest zuzäunen,
Hie Russ', hie Brite, hie Franzos'...
Und alles gegen einen![48]

(They have been surrounding us for years on every border and corner, devised treaties and provisos, and kept an eye out for each other. Now a *battue* begins all around us, to hem us in: here a Russian, here a Briton, here a Frenchman, and all against one).

Phrases like 'in Ost und West vom Feind umstellt' (surrounded by enemies to east and west), 'von Gefahr umringt' (encircled by danger), and 'Feinde zu Land und Meer' (enemies by land and sea) run like a chorus through this poetry. The multiple threat is emphasised when poets use a 'triptych' structure, with a separate stanza devoted to the failings and projected downfall of each of the three major enemies. Julius Bab, the editor of the series *Der deutsche Krieg im deutschen*

Gedicht, rather disparagingly calls this 'Aufzählungspoesie' (counting-rhymes), though two examples are to be found in his first anthology, Gerhart Hauptmann's 'Reiterlied' and 'O Nikolaus, O Nikolaus' (known also as the 'Mainzer Wachtstube' (Mainz guardroom) song) – a soldiers' song to the tune of 'O Tannenbaum'.[49] Although to the retrospective observer the excessive emphasis on the triple threat may seem to be an after-the-event justification for Germany's invasion of Belgium, its widespread recurrence in the poetry suggests that, at the time, the threat to the sanctity of the country's borders seemed to the German people a valid reason for trying to limit the effectiveness of one of the opposing forces before it was too late. One must remember however that these are poems, not political tracts; while the 'triple threat' concept guaranteed their usefulness as propaganda, the repetitive structure also served as a poetic or aesthetic device that validated the act of writing. And undoubtedly the triple threat developed very quickly into a literary convention through imitation, to become something of a German counterpart of the true French patriot's mandatory Reims poem.

In justifying their part in the general outcry at the violation of boundaries, English poets were in a more difficult position than their French and German colleagues, since their home territory was neither attacked nor directly threatened. It is apparent that the majority of them either recognised this difficulty or, more probably, did not even consider invasion to be a possibility, despite Rudyard Kipling's famous warning that 'The Hun is at the gate'.[50] Instead, they took up the issue of the sanctity of borders as a matter of principle, and with heroic alliteration appropriate to the inheritors of the tradition of *Beowulf*, they proceeded 'To fight for freedom for less favoured folk' by defending France and, more particularly, that ' "little" but loyal race', the Belgians.[51] But although many of the poems are nominally inspired by the suffering of the French and Belgian people, much emphasis is placed on Britain's thoroughly unselfish role in the war. Seeking revenge for 'These smoking hearths of fair and peaceful lands, / This reeking trail of deeds abhorred in Hell', Englishmen are urged to 'Haste to the help of a brave nation smitten', or to 'lend a hand / To the woe-struck sons and daughters / Of a war-torn sister land'; they can claim to be 'Fending a little friend, / Weak but unshaken', and are reminded, in a congratulatory manner, 'Ye are holding in your hands / Liberty of little lands, / Seeking nothing, giving all'.[52] Unlike the Germans, who have dealt with the treaty (unspecified, but presumably that of 1839 guaranteeing Belgian neutrality) as a 'scrap of paper', 'torn in pieces', Britain refuses to have anything to do with 'a false, fair-weather friendship', since, as Ian Colvin says in 'The Answer', 'To what England puts her hand, /

Upon that she takes her stand', and 'contracting out of danger were for ever her disgrace'.[53] In 'The Answer' the Germans try to bargain with England to stay out of the war by promising to leave the Belgian ports unoccupied, while England, naturally, remains scornfully aloof. This acknowledgement that an occupied Belgium might pose a direct threat to British soil is, however, unusual, for in general the possibility of such a territorial threat is ignored – in part, no doubt, because the war was taking place 'Abroad', but also because defending a practical policy had less poetic appeal than arguing for an altruistic 'just cause'. And according to James Lill, the author of 'The Issues', altruism would definitely create a better impression on future generations:

And Liberty, Progress, Brotherhood, Peace,
Are the watchwords we now must write;
That our children learn 'twas for these, not gain,
That England stepped into the fight.[54]

Almost certainly the implication in Lill's poem that these capitalised abstractions are merely words to be written to disguise the truth, rather than ideas or causes to be pursued, is unintentional, for the poet is clearly concerned with creating a positive image of England. While the justice of one's nation's cause is perhaps the major battlefield in the poetry, the contest for superiority amongst national images is almost equally important. Each country has what might be termed a 'peacetime' image – the poets' idealised view of the 'homeland' that must be defended from the threatened attack – and a more obviously propagandist and warlike face. The two are by no means clearly separable, and the former is as propagandist as the latter, but in a more subtle way. In view of the popular belief that all Englishmen are countrymen at heart, one should not be surprised that England's ideal self-image is rural – though the capacity of these poets to see only the countryside is rather remarkable. At the end of the eighteenth century William Blake complained about England's 'dark, satanic mills', and seventy years later William Morris observed 'the snorting steam and the piston stroke' and 'the spreading of the hideous town'. By 1914, despite the considerable advance of industrialisation in the intervening years, the country has apparently reverted in poetry to being entirely rural. True Britons who come forth to fight are from 'Sussex, Northumberland, / Cornwall and Cumberland, / Ireland and Scotland and Wales' – a map that neatly encircles and omits the industrial midlands and north. 'Castle and cottage are giving their best', from 'Bideford and Appledore' (two villages in Devon), from 'windy Barrow' (not, at that time, a shipyard), and even from 'Derby's rocks and vales', but not from her coalfields. A rare exception, at first glance, is 'A New Song to an Old Tune' in the anthology *The Fiery Cross*, for it calls on

> Mates of the net, the mine, the fire,
> Lads of the wheel and desk and loom,
> Noble and trader, squire and groom

to rally to the flag. This unusual outburst of realism, however, is by
W.E. Henley, who died in 1903, and the poem dates from the Boer
War – an interesting indication that the nationalistic poetry of 1914
was not necessarily like that of even so recent a conflict. While it is
possible that occasional poems were published in which industry was
part of England's national image, they were certainly not reprinted in
the popular anthologies. Furthermore, when an article in *The Herald*
of 19 December 1914 recommends that the idea of the 'poetic soul' of
England should be applied to the 'industrial hells' and the Black
Country, the implication is that such references were rare. Almost the
only exceptions to this general rule are those poems in which slum-
dwellers are congratulated on their conversion into fine soldiers –
that is to say, where the war offers an escape from an un-English
situation into true citizenship.

Like their English counterparts, French patriotic poets live in an
idealised country committed to the old values. As one might expect,
this ideal nation is deeply religious, and proud that its present trials
place it in the tradition of the saints and martyrs. At the same time,
however, it enjoys its unique link with the classical past, being similarly
proud of its 'âme latine / Éprise d'Art et d'Idéal' (Latin soul, in love
with Art and the Ideal), and of those 'fiers aïeux, ces Grècs et ces
Romains, / Dont l'écho dit encor les exploits surhumains' (noble
ancestors, those Greeks and Romans, whose superhuman exploits are
still echoed abroad).[55] These two aspects of national image are reflected
in the geographical perception of the country as consisting only of
farms and villages, towns with ruined cathedrals, and the cultured
(but not modern) city of Paris. In the struggle between classical and
modern education in France in the last decades of the nineteenth
century, it appears that the honours went to the former, for there is
nothing here to hint at the many French accomplishments in science
and engineering. Germany, on the other hand, definitely sees itself as
a modern nation (though without forgetting for a moment its heroic
and cultural past, or indeed the rural beauty of the present). Poems
sing the praises of the country's splendid modern weapons – U-boats,
famous warships like the *Emden* and the *Königin Luise* (which laid
mines in the Thames estuary), and mammoth guns called 'die faule
Grete' (Lazy Greta) and 'die fleißige Berta' – hard-working (but more
commonly known as 'Big') Bertha.[56] Far from pretending that industry
does not exist, poets venerate men like the steel workers, 'die Helden
im Feuerofen' (the heroes of the furnace), who stay behind to produce

'Blanker, wuchtiger deutscher Stahl' (shining, powerful German steel),
and the stokers on battleships, who carry out the unheroic but vital
task of firing the ships' boilers.[57]

This readiness to make a poetic compromise with modernity is not
necessarily a reflection of a different social attitude in general, for the
treatment of industrial workers in Germany was not significantly
different from that in England. It is, however, linked to a phenom-
enon that seems to have had no counterpart in the other countries –
the existence of a recognised category known as 'Arbeiterdichtung' or
'poetry of the working class'; and one might argue that such poetry
could arise only when the workers were sufficiently aware of them-
selves as a class to recognise their contribution to the cultural as well
as the financial well-being of the nation. (The Social Democratic party
was attracting many more working-class votes in Germany before the
war than the Labour party in England.) The worker-poetry phenom-
enon began to develop from about 1910, mainly through a loose
network of advice and encouragement, eventually involving perhaps
twenty poets. It was given focus by the forming of the 'Bund der
Werkleute auf Haus Nyland' (Union of Workers of the House of
Nyland), whose motivating principle was to bring an appreciation for
modern technology into the framework of the cultural inheritance.
The founding members of the association – Josef Winckler, Jacob
Kneip and Wilhelm Vershofen – were not themselves 'Werkleute', but
they considered that one of their major tasks was to provide encourage-
ment to writers from the working class. While Gerrit Engelke was
possibly the most talented of the poets associated with Haus Nyland,
the most popular was probably Heinrich Lersch, 'der Kesselschmidt
aus München-Gladbach' – the boiler-maker from München-Gladbach
– a title used by Julius Bab when he reprinted 'Soldaten-Abschied' in
his first anthology.

The emphasis on Lersch's occupation is a little misleading, since
although he had trained as a boiler-maker, Lersch had spent the
previous five years travelling around the country, working however
he could. In this respect he is characteristic of the other worker-poets,
few of whom appear to have had been employed consistently at the
same job. (The lathe-turner Christoph Wieprecht, who worked in the
Krupp steel factory in Essen, is therefore unusual.) Not all the worker-
poets were associated directly with the Haus Nyland group – Karl
Bröger, Paul Zech and Alfons Petzold, for example, were all writing
independently, the last in Vienna, where he met and encouraged
younger writers, including Lersch. Ultimately, however, most of their
work during and after the war came from the same publisher, Eugen
Diederichs in Jena. With few exceptions the poets voiced their firm
dedication to the national cause at the outbreak of war, and Bröger's

'Bekenntnis' became particularly well known when it was quoted by the German Chancellor as proof of the commitment of the working class:

> Herrlich zeigt es aber deine größte Gefahr,
> daß dein ärmster Sohn auch dein getreuester war.[58]

(Gloriously, however, your greatest danger shows that your poorest son was also your most loyal).

The verse of these workers-turned-soldiers, together with that of their associates such as Winckler and Petzold (who was ineligible for military service because of his age and poor health), was a major factor in establishing Germany's self-image in the patriotic war poetry as a modern nation proud of its industry. It is worth noting in passing that, although some of the worker-poets were highly regarded in the 1930s, by the time of the Second World War Germany, too, had reverted largely to its rural past as far as poetry was concerned. A link with the soil was a necessary component of the form of nationalism that flourished under Hitler, and almost without exception the poets who supply biographical information in Kurt Ziesel's patriotic anthology *Krieg und Dichtung* (1943) insist that, even if they must live in a city, they are countrymen at heart.

Through what might be termed the 'private' image of the nation, the First World War patriotic poets promote unobtrusively a picture of how they would like to believe their country really is, under normal conditions. In addition, each nation is endowed with a 'public' identity, and it is in this connection that the main verbal battle occurs. Unlike the first image, which is based on elements that can potentially be 'guaranteed by empirical reality', the second involves the conceptualised nation, the nation as a god, endowed with the personal characteristics that its worshippers most admire. Gellner updates Emil Durkheim's contention that 'in religious worship society adores its own camouflaged image' with the claim that 'In a nationalistic age, societies worship themselves brazenly and openly, spurning the camouflage.'[59] Nowhere is this brazen promotion of the ideal 'us' more evident than in the contest for superior national image in the war poetry. While Benedict Anderson maintains that nations are imagined as limited and sovereign, on the evidence of the patriotic verse one must add that they are also imagined as unique. A few of the characteristics of which a nation is proud may be shared by its allies, but ultimately the homeland is superior to all other countries. Because the number of virtues and high-minded causes is limited, opposing nations tend to lay claim to the same characteristics to prove their uniqueness and superiority, so that the effect of the claim is diminished if the poems from different languages are juxtaposed. Even so, the fact that the choice is restricted does not appear to have affected the quantity of verse praising the virtues of the nation, for in this, as in many other respects, conventionality was apparently viewed as an advantage.

Having no territorial interest in the conflict, Britain was in the best position to feel morally superior as the nation that was going to war for purely unselfish and high-minded reasons. It was clearly only a very short step – as in Lill's 'The Issues' – from pledging to fight 'for Belgium's honour and homes, / For the future and fame of France' to the conviction that the country was at war for a variety of high ideals like 'Liberty, Progress, Brotherhood, Peace'. Freedom and Liberty, usually capitalised and without a qualifying 'from', are presented as a 'holy cause', together with Justice and, more enigmatic, 'the Right'. The chief motivating factor as far as England is concerned, however, is Honour, which calls the country to war in Owen Seaman's 'Pro Patria', in Ian Colvin's 'The Answer', R.G. Barnes' 'To the British Army', and in many another poem.[60] The term as it is used in the poetry has a variety of meanings: in 'We are fighting for Britain's honour, too, / For the faith to her plighted word' it refers, presumably, to a reputation for honesty and reliability, but 'Honour of women' (which is to be 'Venged') suggests, rather, that the reputation is for purity; in 'those whose hearts for GOD and honour burn' honour seems to be the equivalent of fame, yet 'Glory sought is Honour lost' denies that equivalence; and in 'England, in this great fight to which you go, / Because, where honour calls you, go you must', the word seems impossible to paraphrase. Nevertheless, there is no doubt that, since defence of the physical homeland was not available as a justification for Britain's involvement, the defence of the nation's Honour served as a satisfactory substitute, to the extent that the two concepts were often interchanged.

Ronald Peacock mentions honour along with freedom and justice as the patriotic ideals that have always 'spurred nations on'; yet interestingly enough, in Betty T. Bennett's anthology of war poetry of the Romantic era, which was also the period of the Napoleonic Wars, 'honour' rarely appears, and only in connection with the death of individual combatants. While a sufficiently strong sense of nationhood prevailed at that time to link the country's name, rather than that of its leaders, with Freedom and Justice, the idea that a nation has Honour was apparently not current amongst English writers of the Napoleonic era (although it was evidently not totally unknown, since Wordsworth has a sonnet on the subject). A German anthology from the same period, *Ergießungen Deutschen Gefühles in Gesängen und Liedern bei den Ereignissen dieser Zeit* (Outpourings of German Feeling in Songs and Poems on the Events of the Present Time), dated 1814, reveals a similar (though again less than total) lack of concern with the honour of the country. If the two anthologies are indeed representative, the explanation for the change in the next hundred years undoubtedly lies in part in the increased tendency to personify or deify the country. Since honour, unlike freedom and justice, is an attribute of the individual, presumably it can be attached to the name of a country only when the nation is perceived as a distinct being endowed with human qualities; and the progress towards such a perception of nations was only in its early stages at the time of the Napoleonic Wars. The change, however – from justifying war on the grounds that the country's sovereignty is challenged, to a justification on the basis of a threat to the nation's honour or prestige – has far-reaching and frightening implications.

The popularity of this particular individual attribute, or at least of this term, undoubtedly owes much to the nineteenth century's interest in things medieval. Mark Girouard in *The Return to Camelot* has described how this taste developed in Britain throughout the nineteenth century, but medievalism was no less prevalent on the Continent, and especially in Germany. The interest can be traced to the precursors of Romanticism, with their concern for the native rather than classical tradition; it manifested itself in the early stages in a revived interest in Gothic architecture (as early as 1770), in historical dramas like those of Schiller and the young Goethe, and, later, those of Victor Hugo, in the Romantic conception of the Middle Ages as the Golden Age, and above all in the popularity of historical novels, where Scott made his mark almost as strongly in Germany and France as in Britain. Medievalism remained alive throughout the nineteenth century with the help of Tennyson, Hugo, Wagner and the Pre-Raphaelites, of literary scholars rediscovering or translating the early masterpieces of the various languages, of railway-station architects and castle-builders, house-designers, schoolteachers and popular novelists. So firmly established was the awareness of this revised version of the Middle Ages that poets in the Great War could use the terminology of knighthood and the warrior ethic, including the all-embracing concept of Honour, with complete confidence that their readers would understand, and would appreciate the sacredness of this particular 'holy cause'.

Although the British situation offered the most scope for selflessness and altruism, there is no intended suggestion that the English poetry held the field unchallenged in the battle over noble causes. In the matter of Honour, for instance, while many true-blooded Englishmen may have subscribed to Robert Bridges' view that 'England stands for Honour', Paul Warncke regards his own homeland as the 'Land der

Treu und Ehre', the land of truth and honour.[61] In Gerhart Haupt-
mann's 'Reiterlied' the war is caused by three robbers who attack
Germany, declaring, 'Deutschland, wir wollen an deine Ehr!' (Ger-
many, we're after your honour) – honour which, in another poem by
the same author, is described as 'untadlig' or blameless.[62] (The problem
of defining the term is no easier in the other languages.) Like Honour,
the Right is a popular cause on all sides, and is similarly undefinable.
'God defend the Right' is almost a cliché in English, as is 'für Reich
und Recht' (for the Empire and the Right) in German, and each side,
in its own way, subscribes to the belief that 'Dem Recht nur bleibt der
Sieg' – only the Right will win. France's national purpose, too, is
clothed in high-sounding ideals. Gabriel Mourey describes the country
as 'la Terre de la Justice et de la Loi, / De la claire Raison et de la
sainte Foi' (the Land of Justice and Law, of clear Reason and sacred
Faith), and few poems in any of the languages carry such a weight of
idealism as the single line in one of Fabre Des Essarts' 'Quatre
sonnets de guerre', where the poet states the cause as 'Le Droit, le
Bien, l'Honneur, la France et la Justice' (Right, Goodness, Honour,
France and Justice).[63] The voice of Ezra Pound, who in 1912 warned
poets to 'go in fear of abstractions', was obviously crying only in the
wilderness.

Innocence of blame in causing the war is an appealing aspect of
national self-image, and all parties are equally certain that the war
was not their fault. The French, perceiving themselves (appropriately
enough) as victims, recognise that they need not justify their position;
therefore, although the French indignation is neither smaller nor less
righteous that that of their friends and enemies, direct debate about
blame is left to the others. R.M. Freeman places the responsibility
squarely on the Germans: 'Came this challenge from the foe; / Naught
we did to court this fight'.[64] Furthermore the English, according to
William Watson, 'can verily say' ... 'our hands are pure; for peace, for
peace we have striven'.[65] In Germany, however, the same theme is
repeated many times – 'Wir haben den Krieg nicht gewollt!' (We
didn't want war), 'Ihr habt den Krieg gewollt, nun habt ihr ihn!' (You
wanted war, now you have it), 'Ihr habt's gewollt, nicht wir!' (You
wished for it, we didn't), to give just a few from a multitude of
examples.[66] When John Drinkwater uses as a title almost precisely the
same phrase, 'We Willed it Not', one is reminded that this is indeed a
feud 'between kin folk kin tongued', as Thomas Hardy described it.[67]

Another supposedly unique feature of each nation's self-concept
that is in fact widely shared is the belief that the survival of humanity
depends on the one country alone. Rudolf Alexander Schröder's claim,
'wenn wir fallen, fällt die Welt' (If we fall, the whole world falls), is
countered with Kipling's question, 'Who dies, if England live?' while

the Italian poet Gabriele d'Annunzio expresses his feeling for France in the words, 'France, sans Toi le monde serait seul' (France, without you the whole world would be lonely) – a sentiment shared by Nicolas Beauduin: 'tu es / La sainte nation qui sauvera le monde' (you are the holy nation that will save the world).[68] The French are particularly attached to the idea that their cause is the general human good. For example, Victorin Baret, promising that France and her allies 'imposeront le joug à l'Ostrogoth immonde' (will impose the yoke on the vile Ostrogoth), justifies the proposed conquest of German territory on the grounds that 'C'est pour l'Humanité que nous travaillerons' ... 'pour le progrés du genre humain' (We will be working for Humanity ... for the progress of the human race).[69] In a later poem, where a hope for peace has replaced the desire for revenge, the same writer remains adamantly patriotic, for the peace that is to bring a new order to humankind, 'un ordre nouveau pour l'Humanité' will be 'la Paix Franìaise' – the French Peace.[70]

Although in this conviction that the country's role is vital for the well-being of humanity the French poets appear to hold the field, neither the Germans nor the English are willing to admit defeat. Friedrich Lienhard is perhaps the strongest proponent of the 'deutsche Sendung', the German mission, which he sees as 'das *Herz* zu sein, / Das fortan allen Völkern Sonne schafft' (to be the *heart*, that henceforth will provide sunlight for all peoples), or 'Den Völkern ein Hort zu sein, / Europas heiliger Hain' (to be a treasure-hoard for all peoples, Europe's sacred grove).[71] For Lienhard the cultural centre, 'Deutschlands Herz', is Weimar, Goethe's home for much of his life, with Wagner's Bayreuth of almost equal importance. He berates those people from abroad who had previously visited the two towns to do homage to the memory of their most famous residents, but who are now intent upon destroying the country which gave them 'Geist' (spirit, mind, intellect).[72] As one might expect of the proverbially pragmatic English, their mission towards humanity is neither cultural nor spiritual, but is expressed mainly in terms of the continuing existence of the Empire, of 'Old England's righteous sway'.[73] Its value ranges from the purely practical – 'I have cleansed the seas, and have opened them / To traffic of many ships' – to the fulfilment of the Empire's idealistic potential:

> Her increase
> Abolishes the man-dividing seas,
> And frames the brotherhood on earth to be!
> She, in free peoples planting sovereignty,
> Orbs half the civil world in British peace –

a peace which, one must assume, is somehow different from Baret's 'Paix Française', noted above.[74]

In the verbal battle for superiority, it is not surprising that all sides claim God as an ally. Since the possibility of divided loyalty on His part may be dismissed on the grounds that the enemy is not a true believer, the majority of poems display a simple confidence that God will know which 'Right' to defend. A few authors are concerned, however, with the subtleties of a situation that sees Christian nations fighting against each other, or with the conflicting demands of their commitment to two gods. Heinrich Keinzl, for instance, recognises that 'Gott ist mit uns, er wird den Feind verderben!' (God is on our side, He will destroy the foe!) is a statement common to Germans, British, French, Japanese, and others; he concludes that, since God is obviously 'kein Fähnrich und kein Kugellenker' – He will not act as an ensign nor determine the direction of the bullets – the Germans must live in a God-fearing manner, so that their ultimate victory, though achieved through their own strength, will be a victory for God.[75] Pastor H.A.F. Tech, the author of *Kampfreime eines Friedfertigen aus dem Kriegsjahre 1914*, contemplates many aspects of the war in an attempt to reconcile the requirements of Christianity and love of the Fatherland, and he is particularly insistent that 'Von Gott erwählt ist nur der Christ' (Only the Christian is chosen by God).[76] Like Tech, J.J. Brown feels that the task of punishing evil should be left to God, and that the war is in fact a judgement upon all, since 'Belgium has its Congo deeds to rue; / Poland its pogroms; Europe has its crimes'.[77] While Tech and Brown place God's cause above that of the Fatherland, for some writers, especially in German, the priority is reversed. Will Vesper and Hans Schmidt-Kestner both confront the Christian edict 'Liebe deine Feinde' (Love your enemy), but feel that, in the present instance, they are unable to obey. Vesper pleads that his hatred is 'die Frucht der höchsten Liebe' – the fruit of the highest love (leaving no doubt which of his two gods takes precedence), while Schmidt-Kestner asks for forgiveness, and promises to love his enemies again when they have been driven 'Ins allertiefste Kellerloch' – into the darkest cellar.[78] The French poetry shows little evidence of questioning on the matter of religion; God is clearly on the side of France against an enemy who, in addition to every other vice, is a follower of Luther and a destroyer of churches. In such a case, the cause of God and that of the Fatherland coincide absolutely.

As ultimate proof of the superiority of their national culture, writers in all three languages are ever ready to call up the names of their country's famous men. Clearly the teaching of national rather than classical history achieved its desired effect. Yet the choice has to be made with care, since the figures must serve to unify rather than divide the nation, and so must be politically uncontroversial. In the matter of military heroes, Germany's champion is undoubtedly Bismarck, the founder of the nation, with Frederick the Great receiving honourable mention (presumably from Prussian writers). France refrains from vaunting the success of Napoleon, perhaps through tact or because of his eventual defeat, or because he remained controversial, but possibly because he was not sufficiently saintly. Instead, French poets prefer to look back to pre-Revolutionary martyrs like Jeanne d'Arc and Roland for military heroes. Britain, on the other hand, is well-endowed with uncontroversial military leaders on whom to call, including King Henry V, Marlborough and Wellington, and especially admirals such as Drake and Nelson. When important people from the humanities are required, however, Germany, which boasts of being 'das Volk der Dichter und Denker' (the nation of poets and thinkers), is far in the lead. French writers summon up Corneille and Racine occasionally, while their English counterparts, in spite of a claim that England is 'the home of poetry', seem to be limited mainly to Shake-speare. Meanwhile, the Germans refer liberally to Goethe and Schiller, Luther and Kant, as well as Wagner, Bach and Beethoven, and a horde of lesser figures such as Dürer and Kleist. In this particular battle, Germany is undoubtedly the victor.

Unfortunately, however, if such famous names from the past may be summoned for the purpose of proving a superior degree of civil-isation, they are also available as a convenient weapon for poets on the other side, who use them to emphasise, through contrast, the present barbarous state of the nation concerned. Thus Friedrich Lienhard's horror at Germany's betrayal by 'die Gäste von Bayreuth' (the visitors to Bayreuth) is expressed equally strongly by the enemy. Maurice Allou argues that 'La grande âme de Goethe est un mirage et meurt' (the great soul of Goethe is a fading mirage), while William Archer imagines 'Luther, Kant, Goethe, Bach, and Beethoven' dis-owning as compatriots the Germans who have sacked Louvain.[79] (Luther is clearly more highly regarded in England than in France.) In 'Emmanuel Kant' Benjamin Buisson points out that 'l'Allemagne actuelle' (present-day Germany) prefers to Kant 'un Nietzsche, en-censeur / D'oppression et de force brutale' (a Nietzsche, censer-bearer to oppression and brute force).[80] Kathleen Knox, too, regrets the passing of the old Germany, which she describes as the 'child-hood land' of the fairy tales, the 'music land' and the 'learned land of wise old books'; none of these can co-exist, she says, with a 'land of hate'.[81] Conversely, some of the German poets feel that it is the English who have abandoned their cultural heritage. According to Richard Schaukal, for instance, England, which had always been 'die erlauchte Schule' (the illustrious school) for other peoples, a 'Walterin

auf hohem Stuhle' (a governor on a throne), has now shown them a
different face, betraying both Shakespeare and the Magna Carta.[82]
Rudolf Herzog is perhaps failing to observe the rules of this verbal
war when he uses Jeanne d'Arc as a weapon against the English – he
describes a statue in which Jeanne is ready to spring into action with
a cry of 'Calais! Calais! Und Tod den Briten!' (Calais! And death to
the British!)[83] That old enmity is treated far more tactfully by Gabriel
Mourey, with a reminder that the English gallantly called France their
'très douce ennemie' (respected enemy).[84]

Although some historians point to rivalry between Germany and
Britain as one of the existing conditions that precipitated the outbreak
of war, such an attitude is not highly prevalent in the poetry. One
finds it mainly in 'triple threat' poems, where the justice of the
German complaint, and accordingly the effectiveness of the poem, is
increased if the enemy powers are presented as conniving against
Germany in the prewar years. For the most part, however, the
England and Germany of the poetry express a sense of mutual dis-
illusionment when they find themselves at war, as though each had
understood and approved of the other's actions, or at least had
believed the other's words of peace. (In French such disillusionment
with Germany's conduct is far less common; presumably the memory
of 1870 endured.) Masks appear as a recurring symbol for the sense of
betrayal – 'Nun sind die Masken alle rings gefallen' (Now all around
the masks have fallen), 'England! du nahmst die Maske fort / Mit
kalten, zynischen Gebärden' (England, you removed your mask with
cold, cynical gestures), 'And now the mask is down', 'You, that flung
/ The gauntlet down, fling down the mask you wore' – to quote a few
examples from amongst many.[85]

A similar sense of betrayal is presented in terms of race. Like
Thomas Hardy from the opposing side, many of the German poets
recognise their blood kinship with the English, and because, as Adolf
Ey puts it, 'Trotz allem sind wir doch durch Blut verbunden' (We are,
after all, bound by blood) they deplore on racial grounds Britain's
choice of allies.[86] A writer who uses the pseudonym 'Caliban' comments
unfavourably on the involvement of the Japanese and the 'Zuaven
und Schützen von Senegal' (the Souaves and the marksmen from
Senegal), and directs his sarcasm against the statesmen who brought
'die Sepoys' into the war.[87] Richard Schaukal and Edgar Steiger also
protest against the Japanese involvement as a racial aberration, while
Gustav Hochstetter objects to the Indians.[88] Racism is not entirely the
prerogative of the Germans, however. Émile Bergerat, for instance,
sees the war as a struggle of 'les Latins' against 'les Germains' and
their allies of similarly unworthy races, while Madelaine Regnault is

scornful of the alliance of 'Turcs, Allemands, Bulgares', amongst whom, she says,

l'on ne sait des trois lequel fut professeur
Des autres, en pillage, exaction, impudeur,
Assassinat, viol, cruauté, perfidie.[89]

(. . . it's hard to know which of the three is the teacher, giving the others lessons in pillage, exaction, effrontery, assassination, rape, cruelty, treachery.)

An anonymous English poem printed in the *Kölnische Zeitung* in September 1914 condemns the British alliance with the Slavs, and calls upon Britannia to 'draw the sword', not against 'our Teuton brothers', but against 'the Russian Bear / With heart as black as night'. In this way, the writer says, the Saxon race will become 'the masters of the world'. Such a breach in national unanimity is rarely allowed to show in patriotic poems – as no doubt the author appreciated, in sending the poem to Germany for publication.

With the masks of the pre-war years removed, some long-standing prejudices of national character come to the fore. Germany, or more particularly Prussia, is seen as ruthless, boastful and pompous; England's main characteristic is its cunning, the old image of 'perfidious Albion'. H.H. Ewers refers to the enemy as 'der Lügenbrite' (the lying Briton), and Ernst Lissauer's 'Haßgesang gegen England' tells how the English nation 'sitzt gedückt hinter der grauen Flut, / Voll Neid, voll Wut, voll Schläue, voll List' (sits crouching beyond the grey tide, full of envy, rage, slyness, cunning).[90] Lissauer's song of hate, described by one German newspaper as 'perhaps the most popular poem of modern times', was first published in August 1914 and reprinted countless times afterwards (rather to the embarrassment of its author, who apparently found the poem a handicap to his literary reputation).[91] Its theme, as the title suggests, is hatred:

Haß zu Wasser und Haß zu Land,
Haß des Hauptes und Haß der Hand,
Haß der Hammer und Haß der Kronen,
Drosselnder Haß von siebzig Millionen,
Sie lieben vereint, sie hassen vereint,
Sie haben alle nur einen Feind,
England!

(Hatred by water and hatred by land, hatred from the head and from the hand, hatred from hammers and hatred from crowns, choking hatred from seventy million people; they love as one, they hate as one, they all have only one foe, England.)

The 'Haßgesang' was the subject of a number of comments in *The Times* during the war, and it appeared widely in both French and English translation, to serve as anti-German propaganda.[92] When Lissauer dismisses the other enemies with the words 'Was schiert uns Russe und Franzos' (What do we care about the Russians and French), to concentrate his hatred against England, he is expressing an opinion shared by many German poets. Ernst Volkmann lists some twenty authors who wrote songs of hate against England, and there are certainly more such poems to be found. Examining this 'arch-enemy' phenomenon in the introduction to his anthology, Volkmann suggests as its primary reason 'England's unexpected declaration of war, which was felt to be unfair'; the English declaration infused an incalculable element (and, one might add, a heavily industrialised power) into the anticipated enmity of France and Russia.[93] By contrast, he says, poems about Russia display a consciousness of moral and political superiority rather than hatred, while the relatively few directed against France are dominated by 'a note of esteem and gentle pity', with the exception of those written by 'Alt-Elsässer' (long-time residents of Alsace) such as Lienhard and Karl Hackenschmidt.[94]

The animosity is not merely one-sided, however. In a situation where the homeland is revered as the representative of justice, freedom and honour, in time of war the physical border between opposing nations must be a psychological border between all that is good and all that is evil. Edward Thomas, by no means a devotee of blind chauvinism, ends his poem 'This is No Case of Petty Right or Wrong' with the words, 'And as we love ourselves we hate our foe.'[95] One might reasonably expect that love would be the inspiration of patriotic poetry, but hatred seems to be the more powerful force. Opening books at random, one finds many such lines as 'Wir haben lang erduldet / Den dreisten Hohn aus schlechtem Mund' (We have long suffered the most impudent scorn from evil mouths) or 'Torn away from loved homes to hurl the savage back', in which almost every phrase is biased and judgemental.[96] *Humanity or Hate – Which?*, the title H.C. Grumbine chose for his anthology designed to persuade Americans to support the French cause, implies that Germany resorts to hatred, while France advocates a humanitarian approach. Yet hatred is much more prevalent in the French poetry than the German. For many of the French patriotic writers, hate is not merely an emotion: it is a virtue, to be deliberately cultivated and used as a weapon of revenge. Henri de Regnier makes it part of a religious oath, 'le double serment de colère et de haine' – the double oath of anger and of hatred; Gabriel Mourey claims that 'la Haine est aussi féconde que l'Amour' (Hate is as fruitful as Love); and Jean Bertot in 'Les Ruines de Reims' advocates that the ruins of the cathedral should be left standing, in order to generate

> La haine sainte, celle où se trempent les cœurs,
> Et la sainte vengeance, implacable et sérène.[97]

(Sacred hatred, that in which hearts are steeped, and holy vengeance, implacable, serene.)

Benjamin Buisson speaks of a secular rather than a religious commitment, but in terms no more equivocal:

> Français, il faut, ou sinon c'est trahir,
> Il faut à mort haïr la Prusse infâme.[98]

(Frenchmen, we must hate to the death the infamous Prussia; anything less is treason.)

'And as we love ourselves we hate our foe' – but one wonders whether Thomas had in mind quite such an orgy of hatred.

In the battle of verbal animosity that these poets are fighting, the alignment between good and bad is made largely through insult and invective, with the occasional help of sarcasm. For French writers the German invasion is a 'crime affreux', a fearful crime, perpetrated upon innocent victims by 'le Teuton bestiale', 'ce fils de Lucifer' (this son of Lucifer), or, even worse, this 'fils de Luther'. The most common form of invective in French, however, equates the Germans with the stateless marauding tribes of the Dark Ages – 'Le Vandale', 'les barbares', 'les hordes d'Attila'. The effect is somewhat spoiled when one finds Germans, in a 'little fleas have lesser fleas' sort of progression, referring to *their* enemies from the east, the Russians, in the same terms – 'Attilas Barbarenheer', or, more graphically, 'die heulenden, mordenden Scharen / Wüster Barbaren' (the howling, murdering bands of vulgar barbarians).[99] English writers definitely favour the term 'Hun' to name the wandering, marauding Germans, though the word became so much a part of the language during the war, as a synonym for 'Germans' or 'the enemy', that its significance was probably forgotten by most of those who used it. Even so, at least one German poet objected to this insulting designation. Taking as his title Kipling's famous line from 'For All We Have and Are', 'The Hun is at the gate', 'Caliban' observes sardonically that 'Tommy Atkins, der Auswurf von Eastend' – the dregs of the East End – is 'feinste Kultur unter Lack' (finest culture, under the varnish), while the German army, made up of 'Beamter und Kaufmann, Professor, Student, / Handwerker und Künstler' (civil servant and merchant, professor and student, craftsman and artist) is a mere pack of Huns, a 'Hunnenpack'.[100] No doubt the poet's anger was exacerbated by the fact that Kipling's name was highly respected in Germany before the war, so the insult was felt particularly severely. Nevertheless, one is reminded of the exchange of offensive remarks that sometimes precedes battle in old epics and Slavic heroic ballads, although in the case of the Great War poetry, the words are the battle in themselves.

Yet despite its often warlike face and extreme belligerence, the patriotic war poetry rarely reached enemy lines. Poetry is notoriously difficult to translate, and foreign languages were not a prominent feature of turn-of-the-century elementary education, whether in board schools or *Volksschulen*. Furthermore (and more important), newspapers and magazines, where most of the patriotic verse originally appeared, rarely circulate outside the country of origin, even in peacetime and when there is a common language. This failure to make contact with the opposition, however, was not a handicap. The rejection of an alien culture often has a significant place in the beginning of a quest for national identity, and although other factors were far more important in generating a sense of nationhood for the peoples in question during the nineteenth century, the war restored animosity to a central position as a unifying element. When poets protested the violation of borders, or when they depicted the homeland as virtuous and superior and the enemy as despicable and villainous, their intention was not to convince the opponents of their wrongdoing, or even to evoke sympathy from unbiased outsiders. It was to generate communal hatred (and as a consequence, unity) in the people at home, and to strengthen their resolve by providing justification for the fighting.

Atrocity stories, as the official government propagandists recognised, were a particularly useful weapon in this verbal war, and being avid readers of newspapers, the patriotic poets were naturally well-informed about such things as

> Villages burned down to dust,
> Torture, murder, bestial lust,
> Filth too foul for printer's ink,
> Crimes from which the apes would shrink.[101]

Marcel Martinet observes in one of his protest poems that the killing of soldiers in wartime is regarded as quite acceptable – 'c'est la guerre' – but when civilians are killed, 'c'est un crime affreux' – it's a fearful crime.[102] The concept of total war, which assumes that all the nation's resources, including the entire adult population, will be committed to the war effort, is a logical corollary to nationalism, and the validity of the concept was taken for granted during the First World War. Nevertheless, the belief was still confined largely to theory, and in practice the war was viewed as a conflict between armies, where civilians, however dedicated to the nation's cause, were innocent bystanders immune from attack. Consequently any incident causing harm to civilians was potentially of immense value from a propagandist point of view. (By the Second World War the concept had come into its own, and civilians of the enemy country were a prime target – ultimately without even the pretence that the attack was aimed at military or industrial sites.) Because the Great War took place mainly outside Germany, most so-called 'crimes' against civilians were perpetrated by the Germans. The U-boat sinking of the *Lusitania* in the North Atlantic in 1915, with the loss of many civilian lives, is considered by historians to have been a major factor in swaying American public opinion against Germany. Even so, the single incident that appears to have made the strongest impact on the French and English poets, perhaps even more powerful than the destruction of Reims cathedral, was the death of Edith Cavell, an English nurse working for the Red Cross in Belgium, who was executed by the Germans as a spy, and whose name occurs time after time in the popular anthologies. The French patriotic poets also appreciate stories about noble children killed by the Germans. Jean Aicard, for instance, tells of 'Le Jeune héros de quatorze ans, Émile Desjardins' (The young fourteen-year-old hero, Émile Desjardins), shot for giving water to a wounded French soldier.[103] Paul Fournier has almost the same story, though with slightly altered circumstances and a different name, Émile Desprès.[104] (This change in name is precisely the kind of alteration one finds in folk-ballad variants – from 'près' to 'prés' (meadows), to 'jardins' (gardens) – where the singer remembers, not quite the original, but something close to it.) Victor d'Auriac, listing the crimes for which the Kaiser must be made to pay, speaks of 'l'enfant au fusil de bois et Miss Cavell' (the child with the wooden gun and Miss Cavell) as though the story of the former, presumably about a child punished by the Germans for defending his country with a toy gun, were as well-known as the latter; and Fleming Tuckerman, an American who writes in both French and English, has a poem called 'Le Boy Scout', prefaced with a passage from a German newspaper boasting of the young hero's death.[105] One of the most astonishing atrocity poems, however, is 'Le Berceau rouge' (The red cradle), which is headed with the words, 'The soldiers of the Crown Prince have sent as a gift to celebrate the birth of the granddaughter of the Kaiser a cradle painted with French blood. The newspapers.'[106] Although it is hard to imagine such credulity, the poet apparently accepted this story as true, presumably because such accounts were not a rarity in 'les journaux'.

It is appropriate that several of the atrocity stories I have cited are associated with the Kaiser, because although Friedrich Lienhard, one of Volkmann's 'Alt-Elsässer', attempts to blame the war on King Louis XIV of France, English and French writers concentrate their venom on a much more modern ruler, Kaiser Wilhelm II.[107] The Kaiser is addressed as 'Destroyer of cities and temples, / Vandal of Louvain and Rheims', 'Marplot of war, Knight of the tarnished mail', and 'the Troubler of the World'; he is described as 'le Néron fou des Allemagnes' (the mad Nero of the Germans), 'Guillaume (William) le bandit, Guillaume le vampire', and 'this monster' who 'has declared / 'Meinself und Gott, will conquerors rise."[108] Despite possible competition from Lissauer's 'Haßgesang', the prize for the most vituperative poem of the war would almost certainly go to one of those in English that attack the German emperor – Abel Aaronson's 'To the Kaiser', perhaps:

> You shameless, perjured, soul-lost renegade,
> You vile abortion in the form of man;
> The eternal future you for self have slayed,
> The basest creature since the world began.
> You loathsome, monstrous, most unholy thing,[109]

or possibly William Watson's 'To the German Emperor, after the Sack of Louvain':

> Wherefore are men amazed at thee, thou Blot
> On the fair script of Time, thou sceptred Smear
> Across the Day?[110]

One can imagine poets like these thoroughly enjoying the liberty of being able to write such virulent condemnation of an opponent, without risking a suit for defamation of character.

The degree to which Kaiser Wilhelm is castigated by the enemy is almost (though not entirely) matched by the adulation he receives at home. His name occurs widely in the German poetry, especially on the occasions of his visits to the trenches or hospitals, or on his birthday, and there is at least one book, *Heil, Kaiser, Dir!*, devoted entirely to poems about him. One might be tempted to see in this German admiration for the Kaiser a foretaste of the idolatry of the Nazi era, and accordingly to believe that such leader-worship is inherent in the German form of nationalism, but the even more marked tendency of English and French poets to focus their invective on the same figure weakens the case. Interestingly enough, the only other leader to receive similar support in verse is King Albert of Belgium, who is the subject of many poems in both English and French, and who clearly serves as a representative figure in much the same way as the German emperor, though not for the enemy's disapprobation. That no individual in France is treated comparably is perhaps to be expected, since elected officials rarely receive universal acclaim, but more surprising is the fact that the English king, George V, appears in very few poems, whether as beneficent ruler or as arch-fiend. In three typical anthologies, Forshaw's *One Hundred Best Poems of the War*, Elliott's *Lest We Forget* and Edwards and Booth's *The Fiery Cross*, all representative of the most common patriotic usage in English, one finds many poems on the subject of the Kaiser, several about King Albert (and one addressed to his wife Elisabeth), but only one concerning the English monarch, James Elroy Flecker's 'God Save the King'. (I exclude the slogan 'Your king and country need you' and the stock phrase 'serving the king', both of which are common.) The most obvious explanation for the disparity is the relative political status of the monarchies, since the English king was mainly a figurehead, while the German emperor was an active decision-maker, but this rationale fails to account for the Belgian monarch's popularity. Perhaps there was a greater need for a symbol of national unity in Germany and Belgium than in Britain (where the full power of the Irish independence movement had not yet been felt), and the respective monarchs were an obvious choice. Or possibly the English veneration of the monarchy was aroused mainly by public ceremonial such as coronations and royal funerals, and otherwise, in the absence of radio and television, it lay dormant most of the time.

But whatever the explanation, this 'Kaiser but no King' phenomenon exemplifies very well the homogeneity of usage in the poetry, both within and across national boundaries. One can almost imagine the poets making an international pact about what was and was not acceptable in patriotic verse – a poetic 'war-crimes agreement', of which a breach like Kipling's use of 'Hun' was greeted with disapproval. Yet the homogeneity was largely spontaneous, the outcome of widely-shared attitudes and assumptions, rather than the consequence of deliberate manipulation. There is a tendency to assume that propaganda comes from 'above' – that it is used by the authorities to direct the thought of the masses; and in the Great War, for the first time, governments established official propaganda agencies for the purpose of influencing public opinion at home. The spreading of atrocity stories about the Germans and the promoting of the image of an evil or monstrous Kaiser were some of the ways in which the British propaganda agency (initially the Parliamentary Recruiting Committee and later the Department of Information) attempted to carry out its mandate.[111] On the evidence of the poetry from the first few weeks of the war, however, one must conclude that a deliberate campaign to vilify the enemy was quite unnecessary, since the public was already convinced. Nor should one assume that the newspapers and magazines which printed patriotic verse so readily were being manipulated by the respective governments. On the contrary, the suppression of information under the Defence of the Realm Act caused considerable conflict between the government and the press in Britain in the first nine months of the war, while the French government's decision to limit or suspend publication of newspapers and magazines in August 1914 reveals a similar lack of confidence that the press would act wholly in the national interest. Consequently, as M.L. Sanders and Philip M.Taylor observe in their study of wartime propaganda, 'the enormous potential of the press as an instrument of official propaganda remained largely untapped during the early part of the war.'[112] The situation changed later, when the so-called 'free' press became more directly a vehicle for government propaganda (an example of lost 'innocence' that Paul Fussell overlooked), but in the beginning, according to Sanders and Taylor, 'if newspapers were propagandist . . . – which they undoubtedly were – it was largely of their own, rather than the government's, initiative.' And just as the publishing of nationalistic propaganda, including poetry, was originally self-motivated, so too was the act of writing, for apart from the relatively small number of poems from well-known writers in response to a request, the patriotic verse was generally unsolicited, like the forty submissions a day Bab received for his early anthologies. The propaganda of nationalism, it seems, came from below rather than above–or perhaps more accurately, 'above' and 'below' shared the same point of view. When poets voluntarily declared their love of the homeland and their hatred of the enemy, and the poem appeared in print, the personal expression of dedication lent support to the official government policy that participation in the war was both desirable and necessary. Herzog's 'Zwei Worte – Feind und Vaterland' (two words – enemy and Fatherland) had been spoken, and the response of an appropriately educated populace was an immediate and almost universal commitment to the nation's cause.

3

We serve you best
The promoting of mass heroism

To go our quiet ways, subdued and sane;
To hush all vulgar clamour of the street;
With level calm to face alike the strain
Of triumph or defeat;

This be our part, for thus we serve you best,
So best confirm their prowess and their pride,
Your warrior sons, to whom in this high test
Our fortunes we confide.

Owen Seaman, 'Pro Patria'[1]

Perhaps because the First World War coincided with the transition from traditional to modern verse, and because the patriotic poetry so obviously belongs to the former, it is easy to assume that the outpouring of loyal dedication in 1914 marked the end of a continuous and full tradition of similar writing. Yet when one attempts to trace the progress of the genre through the ages, it becomes clear that the assumption is largely unjustified. Although a well-established convention links poetry and warfare, patriotism, a sense of dedication to one's homeland, plays surprisingly little part. In traditional epics and heroic ballads, the participants are motivated by loyalty to other people – their leader, their family or clan, a communal group – rather than by a commitment to their native land. A few declarations of patriotic loyalty occur in Shakespeare's historical dramas, and King Henry V's speech before Agincourt is probably the most-quoted patriotic 'poem' in English; nevertheless, the majority of Shakespeare's warriors are inspired by far less altruistic motives. With regard to lyric poetry (as opposed to the epic or dramatic), while patriotic dedication is to be found in occasional examples from as early as the Middle Ages – the Insel anthology *Deutsche Vaterlandslieder* begins with Walther von der Vogelweide – and while there are isolated collections like Gleim's *Preußische Kriegslieder* of 1759, one looks in vain for an extensive pool of such texts in the pre-Romantic poetry of any of the three languages. The ancient tradition of patriotic verse, if it existed, was decidedly spasmodic.

From the beginning of the nineteenth century, as a sense of nationhood gradually impinged upon the general consciousness, and as the size of the potential audience increased, the amount of patriotic poetry grew significantly, especially in wartime. Even so, those anthologists who compiled collections of their nation's patriotic poems at the beginning of the First World War – and who, one must assume, were fully conversant with the tradition – seem to have had difficulty in finding as many examples as they would have liked. Most of them resorted to extracts from verse dramas or epics to fill out the pages (and sometimes even to prose selections), or to poems from other countries, including the national anthems of their allies. In George Goodchild's *England, my England: A War Anthology*, for instance, the subtitle, rather than the title itself, reflects the contents, for the collection offers many poems that have little connection with English patriotism, or even English history – amongst them Thomas Campbell's 'Hohenlinden', Lord Macaulay's 'Horatius', and some of Walt Whitman's American Civil War verse. The school texts to which I referred earlier, from the two decades before the war, are similarly indiscriminate. One begins to suspect that the idea of a tradition of patriotic poetry, or of war poetry in a patriotic vein, had arisen only in the last few years of the nineteenth century – another 'invention' like Bastille Day and royal processions, designed to meet the needs of the 'new form of social organisation'. But whether it was genuinely old or a recent innovation, there can be little doubt that the tradition reached its climax in the intensely homogeneous patriotic poetry of the First World War.

From the viewpoint of poetic technique, the new genre definitely followed established, though limited, practice, in the sense that very few poets chose to express their loyalty in anything other than traditional metre and stanza-structure. Even in France, where the poetic revolution was already several decades old, and where, therefore, one might anticipate more variety, the traditional alexandrine was almost *de rigueur* for patriotic declarations. Admittedly both Paul Claudel and Paul Fort ventured to proclaim their love of country in *vers libre*, while adhering to the convention in other respects, but other previously more adventurous writers, such as the Symbolist Henri de Regnier, reverted to tradition in their wartime poetry. Apollinaire, who combined patriotic (though not chauvinistic) expression with poetic Modernism, was indeed a rarity. English and German writers, while not so rigidly bound as by the alexandrine and its caesura, similarly clung to traditional verse-forms. Yet despite the rich lyric heritage of these two languages, the patriotic poetry shows little of the flexibility and versatility one might expect. Instead, there is a marked preference for simple four or eight-line stanzas, rhyming alternately or in couplets, and a regular trochaic or iambic metre. Sentence-structure tends likewise to be simple, and to coincide with, rather than override, the verse pattern. Apart from the use of the sonnet, very popular in all three languages, and a few English acrostics (where the initial letters of each line combine to make a name), the patriotic poets in general give little evidence of an interest in form for its own sake. One senses that they wrote whatever came most easily, and whatever could most easily be read, and in this respect the poetry is indeed typical of a dying tradition, where the features that survive tend to be those that offer the least challenge to users.

Nevertheless, this metric simplicity is often at odds with the poetic syntax and the archaic or grandiloquent vocabulary. The ostensible purpose of the poetry as a verbal defence of the Fatherland makes for pretentious-sounding diction with a plethora of abstract nouns, including, as I indicated earlier, such traditional and enduring favourites as Liberty, Peace and Justice, together with the popular choices of the moment, the undefinable 'Honour' and 'the Right'. The tendency towards grand abstractions is reinforced by an extensive vocabulary of poetic or what Paul Fussell calls 'elevated' words – terms used by the poets in preference to everyday expressions. Fussell provides a glossary of such terms: 'steed', 'the foe', 'swift', 'staunch', and 'vanquish', amongst many others. A comparable list in French would have euphemisms like 's'endormir' (to fall asleep), and *précieux* words characteristic of the courtly literature of the seventeenth century classical period, such as 'ardeur', 'flammes', 'sacré' and 'superbe'. The French patriotic vocabulary is rich in 'r' sounds, as if the poems were explicitly designed for reading aloud with a full roll of the tongue; and indeed the printed text is frequently accompanied by information about the poem's first performance – 'Dit au Théâtre-Français, le 4 avril 1915, par M. Mounet-Sully', 'Recité pour la première fois à la Réunion patriotique de l'Union Belge' (Recited for the first time at the patriotic meeting of the Belgian Union).[2] (Recitation was popular in German and English, too – though less so, in the latter case, than at the time of the Boer War – but from the relative rarity of 'first performance' notices in those languages one must conclude that writers and publishers placed less significance on the theatrical event.)

In German, as in French and English, the language of the patriotic poetry is 'elevated' above normal usage – as an analysis of this apparently simple oath of allegiance from Kurt Münzer, 'Vaterland', makes clear:

Vaterland, für dich
Waffe, die ich hebe,
Sieg, den ich erstrebe.
Heimat, segne mich!

Vaterland, nur dir
Liebende Gedanken.
Und du sollst nicht wanken!
Eher sterben wir.

Vaterland, nur du!
Opfern Blut und Leben,
Unsre Zukunft geben
Wir für deine Ruh.

Brüder, hebt die Hand:
Friede, Freiheit, Glaube
Und der Feind im Staube,
Für dich, Vaterland.[3]

(Fatherland, for thee the weapon that I raise and the victory that I seek. Homeland, thy blessing on me. Fatherland, for thee alone these thoughts of love. And thou shalt not waver! Rather, we will die. Fatherland, only thou! We offer our blood and our life, give up our future, for thy comfort. Brothers, raise your hand: Peace, freedom, faith, and the enemy in the dust, for thee, Fatherland.)

If Münzer's poem is atypical in being more carefully constructed than many of its kind, with its *abba* rhyme scheme and its application of the second person pronoun – 'dich', 'dir', 'du' – as a structuring device, in other respects it is representative. The vocabulary is remarkably abstract, with few verbs denoting action and a large majority of non-representational nouns. Even the very few concrete terms – 'Waffe', 'hebe', 'Blut', 'Hand', 'Staube' (weapon, raise, blood, hand, dust) – are all used metaphorically, and, significantly enough, there is only one adjective in the entire poem, 'liebende'. The use of the transitive verb 'erstreben' instead of the normal 'streben nach' (strive for), and of the complex parallelism in the third stanza (with 'wir' as the subject of 'Opfern' and 'geben'), may also be considered poetic or 'elevated'. The line 'Waffe, die ich hebe' suggests an ancient weapon rather than a 1914 rifle, and 'Brüder, hebt die Hand' places this oath of allegiance in the context of a secret encounter in the Peasants' War or in the early days of the Swiss Confederacy (at least as presented in Goethe's *Götz von Berlichingen* and Schiller's *Wilhelm Tell* respectively) rather than in a twentieth-century recruiting office.

The tendency to discuss the war in such archaic terms is widespread. A modern reader whose knowledge of the Great War arose mainly from its patriotic verse might assume that almost the only weapon available to the armies of 1914 was the sword, that the troops went into battle following a flag and urged on by a drum, and that they engaged for the most part in hand-to-hand combat. It would appear that they wore shining helmets and mail, kept vigil, were familiar with 'storied scutcheons' and 'Eisenketten' (chains of iron), 'guerdon' and 'Ehrensold' (literally, payment for honour), and, like Münzer and his 'Brüder', made a practice of pledging amongst themselves their loyalty to the homeland. The persistent archaic imagery is reinforced by the poets' extremely limited selection of adjectives. One tends to think of adjectives as contributing to sensory, especially visual, images; in the patriotic poetry, however, such pictures are rarely to be found. There are so few adjectives of colour, and those that recur are so consistently only red, brown, golden and white, that the yellow and black of the Belgian flag in the book title 'Le Rouge, jaune et noir' is quite startling. The adjectives used widely in the poetry, of which there are probably no more than about thirty in each language, are without exception abstract and elevated – words like bold, valiant, earnest, pure, proud, rich, mighty, and their precise counterparts in the other languages. While most of these words are in common circulation, it is surely unusual that so many writers chose them at the expense of almost all others, as if they were writing chivalric or warrior epics (where the repetition of such terms may originally have served as a mnemonic device), rather than modern lyrics.

Undoubtedly a large part of the value of those old heroic epithets for patriotic poets was their applicability to literature's newest heroes, the combatants in the conflict that was named 'the Great War' as early as September 1914. In many of the outpourings of patriotic commitment, the antagonism that serves to strengthen the resolution of the writer's compatriots in the verbal defence of the Fatherland is replaced by a tone of reverence, as poets undertake another important and related task – that of bolstering belief in the complex of myths associated with patriotic heroism. History suggests that such bolstering was unnecessary, for all the armies had an *embarras* of recruits in the early months of the war, even Britain, which relied entirely on volunteers. (In the other countries men not uncommonly reported for duty before they were called.) Whatever may have motivated these young men – patriotism, the wish for a break with the mundane, a sense of adventure, the promise of regular pay, the recognition that such conduct was expected of them, or merely the requirement that they fulfill their military service – there is no doubt that the education they had received prepared them to view going to war on the nation's behalf as a respectable and worthy act. Joining the army had never before been so widely perceived as appropriate, and never before had warring powers been able to muster such enormous forces. Similarly impressive, however, is the amount of verbal support the men received. Owen Seaman in 'Pro Patria' (the epigraph poem for this chapter) preaches that civilians may 'best confirm' the efforts of the nation's 'warrior sons' by remaining stoically silent. Yet the fact that his poem was written and published makes it clear that the poet conceived of his own patriotic duty in a rather different light. His 'part' was to speak out, and like many of his fellow-poets he recognised that he could fulfill his purpose best by promoting the patriotic–heroic ethic upon which, it seemed, the defence of the nation depended.

Nelson reputedly declared at the Battle of Trafalgar 'England expects every man to do his duty.' On the evidence of the poetry, a century later the homelands of Europe no longer merely expected duty of their citizens, for expectations may be disappointed; rather, each country knew with absolute certainty that all the men of appropriate age would be willing to fight and die. Like Jessie Pope's 'Lads of the Maple Leaf', 'Ripe for any adventure, sturdy, loyal and game', young men from throughout the British Empire are depicted as coming 'Quick to the call of the Mother'. Rudolf Herzog envisions Germany's recruits as fields of grain spread far over the countryside:

> Wie Ähren wogt es weit und breit,
> O deutsches Land zur Sommerzeit,
> Das Männer trägt, statt Gärben. [4]

> (There is movement like corn-fields waving far and near, o German countryside that, this summertime, bears men instead of sheaves.)

(Henry Allsopp's account of 'Harvest time in Flanders', where 'Death the Reaper' swings the scythe, is one of many poems that present the same image from a different viewpoint.[5]) The speaker in a French poem offers even her fourth and last son:

> Si la France t'appelle,
> O toi, mon dernier fils, va te battre pour elle.
> . . .
> Allez comme eux gaiment: défendez la Patrie.

> (If France calls you, o my last son, go and fight for her. Go gaily, like the others, to defend the homeland.)[6]

However, the German mother of four who speaks in 'Meine Jungen' (My boys) clearly has no need to remind her sons where their choice should lie, since they are already fighting Germany's four enemies.[7]

(One should not, of course, assume that these poems are auto-biographical; the 'soldier's mother' persona is a favourite device with both male and female writers.)

Many poets endow the combatants with the feeling of being reborn, of having discovered a cause or, as Rilke phrases it in one of his 'Fünf Gesänge', of having found 'Endlich ein Gott' (At last, a god).[8] Although such poems are often the work of civilians, it is not uncommon to find the combatants themselves making similar declarations. A.J.P. Taylor claims that Rupert Brooke spoke for a generation when he wrote, 'Now God be thanked who has matched us with his hour', and one certainly sees many parallels to this mood of self-congratulation in the German poetry – 'Frohlockt, ihr Freunde, daß wir leben, / Und daß wir jung sind und gelenk' (Rejoice, friends, that we are living now, and that we are young and active), the archaic-sounding 'Wir sind gesegnet. Unser ist die Glut' (We are blessed; the flame is ours), and the indisputably modern 'Nun fahr ich in die grosse Zeit / Mit fünfundfünfzig Pferden' (Now I am driving into the great age with fifty-five horsepower), from 'Kriegsfahrt des Automobilisten' (An Automobile Driver's Journey to War).[9] In France, Guillaume Apollinaire – appropriately for this apostle of Futurism – similarly associates the outbreak of war with a car journey. He tells in 'La Petite Auto' how he drove with a friend to Paris, arriving at the moment when mobilisation was announced, and the poem ends with another account of rebirth:

> Nous comprîmes mon camarade et moi
> Que la petite auto nous avait conduits dans une époque
>   Nouvelle
> Et bien qu'étant déjà tous deux des hommes mûrs,
> Nous venions cependant de naître.[10]

(We understood, my friend and I, that the little car had brought us into a new era, and although we were both mature men, we had nevertheless just been born.)

It should be noted, however, that Apollinaire's comment is not an unambivalent welcoming of war, or the discovery of a sense of purpose, so much as a recognition that the conflict will usher in a new age.

In the eyes of the patriotic poets, the recruits who flock to war are without exception fine young men, quite equal in every respect to the heroes of the past – except to the extent that the modern soldier may be superior. It is to be noted, for instance, that 'le poilu' is 'mieux taillé que les guerriers les plus fameux' (better built than the most famous of warriors), and that while those ancient champions were mercenaries who 'Died not for country, but for pay', the modern hero is motivated only by love of the homeland.[11] Friedrich Lienhard, describing the departure of troops from the town of Erfurt, depicts the soldiers, with appropriate adjectives, as

> diese braunroten Männer,
> Deutschlands kräftige Jugend
> Die singend hinauszieht.[12]

(. . . these sunburnt [literally 'brown-red'] men, Germany's mighty youth that goes forth singing.)

A full array of heroic qualities is listed in Laurence Binyon's 'For the Fallen':

> They went with songs to the battle, they were young,
> Straight of limb, true of eye, steady and aglow.
> They were staunch to the end against odds uncounted,
> They fell with their faces to the foe.[13]

The men's spirit of joyful commitment remains with them even in adversity, it seems, for as Victor Compas implies, to fight for the nation's cause cancels all ills:

> Qu'importe le destin! Qu'importe la souffrance!
> À nos braves soldats,
> Ils sont gais, malgré tout, car c'est pour notre France
> Qu'ils s'en vont au combat.[14]

(What does destiny matter! What does suffering matter, to our brave soldiers; they are happy in spite of everything, for it is for our France that they go to battle.)

Even at their most realistic, such collective impressions can make no allowance for individual deviation, whether in the matter of appearance (there were, after all, 'bantam' units made up of soldiers below regular height), or with regard to courage. And as poems like these make clear, the tradition that, in order to be designated a hero, one must be an outstanding individual, has apparently been discarded. Patriotic or nationalistic heroism, unlike the older concept on which it is based, does not make such distinctions, for in the mass army – the army that nationalism produced and that is inspired by a commitment to the nation – all men are elevated to the status of hero.

While in most respects total homogeneity amongst the soldiers is taken for granted, a few poets in all three languages comment on the involvement of ordinary working men in the war. It appears that not everyone was convinced of the equalising effect of general education – perhaps because, in its origin, mass schooling was not designed to promote social equality but to produce literate and satisfied voters and a competent workforce. On the evidence of the poetry it is clear that some people had expected the workers to refrain from contributing to the war effort, while others felt sure that the sacrifice would be less fully appreciated if the victim were from the working class. The former possibility accorded with the expectations of international socialism, but the hopes of the socialists were disappointed when the workers realigned themselves *en masse* with their nation's cause at the outbreak of war. It is the second, however, that concerns Ernst Preczang, himself a worker, in 'Gefallen: ein Mann' (Fallen: A Man). The speaker insists that every death is important, even that of 'ein Arbeitsmann', 'ein armer Knecht, / und unbestrahlt vom Nimbus der Geschichte' (a working-man, a poor labourer, and unilluminated by the nimbus of history), for 'Er auch war ein Held' (He too was a hero).[15] Georges Pioch similarly wishes to ensure that the efforts of the ordinary people, 'les gens simples', are appreciated, particularly since he recognises that many of them will die 'pour servir et défendre / Des honneurs et des biens dont ils n'ont point leur part' (to serve and defend honours and benefits in which they will have no share).[16] Such sympathy is unusual, however, and more commonly the poet's purpose is not to express appreciation but to marvel at the way the lower classes have been ennobled by their participation in the war. In E. Angerau's 'L' Âme des drapeaux' (The Spirit of the Flags), for example, the plebeians ('les plèbes') have at last come into their own:

> Et ces 'hommes-enfants', qui jamais ne sont rien,
> Se trouvent grands premiers au drame shakspearien!'[17]

> (And these 'child-men', who never count for anything, find themselves at centre stage in this Shakespearean drama.)

Like Pioch's 'gens simples', the young man in B.R.M. Hetherington's 'The Patriot' is risking his life for treasures that he does not share, for this slum-dweller has never seen 'an English lawn, / Nor English fields'.[18] Not sympathy with the meek and dispossessed, however, but pride in what the nation can accomplish with even the most improbable material, is the theme of 'The Patriot'. Hetherington's poem offers a vestigial example of nineteenth-century Social Darwinism – the belief that certain classes are endowed by nature with superior characteristics – at its worst:

> Low-browed, ill-nourished, fostered in a slum,
> He had no pride of birthright nor of breed;
> Yet when his country's hour of stress was come,
> Stood up a man indeed!

The stunted mind that laboured dim and dark
Behind that narrow forehead gave small sign,
Till War reached out a hand and lit a spark,
There, of a fire divine.

The implication of racial inferiority here is surely quite as offensive as
'Caliban''s reference to the 'Schlitzgesichter' of the Japanese or his
remark about Tommy Atkins as the dregs from the East End – yet
Hetherington's is supposedly a poem of praise. In spite of examples
like this, however, by far the majority of poems assume that all heroes
are equal. The 'Tommy' of Boer War poetry – coarse on the outside
but with the heart of a lion – has largely disappeared (except perhaps
from the music hall stage), and on the evidence of the Great War
heroic verse one must conclude that the ennobling effect of devotion
to the homeland eradicates social distinctions.

Hetherington's patriot, although clearly a misfit amongst the splen-
did physical specimens in poems like those of Binyon and Lienhard,
is fully in character in his readiness to 'put his life in pawn'. The
soldiers of the patriotic poetry, without exception, are happy to lay
down their lives, not for their friends, but for that 'imagined com-
munity' of compatriots, the nation. The heroic death envisioned by
the poets, however, is far removed from the dynamic final battles of
such arch-heroes as Achilles, Hotspur and the warriors of the *Nibelun-
genlied*. Although there are many references to courage, the new
heroes are rarely shown in action, and one has the impression that in
the edicts of the new heroism the hero simply dies without a struggle.
In 'Happy Warriors', by 'A.L. J.', which appeared in the *Westminster
Gazette* in February 1916, the step from volunteering to dying is
immediate:

Clear came the call; they leapt to arms, and died
As in old days the heroes prayed to do.[19]

Even if one grants full importance to the comma in the first line
(though it is easily overlooked), it is difficult to imagine which heroes
'in old days' served as a model. Did the writer really believe that the
English sailors facing the Spanish Armada prayed they would die in
the battle? – Napoleon's troops at Waterloo? – or the mercenaries who
made up the larger part of the Crusade armies? Even in literature the
hero's prayer is usually for courage and victory, though with the
rider that, if necessary, he prefers to die 'in arms'. But neither victory
nor the gallant struggle has an important place in the heroic creed
promoted in poems like this, since the pathos the poet wishes to
evoke is concomitant only with death:

Deep though our sorrow, deeper yet our pride,
O gallant hearts, in you.

Like most of the writers of patriotic and heroic poetry in the war,
A.L. J. obviously believes that he or she is following literary tradition,
and assumes that the reader shares the same belief. Yet it is apparent
in general that, although the poets of all three languages have taken
inspiration from the heroic literature of the past – from classical or
medieval epics and Shakespeare's historical dramas, as well as more
recent sources like popular historical novels and Wagner's operas –
they have chosen their patterns with care. It is not surprising that
they should have completely ignored such inconvenient anti-heroic
predecessors as Falstaff, who pretended to be dead in order to avoid
having to fight, or Simplicius Simplicissimus, the hero of Grimmel-
shausen's fictional memoir of the Thirty Years' War, who changed
sides as expediency demanded; but many other possible models are
also more notable by their absence than their presence. The new
heroes are confronted with none of the mental conflict that troubled,
for instance, Aeneas and Parzival, nor do they experience the anger of
Achilles or the fear that is acknowledged even in Wordsworth's
idealistic 'Character of a Happy Warrior' (which may have provided
A.L. J.'s title). Their heroism is uncomplicated, since little is required
of them other than the readiness to die. Heroic poetry 'in old days'
was concerned above all with the hero's life and his struggle to defeat
his enemy; the new version is entirely elegiac, though the hero's
death is not mourned but celebrated. When Eden Phillpotts writes,
'you yielded him unto the knife / And altar with a royal sacrifice', he
means to congratulate, not to condemn, the bereaved mother whom
his poem addresses, and Will Vesper is impressed rather than repelled
by the thought of 'heiliges Blut gegossen / Als Opfer auf den Herd'
(holy blood poured in sacrifice on the hearth).[20] So prevalent – and so
unthinking – are the references to sacrificial death that one can easily
appreciate the appropriateness of the metaphor drawn by W.N. Ewer
in his protest poem 'Three Gods', where the Fatherland, proud of
having inspired more human sacrifice than any god before, boasts
that it is 'the bloodiest God of all'.[21]

Accepting without question Horace's edict that 'dulce et decorum
est pro patria mori', most of the patriotic poets are firmly convinced
that to die for the Fatherland is different from any other kind of
death. 'The soldier dying dies upon a kiss, / The very kiss of Christ',
claims Alice Meynell, who apparently had second thoughts after
writing of 'men shot through the eyes' and 'a thousand shattered
men', since the first quotation is taken from her 'Reply' to her own
poem, 'Summer in England, 1914'.[22] Klabund, speaking for a dying

'Freiwilliger' (volunteer), has a last request of his brother soldiers: 'Deckt ein deutsches Fahnentuch / Auf die Todeswunde' (Cover the death-wound with a German flag); bandaged in this way, he will utter his parting cry, which will shine like a sun in the darkness: 'Freies deutsches Land!' (Free German land!)[23] As the young soldiers die, even Death itself cannot take 'The joy of having given from their eyes, / The light of consecration from the brow'. And once dead, they achieve the immortality, whether pagan or Christian, traditionally accorded to heroes, together with everlasting fame and a permanent place in the memory of the nation. Herbert Eulenberg suggests that they may have to wait for the coming of peace before their fame can properly be 'gesagt, geseufzt, gesungen' (praised, sighed for, sung), but most poets (wisely, it seems, since relatively little of the poetry was reprinted once the war was over), accord them immediate and appropriate veneration, like the eulogy offered by Louis Texier:

> Enfants de la patrie, innocentes victimes,
> Soldats, héros obscurs, rien n'est plus grand que vous.[24]

(Children of the fatherland, innocent victims, soldiers, little-known heroes, nothing is greater than you.)

True to their kind, these lines say nothing of the valiant fight or victory; the heroes of the mass army are eulogised – collectively as always – because they are unknown, because they are innocent, and above all because they have died as victims.

While the sense of respect for dead heroes is shared internationally, there are distinct national preferences in the attitude towards heroic death and the afterlife. German poets express pride and sorrow, and recognise the value of the supreme sacrifice, but they are less pre-occupied with death itself than the writers in the other two languages. It is noticeable, for instance, that the German patriotic poetry has more battle narratives in the traditional style, especially concerning the war at sea – and in such stories, although there are casualties, there is also victory. For the French patriotic writers, on the other hand, death is far more important than heroic prowess, and the predominant attitude is summarised in Francis Trochu's line, 'Héros – plus que héros, martyr!' (Hero – more than a hero, a martyr!).[25] Death is implied or mentioned in almost every poem, not merely as a possibility (as in the German 'Sieg *oder* Tod' – Victory *or* death – or 'Deutschland muß leben, *und wenn* wir sterben müßen' – Germany must live, *even if* we must die) but as an accomplished fact. Whereas German patriotic poems frequently end with an expression of determination in the form of a war-cry – 'Deutschland muß bestehen!' (Germany must survive), 'Zum letzten Streit! Zum Sieg! Zum Sieg!'

(To the final battle, to victory), 'Hoch, hoch die Fahne, / Ewig hoch!' (Raise high the flag, for ever!) – their French counterparts almost invariably close with suffering and death: 'De vous nous sommes fiers et sur vous nous pleurons / Soldats, Héros, Martyrs! sans connaître vos noms.' (Of you we are proud and for you we weep, soldiers, heroes, martyrs, without knowing your names); 'O père qui, sans pleurs, sur la joue amaigrie, / As reçu le baiser sanglant de la Patrie!' (O father who, without weeping, have received on your sunken cheek the bloody kiss of the Fatherland); 'Pauvre soldat, ta tâche est faite!' (Poor soldier, your task is done!) – to cite three of many examples in Georges Turpin's two popular anthologies.[26]

National differences of this kind are easier to detect than to explain. Grumbine, the author of *Humanity or Hate – Which?*, suggests that the war poetry reflects an underlying difference in the respective 'self' of the two countries, which he equates with their 'God'. The German God, he says, is 'positive, aggressive, constructive, masculine', while the French God is 'negative in virtue, defensive in war, critical in temper, and feminine in fibre'.[27] (It is perhaps difficult to appreciate from these words that Grumbine's stand is strongly in favour of France.) Religious tradition certainly appears to have played a part, for the Roman church places high value on martyrdom and the promise of sainthood. At the same time, the difference in the tone of the poetry probably also owes something to the circumstances of the moment. Germany perceived itself surrounded by enemies and was convinced that a forceful attack was its best defence; not surprisingly therefore its poetry voices the determination to continue the fight at any cost. France on the other hand was once again, as in 1870, the victim of aggression, and with an obvious military disadvantage, especially after the devastating early battles, martyrdom and noble suffering may have seemed more appropriate than a call for immediate victory. (It is harder to imagine the French soldiers of the Napoleonic Wars in the role of religious martyrs.) Literary antecedents may also have played their part. The German patriotic verse was clearly affected by the revival of interest in medieval German epics in the heroic or warrior tradition (as distinct from courtly or chivalric works), most notably the *Nibelungenlied*. Although the patriotic writers were undoubtedly more familiar with nineteenth-century literary, artistic and operatic representations than with the original epics, the celebration of martyrdom was not particularly characteristic of their models. Meanwhile, the French taste for noble suffering appears to have been reinforced by the overwhelming preference, in the patriotic poetry, for the traditional verse form of that language, the alexandrine. Such a long and carefully-balanced line, consisting of twelve syllables with a break at mid-point, demands a type of poetry that sounds reflective, and it lends itself much more readily to eulogies than to battle-cries. All these factors, and probably others, must be taken into consideration if one wishes to account for the different manifestations of patriotic heroism. Nevertheless, the most striking feature is not the difference from one nation to another but the almost total homogeneity within any one country. The poems, like the heroes whose praises they sing, are a true product of the equalising process of nationalism.

The English patriotic poets celebrate heroic death as frequently as the French, but with an emphasis on immortality rather than martyrdom. Since the heroes are eternally young, they have escaped the burden of living – they are 'free forever', and 'Age shall not weary them, nor the years condemn'.[28] What is more, because they have died, their innocence is equally enduring – an innocence closely tied to both chivalry and sexual purity: 'O lovely youth, slaughtered at Life's new dawn, / In virgin purity thou liest dead', 'Stainless and simple as He made it / God keeps the heart o' the boy unflawed', 'The young white souls, clear-eyed, august, serene, / Pass to God's care'.[29] How remote these 'young white souls' seem from the image of the soldier typified in Shakespeare's line 'Full of strange oaths and bearded like a pard', or in Kipling's *Barrack Room Ballads*. The speaker in Kipling's 'Mandalay', longing to be back in the East with his 'Burma girl', appears almost immoral in comparison with the 'virgin purity' of the First World War heroes. The refining of the image of the ordinary soldier arose in part, no doubt, because the modern army was composed of men from a wide variety of social positions; 'Caliban''s 'Beamter und Kaufmann, Professor, Student, / Handwerker, und Künstler' (Civil servant , merchant, professor, student, craftsman and artist) would apply equally well in Britain and France. To impute to so many respectable young men the coarse masculinity traditionally attributed to the soldier might seem inappropriate – nor would it have accorded well with the taste of most of the writers of the poetry and their presumed readers. But more important was the perception of the ennobling effect of fighting for the nation; since the men were taking part in a holy war, a modern crusade, naturally they were virtuous and noble. (There was a similar sense of participating in a crusade in the Boer War – a crusade on behalf of the Empire – though the image of the knightly and virtuous soldier was far less universal than in the later conflict.[30]) While the new crusade was linked by German poets mainly to warrior epics of Germanic origin (but with Christian overtones), the English inspiration lay in popular modern adaptations of the Arthurian tales of chivalry. Perhaps 'virgin purity' was more important in this version of the Middle Ages than of the one adopted by the Germans, because although there is little implication that German heroes were any less virginal, and their cause was certainly no less holy, their purity is not emphasised. The English concept is in effect much closer to the French, since saints and martyrs are also by implication pure, but whereas the one appropriates its images directly from the religious tradition of the culture – though the god for whom the new martyrs have suffered is of course 'la Patrie' – the other adds a religious veneer to a secular ideal. In all cases, however, it would be a mistake to assume that these soldiers are in a direct line of descent from the Middle Ages – a manifestation of an enduring tradition of 'chivalrous and heroic' warfare, or even of martyrdom on the battlefield. Their origin is recent, a product of the popularisation of the medieval period by writers and artists in the second half of the nineteenth century, combined with a sense of dedication to the modern god, the nation. And by adopting these popular images, the patriotic poets are able not only to endow their heroes with appropriate characteristics, but also to suggest, however inaccurately, that the soldiers are following a worthy tradition – the creed of patriotic heroism which, they imply, has served the country well throughout history.

Heroic death that is even more chivalric than life, high-sounding and virtuous causes, archaic language and the imagery of 'battles long ago', often coupled with book illustrations similarly depicting the accoutrements of earlier wars, all played their part in promoting amongst the poets' contemporaries the belief in a noble tradition of sacrificial heroism. For the modern reader, however, these factors merely enlarge the gap between the words of the poetry and their supposed referent, so that these poems which nominally deal with a factual situation seem to have little contact with reality. Clément Chanteloube's diction in

Héros! jeunes ou vieux, que votre tâche est belle!
Votre sang répandu fait la France immortelle

(Heroes, young or old, how beautiful is your task! Your spilled blood makes France immortal)

bears far more relation to the stage heroism of a character of Racine than to the gruelling life and death of soldiers.[31] It is hard to equate this idea of 'sang répandu' with the 'real' blood in Henry-Jacques' 'Le Charnier' – 'Sous eux le sang s'étale et noircit au soleil' (beneath them the blood dries and darkens in the sun) – or even with the vision of a bloodsoaked world in Maurice Pottecher's 'Le Point de vue des corbeaux' (The Crow's-Eye View), where crows report from all directions throughout Europe that 'La terre est rouge, rouge, rouge' (The earth is red, red, red).[32] The connection between elevated language and remoteness from reality is revealed with particular force in a collection by a little-known French writer, G.A. Fauré. *Mes Impressions sur la guerre 1914–15–16* opens with several poems which present the author's impressions of an earlier conflict, that of 1870–1. The Great War poems abound in verbosity and grandiloquence – 'Il veut, dans une grande bataille, / Sur l'ennemi être triomphant' (He wishes, in a great battle, to be triumphant over the enemy) – and in high-sounding cliches such as 'tombés au champ d'honneur' (fallen on the field of honour) and 'que leurs noms soient sacrés' (sacred be their names), which are quite missing in the earlier work. In 'La Guerre', dated 1871, the speaker has to bring home to his mother the news of his brother's death:

> C'était une nouvelle terrible et bien triste
> Que j'allais bientôt apprendre à ma mère.

> (It was terrible and very sad news that I would soon have to convey to my mother.)

That mother, one senses, would have found little consolation in the words uttered by 'une voix' in the 1914 poem 'La Mère':

> Mère, ne pleure plus!
> Il faut des morts pour faire une victoire,
> Et le soleil un jour sera plus beau!![33]

> (Mother, weep no more! Deaths are needed to make victory, and the sun will be more beautiful some day!)

Although it is unlikely that either of these mothers existed in reality, the former incident, one feels, might have happened; the second mother remains as unreal as Chanteloube's 'sang répandu', since she was so obviously created only to provide an opportunity for the poet's patriotic declaration.

Fauré's progression, it is clear, is not towards the realism that one might expect to result from his experience of the earlier conflict, but towards grandiloquence and the glorification of war. One sees a similar development in the work of a much more successful poet than Fauré, Friedrich Lienhard, whose ballads concerning the Boer War, the *Burenlieder*, are described by M. Van Wyk Smith as 'among the best poems in any language' on the subject of the earlier conflict. Van Wyk Smith comments especially on their 'striking realism' and their lack of didacticism. In the First World War, while Lienhard's poetry remains more realistic than that of most of his confrères (his departing soldiers in 'Soldatenauszug aus Erfurt' are going 'In die Schlacht, in den Tod' – To battle, to death), and while he is more inventive than others in his 'didacticism' (as in 'Münstergespräch', where Bismarck blames Louis XIV for the war), he has nevertheless regressed towards the norm in both respects. His effective technique of focusing on individual soldiers in the Boer poems is entirely absent from his First World War collection *Heldentum und Liebe*. Interestingly enough, there is a parallel development in the case of Thomas Hardy. Hardy's best-known Boer War poem, 'Drummer Hodge', is realistic and closely focused – 'They throw in Drummer Hodge, to rest / Uncoffined – just as found' – and like most of his earlier poetry, it reveals a non-committal or even disapproving attitude towards war. On the other hand 'Men Who March Away', which to contemporaries was his most famous poem of the First World War, is unashamedly an exercise in patriotic propaganda, composed almost entirely of clichés and improbable generalisations. Lienhard's comment on the departing men, who recognise for the first time the beauty that they are leaving, as they depart for the war and death, makes Hardy's seem glib and superficial (Charles Sorley aptly described 'Men Who March Away' as 'arid'), but both poets have moved in the same direction, away from the specific towards the general, and away from a recognition of the reality of war towards patriotic idealism. The poems that result are in both cases disappointingly characteristic of Great War patriotic verse.

Throughout the patriotic poetry, while the nation itself often assumes the role of a single person, one finds that, like Hardy's 'men who march away' and Lienhard's 'braunroten Männer', the inhabitants of the country are almost invariably either collective or plural. Poets write of 'those who die for England', of 'unsre Frauen und Mädchen' and 'les poilus'; of mothers, heroes, men, and, generically, man, but rarely of an individual, apart from an occasional representative type like those mothers of four sons, and the very famous. Individual place-names are similarly limited either to those which help to evoke the desired national image, such as Weimar, Paris and 'Bideford and Appledore', or to those which serve a propagandist purpose, guaranteeing an appropriately outraged response from an informed audience – Reims and Louvain, for instance. Otherwise, location is multiple or general, presented in terms like 'each village', 'durch Feld und Tal' (through field and valley), or 'mes villes en flammes' (my towns in flames). Since effective description that is simultaneously collective and concrete is difficult to produce, the patriotic poets rarely make the attempt. People are described only in 'heroic' terms, and places almost entirely through clichés. Even in English, despite the concept of the nation as a rural society, one finds little of the close observation and familiarity with nature that one might expect of poets writing in a tradition that, as Fussell observes, includes 'a Herrick, a Cowper, a Clare, a Cobbett, a Wordsworth'. Instead, most of the description is in the manner of 'The joy of flow'rs that blow, of birds that sing'.

The principle that underlies both the mentioning of a few propagandist names and the deliberate avoidance of the specific in other reference is that of 'imagining' the community, of calling upon, and helping to enlarge, the pool of shared knowledge, experience and ideas. In making the reference generally applicable instead of attaching it to a single individual or place, one leaves for the reader the possibility of identifying with the circumstances of the poem, and thus of feeling at one with the community. The ultimate non-specific reference in this regard lies in the use of a 'we' speaker instead of the traditional 'lyric I', since the speaker's feelings and beliefs, rather than being those of an individual, must be attributable to the community at large. The collective first person persona is probably the most prevalent international convention of Great War patriotic verse, for in the vast majority of poems the voice that speaks identifies itself as 'we'. Even when the persona is hidden, a single pronoun or possessive adjective usually serves as a reminder that the poetic consciousness is plural and collective. Although in normal usage (including poetry) the French or German counterpart of the English word 'we' may be the impersonal pronoun, *on* or *man* ('On mange à sept heures' – 'We eat at seven'), in the patriotic poetry that impersonal form consistently gives place to the more definite 'nous' or 'wir'. The 'we' voice is more than simply an echo of the 'Wirgefühl' (literally, 'we'-feeling) that is one of the first requirements for a sense of nationhood, since it represents the thoughts and feelings of the nation and yet is at the same time a special literary persona. For this reason, its significance for the functioning of the poetry as communication is far-reaching.

The value of the 'we' persona for writers of Great War patriotic verse rests on two aspects of the poetic that the late nineteenth century inherited from Romanticism: the concept that the poet is a special individual apart from the crowd, with a unique message, and the convention that the 'I' speaker of a poem is normally to be equated with the poet as a person. From the second of these assumptions, as I suggested already, poets had always departed with impunity as the situation required. Readers, on the other hand, apparently liked to think that poets who wrote as 'I' were telling the empirical truth, unless, like Robert Browning, they made their intention clear. Although by 1914 experimental poets were deliberately trying to escape from the confessional mode, most of the readers and writers of the patriotic poetry were traditionalists, so they assumed that the voice that spoke the poem could safely be equated with that of the poet. Even a relatively enlightened critic, Julius Bab, expressed indignation when a particular writer, H.H. Ewers, introduced into a poem some personal 'facts' – a supposed description of the poet's mother's house – that Bab knew to be untrue.[34] At the same time, however, 'we' is different from 'I': when one speaks as a member of a group, one does not speak as an individual, for the collective voice limits the personal. In using 'we', the poet adopts a persona or mask, a public face distinct from his or her own. To the extent that 'we' incorporates 'I', it allows the writer to identify with the group and to be identified by others as a member, while implying also a readiness to surrender his or her individuality for the collective good emphasising the totality of the personal commitment. Yet by placing the writer in a position similar to that of dramatists *vis-à-vis* their characters, who may or may not speak the writer's own opinions, the 'we' voice detracts from the supposed 'confessional' nature of the relationship between poet and speaker. It thus enables the poets to claim for the nation at large (including themselves) the suffering endured by their compatriots directly affected by the war, and it allows them the luxury of vowing to 'fechten für Reich und Recht' (fight for the realm and the right) or to 'Stand up and meet the foe', without requiring, as the 'I' voice might, that their moral commitment be reflected in physical action. The 'we' persona, it is clear, is perfectly suited for the new concept of total war, which requires equal commitment from every member of the nation; and it was especially apposite in a situation like the First World War, where relatively little physical participation was actually expected of civilians.

The second valuable function of the universal 'we' voice in the patriotic verse arises from the Romantic view of the poet as a uniquely gifted individual, with privileged insight and extraordinary powers of imagination. Not only by the very fact of being poets, but also because, in speaking out, they adopted the role of spokesman, the patriotic writers assumed this special status and accordingly were numbered amongst the select. At the same time, the 'we' persona absolved them from the need to demonstrate any extraordinary power of vision, since it spoke for 'all of us', and merely reiterated the accepted and popular point of view about the war. Thus although the image of the poet as a priest was retained, the skill required to fill the position was not commensurate with exclusiveness. The priest was demysticised, as if to coincide with the demands of that new priestless or 'unmediated' religion, the worship of the Fatherland; but instead of the destruction of the priesthood, the consequence was an enormous increase in the number of priests. Unlike most published literature, which is the work of a relatively small number of professional or expert writers, this poetry came from a very large and diverse group, varying in both occupation and literary ability. The more prolific writers were usually professionals, often commissioned by newspapers (formally or informally) to produce poems that gave support to the country's cause, and their work was readily available to the reading public. Most poets, however, were amateurs, who had perhaps only recently progressed from being readers themselves and who, one may assume, were inspired both by poems they had read and by their role as members of a nation in crisis. It is this constant intermingling of writers and readers, this obviously influence-based yet also spontaneous or 'unmediated' mode of production and communication, that makes Great War patriotic poetry such an unusual literary phenomenon.

Yet despite its obvious popularity, the patriotic verse is not 'popular literature' as the term is used to describe such genres as the Western novel and the detective story. These are the work of a few authors skilled in literary manipulation, who often earn their living by writing, and whose books are intended before everything as entertainment. The patriotic poetry, on the other hand, was produced by a very large number of amateur writers, and its primary purpose was neither to make money for the author nor to entertain. Nor is it related in its functioning to another category of popular literature, folk poetry, for that term is usually reserved for work which emanates exclusively from the lower social classes, and is transmitted by oral rather than printed means. Nevertheless, the most appropriate parallel may indeed be a form that is accepted as folk literature, the English broadside ballad, which was popular in the eighteenth and nineteenth centuries. The ballads were printed poems sold cheaply on the street or at a fairground, and they owed their existence largely to the increased literacy of craftspeople and artisans in the eighteenth century, which brought a corresponding growth in the market for inexpensive, unostentatious and easily available reading material. Great War patriotic verse was similarly a form of popular verse in print, and it arose because almost universal literacy made the publication of patriotic poems a worthwhile undertaking during the war. Normally, in the case of printed works of literature, editors and publishers intercede between writers and readers, ensuring that some texts reach their intended audience, and determining that others will not. The dissemination of broadside ballads was unimpeded by the controls of the literary system, since writers paid for the services of a printer (or printed the poems themselves), and sold their work directly to the public. With regard to the patriotic poetry an element of the same immediacy prevailed, because publishers, in this instance, appear to have served as a conduit rather than a filter, printing innumerable poems in inexpensive and easily accessible form – in national or local newspapers, for example – and bringing a wide range of poets into contact with their wished-for audience. (In the process, of course, the publishers also gave proof of their own patriotic dedication.) There is, however, a major difference. The ballads circulated only on the periphery of literate society of their time, apart from the few that made their way into the folksong collections popular with the sophisticated middle class towards the end of the century. The patriotic war poetry, on the other hand, clearly belonged to the literary mainstream, regardless of the social status of its author. The tradition of printed popular verse that began with the ballads thus came to fulfilment with First World War patriotic poetry, in a form that permeated the whole of society.

The link between these two kinds of popular verse is underlined by the fact that many patriotic poems were actually published as broadsheets or on postcards. Some of the broadsheets were reprints from newspapers or magazines – Hans Limburger's 'Frisch auf', the first poem the *Kölnische Zeitung* published in the war, for instance, or 'The Day', by 'Mr Henry Chappell, the Bath railway-porter'. Chappell's poem appeared first in the *Daily Express*, and the paper immediately proceeded to advertise reprints, recommending that each recruiting meeting (or, in the preferred term, 'patriotic demonstration') should include a recitation of 'The Day'. This broadsheet came with a red, white and blue border, while Limburger's poem was decorated with the German imperial eagle. The *Express*, incidentally, published far fewer poems than most of the national newspapers in England, but it must have received a good return on those few, both in money and in reputation, through the sale of reprints, which it advertised repeatedly. While 'The Day' as a broadsheet seems to have been intended for a civilian audience (or, recited, for potential recruits), poems printed on postcards were often designed for mailing to combatants. The Birmingham collection has several such poems by Marie E. Clay, written for the Warwickshire Poem Aid Society.[35] This society had a dual objective: 'To aid in the Spiritual Welfare of our Soldiers by means of Poems written for this purpose', and 'To aid in the Material Welfare in necessitous cases by means of funds raised from the sale of other Poems sold to the Public'. (The idea of two distinct types of poem has interesting implications; one wonders why the poems written for the spiritual welfare of soldiers could not also be sold to the public.) Many of the single-sheet publications, like the earlier broadside ballads, were printed at the author's own expense, though they were probably circulated to friends and relations, rather than sold in the market square. Elsie Mewis, who contributed some of her broadsheet poems to the Birmingham collection after the war, raised £120 for the Belgian refugees and 'our own Tommies' – an astonishing total of more than twenty thousand copies, if all were sold at the asking price of one penny.[36] This, surely, is a form of folk poetry, even though it is not confined to the poorer classes or propagated by oral means: the folk poetry of a 'high (literate) culture'.

In the letter that accompanies her submissions to the Birmingham library, Mewis mentions how proud she is 'to have been able to help a little in the hour of need'. Undoubtedly a personal sense of having contributed to the nation's cause was a significant factor in making the writing of poetry of this kind a popular occupation, but equally important was its function in establishing the writer's public reputation, both as poet and as patriot. To be placed amongst the *literati* was an especially valuable consideration for those who belonged to a class that was not normally expected to read or write verse; Mewis sounds humble and almost apologetic when she remarks, 'I am employed at Cadbury Brothers but I am very fond of poetry'.[37] Without extensive and difficult biographical research it is impossible to know how typical Mewis is of the 'unknown' writers of patriotic verse. Evidence that is readily available suggests that poetry of this kind in all three languages came predominantly from such representatives of the middle class as schoolteachers, public officials, and clerics (or their wives), but there were obviously many exceptions of both lower and higher rank, including Mewis, Henry Chappell, the German worker-poets, and the Austrian aristocrat who signs himself 'Altgraf Erich'. (My general impression is that most of this poetry was produced by the type of people who wrote, and still write, 'letters to the editor' in newspapers – that is, the more vocal members of each social group – though with a significantly larger proportion of women than the 'letters' page usually reveals.) For poets of all classes, however, the writing of patriotic verse proved that one was a true patriot, in that the public declaration of loyalty was in itself a patriotic deed. One of the many ironies of the war poetry lies in the fact that, while innumerable poems promise undying fame to unnamed combatants, the fame they promise is inseparable from the existence of the poem, and therefore from the poet's own reputation. Few of the visitors to war memorials study the names of the men who died, yet almost all read the inscribed lines of verse and, if it is provided, the name of the poet.

The collective first person 'consciousness' that opens up poetry to such a wide range of writers also affects the role of the reader. In normal poetic usage, when a writer adopts a first person singular voice, or even when there is no explicit persona, the words are directed towards an implied reader, a distinctive 'you', or at least 'other'. When the voice is an unspecific 'we', such a distinction between speaker and reader is weakened, since the reader is encompassed by and implicated in the poet's statement. A necessary condition for the proper functioning of propaganda literature is that the actual audience recognise and equate itself with the writer's implied reader. In the patriotic verse the bond of compatriotism provides for that identification, linking speaker and implied reader, poet and audience. To place oneself outside this sense of community with one's fellow citizens in time of war is to risk an accusation of disloyalty, while to dissociate oneself from one's share in the words which the poet, through the 'we' voice, imputes to the reader requires a conscious act of rejection. Without doubt, compliance is easier. Accordingly, Karl Strecker's confident 'Wir zagen nicht, bricht auch die Welt zusammen' (We do not waver, even if the world falls apart) is persuasive as well as assertive, particularly with its present tense predicting the future as an absolute, just as Laurence Binyon's 'We step from days of sour division / Into the grandeur of our fate', by linking all readers into the same destiny, eliminates the possibility of continued disunity.[38] Propaganda of this kind aims to reinforce existing attitudes rather than to inculcate new ones. The 'we' voice, encompassing all compatriots and excluding those who do not belong, eliminates the need for subtle or complex argument, since it preaches only to the converted. In this way it reinforces the inclination of nationalism to inspire extreme and simplistic attitudes and a completely black-and-white viewpoint, for the enemy outside the magic circle drawn by the 'we' persona – a circle that coincides with the boundary of the nation – is different in every possible way from those on the inside. 'Civilised ambiguity', to borrow Fussell's phrase, is irrelevant.

But although patriotic poets consistently draw a contrast between 'the Fatherland' and 'the enemy', this division (surprisingly enough) is not usually presented in terms of 'us' and 'them'. More commonly, the enemy is addressed as 'you' or referred to as 'he', while the 'we'–'they' dichotomy is reserved for a different purpose – to voice praise for the nation's heroes: 'they' who, for 'our' sake, have left their 'loved homes', have sacrificed their youth, and have moved on to heroic or saintly immortality. The division reflects in part the acknowledgement that 'we' are safe while 'they' are in danger and discomfort, or 'we' are alive and 'they' are dead, but the choice of pronouns also underlines the propagandist function of the heroic verse. The usage allows the poet to link his or her own patriotic commitment to that of the 'warrior sons', without the immodesty of claiming too large a share in the suffering. At the same time it excludes the combatants from the circle of ordinary citizens and places them on a higher plane, where they can be utilised as an example to promote the patriotic–heroic ethic within the ranks of people not on active service. Just as invective against the enemy in songs of hate strengthens the nation's resolve and reassures the poet's compatriots about the rightness of the country's cause, so through heroic poems both writers and readers convince themselves that the sacrifice in terms of human life is worthwhile and in a noble tradition. And because at the same time they confirm their resolve to encourage the young men of their acquaintance to carry on the fight, at whatever personal cost, the poetry has a consequence in the world of reality, if not immediately on the heroes themselves, at least on the public at large. Brian Gardner may be right in suggesting that Rupert Brooke was directly influential in inspiring a death-wish in some of his contemporaries, but in general the consequence of patriotic–heroic verse like Brooke's and Seaman's was both more subtle and more pernicious.[39] Its effect was to encourage a large part of the population of each country to believe in a set of standards of heroic behaviour that owed a little to literature, less to history, and nothing at all to the reality of warfare, and to apply those standards in judging the conduct of a group of their fellow citizens. One can appreciate why combatant protest poets often adopted the same 'we-they' opposition from the reverse angle.

One of the most obvious indications of the pernicious effect of the 'heroic' standard of judgement is in recruiting poems, which address the possible recruits who have failed to volunteer. Probably because the British army relied entirely on volunteers until 1916, whereas France and Germany both had compulsory military service and a large number of reservists, poems of this kind occurred more commonly in English, where the writer could pretend to be serving a useful function. Some of the appeals are expressed in general terms, like 'Come forward, Sons of Britain', or 'Rouse ye, my men, are ye waking or sleeping?' Others, however, atypically for patriotic verse, focus on individuals; perhaps here too villains are more worthy of attention than heroes. J.A. Brooke's 'What Will you Say?' is an echo of the famous poster caption, 'What did you do in the war, Daddy?'

> What will you say in the years to come?
> You who are deaf today
> To the call of the bugle, fife and drum –
> O young man, what will you say?
>
> 'Into the shadow I feared to ride',
> This must your answer be
> To the stalwart son who walks by your side
> The child who stands at your knee.[40]

Although the poster itself shows contemporary – indeed, stylish – figures, Brooke's interpretation is typically archaic, with its traditional rallying-call, the description of the son as 'stalwart', the metaphorical image of a horseman riding (or not riding) 'into the shadow', instead of a soldier going to the Front by train or on foot, and above all in the assumption that a man who has once been afraid will feel ashamed for ever. Walter Sichel's 'What are You Waiting for? To the Slackers: A Recruiting Song', also takes up a familiar picture, that of a *fin de siècle* aesthete. The potential recruit is addressed as 'Boy with the willowy figure, / Lad with the lacklustre eye', and urged on with the words, 'Can you not *try* to try'.[41] Ironically enough, in actuality much of the controversy about recruitment in Britain centred on two groups of young men who certainly did not match Sichel's image of the 'slacker' – skilled workers in heavy industry and professional football players. Sichel's poem, with its hint of the (apparently misplaced) belief in the moral superiority of the athlete, is possibly another remnant of the Social Darwinism which, as Van Wyk Smith shows in *Drummer Hodge*, was characteristic of Boer War verse. For the most part, however, in the Great War poetry homogeneity is taken for granted: the unwilling recruits are perceived to be different only in their failure to respond with enthusiasm to the thought of going to war.

Recruiting poems are an obvious example of propagandist writing, and their purpose, on the surface, is clear: to persuade young men to volunteer for service. It is doubtful, however, whether the poems fulfilled that aim, if only because young men who were sufficiently impervious to the appeals of patriotic idealism to refrain from volunteering are unlikely to have been avid readers of such poetry. And surely they would react with indignation or cynicism, rather than with compliance, to constant reminders of their duty, like Louisa Prior's 'To a Hesitant Briton' – 'You have not gone – no doubt you have a reason' – or Marjorie Pratt's 'To a 'Shirker'' – 'Some have left wives and kiddies behind them, / And they're fighting for you – yes, for you' – especially when the reminder comes from a woman who is herself a non-combatant.[42] It is clear that like the kind of patriotic poem that appears to be directed at the enemy, these propagandist texts are not intended for their ostensible target – in this case, the recalcitrant young men. Their appeal rather is to an audience already convinced that the only appropriate action is to volunteer, and they perform a dual function. In the first place they provide the poet, who is usually not in a position to volunteer, with a means of fulfilling his or her duty by pretending to persuade other people to do so. And secondly they serve to reinforce the community's belief in the appropriate heroic attitude. Recruiting poems, in effect, are merely the obverse of the innumerable poems about heroes, and in neither case is the ostensible purpose – · whether of praising heroes or of reprimanding the unheroic – the major reason for the poem's existence as a printed text.

Despite its serious propagandist purpose of sustaining officially-sanctioned attitudes throughout the nation, the patriotic and heroic poetry rarely succeeds in convincing modern readers to treat it seriously, although they may occasionally be shocked by the apparent callousness of lines like 'Happy is England in the brave that die' or 'Herz, dein Glück sei Opfermut' (Heart, may your happiness lie in the courage for sacrifice). So much of the work is clearly incompetent as verse, and often amusingly so – Forshaw's anthologies have several 'gems' of this kind, such as the splendid lines addressed to the moon, supposedly by a soldier's mother: 'I know'st thou see'st him lying / 'Midst his Comrades dead and dying'.[43] Mostly, however, the problem lies in the fact that the poems are so much like each other; as a result one feels that the poets were merely playing a game of variations on a theme, reminiscent of other highly conventionalised literary games, such as the medieval poetry of courtly love. In a December 1914 review Edward Thomas described the process of creating patriotic poems:

> It is the hour of the writer who picks up popular views or phrases, or coins them, and has the power to turn them into downright stanzas. Most newspapers have one or more of these gentlemen. They could take the easy words of a statesman, such as 'No price is too high when honour and freedom are at stake', and dish them up so that the world next morning, ready to be thrilled by anything lofty and noble-looking, is thrilled.[44]

While this assessment fails to make any allowance for the extent to which patriotic verse was written 'by the people' as well as for them, it is valuable in pointing to the conventionality of the poetry. What Frederick Goldin says about the courtly love lyric of the Middle Ages – 'The song we read today was first written as an arrangement of the audience's expectations' – applies equally well to Great War patriotic verse.[45] Courtly love poetry, however, was recognised as a game by all participants in the communicative act, whether the troubadour or Minnesänger establishing his position at court by telling of his undying love for his noble mistress, the lord or duke who paid this upstart visitor to sing love-songs to his wife, or the guests who waited to hear their favourite variations on the theme of love; and no-one considered the possibility that the poet's 'love' had any connection with physical reality. Patriotic verse, on the other hand, claimed to deal directly with an important issue of the time, and was taken seriously by many contemporary readers, even while its themes, attitudes and style all helped to destroy its connection with the reality to which it nominally referred.

Nevertheless, a few poems depart from the ordinary, and accordingly become not only more interesting but also (for my purpose) more useful. It is hard to demonstrate the almost universal validity of the conventions that govern the poetry merely by quoting a few from amongst many thousands of examples; to discuss the exceptions that proverbially prove the rules may be more convincing. Since one striking feature is the prevalence of the first person plural 'voice', atypical patriotic poetry may be considered as that in which the author expresses his or her commitment to the nation's cause through an 'I' persona instead of 'we'. Sometimes the 'I' voice proves to be nothing more than a formulaic usage, such as 'mein Vaterland', 'je te salue', 'I pray', within an otherwise collective expression of dedication, but in other cases, especially in German, 'I' and 'we' are explicitly merged. In what might be called 'oath' poems, a vow of loyalty and sacrifice made through the 'I' persona is incorporated into a collective pledge. Kurt Münzer's 'Vaterland' (which I quoted earlier in the chapter) is of this type, as are Walter Flex's 'Preußischer Fahneneid' (Prussian military oath) and Gerhart Hauptmann's 'O mein Vaterland'. Amidst the generalisations that dominate patriotic poetry, the 'I' persona in these poems has the effect of making at least one of the referents specific and, accordingly, more credible. For instance, Flex's lines 'Ich habe dem König von Preußen geschworen / Einen leiblichen Eid' (I have sworn to the King of Prussia my personal oath) evoke a picture which, if not immediately transferable into the empirical world, is at least a realisable image, and it is not difficult to believe that the poet may have conceived of his own military pledge of allegiance in just such a light.[46] One cannot safely assume, however, that the 'I' voice is always autobiographical. In Heinrich Lersch's 'Soldaten-Abschied', for instance, the illusion that the soldier who pleads 'Laß mich gehen, Mutter, laß mich gehen!' (Let me go, Mother, let me go!) may be Lersch himself is destroyed when the 'I' speaker takes a fond farewell of his wife, and then of his 'Liebste' (sweetheart). Lersch's 'I' persona is not to be taken as voicing the poet's personal commitment (although, of course, it may exemplify it), but is used for the aesthetic purpose of evoking sympathy, while the alternation between 'I' and 'we' underlines the theme of the poem, the voluntary sacrifice of the individual to the general cause.

Although the idea of giving oneself for the collective good is not uniquely German, it apparently did not inspire the same form of expression in the poetry of the other two languages. Personal declarations of patriotic devotion are not common in French, although Nicolas Beauduin's *L'Offrande héroïque*, obviously influenced in style by Whitman, compensates liberally for their absence elsewhere. In 'À la France', the first poem in the collection, Beauduin writes, 'Mon chant est un hymne d'amour' – My song is a hymn of love – and he goes on to proclaim his love effusively in both secular and religious terms: 'Je t'adore et je te dis mon amour, ô ma France' (I adore you and declare my love for you, o my France), 'Ma mère, ma patronne et ma sainte épousée' (Mother, patron-saint and holy wife).[47] In view of the English reputation for 'reserve and self-consciousness' (as Charles Sorley terms it), one is not surprised to find that the English voice their personal patriotism, if at all, in a more restrained manner. Such declarations almost always focus on a particular location, usually rural, like the Gloucestershire scenes that are central to Ivor Gurney's patriotic dedication, and the commitment tends to remain private and deliberately exclusive, rather than seeking to encompass the nation as a whole. 'The Soldier Speaks', by F.W. Harvey, a friend of Gurney and author of *A Gloucestershire Lad*, displays something of Beauduin's effusiveness – 'Still must I love you, yearn to you, / England, how truly mine' – but the poem's title hints at impersonality, as though a personal expression of dedication to the nation (rather than to the physical terrain) were not quite respectable.[48] The same is true of Rupert Brooke's 'The Soldier', where not only the title but also the major part of the poem counteracts the personal tone of the opening line, 'If I should die, think only this of me'.[49] After this casual and self-effacing beginning, which could easily be the antecedent for a comment like Sorley's 'many a better one has died before' (and which is quite characteristic of Brooke, both as poet and as person), the 'I' voice disappears and, except for the fact that the soldier in question is singular rather than plural, the rest of the poem is scarcely distinguishable from others concerning the nation's heroes.

Like the German 'oath' poets, Edward Thomas in 'This is No Case of Petty Right or Wrong' uses both an individual and a collective voice. But instead of making through the 'I' persona an individual pledge that represents a minute part of the general commitment, Thomas uses it to deny the validity of a love in which all are expected to join.[50] He deliberately refutes automatic and extremist patriotism, and declines to take a judgemental position. Yet, having established his individual and unbiased viewpoint, he makes a statement of patriotic commitment that is largely in keeping with the principles he has rejected, not least in the use of the 'we' persona characteristic of patriotic verse. The linking of the name of God with that of England, the personification of the country as 'she' – thus paradoxically reminding the reader that 'England', in this case, is not a physical entity but a concept – and such 'poetic' vocabulary as 'perchance' and 'ken', are not commonly found in Thomas's work. Jon Silkin's comment that in this poem Thomas inclines, 'however slightly', towards 'the rhetorical position that any patriotism, no matter how moderately expressed, tends to lead one into', is undoubtedly true. It would, however, be more appropriate to identify nationalism rather than patriotism as the culprit, since the responsibility for the rhetoric lies mainly with the collective voice and the technique of conceptualising and then personifying the country.[51] So grand a figure as 'an England beautiful' must of necessity be associated with grandiloquence, while the use of a persona that speaks for the entire nation apparently limits the possibilities of expression available to the poet.

A more consistently unusual patriotic poem is Arnold Ulitz's 'Belagerung' (Siege).[52] For Ulitz's speaker the 'Vaterland' is neither an idea called Germany nor, in a general sense, a territory bearing that name, but his home town. Yet unlike the English poems in which patriotism is linked to a specific location, 'Belagerung' is set in a modern city rather than a rural and private corner of an industrialised country. Although the opening line, with its collective persona, sounds typical of patriotic verse ('Russische Reiter jagen durch unser Land' – Russian cavalrymen are charging through our country), in the rest of the poem the voice is 'I'. Since the threat is above all to the physical structure, the town's streets and buildings serve as the focal point for the speaker's love. He proposes to relive his childhood discovery of the town, not through the publicly-shared senses of 'sights and sounds' (to quote Brooke in 'The Soldier'), but through the most intimate, the tactile:

> Wenn wir umkreist sind, will ich noch einmal wildern
> Durch alle meine Lieblingstraßen wie als Kind,
> Will buchstabieren an funkelnden Ladenschildern,
> Und auf die Straßenbahnschienen will ich die Hände legen
> Und spüren, wie sie warm von der Sonne sind.

> (When we are surrounded, I will wander through my favourite streets once more, as I did as a child; I will spell out the letters on the shiny door-plaques, and place my hands on the tram rails, to feel how warm they are from the sun.)

By comparison, the experiences that Brooke enumerates as contributing to the 'awareness' of his soldier, to whom England 'Gave, once, her flowers to love, her ways to roam', and who was 'Washed by the rivers, blest by suns of home', are seen to be far too general and abstract to belong to any individual 'I'.

Ulitz's poem is atypical of patriotic verse in many ways, not least in the use of 'non-poetic' words like 'Straßenbahnschienen' and 'Ladenschildern', and in the complementary dearth of high-sounding terms and of invective against the enemy. Equally out of character, at least for German patriotic poetry, is the ending, for instead of the usual 'Sieg oder Tod!' type of war-cry, one finds in the last lines a ready acceptance of both death and defeat, a reaction that is much more typically French:

Und wenn sie dich treffen ins Herz, und wenn du fällst,
Du meine Stadt, dann will ich mit dir fallen, Leib an Leib!

(And when they hit your heart, and when you fall, you, my town, then I will fall with you, body to body.)

Ulitz's town is personified, not as a symbolic figure like Thomas's 'an England beautiful' rising from the witches' cauldron of war, but as a physical entity capable of being destroyed 'Glied um Glied' – limb by limb. In some respects, especially in its concentration on the physical and specific, 'Belagerung' is much more typical of Thomas than Thomas's own patriotic declaration – although the English poet, whose writing is characterised by a temperate and modest tone, would certainly have minimised the 'I' persona and made the total effect less obviously dramatic. Even so, when Ulitz's speaker, referring to the 'Erdenkörner' (kernels of earth) that he has gathered from cracks and crevices as he wandered around the town, says

Mein Häuflein Erde in der Hand,
Küssen will ich's und sagen: Vaterland!

(My little pile of earth in my hand, I will kiss it and say, 'Fatherland!')

one is reminded of an incident reported by Eleanor Farjeon concerning Thomas, which both Silkin and E.D. Blodgett consider central to the understanding of his poetry.[53] When, after volunteering for the army, Thomas was asked if he knew what he was fighting for, he picked up 'a pinch of earth' and replied, 'Literally, for this'.

It is interesting to note that many Belgian poets reveal an attitude towards their country similar to that of Ulitz and Thomas (in his normal mode), and markedly in contrast with their French counterparts writing in the same language. The distinction is particularly clear in poems concerned with physical destruction. The poets of France itself are primarily intent on demonstrating the wickedness of the Germans and on emphasising their own country's role as the innocent victim, as well as their right to seek revenge. In the propaganda game they are playing, the uniqueness of any location that has suffered damage is important only in its potential for generating a sense of outrage, Reims Cathedral being the most popular example. For the Belgians the propaganda aspect is decidedly secondary to their concern for the loss of the special material object and the centuries of human culture that it represents. The most consistently striking characteristic of the Belgian poetry is the writers' capacity to make things, objects, seem real and therefore important. It is no coincidence that the one memorable poem about Reims is by the Belgian Émile Verhaeren. Another Belgian poet of the same generation as Verhaeren, Émile Cammaerts, lived in England during the war, and Edward Thomas reviewed the English translation of his *Chants patriotiques*, along with Ella Wheeler Wilcox's *Poems of Optimism*.[54] Thomas writes of Cammaerts, 'When he says that grass and flowers will grow over the dead in Belgium, it is real grass and flowers that we see, and not the somewhat spectral 'violet of his native land' that poets cause to spring from human ashes.' Although Wilcox writes of 'rivers of blood' in Belgium, he observes, 'she says only what is a possible thing, for a mind with no grasp of reality, to say. Mr Cammaerts knows, and makes us feel, that it is a fact.' Another Belgian poet temporarily in England, Marcel Wyseur, has a similar sense of the reality of the object. In 'Les Mortes' (The Dead), for instance, he wonders what has happened to the old buildings in the ruined towns of his native land:

> Où sont vos toîts penchés comme d'anciens visages,
> Et l'exquise douceur des calmes béguinages,
> Dixmunde, Ypres, Nieuport, où sont vos lourds beffrois,
> Vos cloches qui chantaient les chansons d'autrefois?[55]

(Where are your roofs drooping like ancient faces, and the exquisite sweetness of your peaceful convents, Dixmunde, Ypres, Nieuport, where are your heavy belfries, your bells that sang the songs of other times?)

The implication is that they are in ruins or, as the title says, 'dead'; but the tone at the end is of sadness rather than the outrage that one expects of poems of this kind in French:

> La Mère Flandre pleure, et les bises sauvages
> M'ont apporté ce soir quels râles dans leurs voix?..

(Flanders our Mother weeps – and what death-rattle have the savage north winds brought me in their voice tonight?)

When a French poet, Alfred Droin, writes on a similar theme, even his title, 'Le Carnage', suggests that his aim is to incite anti-German feeling rather than to express a sense of loss. As one might expect, his village which 'riait, calme' (smiled, calm), in the early morning is nothing but 'un braiser rouge et noir' (a black and red cinder) by evening, after its encounter with 'les reitres'.[56] Unfortunately Droin's nameless village, where, he would have one believe, 'le bonheur habitait la plus humble chaumière' (happiness dwelled in the humblest cottage), never seems to be more than a literary device or cliché, reminiscent of Samuel Rogers' bucolic 'cot beside the hill'. In strong contrast with this, or with the devastated fields and towns in flames by which Henri de Regnier's France swears vengeance, stands A. Marcel's lament for the destruction of Ypres, 'Mai 1915', in the Belgian anthology *Poètes-Soldats*.[57] Marcel's poem has all the life, colour and detail of a Flemish painting. It describes how the citizens of Ypres from the past,

Nous les drapeurs pour qui l'on construit les Halles,
Nous les maìons qui bâtissions les cathédrales,

(we drapers for whom the Halles were constructed, we masons who built the cathedrals),

and many others, dressed in 'voiles, pourpoints, guenilles, / Robes sombres, costumes colorés, / Bure velours soie et casques dorés' (veils, doublets, rags, dark robes, colourful costumes, homespun, velvet, silk, and gilded helmets), come forward to insist that, although their work is being destroyed, the spirit of Ypres will remain. One finds more concrete nouns and adjectives in this single poem than in the total of many volumes of French (as distinct from Belgian) patriotic poetry. To come upon a picture like this, or Verhaeren's image of Reims Cathedral moving towards the traveller, Wyseur's 'toîts penchés comme d'anciens visages', or the many examples of 'real' objects in the *Poètes-Soldats* anthology, amidst all the abstractions and generalisations that characterise the patriotic verse as a whole, is like finding the proverbial oasis.

The Belgian poems are also unusual in their sense of history – the poets' awareness that buildings which have stood 'Depuis des jours sans fin, depuis des jours sans nombre, /Et puis des jours encor' (From endless days, from days without number, and still more days), as Wyseur says of the Tour des Templiers at Nieuport, are being destroyed.[58] Fussell writes that 'the Great War was perhaps the last to be conceived as taking place within a seamless, purposeful "history" involving a coherent stream of time running from past through present to future.'[59] His observation may be true in general, but as far as the patriotic verse is concerned, the 'stream' metaphor, with its implication of forward movement, is inaccurate. Rather, typical patriotic poets give little indication of any historical awareness; in the view they promote, the past was unchanging and the future, after the aberration of the war, will be the same. By contrast, the idea which finds expression in the Belgian poetry – that, although life will continue, an important link with the past has been irretrievably destroyed – shows a much more rational acceptance of the facts, and implies accordingly a readiness to deal with them. One looks in vain for a similar historical sense in the French writing, or indeed in the patriotic verse in the other two languages. Perhaps the closest comparison is with English poems concerning the continuity of rural life, like Hardy's 'In Time of 'The Breaking of Nations'', Kipling's 'The Land' (which is presumably to be considered a war poem, since the author is careful to locate it, through the narrator's 'Georgii Quinti Anno Sexto' – the sixth year of King George V – in 1916), and, on a theme similar to Kipling's, Edward Thomas's 'Lob', which reveals a more subtle awareness of the interplay of change and permanence.

Such historical sense as these English poems evince, however, is that of a peaceful rural setting. Thomas's poetry offers a reflection on war from a civilian perspective, rather than a report on combatant experience. And it may be significant that, although the period before he left England at the end of 1916 was highly productive, Thomas wrote no poems in the three months he was in France before he was killed; one wonders whether his vision of continuity had difficulty in accommodating the reality he encountered. In the war poetry of Edmund Blunden, another 'country' poet, a persistent theme is the failure of his old perceptions about the consolatory effect of nature (including rural traditions), in face of the chaos caused by war. Could Hardy have located the same poem about the unchanging patterns of human life in a part of Belgium or northern France where the farmland and woods had been destroyed by shells? A. Marcel's account, in 'La Dentellière', of an old lacemaker fleeing from the Germans seems much more true to reality. The old woman, who like her mother and grandmother before her has laboured throughout her life, sits by the cottage door working at her lace, watching the fleeing peasants and the retreating soldiers. At last she, too, must join the stream of refugees:

> Silencieuse elle s'enfuit
> Sans même un regard en arrière,
> Abondonnant tout, mais tenant
> Contre elle, de ses bras tremblants,
> Son vieux carreau de dentellière.[60]

(Silently she flees, without even a backward glance, abandoning everything, but clutching against her, in trembling arms, her old lace-maker's pillow.)

To reinforce his message, Marcel adds:

> Je vous raconte ce départ
> Pour que chacun puisse comprendre
> Qu'on ne détruira ni la Flandre
> Ni son dur travail, ni son art.

(I am telling you of this departure so that everyone may understand that Flanders will never be destroyed, nor its hard work, nor its art.)

The English poets invite one to place the war in a cosmic perspective, to see it as part of the cycle of human experience, like the recurring patterns of country life. Marcel and his compatriots, on the other hand, perceive the destruction in more immediate terms, and with a sense of urgency that cannot allow for such objectivity and detachment. As citizens of a small nation caught in the middle of a war, they recognise that their entire culture is threatened. Their purpose extends far beyond that of the patriotic poets of the other countries, playing games of insult and invective and ringing changes on a theme, and they are not concerned with taking comfort in name-calling. While their aim is to strengthen the resolve of their compatriots, they also recognise that their poems must serve as a permanent memory, representing for the future a past that seems close to irreversible destruction. In such a situation, survival depends, not on natural cycles, but on individual determination. And in striving to ensure the continuity of their nation, by recreating in their poems a remnant of the culture that is being destroyed by the war, as the old lacemaker salvages one small but vital part of her family's history, these Belgian writers are indeed serving their country as well as any poet may.

4

Cruel thy sword
The war against words

Thou art the Disillusioner. Thy words
Are desolate winds and jagged spurs of rock,
Whereon they urge the frigate of our pride
To wreck her gaudy cargo. Cruel thy sword,
To strip our sword of glamour, leaving steel
Naked! and wounds inglorious! grief laid bare!
O Still Small Voice, the louder roars the whirl,
More clear thou comest, and more terrible!

E.H. Visiak, 'The Pacifist'[1]

Towards the end of 1915, the number of patriotic poems in news-papers and magazines began to diminish. It is tempting to perceive in this decline the reflection of a change in public attitude, since such a fervour of commitment and hatred as that which prevailed a year earlier would presumably be difficult to sustain. Yet to assume that the nations in question were beginning to abandon the principles that had inspired the initial outburst would be a mistake. On the contrary, news reports, editorial columns and readers' letters all suggest that the conflict was still seen by many people in terms of total opposition, and even much later in the war hints of compromise with the enemy were dismissed with anger, as a betrayal of the cause for which so many men had died. Victory was believed to be possible, and without victory there must be no peace. The decline in the kind of verse that had provided a powerful voice for divisiveness cannot, therefore, be attributed primarily to a lessening of patriotic sentiment. The explana-tion for its passing lies almost certainly in the nature of the poetry itself, for its demise is inherent in the genre's own intense and necessary homogeneity. The simplistic attitudes and simple form of the poetry, together with its public persona and the limited range of motifs, allowed for only a restricted number of possible variations. After a year of war all the variations had been played many times, and both writers and readers apparently found that this literary game had lost much of its appeal. Furthermore, the poetry had already fulfilled its initial purpose, both in helping to incite hatred of the enemy and strengthen resolve amongst compatriots in the early months of the war, and in granting many people the opportunity to make their personal contribution to the national war effort. Minor resurgence occurred when new possibilities were offered by an unusual event, such as the visit of a dignitary to the trenches, the Kaiser's birthday, or (in Germany) Britain's rejection of the peace offer of December 1916, but for the most part the deluge had passed.

Nevertheless, it would be misleading to imply that the taste for patriotic verse evaporated completely after 1915. Innumerable poems that had already appeared in ephemeral form were collected and reprinted in books, most commonly in individual volumes filled out with a few poems not concerned with the war. Anthologies are a particularly good indicator of what editors and publishers expect the reading public to appreciate, and patriotic anthologies continued to appear. Not all of them were reprints or new editions of earlier volumes. For example, the two anthologies from which many of my examples of French patriotic poetry are taken, Georges Turpin's *Les Poètes de la Guerre*, were published for the first time in 1916 and 1917 respectively, and Reinhold Braun's *Heil, Kaiser, Dir!*, from 1916, is quite as patriotic as its title suggests. Yet although much of the continuing taste for patriotic poetry was filled by the reissuing of older poems, the publication of new verse did not by any means cease, and magazines in particular still offered poets the opportunity to display their loyalty. There is, however, a noticeable change in tone if one views the poetry collectively, for the emphasis moved, as D.S.R. Welland observes in a similar connection, 'from the righteousness of the crusade to the knightliness of the crusader'.[2] At the beginning of the war, poems of hate and those of heroism had been equally abundant, but while the former lost ground after mid-1915, songs of praise for the nation's heroes continued to flourish, quite unimpeded by whatever accounts of their actual experience the 'heroes' themselves might supply. An especially popular device was to dedicate such a poem to an individual combatant, particularly as a eulogy. Even the magazine *The Nation*, which from late 1916 was printing the work of combatant protest poets, had difficulty in persuading itself to abandon the heroic tradition, with the result that patriotic heroism and the protest against it co-habited (though not in precisely the same issues) for several months. Contrary to what conventional wisdom might suggest, E. Hilton Young's 'Air Service', in the issue of 19 May 1917, marked by apostrophes like 'Not, golden lads, in vain / The royal gesture of your offerings', postdates by over two months the publication of 'Died of Wounds', where Siegfried Sassoon seeks to invalidate such rhetoric, with a picture of the mental agony and the 'wet white face and miserable eyes' of a 'real' dying man.[3]

Hilton Young's poem, however, gives a hint of the reason for the relative longevity of the heroic or chivalric poetry, which continued to be published or reprinted to the end of the war, and even afterwards. As the length of casualty lists increased, and the public at home became aware of the awesome tally of human destruction that the war was causing, the need remained strong for people to be convinced, and to convince themselves, that death on behalf of the nation was different from ordinary death, and that the sacrifice, the 'royal gesture', was indeed not 'in vain'. It is possible, too, that the families and friends of the men who were killed found consolation in the thought of the noble sacrifice, for the alternative, to accept that the death of one's son or fiancé or brother had accomplished nothing, would undoubtedly have been harder. That heroic poems maintained their appeal despite growing awareness of the horror of the Front is therefore not entirely surprising. In the meantime, however, the poetry that protested against the war, or against the beliefs that inspired and sustained it, was also finding a sympathetic audience, though never by any means so large as that which, even in 1918, continued to appreciate patriotic and heroic verse.

The widely-held conviction that Great War patriotic verse is typical of war poetry through the ages leads readily to the conclusion that, before this conflict, there had been no poems of protest. Such an apprehension (as some of the war-poetry critics admit) is far from valid. Even the so-called 'heroic' epics, of whatever progeny they may be, do not hide the horror of bloody corpses or the feelings of despair that war engenders. Nevertheless, since any explicitly anti-heroic voice is usually ascribed to a woman (Dido in Virgil's *Aeneid* and Herzeloide in Wolfram von Eschenbach's *Parzival*, for example), it might justifiably be argued that epics ultimately validate the heroic, masculine standard. The same is not true, however, in poetry that deals with war as a contemporary or recent event, rather than as a historical or fictional subject. Many poets in the past have objected unequivocally to war, or to a particular conflict, on political, religious or humanitarian grounds, and poems about the destruction and sorrow caused by warfare are more common than those that talk of comradeship and heroism. Folksongs concerned with war, from 'Bonnie George Campbell' to 'Johnny I hardly knew you' have often emphasised the pathetic at the expense of the heroic. The Thirty Years' War in the seventeenth century inspired a surprisingly large amount of poetry in German, but the dominant mood is of confusion and resignation, rather than of commitment to heroic values (or, indeed, to any other cause). There is little praise for the warrior ethic in the poetry of the Civil War period in England (including Milton's). In Betty T. Bennett's anthology of English war poetry of the period from 1793 to 1815, what is particularly striking, within this representative selection of 350 poems from the 3000 that Bennett collected, is the large number that criticise the government's position or the decisions of military leaders in the war against France. Amongst English poets of the Boer War there was a considerable voice of dissent, even from such unlikely figures (in view of their fervently patriotic contributions to First World War poetry) as William Watson and G.K. Chesterton, and according to Van Wyk Smith, the recognition of the disparity between expectation and reality – supposedly a discovery made by Great War poets – was in fact no rarity amongst combatant poets in the earlier conflict. First World War protest poetry, as anthologies like Scott Bates' *Poems of War Resistance* and Archim Roscher's *Tränen und Rosen* make clear, is more appropriately to be viewed as part of a tradition than as something unique.

Nevertheless, as a corpus the Great War protest poetry is not entirely in accord with its precursors. Perhaps because of the nature of this particular conflict, with its clear alignments and obvious national causes (unlike the rather complex Boer issue, for instance) one sees relatively little criticism of particular government policies in foreign affairs, apart from the decision to engage in war in the first place. More surprisingly, with the major exception of the British expedition to the Eastern Mediterranean, specific military decisions also escape condemnation. A possible reason is that this conflict which started with such clear-cut oppositions became one of chaotic stagnation, so that it was hard for potential critics to prove that a battle had actually been lost – though they might presumably have condemned the military leadership for the large number of casualties, and for persisting with the murderous futility of advances under fire. Instead, much of the protest in the poetry is centred on a single feature, which recurs with astonishing frequency. From August 1914, when Franz Werfel condemned 'Die Wortemacher des Krieges', the word-makers of the war, as a plague of rats, to November 1918, when George Willis, speaking for 'Any Soldier to his Son', prayed, 'May the lies they've written choke them like a gas-cloud till they're dead', the focus of the attack was words – 'Worte, berauschende Worte' (words, intoxicating words), 'les grands mots, les mots doctes, les nobles mots, les mots sonores' (great words, words of doctrine, noble words, sonorous words), the words employed to convince people that fighting a war for the sake of the nation was both a necessity and a virtue.[4]

In all three languages, a substantial amount of protest poetry was the work of combatants. The incongruity between their anti-war sentiments and the fact that they were on active service was recognised by at least two of the well-known English writers. Wilfred Owen, who hesitated for a year before deciding to volunteer, wondered later whether he was not 'a conscientious objector with a very seared conscience'.[5] Charles Sorley, on the other hand, volunteered within the first week of the war, but with little of the spirit of idealism usually attributed to the poets. He wrote in a letter to a friend in November 1914, 'What a worm one is under the cart-wheels – big, clumsy, careless, lumbering cart-wheels – of public opinion', and observed that fighting because to do so was the only socially acceptable course of action was 'a refinement of cowardice'.[6] Yet, with regard to the poetry at least, the conflict between sentiments like these and the poets' active participation in the war is more apparent than actual. The protest verse of combatants on the whole, while not condoning the example of 'man's inhumanity to man' in which the writers are engaged, attacks neither the idea of war nor this combat in particular, but the propaganda that is used to make war acceptable. The same is true of the majority of protest poems of civilians; they are not anti-war but, to borrow a term from Bertram Lloyd, anti-'cant', and especially they are opposed to the use of cant to influence people's attitudes and conduct. The dissenting poetry of the Great War is distinctive en masse because it protests, not against war – even this most horrible of wars – but against propaganda and propagandists.

Wilfred Owen's 'Dulce et Decorum Est' shows clearly the direction of the protest. The poem opens with a description of weary soldiers, 'Bent double, like old beggars under sacks' and 'coughing like hags' as they curse their way through trenches, and then marching half-asleep, lame and 'Drunk with fatigue', towards their base.[7] Their somnolence is shattered by a cry of 'Gas! Quick, boys!' and 'an ecstasy of fumbling' as they struggle for gas masks. One man, however, is too slow, and, as the narrator watches helplessly, the other stumbles and yells through the 'thick green light', 'guttering, choking, drowning'. The final stanza tells of the futile attempt to save the man, and of the agony of his dying:

> If you could hear, at every jolt, the blood
> Come gargling from the froth-corrupted lungs,
> Obscene as cancer, bitter as the cud
> Of vile, incurable sores on innocent tongues,
> My friend, you would not tell with such high zest,
> To children ardent for some desperate glory,
> The old Lie: Dulce et decorum est
> Pro patria mori.

The descriptions in this poem could easily have stood as a condemnation of the inhumanity of war itself, or of the new marriage of warfare with science. Instead, the poem is directed against 'wordmakers', and in particular against any who, failing to consider what death on the battlefield is really like, persist in repeating 'To children ardent for some desperate glory', the edict that 'dulce et decorum est / Pro patria mori' – to die for the homeland is sweet and decorous. Owen's poem does not deny that fighting and dying for one's country may be appropriate (as the poet himself fought and died, despite his reservations about where his conscience lay), but it insists that to persuade other people to fight by telling them something so far from the truth is immoral. One might be tempted to attribute Owen's attitude to his discovery that new and terrible weapons like chlorine gas rob war of the nobility it may have had in the past, as Gertrude White does when she talks of the poet's anger at 'the traditional heroic sentiments so wholly inappropriate to mechanized warfare'.[8] It is important to note, however, that Owen calls Horace's words 'the old Lie', which suggests, not that he finds the archaic standard out of date, but that he believes it has never been valid. (And it is certainly hard to imagine that a spear through the lungs or a sabre through the skull made for a pleasant way of dying – by no means either so 'dulce' or so 'decorum' as passing away peacefully at home.)

Criticism of the English war poetry has said much about the 'graphic fidelity' and 'photographic realism' of poems like Owen's, which apparently seek to convey to the reader a factual picture of the war. Owen is certainly concerned with realistic representation, in that he pretends to substitute for whatever concept Horace's words may evoke the reality of one man's death (though one must remember that the specific incident Owen describes exists only through the poem). His propagandist purpose here, however, is not so much to inform his readers about the reality of war, as to draw their attention to the unethical use of words in perpetuating the tenets of patriotic heroism. Since he recognises that people like the one he addresses sardonically as 'my friend' repeat such phrases thoughtlessly, his immediate goal appears to be to force upon them an awareness of literal meaning, to insist (one might say) that, if words are used to persuade people to a course of conduct in the world of actuality, they must refer to the actuality of that world. His concern with realism, then, is primarily as a means of showing the inadequacy of the link between the words that propagate the myth and their supposed referent. Many protest poets share precisely the same goal, whether explicitly or implicitly, while others focus on different aspects of the communicative process – the complicity of readers, for instance, the dubious motives of some of the speakers who spread the nation's message, or the wider significance of the message itself. In general, however, as words are the weapon of the protest poets, so words and the users of words are their target.

Not all the accusations of lying are made, like Owen's, by matching words against reality. The poem that provides the title for this chapter, 'The Pacifist' by E.H. Visiak (himself a pacifist and conscientious objector) takes up the story of Christ's quieting of the storm with a 'still small voice' calling for peace. Here, however, the words of peace are themselves a storm, a treacherous threat to all the illusions about war, offering instead the fearful desolation of the truth. Franz Werfel in 'Krieg' depicts the present age, rendered sleepless by the noise of lies, as a warrior riding into the nightmare of war, his accoutrements the empty values of the heroic myth:

> Auf einem Sturm von falschen Worten,
> Umkränzt von leerem Donner das Haupt,
> Schlaflos vor Lüge,
> Mit Taten, die sich selbst nur tun, gegürtet,
> Prahlend von Opfern,
> Ungefällig scheußlich für den Himmel –
> So fährst du hin,
> Zeit,
> In den lärmenden Traum,
> Den Gott mit schrecklichen Händen
> Aus seinem Schlaf reißt
> Und verwirft.[9]

(On a storm of false words, your head wreathed with empty thunder, sleepless with lies, girded with deeds that are of use only to themselves, boasting of sacrifices, displeasing and abominable in the sight of heaven – so you journey, Time, into the noisy dream that God, with terrifying hands, rips out of his sleep and discards.)

The same poet's 'Die Wortemacher des Krieges' opens with the sardonic reiteration of a popular phrase, 'Erhabene Zeit!' – Supreme moment! – and goes on to tell how, in this supreme moment, 'des Geistes Haus' – the home of the intellect – has been destroyed, with the result that the vermin which inhabited its cellars and drains have all escaped and are rejoicing in their freedom.[10] A later poem by an anonymous English writer evokes a similar image of infestation, when it talks of the need to 'pick the crawling catchwords from the brain' of politicians.[11]

Like Werfel, E.G. Kolbenheyer in 'Chronica II, 1915' makes use of a demonic rather than a realistic image, depicting war as a bloodthirsty Leviathan. He pictures the monster drawing a wagon which is 'Vom Lügengift tausendzüngiger Rede und Schrift / Hoch wie ein Erntewagen gefüllt' (piled high like a harvest cart with the lying poison of the speeches and writings of a thousand voices). The poem explains how the lies achieve their effect, washing out any trace of conscience and 'Menschheitsglaube' (belief in the cause of humanity) in a flood of written and spoken words ('ein Schwall von Rede und Schrift'), and soothing away fear with

Lieder, gläubige Lieder,
Die das Herz bedecken wie eine Mutterhand,
Schirmend vor Furcht und Tod.[12]

(. ... songs, credible songs, which cover one's heart like a mother's hand, protecting one from fear and death.)

Kolbenheyer's monster insists that it should be called only by such names as 'Menschentum. Freiheit. Recht' (Humanity. Freedom. Justice), and its crest bears in large letters the words, 'Ich will den Frieden' (My goal is peace). The poem ends, as it begins, 'Wirst du erwachen, Menschheit, an der Lüge?' (Mankind, will you awaken to the lie?) While many of the German poets of protest were ultimately oriented towards the political left, Kolbenheyer became a strong supporter of National Socialism, to the extent that he was placed briefly under 'Schriftverbot', a ban on writing, in 1948. It is hard to reconcile those later beliefs with the urgency of his plea to humanity, in 'Chronica II, 1915', to 'awaken to the lie' about war.

The specific lie that Kolbenheyer condemns at the end of his poem, the concept of a war for peace, a war to end war, was widely proclaimed in nationalistic propaganda from both sides. Since there appears to have been little evidence to support the claim, it was often mocked by protest poets. 'A.E.' (George Russell) in 'Statesmen', published in *The Times* in May 1915, challenges the propagandists directly:

They tell us that they war on war. Why do they treat
    our wit with scorn?
The Dragon from the Dragon Seed, the breed was true
    since life was born.

In Osbert Sitwell's 'Sheep Song' a black lamb asks innocently, 'Why did we start this glorious Gadarene descent?' and the herd replies angrily,

It is a noble thing to do.
We are stampeding to end stampedes.
We are fighting for lambs
Who are never likely to be born.[13]

The herd, incidentally, 'went in with clean feet, / And [. . .] will come out with empty heads'. A.O. Weber, a satirist like Sitwell, deals with a related lie – that of arming for peace:

 Vierzig Jahr hat man gerüstet,
Um den Frieden zu erhalten;
Auch nicht einer hat's gelüstet,
Kriegesfahnen zu entfalten.[14]

(For forty years they were arming to keep the peace. Not even one of them had any desire to unfurl the flags of war.)

He tells how everyone built cruisers, mortars, hand-grenades, just to emphasise their love of peace. And when he continues,

Wüchsen die Verteidigungslasten
Auch zu ungeahnten Höhen,
Gab es hierbei doch kein Rasten,
Stillstand heißt stets Rückwärtsgehen,

(Even when defence taxes grew to unsuspected heights, there was still no resting. Standing still means going steadily backwards.)

his words have an even more uncomfortable familiarity for modern readers.

It is interesting to note, however, that Weber's satires are not consistently poems of protest. While some are opposed to 'Krieges-hetzer' (warmongers) and to excessive chauvinism ('Und sahst du auch nur englisch aus, / So bliebst am besten du zu Haus' – And if you looked even a little bit English, it was better to stay at home), others are directed against the official enemy, or against people who decline to play their part in the nation's war effort, including the frequenters of the former 'Cafe des Westens', a favourite haunt of Expressionist writers in prewar days.[15] An English counterpart of Weber in this respect is J.C. Squire, who similarly finds his targets in any words that seem to him ridiculous, of whatever persuasion the speaker may be. In the epigram 'The Entente', for example, he ridicules a German speech that proclaims 'Turkey is our natural ally'; Squire agrees, since, as he says, 'Deep calls to deep, Armenia to Louvain'.[16] More frequently, however, he attacks the propagandists who justify the war on the wrong grounds – the people who speak, with the confidence that only nationalism could breed, about the value of war as a means to racial regeneration (in 'The Survival of the Fittest'), about the correct way of teaching poor children to be good patriots (in 'Christmas Hymn for Lambeth'), and about the absolute determina-tion to win the war at any cost ('The Touch of Nature'). And in his best-known war-poem, an epigram called 'The Dilemma', he mocks the sacred conviction that 'our' side is in the right:

God heard the embattled nations sing and shout
'Gott strafe England!' and 'God save the King!'
God this, God that, and God the other thing –
'Good God!' said God. 'I've got my work cut out.'[17]

Even so, there is something refreshing in the apparently ambivalent attitude of the few poets like Weber and Squire who refuse to accept nonsense or bigotry from any side.

For most of the protest writers, however, ambivalence is out of the question; they have no doubt that their target is not the official enemy but the people in their own country who use words for the wrong purpose. Poets, of all people, should be aware of the importance of language; consequently it is not surprising that those who, in the opinion of their opponents, are guilty of misusing their craft, should be treated with particular scorn and acrimony. Lois Cendré, one of three women represented in the French protest anthology *Les Poètes contre la guerre*, accuses poets in general of ignoring what should be their central concern:

Le sang coule inutilement dans les fossés immenses que
    ne veille nulle idéale moisson.
Et vous, ô poètes mes frères, ô les plus manqués des prêtres!
Devant cet Univers livide vous chantez encore votre table
    et votre lit, les murs de votre chambre, vos
    digestions, vos amours.[18]

(The blood runs uselessly in immense ditches that serve no harvest of ideas. And you, my brother poets, most failed of priests! Confronted with this blood-stained universe, you still sing of your table and your bed, the walls of your room, your digestion, your love affairs.)

More commonly, the complaint is not that poets ignore the war but that they misrepresent it, by reiterating patriotic and heroic phrases without regard for the applicability of their words to real life. In one of its early drafts 'Dulce et Decorum Est' was addressed 'To a Certain Poetess', presumed (on the evidence of another draft) to be the perhaps undeservedly notorious patriotic writer Jessie Pope.[19] Even without that subtitle, however, the direction of Owen's condemnatory message is clear. Another writer in a position to match experience against the patriotic–heroic ethic, Arthur Graeme West, attacks his fellow poets more directly, and not civilians but combatants:

God, how I hate you, you young cheerful men
Whose pious poetry blossoms on your graves
As soon as you are in them, nurtured up
By the salt of your corruption, and the tears
Of mothers, local vicars, college deans,
And flanked by prefaces and photographs
Of all your minor poet friends – the fools –
Who paint their sentimental elegies
Where, sure, no angel treads; and, living, share
The dead's brief immortality.[20]

After this tirade against the system that both lends support to the writers of 'pious poetry' and preys upon their death, West chooses a specific victim. H. Reginald Freston, a combatant killed in 1916, was the author of 'O Fortunati', which begins,

> O happy to have lived these epic days!
> To have seen unfold, as death a dream unfold,
> These glorious chivalries, these deeds of gold.[21]

West's attack continues,

>   Hark how one chants –
> 'Oh, happy to have lived these epic days' –
> 'These epic days!' And *he'd* been to France
> And seen the trenches, glimpsed the huddled dead
> In the periscope, hung on the rusty wire,
> Choked by their sickly fœtor, day and night
> Blown down his throat. . .

West's war poems, according to the friend who edited his diary for publication, were written in the summer of 1916, when the poet was on leave in England. At that time, the diary entries show, West admitted to himself that he no longer supported the war but he could not persuade himself to mail the letter which, in announcing to his commanding officer his resignation from the army, would have brought him at the very least a term of imprisonment. (He returned to the Front and was killed in 1917.) In comparison with West's mental turmoil, Freston's attitude seems facile rather than heroic. Nevertheless, it is hardly surprising that, although 'O Fortunati' was considered worth reprinting in John L. Hardie's Second World War anthology, *Verse of Valour*, published in 1943, West's response was not included.

While West implies that even an intimate familiarity with the facts is inadequate as an antidote to the urge towards 'pious poetry', Helen Hamilton suggests that such experience should not be necessary, that civilians are sufficiently well informed to recognise the inconsistency between such a literary response and the reality of the war. She condemns the 'Romancing Poet', therefore, for a failure of imagination:

> If you must wax descriptive,
> Do get the background right,
> A little right!
> The blood, the filth, the horrors,
> Suffering on such a scale,
> That you and I, try as we may,

> Can only faintly vision it.
> Don't make a pretty song about it.[22]

Alfred Lichtenstein, who has the dubious honour of being almost certainly the first protest poet to be killed in the war (on 25 September 1914), was similarly concerned with the distance between the literary concept of war and the reality. Although his critique of war poetry in 'Abschied' (Departure) is much more subtle that that of the English poets I have quoted, the irony of his statement is none the less effective. The brief poem is a masterpiece of careful construction, and offers a serious message in an amusing form:

> Vorm Sterben mache ich noch mein Gedicht.
> Still, Kameraden, stört mich nicht.
>
> Wir ziehn zum Krieg. Der Tod ist unser Kitt.
> O, heulte mir doch die Geliebte nit.
>
> Was liegt an mir. Ich gehe gerne ein.
> Die Mutter weint. Man muß aus Eisen sein.
>
> Die Sonne fällt zum Horizont hinab.
> Bald wirft man mich ins milde Massengrab.
>
> Am Himmel brennt das brave Abendrot.
> Vielleicht bin ich in dreizehn Tagen tot.[23]

Each stanza consists of two dissociated lines, one representing a not-very-successful soldier-poet's attempt to write in the heroic manner, and a second where the illusion is destroyed by a bathetic 'aside'. The first couplet shows the writer persona engaged in his last literary effort (and one can almost imagine him biting the end of a stubby pencil): 'Before I die, I must write my poem.' To this his mundane self adds, 'Quiet, friends, don't disturb me.' (The persona is not to be confused with Lichtenstein himself, though it may be the *alter ego* who appears in some of his other writings, Kuno Kohn.) In the second stanza, noble and stoical acceptance of the prospect of death, 'We are going to war. Death cements us together', is tempered by, 'Oh, if only my girlfriend wasn't howling.' The poet persona in the third stanza proclaims proudly, 'I have my part to play. I'm going gladly,' while his less imperturbable other self observes, 'My mother's crying. You have to be as tough as iron.' The fourth couplet offers sunset and death, a standard parallel in heroic poetry, but here the former, appropriately for this Chaplinesque 'little man' of a writer, is presented as a cliché, 'The sun sinks down to the horizon,' while the latter is far

from heroic: 'Soon they'll be throwing me into the gentle mass grave.'
(The phrase "das milde Grab", possibly derived from Shakespeare's
"gentle grave", becomes decidedly less consolatory in its new context.)
Finally, as the traditional poetic glory of the afterglow completes his
poem ('In the sky burns the noble red of evening'), to the soldier
himself comes the fearful recognition that death is not merely a word,
but an imminent possibility: 'In less than a fortnight I could be dead.'
If one lists the 'heroic' lines, it is clear that they become increasingly
poetic and non-realistic, whereas the anti-heroic lines move in the
opposite direction, from a minor inconvenience towards the soldier's
understanding of the full implication of what he is writing about. The
struggling poet has failed to persuade himself by his own rhetoric
(such as it is), for his heroic sunset is made to appear totally irrelevant
to the reality of his impending death.

In 'Gebet vor der Schlacht' (Prayer before the Battle), Lichtenstein
again uses an unheroic persona to mock the ideals associated with
patriotic heroism, especially as they relate to the reality of the ordinary
soldier's view of war. While Lichtenstein's speaker is undoubtedly a
descendant of Simplicius Simplicissimus, Grimmelshausen's prag-
matic hero from the Thirty Years' War, he also bears a family resem-
blance to many later unheroic soldiers, not least the Good Soldier
Schweik. The immediate association, however, is with poetry, for
'Gebet vor der Schlacht' parodies a type of poem where the speaker
prays for courage and voices his willingness to die. Patrick Bridgwater
points out in *The German Poets of the First World War* that Lichtenstein
was probably inspired by two poems by Thomas Körner from the
Napoleonic wars, published in 1814.[24] The type became popular again
a century later, though Lichtenstein, engaged in military action from
very early in the war, was probably not familiar with any of the new
versions. Nevertheless, 'Gebet vor der Schlacht' sounds very much
like a parody 'before the fact' (if such a thing were possible) of an
English example published in 1916, W.N. Hodgson's 'Before Action',
which tells of the poet's joy in life, and ends with the dramatic plea,
'By all delights that I shall miss, / Help me to die, o Lord.'[25] Hodgson's
persona, celebrating 'The laughter of unclouded years, / And every
sad and lovely thing', seems very pure and innocent in comparison
with Lichtenstein's, whose ambition is to 'Mädchen stopfen' – stuff
girls – and 'Mich noch manches Mal besaufen' – get drunk a lot more
times. This speaker, who is actually every soldier in the company
praying silently on his own behalf, pleads not for the courage to die
nobly, but for survival, and his approach is far from altruistic. He
asks God – Father, Son and Holy Ghost – to protect him from
misfortune, so that he will not die like a dog ('wie'n Hund verrecke')

for the beloved Fatherland. Since he would prefer to remain alive, he offers God a pact:

> Sieh, ich bete gut und gerne
> Täglich sieben Rosenkränze,
> Wenn du, Gott, in deiner Gnade
> Meinen Freund, den Huber oder
> Meier, tötest, mich verschonst.[26]

(Look, I'll happily say seven rosaries a day without fail if you, God, in your goodness, will kill my friend Huber or my friend Meier and spare me.)

In this way Lichtenstein disposes not only of the myth of the ordinary soldier's dedication to the homeland, but also of the belief in his innate goodness and selflessness and, more significantly, in the noble comradeship amongst men who fight together. That particular aspect of the heroic ethic survived the war almost unchallenged in poetry, apart from Lichtenstein's 'Gebet'.

While most of the protest writers I have mentioned are concerned with the failure of poetry to accommodate reality, the French socialist Marcel Martinet, ever conscious of divisions and alignments within society, offers a different perspective on the war amongst the poets. His 'Poètes d'Allemagne, ô frères inconnus' (Poets of Germany, my unknown brothers) serves as a reminder that two sides are involved in the secondary conflict, as well as in the primary one, for this, to adapt a term used by Paul Fussell, is 'a literary war'. The poem is addressed to young and unknown German poets whose message from the trenches calls for an end to the war, and Martinet sees the traditionalists, rather than the protest poets, as the attackers. The enemies of the young 'poètes d'Allemagne', and his own, are the old and famous writers of France and Germany, 'Dans leurs bons fauteuils dorés, / Belliqueux et satisfaits' (in their fine gilded armchairs, bellicose and self-satisfied), who accuse young combatant protest poets of treachery. As Martinet recognises, the battle is not wholly verbal, for in addition to their almost unanswerable appeal to the concept of loyalty to the dead, the older poets can claim the advantage of both reputation and financial success to demolish the pretensions of their younger adversaries:

> 'N'écoutez pas ces jeunes gens.
> Traîtres à la cause sacrée
> Des morts et des agonisants,
> Ce sont des sots, des fous, des lâches,
> Ils ne respectent pas les honneurs qu'on nous rend,

Et qui sont-ils? Des inconnus!
Nous, nos livres se vendent,
La gloire du pays, la conscience du monde;
Nous avons vécu, nous; nous connaissons la vie,
Nous sommes sages.
N'écoutez pas ces inconnus. Tuez, mourez.'[27]

('Don't listen to those young people. They are traitors to the sacred cause of those who have suffered and died; they are madmen, fools, cowards, and they don't respect the honour that is paid to us. And who are they? They are unknown! As for us, our books sell, and are the glory of our country, the conscience of the world. We have lived; we know about life, we are wise. Don't listen to those unknowns. Kill! Die!')

Martinet appeals to his brother poets in Germany, unknown to him in both name and person, but 'unknown' also in terms of literary reputation, to continue their fight for peace, and promises that together these 'amis des prochains jours' (friends of future days) will overcome through love the lust for revenge that their more famous opponents promote.

Although poets are an obvious target for the protest, they are by no means the only one, for no propagandist or 'wordmaker' is immune. Martinet in 'Civils' chooses some of the more popular targets – journalists, public speakers, raconteurs, churchmen, politicians – and condemns them collectively for the part they play in the continuation of the slaughter:

Vous qui luttez si bien, la plume en main,
Héros cachés, cachés derrière ceux qui meurent,
Derrière ceux que vous jetez à la mort.[28]

(You who fight so well with the pen; hidden heroes, hidden behind those who are dying, behind those whom you are sending to death.)

Siegfried Sassoon also takes aim at a variety of wordmakers, including journalists in 'Fight to a Finish' and 'The Effect', the local squire who 'nagged and bullied' a young man to volunteer in 'Memorial Tablet', and, more generally, the 'Great Men' who are responsible for the war, and whom he urges now to 'keep [their] mouthings for the dead'.[29] In 'They' Sassoon's target is the Church, which he condemns for its failure to consider the consequences of what it preaches. 'The Bishop' in the poem announces that, when 'the boys come back / They will not be the same', having been challenged and ennobled by their experience.[30] The soldiers agree that the war has altered them, though the change is not quite as the Bishop had anticipated:

'We're none of us the same!' the boys reply,
'For George lost both his legs; and Bill's stone-blind;
Poor Jim's shot through the lungs and like to die;
And Bert's gone syphilitic: you'll not find
A chap who's served that hasn't found *some* change.'

To which the Bishop replies, 'The ways of God are strange' – a phrase expressly designed to hide the inadequacy of words as an intermediary between God's will and its manifestation in human life. The Church is the target also for Bruno Schönlank, who claims that it is now occupied by false priests slandering the name of God, and for Oskar Kanehl, who offers in 'Soldatenmißhandlung' (Maltreatment of Soldiers) an example of civilian insensitivity.[31] This poem tells how a group of soldiers, exhausted after a day's march, is forced to endure a church service, where the preacher

schmeißt auf uns geduldige Gemeinde
im Namen Gottes
Beleidigung aller unsrer Feinde.

(. . . hurls down on us, his patient congregation, in the name of God, curses upon all our foes).

In this case the Church is condemned not only for contributing to an ethic of hatred, but also for increasing the burden on the weary soldiers by making them serve as an audience.

As some of these poems make clear, the problem which many poets perceive in the rhetoric of the wordmakers is not simply that it spreads hatred, but that the promotion of the national cause serves the interest of the people in power, at the expense of those who are subject to control. W.N. Ewer's 'Five Souls', first published in *The Nation* on 3 October 1914, already draws the victim–manipulator dichotomy usually considered to have evolved as a consequence of war experience: the perception that the soldiers of all countries are on one side, in opposition to all the civilians who sent them to war.[32] The 'souls' here belong to five representative working men from different countries of Europe, each of whom tells, according to the official version, the story of the events that led to his death. The 'third soul', for instance, explains,

I worked in Lyons at my weaver's loom,
When suddenly the Prussian despot hurled
His felon blow at France and at the world;
Then I went forth to Belgium and my doom.

Patriotic sentiment indeed, recited precisely in accordance with the official lesson, including such 'elevated' phrases as 'Prussian despot' and 'felon blow'; but the credibility of the account is shattered, and the author's anti-nationalistic position made plain, when all five narratives end with the same refrain:

I gave my life for freedom – This I know:
For those who bade me fight had told me so.

Like Ewer, Charles Vildrac in 'Élégie à Henri Doucet' perceives in international terms the manipulation that kills, and he deplores in particular the anti-human attitude of 'les trafiquants du monde' (the traders of the world), whose values are

Patrie, population, territoire, effectifs,
Main-d'œuvre, marchandise,
Toutes choses qu'on divise
Ou qu'on additionne.[33]

(Fatherland, population, territory, possessions, workforce, merchandise: anything that one can divide or add up.)

'Miles' (Osbert Sitwell) assaults the same kind of people, but through a prototype; his 'modern Abraham', fat and purple-fingered, would rather give another son than contribute to the Disabled Soldiers' Fund any of the money he has made from the manufacture of explosives.[34] J.C. Squire, meanwhile, focuses not on a type but on a specific individual, Lord Devonport, a member of the House of Lords, who has urged that in the interests of national economy Army pay and allowances should be reduced. Squire suggests, however, that such a proposal is not unexpected from 'Lord Molasses':

Oh no! A peer of new creation
Broad-based on wholesale groceries
Will still preserve an inclination
For paring other people's cheese.[35]

The most readily identifiable victims of war are soldiers, and military leaders are an obvious target for attack as the people responsible for their suffering and death. Sassoon tells of a general, cheerful but incompetent, who greeted 'Harry' and 'Jack' in a friendly manner on their way 'to the line', but who 'did for them both with his plan of attack'.[36] Georges Chennevière depicts the leaders as calculating rather than incompetent –

Le massacre est prévu, compté, réglé d'avance,
Pour cent mètres de terre et de la gloire en mots[37]

(The massacre is predicted, counted, ruled in advance, for a hundred metres of ground and some words of glory)

but for Walter Hasenclever in 'Die Mörder sitzen in der Oper' (The murderers are at the opera) they are merely uncaring:

Zweitausend sind in dieser Nacht gefallen!
Die Mörder sitzen im Rosenkavalier.[38]

(Two thousand men died tonight! The murderers are watching *Der Rosenkavalier*.)

Yet despite the enormous slaughter of combatants in the war, and despite what to a retrospective view seems to be obvious and terrible errors of judgement on the part of military decision-makers, these men escape surprisingly lightly. (The Gallipoli disaster, which generated some protest, was blamed on politicians.) In trying to understand why there was not more outcry, whether from the poets or from the public at large, against military decisions, one is led to wonder whether the slaughter was not indeed in some sense 'prévu' – foreseen – to use Chennevière's term. The large armies that made possible the unprecedented scale of the killing existed because the population in general of the countries in question considered it right and fitting that the physically-able young men of combatant age from every family should share the responsibility for defending the country. At the same time, this duty to the nation was widely promoted and perceived as a heroic undertaking – not least in the patriotic poetry, which, notwithstanding the socialist cry of 'manipulation', appears to have been generally in alignment with popular opinion. But whereas warriors in the literary and historical heroic tradition were admired for their ability to fight and to win, on the evidence of the poetry one must conclude that their modern counterparts were valued mainly for their willing sacrificial death. Long before the enormous destructiveness of the war was recognised, patriotic poets and other wordmakers were singing the praises of the newest national heroes, not because they had fought valiantly, but because they had died. (One of the best-known of these poems in English, Binyon's 'For the Fallen', does not date from the end of the war, as one might expect, but from September 1914.) To suggest, on the grounds that patriotic poets preached the virtue of dying *pro patria*, that the population at large was quite prepared to accept the terrible slaughter, perhaps seems far-fetched. Yet the patriotic verse is in many respects a manifestation of the creed, the way of thinking, to which the majority of citizens of each country subscribed, and which also determined the conduct of the war. Since the kind of people who might have voiced a protest – that is, those who were prepared to make their opinions known – had committed themselves publicly to the belief that to die for the Fatherland was the perfect death, one should not be surprised that they raised no objection when the length of the casualty-lists grew. Nor can one doubt that the larger part of the population, whether combatant or civilian, simply accepted without question the right of the nation to demand the lives of its young men, and the appropriateness of the view that victory was both necessary and possible, whatever the cost.

It is fitting, therefore, that instead of blaming the military leaders who were implementing what appeared to be the wishes of the people, by continuing the struggle as long as men were available, the protest poets attacked the people themselves, for adhering to an ethic that was condemning many thousands of their compatriots to death. As a representative of the civilian population as a whole, the proverbial man-on-the-street is treated with no less acrimony than the more obvious manipulators and profiteers who use the war for their own advantage. He is criticised both for his unquestioning acceptance of the official viewpoint and for his lack of real concern about the suffering of combatants. André Spire accuses the 'petits gens' – ordinary people – of indifference:

> On tue, on assassine,
> Ce n'est pas ton affaire, crois-tu.
> Pense à ta petite besogne
> Et fais-y ton gain si tu peux.[39]

> (People are being killed, being assassinated. It's not your concern, you say. Think about your own little affairs, and make something on the side if you can.)

Wilfred Owen's 'Insensibility' makes the same accusation – that indifference is a deliberate choice rather than an accident of circumstance. The poet contrasts the blessing of insensitivity that comes upon the soldiers, to protect them from the horror of the war, with the genuine lack of compassion to be found at home amongst the 'dullards whom no cannon stuns', and who have 'made themselves immune / To pity'.[40] But as Martinet points out in 'Droit des gens' (The rights of the people), the accepted standard, while deploring the mistreatment of civilians as a crime, condones the slaughter of soldiers as a fact of war. The combatants can clearly expect little support from those who (in an image drawn by Rose Macaulay) have built 'guarding walls' between themselves and the men who suffer.[41]

As an extension of the division between soldiers and uncaring civilians, the age gap contributes to the bitterness. The repetitive structure of the opening lines of Eliot Crawshay-Williams' 'Sonnet of a Son' places both the division and the bitterness very clearly:

> Because I am young, therefore I must be killed;
> Because I am strong, so must my strength be maimed.[42]

Nevertheless, Crawshay-Williams does not direct his lament specific-
ally towards the old, but towards

> Poor mad mankind! that like some Herod calls
> For one wide holocaust of youth and strength!

F.S. Flint is more particular in his attack:

> The young men of the world
> Are condemned to death.
> They have been called up to die
> For the crime of their fathers.[43]

Flint links to the age–youth or parent–child dichotomy the contrast
both between guilt and innocence and between safety and vul-
nerability; the young must suffer, and their suffering is for the benefit
of the old. The self-satisfied persona in Osbert Sitwell's 'Armchair',
contemplating how he might (under other circumstances) play his
part in the war, carries this imposition a stage further, when he
declares,

> I'd send my sons, if old enough, to France,
> Or help to do my share in other ways.

The inference is not only that the giving of sons is no different from
other ways of doing one's patriotic duty, but also, more importantly,
that the young belong to the old, and are theirs to give.[44] A similar
sense of possession is implied in Karl Otten's 'Für Martinet', though
the owner in this case is the state as a whole:

> Man wartete ihr neunzehntes Jahr ab, um sie nach dem
>   Kodex zerhacken zu können.
> Man lauert auf die Kinder, prüft ihre Gelenke, ihre Muskeln,
> Und fragt sich ob es bald so weit ist.[45]

(They awaited their nineteenth year, in order to be able to chop
them to pieces according to the law. They watch and wait for the
children, feel their limbs, their muscles, wondering whether they're
ready yet.)

The children's story of Hansel trapped in the witch's cage, being
fattened for slaughter, has become a metaphor for the nightmare
reality of adulthood, in a world where, in Alec Waugh's words, 'Old
men, secure in length of days, / Have whispered, "Kill".'[46]

That women, almost as much as the old, were an arch-enemy of the
combatants (a counterpart, perhaps, of Hansel's witch) is well-
recognised by anyone familiar with the English war-poetry criticism.
Siegfried Sassoon has two especially bitter poems about the response

of women to the war. 'Glory of Women' portrays them as concerned chiefly with decorations, wounds 'in a mentionable place' and 'laurelled memories', and hints that they are quite unable to believe that war is nasty and 'heroes' unheroic; moreover, their unfailing patriotism renders them incapable of recognising, as the poet does, that German women are equally misguided:

> O German mother dreaming by the fire,
> While you are knitting socks to send your son
> His face is trodden deeper in the mud.[47]

The women portrayed in 'Their Frailty' are entirely selfish; so long as their own husband or son or lover is safe, they care nothing for the suffering of the other men.[48] Marcel Martinet, though not himself a combatant, draws with equal sharpness the line of opposition between women and soldiers. His 'Elles disent. . .' (They say. . .) depicts some women at a tea-party discussing Latzko and Barbusse, the authors of protest novels which claim to present a realistic picture of life at the Front. The women conclude:

> N'est-ce pas, si c'était comme ils disent,
> Tellement horrible,
> Nous ne pourrions pas supporter,
> Nous n'avons pas le cœur si dur.
> Ce n'est pas possible.

> (Don't you agree, if it was as horrible as they say, we wouldn't be able to put up with it, we're not so hard-hearted. It just isn't possible.)

Having thus dismissed the reality of war, they proceed to their next cup of tea.[49] With less bitterness but no less condemnation, Laurence Housman's 'Caesar's Image' tells how, through the ages, once woman has helped man to recover from war, she has encouraged him to set up a statue to Fame, 'the very image' of himself, thus helping to perpetuate the cycle of recovery and destruction.[50] And Helen Hamilton attacks the 'jingo-woman' who hands out white feathers (symbols of cowardice) and insults to young men not in uniform, trying to 'flout and goad' them into doing what she is not required to do herself.[51]

As the last two poems indicate, however, the opposition between women and combatants is far from absolute. In Housman's picture the two groups are on the same side, contributing equally to the perpetuation of the heroic myth, while Hamilton proves by the very act of writing that, contrary to what Sassoon implies in 'Glory of Women', some women refuse to believe that 'chivalry redeems the war's disgrace'. In fact, some of the most scathing attacks on women who decline to oppose the myth come from poets of their own sex, rather than from combatants. Pauline Barrington, for example, raises a question that is still a major concern, even in peacetime – the part played by mothers in promoting the acceptability of violence. The speaker of 'Education' addresses a woman who sits sewing while her children play with toy soldiers and engage in a 'mimic battle'.[52] The last stanza (of which the opening reflects the rainy day in the initial scene) reads:

War is slipping, dripping death on earth.
If the child is father of the man,
Is the toy gun father of the Krupps?
For Christ's sake think!
While you sew
Row after row

The fourth line echoes a much-repeated criticism – that women prefer not to think about the war and their own part in it. Above all, as other poets suggest, they refrain from voicing any protest. Cécile Périn, speaking of 'Les Femmes de tous les pays' (The women of all countries), wonders, 'A quoi songent-elles, muettes?' – What are they thinking of, in keeping silent?[53] Margaret Sackville offers an explanation in 'Nostra Culpa', when she suggests that, despite their special knowledge, gained through childbirth, of the value of human life, women keep silent because of their need for approval:

We knew that Force the world has deified,
How weak it is. We spoke not, so men died.
Upon a world down-trampled, blood-defiled,
Fearing that men should praise us less, we smiled.[54]

Because of this betrayal of their intuitive feminine wisdom, they must now reap the harvest of their own sowing:

This is the flesh we might have saved – our hands,
Our hands prepared these blood-drenched, dreadful lands.

Just as the existence of protest poems by women denies the validity of the view that all women were warmongers, so the protest poetry invalidates another of the oppositions that make up the established 'memory' of the war, the total alignment between combatants who suffer and the civilians who are responsible for the suffering. Perhaps because the patriotic myth promotes the belief that people gladly give their loved ones in the cause of the nation, protest poets tell of the anguish of the secondary victims of war – the bride in Yvan Goll's *Requiem: Für die Gefallenen von Europa*, for instance, who finds that, because she is unable to rejoice as other people do in her hero's death, she must weep alone; the bereaved father in Alec Waugh's 'The Other Side', 'with nothing left in life / But the will to die'; or, in the same poem,

> A young girl born for laughter and Spring,
> Left to her shame and her loneliness.[55]

After all, the speaker asks,

> What is one woman more or less
> To men who've forgotten everything?

In Squire's 'Christmas Hymn for Lambeth' the victims are the pauper children of the London borough of Lambeth.[56] Squire quotes as an epigraph an item from *The Times* of 12 November 1914:

> The Lambeth Guardians yesterday decided that, in order that the Poor Law school children might have an opportunity of appreciating the position of national affairs, the usual practice of allowing each child an egg for breakfast on Christmas morning be suspended this year. The Chairman of the Board remarked that it was better to let the children go without eggs than to give them shop eggs.

The speaker in Squire's poem wonders why the Guardians do not go farther, to the extent of selling the beds and starving the children, to teach their patriotic lesson more thoroughly and to 'save the rate-payers expense'. Then the Guardians, justly proud of their accomplishment, may withdraw to 'Chatsworth Terrace, or 'St Ann's,' / 'River View,' 'The Den,' 'The Manse'' for Christmas dinner, and 'eat and eat until [they] snore'. Similar maltreatment of poor children in the interests of economy is observed by G.E.D.S. in 'The Kiddies He's Left Behind Him' in *The Herald* of 12 February 1915 – 'he's risked all for a country that can't keep its kiddies fit' – while M.E. Powell's 'The Reward' (7 November 1914) condemns the parsimonious attitude of officialdom towards war widows, who must be content with 'five bob a week' now that the men whose 'valour, / Gay temper and grit' the nation applauded are dead.

While some of these examples may suggest that the protest poets were interested chiefly in propaganda and little in poetic technique, Erwin Piscator's 'Der Mutter zweier Söhne, welche fielen' (To the mother of two sons who died in the war) merges the two concerns in a highly effective protest against the secondary suffering produced by the war.[57] The woman who is the subject of the poem is reduced by her sorrow to a degree of passivity so intense that even the act of dying is too positive – she simply disappears from life. As Piscator recognises with remarkable sensitivity, the problem is not only that the life the woman knew and anticipated is totally destroyed, but that this painful knowledge is encountered repeatedly in all her thoughts and actions:

Nun liegen die Trümmer deines Lebens spitz in
    den Lüften
daß du überall dich daran stößest.

(Now the ruins of your life are projecting into the air with jagged points, so that you stab yourself on them everywhere.)

Piscator describes compassionately and skilfully the change in the woman's appearance, her slow withdrawal from life, until finally, since there is no-one left to whom she matters, she is seen no more:

Deine Hände verschrumpfen, dein Gesicht und
    das Haar ist nächtens weiß.
Und aus allem ziehst du langsam deine Anwesen-
    heit zurück,
dein ganz schmal gewordenes Gesicht und die
müden, müden Hände,
ganz langsam und insgeheim
– und dann weiß niemand mehr etwas von dir.

(Your hands shrivel up and your face, and your hair becomes white overnight. And you slowly withdraw your presence from everything, your face that has become very thin and your tired, tired hands, quite slowly and secretly – and then no-one any longer knows anything of you.)

Piscator's poem serves as a powerful antidote to those examples of patriotic verse that tell of women who, happily and without qualm, sacrifice several sons for the Fatherland. The protest is made explicit, however, when the poet aligns the woman's anguished passivity against the deliberate will of the 'powers-that-be' who, by killing her sons, have taken away her reason for living; she too is a victim of murder, though in her case the process of killing is different – 'Dich aber mordet man ganz langsam' (But they are murdering you quite slowly). Piscator was to become famous for his work with the political theatre in Germany in the 1920s, and, during his exile under the Nazi regime, in the United States. As a poet he is little known, and in total only seven of his poems were published, all by Franz Pfemfert in various issues of *Die Aktion*.[58] Yet, in addition to the remarkable compassion that this poem reveals (especially from a young man – by comparison, Owen's range of sympathy seems very restricted), Piscator also has the ability to create precisely the image that is needed for his purpose: this woman's thin face and tired hands; in 'Denk an seine Bleisoldaten' (Remember his Lead Soldiers), the impression of men all lined up ready for battle, and all dying 'plumps und stumm' (just dropping down dead) like toy soldiers; and in 'Einer ist tot' (A man is dead) a young soldier recently dead, whose lips are pressed against his gently curved left hand and his still ticking wristwatch. Perhaps because the use of such precise visual focus as a tool for rousing compassion is less common in the German war poetry than in the English, Piscator's poems, though they are few in number, make a strikingly effective contribution to the protest.

Piscator, according to his later recollections, was shocked by the blind enthusiasm of his compatriots in August 1914, and 'Denk an seine Bleisoldaten', written within the first few days of that month, reflects his refusal to comply with what he saw as the obviously misguided teachings of the patriotic ethic.[59] In the course of the war, especially after he was drafted in 1915, he became increasingly aware of the division between those who suffered and those who caused the suffering, and he eventually came to see this opposition in political terms (though his stance was not sufficiently left-wing for Pfemfert in the postwar years). A few other protest poets – Sassoon and Ernst Toller amongst them – followed a similar path towards the political left, though Sassoon's political involvement was decidedly less dramatic than Toller's (who was jailed for his part in the 1918 Munich uprising) and the initial war-enthusiasm of these two writers is less characteristic than Piscator's mild scepticism. Indeed, in few cases can one trace in the war poetry of an individual the different stages of development towards political commitment, because most of the political protest poetry did not come from writers converted by their war experience, but from those who perceived the victim– manipulator dichotomy as a political issue right from the beginning. Amongst the protest writers in French Georges Pioch, René Arcos and Marcel Martinet were already committed to socialism from the beginning of the war, as were Oskar Kanehl and Karl Otten in Germany. In England *The Herald* offers many protest poems that present the alignment in terms of a struggle between the working class and those in power. 'The Hero' by 'J. G.', in the issue of 13 April 1915, refers the victim–manipulator distinction specifically to a favourite patriotic image – that of rural England. This hero 'has died at Mons to save an English home,' but the home is located 'mid dustbins, grime and asphalt, with no trees'. A. St. John Adcock in 'The Way of Peace' (26 August 1914) puts the same complaint into a historical context:

We are the common people; from of old
We have been duped and driven, bought and sold,
Ours but to blast each other down in hordes,

And thus exalt our Kaisers and our Lords.'

As a result of 'one War Lord's raw, barbaric laws', the speaker maintains, the present situation leaves no alternative but to fight. In the future, however, because they are 'untaught, unlettered now no more,' the 'workers of the world' will be less ready to fight against each other, and instead will 'find / A kinship in our common human-kind'. G.E. Slocombe's 'To the War Lords of Europe', of 24 August 1914, is less accommodating to present needs, in that it posits the coming change, not in terms of a humanistic awakening, but as a threat of revolution from people who are being manipulated:

Take this into account, my lords,
When you come to your reckoning,
When you decide to sheathe our swords
And send us back to bartering,
Think you the humbling of a king
Will hold in check our hungry hordes?

These examples, in addition to their usefulness as indicators of thematic tendencies, also serve to demonstrate that protest poetry of a political kind is no less prone to cliché than patriotic verse. After encountering phrases like 'the workers of the world' and 'hungry hordes' in the early poetry, one is not at all surprised to discover, when the Russian uprising in 1917 brings new inspiration, not only a resurgence of political protest (which was simmering rather than boiling in the middle of the war), but also a proliferation of Red Dawns.

Yet all of these poems, together with the extra-literary protest that they represent, are hardly sufficient to disturb the impression of unanimity in the way the various countries welcomed the war in 1914. While historically there was certainly more objection than the established 'memory' maintains, it is clear that a very large number of people greeted the outbreak of war with enthusiasm. As perhaps no other writer on either side in the poetic conflict, the protest poet Oskar Kanehl captures the sense of excitement, of a holiday spirit, that arose in the major cities of Europe, when he asks,

Was jubelt ihr und schwenkt die bunten Tücher?
Und brüllt den Krieg?[60]

(Why are you cheering and waving gaily-coloured rags and roaring a welcome to war?)

Many explanations have been offered for this enthusiasm, but it remains, as Jon Silkin observes, 'a puzzle'. Common sense suggests that such eagerness could arise only amongst people unfamiliar with war – and the last widespread conflict involving the main European powers had ended almost a hundred years earlier. But common sense also points out, and with equal persistence, that the English had been at war in South Africa only fourteen years previously, and that the Franco-Prussian War of 1870–1 was still well within living memory. People who had been directly affected by these wars must surely remember them; and it is hard to believe that others were not aware, whether from literature or from history, that war inevitably brings suffering and death. W.N. Ewer's poem '1814–1914: On Reading *The Dynasts*' helps to reconcile this conflicting logic, for Ewer makes it clear that the lessons of both history and literature were either forgotten or ignored. The title refers to Thomas Hardy's verse drama about the Napoleonic Wars – a story, as Ewer reminds his readers, of how a century earlier ordinary Englishmen went off to fight, persuaded by the rhetoric of statesmen who declared, 'Europe in danger – her liberties imperilled.'[61] The reward of those soldiers, instead of freedom, was Peterloo (an incident in Manchester in 1819 when the militia, called in by civilian authorities, fired on a crowd at a protest demonstration). Yet now once again, Ewer says, Englishmen 'march cheerfully away' to war, 'nowise disbelieving' what the statesmen tell them, and 'Heedless of the story of their fathers' "War for Freedom" / Under Pitt and Castlereagh.'

Another popular explanation for the enthusiasm, especially in literary–critical circles, is that the war gave meaning to existence – that young men turned gladly to combat as a release from what Rupert Brooke calls 'a world grown old and cold and weary', happy to have found a cause. Yet although the mood described by Brooke and other poets represents appropriately the reaction of many combatants, the suggestion that this mood replaced one of indolence and world-weariness is not supported by the evidence of history. On the contrary, in the artistic community throughout Europe (including the Georgian group in England, of which Brooke was a central figure), the period just before the war was a time of innovation and exuberance, rather than of ennui. Nor was there any lack of causes, for the war arrived at the moment when, in Henry Bataille's words, Europe was 'en plein rêve humanitaire' (in the midst of a humanitarian dream) – a dream that included the 'pacificist' movement (as it was originally called), instigated around the turn of the century to counter the growth of militarism.[62] The sense of change and of causes to be fought was not confined to intellectuals. Socialism and other movements involving the working classes (such as the Workers' Education Association) had been gathering strength for several decades, while the campaign for women's suffrage was attracting increased attention, not only in Britain. The dismay expressed by Marcel Martinet in 'Tu vas te battre', that the workers of Europe, who should be fighting 'Contre les riches, contre les maîtres' (against the rich, against the bosses) are now aligned against each other, is echoed in Kanehl's anger at the abandoning of humanistic values:

Was schießt ihr plötzlich auf euren Menschenbruder,
den ihr geliebt?
Fällt sengend über sein Gut und Habe her?
Staaten- und Völkerrecht. Wißt ihr nicht mehr,
daß es Menschenrecht gibt?[63]

(Why are you suddenly shooting your fellow man, whom you loved? Why are you burning his house and home? The rights of states and peoples! Have you forgotten that there are also human rights?)

The protest poets complain neither of their compatriots' ignorance, nor of their indifference and self-centredness in the preceding years, but of their readiness to abandon old causes – all the things that, in Margaret Sackville's words, they had 'worshipped and held good' – in favour of a commitment to war.[64]

The problem remains, however, of explaining why history was forgotten and causes abandoned, and why people were suddenly possessed of a new sense of purpose, to the extent that their former campaigns and creeds seemed unimportant. For the combatants, no doubt, there was the appeal of a new venture, a change from the ordinary, and, according to the worker–poet Gerrit Engelke, the release from having to make decisions or be responsible – 'dies: Vom Schicksal gefaßt sein, ohne Gefragt-sein' (this being carried along by fate, instead of being asked).[65] The war appeared to the general public to be a straightforward problem, a matter of defending or restoring national boundaries, and it was promoted as a short-term undertaking, which would be 'over by Christmas'; to volunteer, therefore, was to commit oneself to an uncomplicated and finite task, for which no justification was needed. The venture carried social approval, and brought the combatant, in a variety of ways, the personal satisfaction that comes from doing by choice what is required of one as a duty. Those initially less enthusiastic were probably influenced, as Sorley was, by the 'cart-wheels of public opinion' or inspired by the commitment of their friends. And for people who were not in a position to volunteer to fight, there was a similar sense of willingness to contribute what one could to the cause, whether by knitting socks and rolling bandages, by writing poems of loyalty and support, or merely by resolving, as Owen Seaman does on behalf of his countrymen in 'Pro Patria', 'To go our quiet ways, subdued and sane'.

Propaganda certainly played its part, though not with the straightforward manipulative effect implied in the accusations of the socialists. Ewer in '1814–1914' blames the statesmen who persuade his 'stern stupid Englishmen' to volunteer, but he is apparently not convinced that propaganda functions so simply, for he also acknowledges the men's cheerful compliance in their own downfall. In reality, both persuasion and ready compliance contributed to the war enthusiasm. The propaganda was immediately and powerfully successful because it fell on well-prepared ground – the result of a form of manipulation that had taken place over many years, and in a cause which, if not without ulterior motives, was certainly both well-intentioned and worthwhile – the principle of general education. It is unlikely that any historical circumstance could have prompted such widespread and sustained commitment to war without the help of popular education – the system that had produced, in each of the countries under discussion, not only the desired versatile workforce, but also a population in which individual identity and national identity were inseparably linked, and which was therefore wholeheartedly committed in its support of what it perceived as the nation's cause.

In 'The Way of Peace', St. John Adcock foresees a peaceful future for the world (once the war is over), on the grounds that, because of their education, the workers will no longer be persuaded to fight against each other. But the French sociologist Jacques Ellul views the role of education differently, arguing that, far from helping people to avoid being 'duped', literacy actually renders them more susceptible to propaganda.[66] On the evidence of the war enthusiasm that prevailed at the time Adcock was writing, it is clear that Ellul's contention has considerable validity – especially since Adcock himself had obviously been persuaded to believe in the need for English involvement. Yet the enthusiasm was freely given, and the propaganda that helped to generate it came not only from the 'statesmen' and others in power, but from members of nearly every social group and class throughout the different nations. Manipulation and compliance, in this case, were almost indistinguishable. The outcome, however, was an unprecedented outpouring of chauvinistic rhetoric which emphasised all the most destructive characteristics of the new creed, the worship of the Fatherland. Observing their compatriots rejecting the causes they had 'held good', ignoring the lessons of history, going with enthusiasm to fight and kill, 'lying' and believing lies, and, as time passed, continuing to promote a war that was immeasurably more devastating than anyone had imagined possible, the protest poets saw their goal clearly. It was to counter the 'Schwall von Rede und Schrift', the flood of speech and writing that nationalistic commitment inspired, with the 'Still Small Voice' – but a disturbing voice none the less – of reason and 'Menschlichkeit'.

5

Laissez-les donc dormir
Protest against the heroic ethic

Laissez-les donc dormir en paix,
Ces morts! Que vous ont-ils donc fait,
Pour être pourchassés dans leur funèbre asile?
Marc Larreguy de Civrieux, 'Debout les morts!'[1]

The 'cruel sword' of the Disillusioner, stripping the glory from war, is nowhere more active than in the protest writing that addresses one of the patriotic poetry's main concerns, heroism. The strong anti-heroic element of the protest verse might seem to be a direct consequence of twentieth-century weaponry, which, as many commentators have observed, limited or altered the opportunity for personal heroism. Yet if one acknowledges that not only technology but also national attitudes had changed substantially in the course of the previous hundred years, one can perceive anti-heroism as a consequence as much of the latter as of the former. The Great War was a perfect war for nationalism, for there was nothing to question but the morality of war itself. None of the main participants was fighting for a creed other than the sanctity of borders, so with socialism temporarily *hors de combat*, the conflict involved no major cause where sympathy and antipathy might override national commitment (as they did in many ways in the Second World War, for instance). It was almost as though the war had been designed expressly to prompt the kind of response for which the educational system, both directly and indirectly, had prepared the populations of most of the countries involved – a strong and almost unanimous sense of patriotic loyalty and dedication.

Despite this unusual fervour, however, and despite the vastly increased size of the armies, the burden of fighting fell, as it always had, on a relatively narrow segment of the population, the young men. For the rest of the people, no matter how great their patriotic zeal, fighting had to be a vicarious activity, carried out on their behalf by the nation's 'heroes'. There is no reason to doubt the sincerity of the old men and young women who expressed a longing to be at the

Front; such a feeling – a commitment to the concept of total war – was a natural consequence of their education and the mood of the times. Their longing was fulfilled in the Second World War, when the Home Front was the scene of much dramatic action, but the Great War offered little opportunity for civilian heroism. Consequently, if civilians (including combatants who had not yet been to the Front) wished to prove that their own patriotic dedication was extraordinary, almost their only recourse was to words, and one of the favourite devices was an expression of praise or support for the nation's 'warrior sons'. As a result of these verbal outpourings – in sermons, political speeches, and newspaper articles as well as poems – the young combatants were presented with a double burden. They volunteered, or were compelled by law, to risk their lives in the defence of the nation or its prestige, and at the same time they had to carry the full weight of their countrymen's patriotic idealism and devotion. What is more, the civilian patriots did not pause to consider whether the edicts of heroism that they promoted had ever been applicable in real life, or to recall that 'dulce et decorum est pro patria mori' was in its origin a literary concept. Nor did they hesitate to attribute the characteristics of legendary heroes, famous because they were outstanding, to the mass of very ordinary young men who comprised the nations' armies. In the enthusiasm for heaping praises upon the heroes, no-one wondered whether the individual soldier might prefer not to be confronted with the demands of an unrealistic code of honour and heroism, or whether the nation would benefit from the death of hundreds of thousands of its young men on the battlefield. The patriotic 'word-makers' had no doubt about the right of the nation to demand the ultimate sacrifice, and they were similarly convinced that the readiness for sacrifice reflected gloriously on the nation as a whole – and therefore of each of its citizens. The anti-heroic poetry of the war, including many of the well-known English protest poems, is a challenge to all these assumptions, an attempt to ease the extra burden placed upon the young men by this large-scale promotion of the creed of patriotic heroism.

The English soldiers in Laurence Binyon's 'For the Fallen' – 'steady and aglow', going 'with songs to the battle' and 'staunch to the end against odds uncounted' – represent not only the kind of heroes the patriotic poets envision, but also the ideal that the anti-heroic poetry often seeks to discredit. The historically-verifiable image of the soldiers singing as they left their home town or training-camp clearly appealed to patriotic writers, whether as proof of the men's enthusiastic and heroic commitment, or on account of the pathos in the combination of joyful setting-out and portended death – the image, for instance, in Lienhard's lines, 'Deutschlands kräftige Jugend, / Die singend hinauszieht [. . .] In die Schlacht, in den Tod' (Germany's mighty youth, departing with song . . . for the battle, for death).[2] When Charles Sorley writes, in 'All the hills and vales along', 'And the singers are the chaps / Who are going to die perhaps', the words seem to mock the solemn tone of poems like Lienhard's, and to underline Sorley's refusal to subscribe to the concept of heroic immortality.[3] Other poets indicate their rejection of the myth by showing that, although the departure from home may be joyful, going 'to the battle' is not. H.d'A. B.'s 'The March' tells of the silent misery of a 'khaki column' trudging through the rain, while Ernst Toller's ironically-named 'Marschlied' (Marching song) ends 'Wir Waisen der Erde / Ziehn stumm in die Schlacht' – Orphaned by the world, we go in silence to the slaughter.[4] In Oskar Kanehl's 'Auf dem Marsch' (On the march) the weary soldiers still sing, but barely, and the rejection of the image of ideal patriotic heroes, implied by Toller and H.d'A. B., is made explicit here:

Aus müden Münden fallen lalle Lieder.
Nur um den Takt.
Kein Mensch freut oder ärgert sich
über den lieben Gott oder das Vaterland,
von dem sein Sang singsangt.[5]

(From tired mouths fall babbled songs, but only for the sake of the rhythm. No-one cares in the least about dear God or the Fatherland, of whom the sing-song verses tell.)

Wilfred Owen attacks the image in a different way in 'The Send-Off', as he pictures with characteristic compassion the homecoming of the men who, at the beginning of the poem, 'sang their way' to the train:

Shall they return to beatings of great bells
In wild train-loads?
A few, a few, too few for drums and yells

May creep back, silent, to village wells,
Up half-known roads.[6]

From such a return, which suggests a weary animal seeking the safety of its den, most of the patriotic poets shy away, taking refuge in the thought of heroic death and the country's eternal gratitude and remembrance.

As one explores the patriotic poetry of the Great War in the three languages, one becomes strongly aware of how very thoroughly its writers romanticised their subject. In few places is this romanticising more difficult to appreciate than in connection with the wounded.

Admittedly Shakespeare's King Henry V anticipated in his address before Agincourt that his soldiers would in the future be proud of their scars; but it is hard to imagine anyone believing, in 1914, that soldiers who came home handicapped would revel in the honour of having been badly injured for the sake of the nation. (The only desirable wound outside literature was what the English soldiers called a 'Blighty', an injury bad enough to ensure one's return to 'Blighty' – that is, England – but unlikely to cause permanent harm: perhaps something like the 'leichte Beinschuß' – light injury to the leg – that the unheroic hero of Alfred Lichtenstein's 'Gebet vor der Schlacht' prays for.) Yet patriotic poems and other contemporary writings of the same kind commonly express the belief that the soldier's commitment to the national cause will make the suffering less, and the lasting consequences easier to bear. When a poet known as Altgraf Erich, in his 1915 'Neujahrsbrief' (New Year's Letter), attributes this effect to a mythic agent – laurel-crowned warriors of long ago coming down from Valhalla to kiss the wounds of the new heroes – one recognises the inanity but dismisses it as excusable in the context of the poem.[7] On the other hand, when the setting is contemporary and realistic, and the poet also attempts to arouse compassion for the disabled soldiers, the promise of consolation sounds, at the very least, insensitive. Th. Mary, a Red Cross nurse who was the author of a small volume called À nos chers Blessés (To our dear Wounded), addresses a poem 'To those blinded in the war' ('Aux Aveugles de la guerre'), whom she describes with compassionate understanding as captives 'En leur prison de chair, dans une nuit profonde' (In their prison of flesh, in a profound night).[8] Unfortunately, towards the end of the poem Mary's patriotism overcomes her sympathy as a nurse, and she offers the blind men consolation of a kind that is no more probable than Altgraf Erich's mythology:

Courage, mes amis, voici les coeurs de France
Qui viennent adoucir vos tourments si cruels.

(Take courage, my friends, French hearts are coming to soften your cruel torment.)

The difficulty does not lie entirely in the unlikelihood that the men will find much consolation in this idea (even if the 'French hearts' bring some practical assistance); it rests also in the fact that, although the soldiers represented by those in the poem have already given their sight, they are still being used for a patriotic purpose. Joseph Bayer in 'La Manche vide' (The Empty Sleeve) carries such an imposition upon the war-wounded a stage further, when he makes use of the persona of a combatant who has lost an arm.[9] While 'Aux

Aveugles de la guerre' was probably inspired by true sympathy for the blind soldiers the writer had encountered in the course of her work, Bayer's 'mutilé' was almost certainly invented merely to give scope to the poet's own patriotic declaration. This disabled man, though his sleeve hangs sadly against his side, does not wish for sympathy, for he claims to be little affected by a handicap that was acquired in so worthy a cause:

Oui, qu'importe après tout que ma manche soit vide,
Si de fierté mon coeur est plein!

Qu' importe que mon sang, hélas! avec tant d'autre. . .
Ait rougi fortement le terrain reconquis!
J'ai l'honneur d'avoir pu défendre mon pays.

(Yes, what does it matter, after all, that my sleeve is empty, if my heart is full of pride! What does it matter that my blood – mingled, alas, with that of so many others – has stained to a deep red the ground that we recaptured! I have the honour of having been able to defend my country.)

In these two poems one sees how the double burden placed on the combatants might accomplish its effect. It is unlikely that Mary would greet the young men in her hospital ward with words like those at the end of her poem, 'Honneur, honneur à vous, Mutilés glorieux!' (Honour to you, glorious disabled!), while Bayer's 'hero' is so obviously a convenience for the author that one is inclined to dismiss the poem as merely literary, and totally irrelevant to reality. At first glance, then, it appears that such sentiments would have little effect on the combatants, except perhaps in offering them consolation if they were romantics, or in provoking bitter laughter in the cynics amongst them. Yet because the two poems subscribe to and propagate the same myth, they reinforce each other and, by being printed and circulated, they help to establish an attitude like that of Bayer's hero as an ideal against which real people may be measured. It is hardly surprising, therefore, that protest poets try to depict as it actually is the situation of men who have returned handicapped from the war.

One of the most powerful statements against the myth of the 'mutilé glorieux' is Wilfred Owen's 'Disabled', a picture of a former football-player, handsome and virile in the old days, who has lost both legs in the war. Owen perceptively compares the man's present existence with his past, and projects the future – 'a few sick years in institutes' – for this young man who, only a year ago, was 'carried shoulder-high' after matches, and of whom 'Someone had said he'd look a god in kilts'.[10] The protest in this poem lies mainly 'in the pity' (to use Owen's own phrase), achieved largely through the poet's use of a voice which speaks as an observer, yet which imputes thoughts and feelings directly to the disabled man himself:

> Now he will never feel again how slim
> Girls' waists are, or how warm their subtle hands.
> All of them touch him like some queer disease.

By using a technique more commonly found in prose narratives than in verse, Owen has created a character that exists in much the same sense as the protagonist of a realistic novel: that is, a personality whose existence one accepts without question, and with whom one can readily empathise. In contrast to 'Dulce et Decorum Est', where the poet resorts to an explicit message delivered in the voice of the speaker, here the only hint of direct protest lies in the reported recollections of the young man – when he wonders why he volunteered, for instance:

> Aye, that was it, to please the giddy jilts
> He asked to join. He didn't have to beg;
> Smiling they wrote his lie: aged nineteen years,

or when he thinks of his homecoming:

> Some cheered him home, but not as crowds cheer Goal.
> Only a solemn man who brought him fruits
> *Thanked* him; and then enquired about his soul.

In these few lines Owen succeeds in attacking several targets: women who persuade the men of their acquaintance to go to war, recruiters who turn a blind eye to under-age volunteers, a populace that is little concerned with the consequences of its own enthusiasm for war, and the Church which expresses thanks (in keeping with the myth) rather than commiserating, and which passes over the terrible destruction of the body in the interest of the soul. Nevertheless, the effectiveness of the protest rests mainly with the image of a human being destroyed by war – a picture drawn with precisely the right detail to evoke compassion without sentimentality.

Like Owen, Georges Pioch, a Belgian socialist (and a civilian), is highly conscious of the suffering caused by 'La haine et tous ses maux, la gloire et tous ses crimes' (Hatred and all its evils, glory and all its crimes), and his protest against the glorification of war is equally strong.[11] In 'Mutilés' Pioch attacks directly the myth about the value of glory for men who have been disabled in battle. Though they wear medals on their chest, 'Des signes qu'on nous dit être ceux d'honneur' (Signs which, we are told, are those of honour), the disabled are

> si las d'être glorieux,
> Ils condamnent, par la tristesse de leurs yeux,
> L'excès d'une grandeur qui ne sert point la vie.[12]

(. . . so tired of being glorious that they condemn, through the sadness of their eyes, the excess of a greatness that serves no purpose in their lives.)

Nor does the future hold much hope for them, when, poor and ignored, their only consolation will be in remembering that they used to be called heroes, while the war lasted. A similar point is made by Pastor Tech in 'Der Krüppel in der Siegesallee' (The Cripple in the Siegesallee). Here the disabled hero is greeted with friendliness by a young woman, but the speaker remarks,

> Noch tobt der Kampf. Doch wer will *nach* der Schlacht
> Noch von den schweren Opfern sehn und hören?[13]

(At present war is still raging. But *after* the battle, who will still wish to be reminded of the heavy sacrifices?)

While the former soldiers in all these examples may be in a better position than those whom Falstaff callously condemned 'to the town gate, to beg for life', the protest poets make it clear that heroism in the name of the country guarantees neither the enduring sympathy of the community in general nor the spiritual comfort the myth might lead one to hope for.

Although the patriotic–heroic ethic is quite able to accommodate the wounded and maimed through the concept of the 'mutilé glorieux', it has no place for the most pathetic casualties of the war, the insane. That the war would drive a substantial number of men to madness, and that mental as well as physical endurance would be required of 'our heroes', simply did not occur to the exponents of the myth in 1914. Historically, many factors contributed to what became known generally as 'shell-shock', especially the sense of the war's inescapability. Nowhere was the soldier so conscious of his helplessness as during a prolonged bombardment, and poems by combatants frequently tell of the struggle to keep one's sanity at such a time – when, as Richard Aldington says, each blow to the earth seems like a blow to oneself. But visual memories are usually the most enduring, and the war provided a multitude of nightmarish sights that might return to haunt the observer. In Owen's 'Mental Cases' the victims, these 'purgatorial shadows' condemned for ever to relive in their minds their experiences of the war, are 'Men whose minds the dead have ravished'.[14] Toller tells of the thoughts of one of his comrades looking into a mass grave, and the horror is magnified considerably by the linking of the macabre scene to childhood and innocence:

Einer träumt am Massengrab
'Solchen Haufen Weihnachtskuchen
Wünscht ich mir als Kind,
Soviel.'[15]

(One man stands dreaming beside the mass grave: 'When I was a child I used to wish for a heap of Christmas cookies like that – so many.')

Like Toller, Ivor Gurney juxtaposes past and present, with similarly horrifying effect, in 'To His Love'. This seems to be a simple and gentle lament for the death of a friend (the 'passionate shepherd' to whose 'love' the poem is addressed) and for lost pastoral days 'On Cotswold / Where the sheep feed'.[16] Only at the end does one appreciate the poem's many complexities, amongst them the fact that the speaker's real concern is with neither past nor present, but with the future:

You would not know him now.
But still he died
Nobly, so cover him over
With violets of pride
Purple from Severn side.

Cover him, cover him soon!
And with thick-set
Masses of memoried flowers –
Hide that red wet
Thing I must somehow forget.

Gurney distinguishes not only between the dead and the living, but also between the two groups of survivors: those, like the dead man's 'love' ('you' in the poem), for whom 'violets of pride' and the thought of noble death provide adequate consolation, and those like the speaker, for whom such means are, at best, a desperate recourse in the attempt to live with the experiences of the war. When 'the Fallen' have become hideous objects, a 'red wet / Thing', 'wobbling carrion roped upon a cart', or 'Die Bündel Blut auf den Tornistern klebend' (bundles of blood attached to knapsacks), a pledge like Binyon's 'We will remember them!' is an expression of dread rather than a promise.[17]

Fear and madness are often closely related, and in the heroic literary tradition the overcoming of fear is part of the process of becoming a hero. In the tenets of the creed as it is preached in the Great War, however, the fearlessness of each nation's heroes is taken for granted; these young combatants, without exception, are 'staunch to the end'. This aspect of the myth is countered in a variety of ways in the protest writing – not least in Lichtenstein's 'Gebet vor der Schlacht', where all the men admit secretly that they would rather not die in battle. Hermann Plagge in 'Nacht im Granatenfeuer' (Night under shell-fire) emphasises the unheroic by showing how fear reduces men to an animal-like state, as the speaker describes the faces of his companions during the bombardment:

> Die Augen um mich her sind lauernd in Angst und geduckt
> wie gepeitschte Hunde.
> O nicht sterben.[18]

> (The eyes around me are lurking in fear, cowering like beaten dogs. O let me not die.)

Herbert Read's 'The Happy Warrior' contrasts the reality of fear directly against the literary myth – William Wordsworth's 'Character of the Happy Warrior'. This prototype of what 'every man in arms should wish to be' is governed by reason, and even in 'the heat of conflict' he controls and subdues those necessary companions of the soldier, Pain and Fear. Read shows instead a man driven by fear far beyond the reach of reason:

> I saw him stab
> And stab again
> A well-killed Boche.[19]

To reinforce his point, Read ends his poem with Wordsworth's own words – 'This is the Happy Warrior, / This is he.' 'The Execution of Cornelius Vane', by the same author, is a narrative poem about the ultimate expression of fear, desertion.[20] The desperate 'hero' flees to escape the war, but once his fear has abated he loses 'the strength of his will' and is arrested. Moments before his death he speaks in his own defence, and the question he poses is far from an innocent enquiry:

> The morning was bright, and as they tied
> The cloth over his eyes, he said to the assembly:
> 'What wrong have I done that I should leave these –
> The bright sun rising
> And the birds that sing?'

Naturally he receives no answer. Cornelius Vane asks to be judged by civilian standards, where fear is a normal human reaction. But in a military situation, which demands that men must remain more afraid of deserting than of fighting, such standards cannot be permitted.

The existence of the dual standard implied in Read's ending is addressed explicitly by Winifred Letts in 'The Deserter'. Letts observes

that, since 'God makes a man of flesh and blood / Who yearns to live
and not to die', few of us are in a position to pass judgement upon
such a man if, one day, trapped between fear and death, he simply
runs away.[21] The protest is carried yet further when Letts adds a
conclusion that demonstrates what she calls 'the irony of life'. Although
her deserter protagonist died with 'an English bullet in his heart', his
mother believes he 'fought and fell / A hero':

> So she goes proudly; to the strife
> Her best, her hero son she gave.
> O well for her she does not know
> He lies in a deserter's grave.

Owen's 'S.I.W.' (which, incidentally, postdates Letts' poem by at least
a year) has a similar ending. The 'hero' of 'S.I.W.' is a young man
who, after struggling in vain to overcome his fear, shoots himself
through the mouth to escape from the terror of the war ('S.I.W.' being
the official abbreviation for 'self-inflicted wound').[22] Like Letts, Owen
adds a postscript to underline the irony of the fact that the truth
cannot be told, even (or especially) after the victim is dead:

> With him they buried the muzzle his teeth had kissed,
> And truthfully wrote the Mother, 'Tim died smiling.'

These two unheroic deaths exemplify the way the patriotic-heroic
creed may be used deliberately to veil the truth, and they also represent
another of the major disparities between truth and myth that protest
poets like to point out: the notion that soldiers fighting for their
country all die like heroes. Siegfried Sassoon in 'How to Die' devises
a poetic version of this concept and juxtaposes it against the other
possibility, while pretending to agree that the myth is correct.[23] The
first stanza sets the heroic scene – dawn, and

> The dying hero shifts his head
> To watch the glory that returns.

The 'holy brightness' of the sky is reflected in his eyes, and 'on his
lips a whispered name'. The speaker continues,

> You'd think, to hear some people talk,
> That lads go West with sobs and curses,
> And sullen faces white as chalk,

but in fact, he assures his readers, 'they've been taught the way to do
it / Like Christian soldiers', 'with due regard for decent taste'. Osbert
Sitwell, writing under the pseudonym 'Miles', suggests in 'Rhapsode'
that even Christ was guilty of failing to die heroically, by the standards
of the 'Pharisees and Sadducees'. Sitwell quotes Christ's 'blessed,

humble, human words of doubt' at his crucifixion – his cry of 'My God! My God! why hast thou forsaken me?' – and pictures the bystanders 'Pained beyond measure' as they exclaim,

> At least he might have died like a hero
> With an oath on his lips,
> Or a refrain from a comic song,
> Or a cheerful comment of some kind.[24]

The bystanders are afraid that Christ's outburst will reflect badly upon themselves, as having perhaps 'gone too far'. Such unheroic conduct, they say, is 'very unpleasant for all of us'.

An example of an unexpected and possibly accidental confrontation between unheroic death and the myth is 'The Everlasting Terror', a poem printed on the back of a concert programme for a performance at an army barracks in England in November 1916. (Its author is identified only as J.R. A., with no indication of rank.) As the speaker acknowledges the reality of death on the battlefield, his choice of words is interesting:

> Oh, God, I've heard the screams of men
> In suffering beyond our ken,
> And shuddered at the thought that I
> Might scream as well if I should die.[25]

The echo of Brooke's famous 'If I should die, think only this of me' in the last line may be unintentional, although the title of the poem, a parody of John Masefield's 'The Everlasting Mercy', which was published in 1911, indicates that the author was familiar with modern literature. But whether intentional or not, the use of Brooke's words certainly serves as a measure of the reality of 1916 against the confidence of 1914, as far as the reader is concerned. (Brooke's soldier imagined himself peacefully mingling his English dust with the earth of 'a foreign field', without any thought of the unpleasant process of dying.) Because its unusual context distinguishes it from poems published after a process of editorial selection, 'The Everlasting Terror' is especially interesting as an example of unmediated combatant response to the war. One might anticipate, since the concert in question is held 'by kind permission' of the commanding officer, that the poem would subscribe to the patriotic norm, but the reality of war is recognised quite as clearly here as in many combatant protest poems. The attack in this instance, however, is not upon the concept of heroism, but upon the belief that one can be educated to be a 'gentleman'. The poet says that, after fourteen years of such training, he 'took [his] righteousness to War', and there, in this hellish 'place of misery', he discovered that one's behaviour towards the enemy can be very ungentlemanly. He also discovered, however, that war diminishes pride and brings out 'gentleness', which is not a mode of behaviour that can be taught in school, but an innate quality that is to be found very commonly in 'the Tommy'. Although the poem hovers on the brink of protest, especially with regard to the evil of killing and the reality of dying, the lesson about 'gentleness', the poet seems to suggest, helps to justify the Hell that produces it. Consequently, the reader has an impression of ambivalence, which is nowhere more apparent than when the speaker looks back to the beginning of the war:

> The one thing that I can't recall
> Is why I went to war at all;
> I wasn't brave, nor coward quite,
> But still I went, and I was right.

The ending leans once more towards protest, as the speaker (a young man who sounds old and weary) talks of the 'lonely life' before him, acknowledging that 'the lasting terror of the war' will be with him for ever, mitigated only by the recollection of comradeship. Nevertheless, the feeling of ambivalence remains, and in this respect J.R. A.'s attitude, hovering between hatred of the war and a recognition that there is no alternative but to fight, is highly typical of the response of combatant poets, from Apollinaire to the 'merest rhymster'.

As a whole, the war poetry of Robert Graves is similarly ambivalent, but in 'The Leveller' the poet leaves no doubt of his intention of mocking the heroic ethic, or at least the civilians whose taste for heroism must be satisfied. 'The Leveller' describes the death of two men who were struck by the same shell, the one 'a pale eighteen-year-old, / Blue-eyed and thin and not too bold', and the other an experienced soldier 'With bristling chin and whiskered hands'.[26] The latter, as he died, 'Groaned "Mother! Mother!" like a child', while the former, 'that poor innocent in men's clothes, / Died cursing God with brutal oaths'. Thereupon their sergeant wrote 'his accustomed funeral speech / To cheer the womenfolk of each: // 'He died a hero's death'. Although this outcome is similar to the endings of Owen's 'S.I.W.' and Letts' 'The Deserter', Graves' title adds to the irony of his comment. The two men are made equal not only by death, the traditional 'great leveller', but also by the way they, and potentially (one may assume) all other combatants, are disguised as heroes for the benefit of the people at home, regardless of their military record. A similar levelling, and a similar attack on the myth, is evident in Erwin Piscator's 'Denk an seine Bleisoldaten'. While the death of the combatants here is perhaps less obviously anti-heroic than that of the two men in Graves' poem, it is far from the splendid finale implied in the message the mother receives:

Mußt nun weinen, Mutter, weine –
Wenn du's liesest: 'Starb als Held.'
Denk an seine Bleisoldaten.
Hatten alle scharf geladen.
Starben alle: plumps und stumm.[27]

(You'll weep now, Mother, weep, when you read the message: 'He died like a hero.' Think of his lead soldiers; they were all lined up, ready to take aim; and they all just dropped down, silent and dead.)

Interestingly enough, however, this anti-heroic death is a rare German example of a convention that appears far more commonly in the English protest poetry than in that of the other two languages. The most probable explanation for this disparity lies in the far stronger tendency of English patriotic poets to view the process of dying in war in a romantic way, leading to a correspondingly strong desire amongst the English protest writers to prove them wrong. German patriotic poets, as I indicated earlier, appear to be considerably less preoccupied with death, and their French counterparts, though totally committed to the concept of 'the glorious dead', seem to recognise that, in order to die as a martyr, one must suffer. In English, on the other hand, there is apparently a firm conviction that soldiers die both nobly and joyfully. 'One short last sigh, the warrior / Lay quiet, still and calm', M. Hall writes in 'After the Battle', one of Charles Forshaw's 'One Hundred Best Poems by Women Poets of the Empire', while Katherine Hale's 'Grey Knitting' (which Forshaw somehow overlooked) is enough to make one hang one's head in shame for one's sex:

I like to think that soldiers, gayly dying
For the white Christ on fields with shame sown deep,
Will hear the fairy click of women's needles
    As they fall fast asleep'.[28]

Alongside poems like these, Sassoon's 'How to Die' scarcely seems exaggerated, and one is not surprised to hear from the protest poets a resounding cry of 'Not so!'

Nevertheless, in one respect at least opponents and proponents of the myth come close together: in the conviction that the soldiers are destined to die in battle. Although the upholders of the patriotic–heroic ethic pay lip-service to heroism, it is clear that what they really appreciate is the heroic dead – the men who have gone to battle with what Richard Dehmel calls 'ein Herz voll Opferfreudigkeit' – a heart full of the joy of sacrifice – and who have died appropriately. As the combatant protest poets perceive it, however, the sacrifice is far from joyful or heroic, having much in common with the fate of sacrificial animals. In Edmund Blunden's 'Vlamertinghe: Passing the Château, July 1917', the sight of the Château and its flower-filled gardens reminds the speaker of Keats' line, 'And all her silken flanks in garlands drest'. This richness of flowers serves in place of garlands for the ritual slaughter, but here the soldiers, instead of Keats' heifer, are 'coming to the sacrifice'. While the profusion of colour affords these men momentary pleasure, the victims in Ernst Toller's 'Marschlied' are less fortunate, for these 'Wandrer zum Tode' (wanderers towards death) going silently to battle are 'kranzlose Opfer' – wreathless offerings – who lack even the consolation of believing that their slaughter is sanctified as a religious sacrifice. Wreaths and garlands are granted to heroes as well as to sacrificial victims, but, as Richard Fischer points out in 'Feld der Ehre' (Field of Honour), the docile and animal-like acceptance of impending death that is required of the soldiers is totally incompatible with heroism:

'Ehre' – Willenlos werden wir hingeschleppt,
Eine stumpfe, todesangstschwitzende Herde.

('Honour' – we are dragged along without any will, a spiritless herd sweating with the fear of death.)

Heroism, Fischer implies, requires the freedom to choose one's course of action, but for soldiers like these, 'poor sheep, driven innocent to death', as Max Plowman describes them, the power to make decisions has been taken away, and they have become entirely inactive – no longer, in these two examples, destined even for the sacrificial altar, but for the slaughterhouse.[29] Joseph Billiet emphasises the extent of their enforced passivity, and accordingly of their dehumanisation, by both the passive voice and the meaning of his verbs, when he depicts the men as

Parqués dans les frontières,
numerotés,
marqués du signe de la bete,
comme des moutons[30]

(Penned inside frontiers, numbered, marked with the sign of the beast, like sheep.)

But though the heroes have been transformed into animals going to be slaughtered, the sacrifice against which these poets protest is still in keeping with what the myth anticipates, when it assumes that all young men are ready to die in the nation's cause.

An almost inevitable consequence of the commitment to mass armies is mass destruction, an aspect of the First World War particularly remote from the individual battles of heroic literature that the patriotic poets apparently believe to be the norm. Piscator's 'Bleisoldaten', written in August 1914, foreshadows remarkably well this character-istic of the Great War scene, where men die in large numbers, for no apparent purpose, and without any opportunity to take action – 'Starben alle: plumps und stumm'. Max Plowman describes the after-math of just such an apparently futile, and certainly unheroic, incidence of mass death, in the first of a series of sonnets called 'The Dead Soldiers':

> Just as the scythe had caught them, there they lay,
> A sheaf for Death, ungarnered and untied:
> A crescent moon of men who showed the way
> When first the Tanks crept out, till they too died:
> Guardsmen, I think, but one can hardly tell. . . .[31]

To underline his refusal to subscribe to the myth that the men's death was heroic, Plowman goes on to tell how these corpses were left to sink gradually into the mud, and how 'At night one stumbled over them and swore'. The many references in all three languages to large numbers of unidentified corpses left on the battlefield similarly serve to emphasise the distance between the myth of meaningful heroic death and the futility of the fact. (It is worth adding, however, that the promoters of the ethic of mass heroism – and correspondingly of mass sacrifice – succeeded in accommodating this aspect of the new warfare, through the ceremonial burial of a representative 'unknown soldier' whose tomb became a national shrine.) If the soldiers who die are blown to pieces, so that even their corpses cease to exist, the gap between significance and futility is magnified, increasing also, it seems, the temptation for protest poets to confront the myth directly with the truth. Henry-Jacques, in an uncharacteristic French example of anti-heroic death, begins 'Les Martyrs' with a heroic phrase that he proposes to illustrate, 'Mourir, c'est le sort le plus beau' (To die is the most beautiful destiny).[32] The poem then recounts an incident involving the death of twenty men carrying explosives, of which the outcome is far from beautiful:

> Il ne reste rien d'eux qu'en débris mélangés
> Des parcelles de chair et des bouts de capote.

> (Nothing remains of them but, in a mixture of debris, a few pieces of flesh and some bits of their caps.)

H.F. Constantine uses a similar confrontation in 'The Glory of War', telling of a victory – the retaking of a village – that was achieved at the cost of the destruction of all the buildings and the death of a thousand men.[33] What troubles Constantine particularly is the persistence of the belief (also implicit in Henry-Jacques' 'le sort le plus beau') that combatants are glad to die for their country. Addressing an imagined listener who is an after-the-event observer of the scene, the narrator tells of one particular death:

Our sergeant-major's dead, killed as we entered the
   village;
You will not find his body, tho' you look for it;
A shell burst on him, leaving his legs, strangely enough,
   untouched.

This description, especially with the narrator's detached 'strangely enough', is already horrifying, but it is made increasingly so by the next line, as the scene is juxtaposed against the major tenet of patriotic heroism:

Happy man, he died for England.

When patriotic civilians, including poets, talk of 'the Fallen', they rarely mean corpses, except to the extent that the latter are safely buried. For combatants, on the other hand, fallen comrades (except perhaps close friends) are, first and foremost, bodies – objects that must be disposed of, that impede one's progress, that continue to exist in gory fragments, that rot and produce a foul odour. The poetry of combatants reflects this reality, and, whether intentionally or not, takes on a tone of protest simply by its insistence on the physical object, as distinct from the immortality of the spirit. 'Only the dead were always present', Arthur Graeme West writes in 'The Night Patrol', ' – present / As a vile sickly smell of rottenness.'[34] Hermann Plagge's account of a battle tells how 'Ein Toter wird über die Brustwehr geworfen wie Ballast aus einem Schiff' – a dead man is thrown over the parapet like ballast out of a ship.[35] By civilian standards, this practical method of disposing of a dead comrade who is interfering with the necessary tasks of the soldiers sounds callous and disrespectful – and intentionally so.

Corpses, especially in large numbers, are also useful to protest poets as a direct antidote to nationalism. Toller's 'Leichen im Priesterwald' (Corpses in the Priesterwald) describes a 'Düngerhaufen faulender Menschenleiber' – a dungheap of rotting human corpses – belonging to both French and German soldiers, and by implication contrasts this ultimate result with the spirit that sent the men to war:

O Frauen Frankreichs,
Frauen Deutschlands,
Säht Ihr Eure Männer!
Sie tasten mit zerfetzten Händen

Nach den verquollnen Leibern ihrer Feinde,
Gebärde, leichenstarr, ward brüderlicher Hauch,
Ja, sie umarmen sich.[36]

(O women of France, women of Germany, if only you could see your menfolk! They reach with ragged hands towards the bloated bodies of their enemies. A gesture, in the stiffness of death, has become the breath of a brother. Yes, they even embrace.)

Death in the war has destroyed the relationship between husbands and wives by making the men, as corpses, physical lovers of each other. (A similar topic is addressed in Wilfred Owen's 'Greater Love', where the physical love of women is compared unfavourably with the 'greater love' of giving one's life for one's friends.) More than that, however, death has invalidated the very purpose for which the men were killed – the aim of maintaining the separateness of their two nations. Like Toller, René Arcos believes that death defeats nationalism, for in separating the men from their flag it has also removed their hatred:

Serrés les uns contre les autres,
Les morts sans haine et sans drapeau,
Cheveux plaqués de sang caillé,
Les morts sont tous d'un seul côté.[37]

(Leaning one against the other, the dead without hatred and without flags, their hair coated with dried blood, the dead are all on the same side.)

Laurence Housman takes up the same theme, but with much more bitterness, in 'Armageddon – and After', a comment on the aftermath of a battle in the war against the Turks:

We fought at Armageddon for the freedom of the world!
I fought, and you fought, and here our bones lie mixed.[38]

Housman relates this result explicitly to political manipulation: while the soldiers of east and west struggled to take each other's lives, the freedom for which they believed they were fighting was 'bought and sold' by 'tricksters' 'safe within their fences'. Consequently, although the bones are stripped of flesh, 'the chains remain behind'.

While the protest poetry in many respects echoes the preoccupation with death to be found in patriotic verse, one topic that the latter never broaches is the problem of killing. In the heroic tradition in literature, one respects one's enemy but nevertheless admits that one may be forced to slay him – and indeed, heroic epics and ballads dwell at length on the actual struggle between men trying to kill each other. As the tradition is interpreted by patriotic poets of the First World War, the converse is true: one hates the enemy, seeing nothing in him that might be worthy of respect, but the possibility of killing is never mentioned. In German, where the verbal forms are most similar, it is particularly noticeable that the patriotic verse is rife with 'der Tod', 'der Tote', 'tot' and even 'getötet', but one rarely finds the active form, 'töten', even in battle narratives like those of Albrecht Schaeffer. The writers of the modern heroic poetry, one must assume, prefer to believe that enemy soldiers succumb to an impersonal Death or have somehow become dead, without the agency of a killer; to suggest that the nation's heroes are killers would clearly be in bad taste. Not surprisingly, then, protest poets refute this deliberate avoidance of a crucial word by taking up the conscientious objector's cry that the main purpose of war is to kill. The words 'Tue! tue!' (Kill! kill!), coming from the wisest and holiest voices of Europe, form a refrain in Pierre-Jean Jouve's 'Les Voix d'Europe'.[39] Martinet in 'Tu vas te battre', his bitter lament for the end of international socialist unity, reminds the workers that their task will be to kill men like themselves:

> Mineur de Saxe, devant toi
> Il y a un mineur de Lens,
> Tue-le.
> Docker du Havre, devant toi
> Il y a un docker de Brème,
> Tue et tue, tue-le, tuez-vous,
> Travaille, travailleur.[40]

(Miner from Saxony, in front of you is a miner from Lens; kill him! Docker from Le Havre, in front of you is a docker from Bremen; kill and kill, kill him, kill each other; worker, do your work.)

Siegfried Sassoon's 'Remorse' deals explicitly with the failure of the heroic ethic to allow for the reality of how men kill others – though presumably the father's reading, in this case, was modern:

> 'Could anything be worse than this?' – he wonders,
> Remembering how he saw those Germans run,
> Screaming for mercy among the stumps of trees:
> . . .
> Our chaps were sticking 'em like pigs ....' O hell!'
> He thought – 'there's things in war one dare not tell
> Poor father sitting safe at home, who reads
> Of dying heroes and their deathless deeds.'[41]

But even when the soldiers are behaving in a seemly and heroic manner, their task remains that of killing their fellow-men. For Edlef

Köppen the ultimate daydream, 'diesen schwarzsamtnen, singenden Traum' – this black velvet, singing dream – is not, as one might expect, to be free of the risk of being killed, but to pass one whole day without killing – 'Einen Tag lang nicht töten'.[42] The speaker in Karl Stamm's 'Soldat vor dem Gekreuzigten' (A Soldier before the Crucified Christ) sees, scratched on the face of his enemy, the words, 'Mord, Mord', (murder) and he knows that he will never escape from that knowledge.[43] Oskar Kanehl states the equation simply: 'Ich bin Soldat und werde Mörder sein' (I am a soldier and shall become a murderer), and insists that any celebration of victory is a celebration of murder.[44] While Stamm's image, in particular, could relate to any war in which enemies are face to face, Paul Bewsher's 'Nox Mortis' places the problem in a specifically modern context – a bombing raid, where the speaker must cause death to pour down from the sky, filling 'nameless hearts with nameless sorrow' without even seeing his enemy.[45] Like other men of conscience who are caught between their duty to kill and their reluctance to do so, the airman in this poem can only pray for peace – and the poet himself can only write his poems and publish his views.

By ignoring the reality that heroism in war involves killing, patriotic poets and other exponents of the myth avoid having to make a commitment on the issue that troubles writers like Kanehl and Bewsher. Consequently, the guilt for performing the act of killing rests on the 'heroes' alone, not on the people who incited them to go to war, so that the burden the young men must bear is made yet heavier. Marc Larreguy de Civrieux's 'Debout les Morts!' (Let the Dead Arise!), written in September 1916 two months before the author's death, pleads on behalf of the dead that they should be relieved of at least a part of their burden. The words of the title are a favourite expression in French patriotic circles, and the poet draws attention to the function of this cliché by pretending to interpret it literally (though his message lies in the metaphorical usage):

Laissez-les donc dormir en paix,
Ces morts! Que vous ont-ils donc fait,
Pour être pourchassés dans leur funèbre asile?
Après avoir porté le faix
De tant de maux et de forfaits,
Après s'être damnés pour vos haines civiles,
Avoir sacrifié leur jeunesse et leur sang,
N'ont-ils pas le droit que le passant,
À leur trépas compatissant,
Les laisse enfin pourrir tranquilles?[46]

(Let them rest in peace, these dead! After all, what harm have they done you, that you pursue them even into their dark refuge? Having carried the burden of so many evils and so many forfeits, having damned themselves for your civic hatred, having sacrificed their youth and their blood, don't they have the right that the passer-by, sympathising with their sin, should leave them to decay quietly at last?)

Far from revelling in heroic immortality, the weary young combatants whom this compassionate speaker imagines wish only to be left in peace. After giving up their youth, their blood (whether in the sense of life or of progeny), and their conscience, they surely should not be required, he implies, to contribute also to whatever cause the patriotic zealots have in mind with their cry of 'Debout les Morts!' The form of rest that the poet calls for, however, is not the peace of the soul, but 'the eternal and kindly nothingness' of the decaying body:

Laissez-les donc dormir en paix,
Sous la terre glacée et les gazons épais,
Dans le bon nirvâna de leur suprême pose!
Afin qu'ils ne sentent jamais
Le ver en eux qui se repaît
Et par qui, lentement, leur chair se décompose!
Afin que jamais plus ils ne rouvrent leurs yeux,
Et qu'ils oublient ce monde odieux,
Au néant éternel et miséricordieux,
Où leur cadavre se repose!

(Let them sleep in peace, beneath the frozen earth and thick grass, in the comforting nirvana of their ultimate pose. So that they will never feel the worm feasting on them, slowly decomposing their flesh. So that they will never again open their eyes, and will forget this odious world, in favour of the eternal and kindly nothingness in which their corpse reposes.)

Through this mystical and yet realistic image of the decaying body, Larreguy de Civrieux implicitly denies any belief in the immortality of the soul, upon which the heroic myth depends. Yet by insisting that the dead have a continuing existence of some kind, he validates his own argument that, since the world was made odious for them, having now escaped from it they deserve peace.

Like Larreguy de Civrieux, Charles Sorley was a young combatant surrounded by death, writing poems that explore its meaning, and Sorley, too, concluded that the heroic immortality preached by the myth was not part of his vision. If the French poet seems to have resolved for himself the problem of the form of continuing existence, Sorley has not. He knows 'the end not yet', that death is not simply

'Life effete, / Life crushed', but otherwise for him death is an unknown land, 'a homeless land and friendless' possibly, but one that he is prepared to explore.[47] He is convinced, however, as Bernard Bergonzi observes, of the 'absolute "otherness" of death, of the lack of any possible rapport between the dead and the living, or even between the past and the present of those who have died:[48]

> Ghosts do not say
> 'Come, what was your record when you drew breath?'
> But a big blot has hid each yesterday.

In his last poem, the sonnet 'When you see millions of the mouthless dead', Sorley strips away one by one the consolatory devices that the living find in the myth of heroic death:

> Say not soft things as other men have said,
> That you'll remember. For you need not so.
> Give them not praise. For deaf, how should they know
> It is not curses heaped on each gashed head?
> Nor tears. Their blind eyes see not your tears flow.
> Nor honour. It is easy to be dead.
> Say only this, 'They are dead.' Then add thereto,
> 'Yet many a better one has died before.'[49]

In comparison with 'Debout les Morts!' this poem sounds almost brutal in its denial of the myth: firstly towards the living, who are urged both to recognise that they have no connection with the dead, and to admit to the emptiness of phrases like Binyon's 'We will remember them'; and secondly towards the dead themselves, whose efforts in life go totally unrewarded, even by a 'kindly nothingness'. From Sorley's recognition that 'it is easy to be dead', to the attitude towards death in some of the English poetry of the Second World War, with what Fussell calls its 'laconic refusal to reach out to any myth', is a direct path.[50] In this sense Sorley appears more modern than most other First World War protest poets, who often replace one myth with another, and who, at the very least, feel that the death of others must retain some meaning – even if, as in Owen's 'Anthem for Doomed Youth', traditional religious symbol and ritual are transmuted into elements more appropriate for 'these who die as cattle' or, as in 'Debout les morts', their slow and peaceful putrefaction must be respected.

Yet on the evidence of these two poems one might argue that, in one sense at least, Larreguy de Civrieux is more perceptive than Sorley: in his fuller appreciation of the function of the heroic myth. It is safe to assume that neither poet believes veneration will in any way affect the dead, but the poems imply different interpretations of its purpose for the living. Sorley seems to suggest that its function is primarily to console those who 'remember', and, if he has a propagandist intent, it is to urge people to reject the patriotic–heroic ethic as a lie – a move that, in practical terms, will presumably make them less eager to promote the sacrifice of the young men they know. Larreguy de Civrieux, on the other hand, reaches beyond the individual level to object not only to the myth itself, for its dire effects upon the young men, but also to the way it is sustained in society, and especially to its propagation through its victims. Ghosts may indeed not ask, 'What was your record?' but for the kind of people whom 'Debout les Morts!' addresses, the records and stories of dead soldiers are important; and their name, to misquote another patriotic cliché, must appear to live for ever, in order to uphold the belief that heroic sacrifice brings special rewards. Without the contribution that, according to Larreguy de Civrieux's reasoning, the dead are forced to make, the task of maintaining the ethic would be much more difficult for its proponents.

Although it is unlikely that Bertolt Brecht read 'Debout les Morts!' before the end of the war, his 'Legende vom toten Soldaten' (Legend of the Dead Soldier) carries to its logical conclusion the attitude to which Larreguy de Civrieux objects. Brecht's satirical 'folk-ballad', written in 1918, tells how the Kaiser, disappointed that his heroes die so quickly, gives orders that one of them should be resurrected.[51] The soldier's corpse is treated to make it look more respectable and to disguise the smell, and then it is paraded through the streets, a symbol of the fatuity of the 'fight to the finish' principle, and proof of the vulnerability of society to manipulation in the guise of the veneration of heroes. While Brecht makes his point by extending to a ridiculous extreme the concept of the exploitation of the dead, Helen Hamilton has found in 'Ghouls' a related image that perfectly blends the metaphorical and the realistic. Her 'ghouls' are the old men who pore over the lists of war-casualties, looking for names they recognise:

> You strange old ghouls,
> Who gloat with dulled old eyes,
> Over those lists,
> Those dreadful lists,
> To see what name
> Of friend, relation,
> However distant,
> May be appended
> To your private Roll of Honour.[52]

Here, as in 'Debout les Morts!', more is required of the young men who have already given their lives: in this case, their names. In modern Western culture personal names are entrenched as the sign for the unique identity of the individual, a relationship so intimate that any conditions under which it is threatened or disregarded are considered to be dehumanising. When the 'ghouls' in Hamilton's poem place a name on their 'private Roll of Honour', they disrupt that relationship, for instead of functioning primarily as a reference to a particular young man and the fact of his tragically early death, the name becomes merely a series of words to be used for another purpose. Its value now lies in its usefulness to the old men, increasing their personal glory in a circle of people like themselves, who take gruesome pleasure in tallying the names of acquaintances who have been killed. Even after death, it is clear, the young victims are required to provide sustenance for their older compatriots:

Unknowingly you draw, it seems,
From their young bodies,
Dead young bodies,
Fresh life,
New value,
Now that yours are ebbing.
You strange old ghouls,
Who gloat with dulled old eyes,
Over those lists,
Those dreadful lists,
Of young men dead.

But Hamilton's image of the old as ghouls sucking blood from the corpses of the young may also be seen as a symbol for the country at large – for all the members of a nation that not only demands the death of its young men but also uses them in other ways to promote its cause. The ghouls are the poets who attach their words like parasites to the nation's 'warrior sons'; who glory, not in heroic action, but in sacrificial death; and who make a name for themselves with lines like 'Happy is England in the brave that die' or 'Herz, dein Glück sei Opfermut' (Heart, let your joy be the courage for sacrifice). And they are the readers who, without questioning the implications, take pleasure in such lines, helping to perpetuate both the poems and the creed of sacrificial death. They are the churchmen who condone and prolong the suffering by preaching for their own fulfilment the edicts of heroism and hatred, the women who add to their self-righteousness by handing out white feathers to the 'cowards', and the politicians and profiteers who promote the war and use it for their own advantage. They are, in effect, all the individuals, in all the combatant countries, who draw self-worth, 'Fresh life, / New value', from a conflict that is creating 'those lists, / Those dreadful lists' of eight million young men dead.

6

A few alone
Readers, non-readers and protest

And those – a few alone amid the mass of men –
Who see the gangrened spectral form upon the throne,
For what it is in truth,
And strive to tear away the enshrouding draperies,
They brand as liars and iniquitous,
At best as fibreless fools....

Anon., 'Europe – 1916'[1]

Although the ethic that lends respectability to the taking of life in battle is preached widely and vociferously in the patriotic poetry of the war, one fundamental precept of the heroic tradition is almost totally ignored: the old belief in a unique sense of comradeship amongst men who fight together, the intense loyalty of 'brothers in battle'. The reason for this omission is not difficult to perceive. While the poets and other wordmakers who promote the patriotic–heroic myth in the war often make a distinction between 'us' and the combatants, their intention is nevertheless to establish that 'they', the heroes, belong to the nation as a whole. This goal is clearly incompatible with the traditional heroic belief that the only true belonging, the comradeship amongst a special 'band of brothers', necessarily excludes those who did not take part in the battle. To insist that combatants share an exclusive companionship is therefore to protest implicitly against the claim of civilians to be part of the unique fraternity.

But in order to make use of this device, protest poets must voice support for one of the principles of a creed that they otherwise reject. The result is a note of ambivalence, which sometimes approaches a commitment to war – in Robert Graves' 'Two Fusiliers', for example:

Show me the two so closely bound
As we, by the wet bond of blood,
By friendship blossoming from mud,
By Death: we faced him, and we found

Beauty in Death,
In dead men, breath.[2]

In keeping with tradition, the special comradeship that this speaker
describes validates the suffering from which it arose, with something
akin to the 'bloodlust' that Graves deplores in 'A Dead Boche', and
with an image of death far removed from the usual realism of protest
poetry. One can appreciate the appeal of such an uncommon bond of
friendship as a consolatory device, in a war that offered few consola-
tions; and no doubt many people would argue that the comradeship
of the trenches was fact rather than myth, the consequence of the
close physical proximity, shared hardships, and sense of isolation as a
community that characterised trench warfare. In this regard, it may
be significant that one of the few poems to denigrate this aspect of the
heroic tradition, Alfred Lichtenstein's 'Gebet vor der Schlacht', was
written in August 1914, before trench living became the predominant
feature of army experience in the war. On the other hand, one cannot
ignore the fact that Graves' diction in 'Two Fusiliers' has much more
in common with patriotic verse than with his 'factual' poem 'The
Leveller', while the fusiliers themselves are certainly far less con-
vincingly real than the sergeant 'with bristling chin and whiskered
hands' in the latter. A similar problem arises with Owen's 'Greater
Love', where the poet's determination to distinguish between com-
batants and civilians leads him to the standard (but for Owen highly
uncharacteristic) patriotic phrase, 'the English dead'. If these are
intended as poems of protest, one can only conclude that the 'brothers
in battle' concept is too close to the heroic tradition to be an effective
protest device in its own right. Had he lived, the more cynical Lichten-
stein might well have continued to promote the unromantic view of
war, by insisting that becoming a soldier does not automatically
eradicate the innate self-interest in man.

The exclusive friendship amongst combatants, however, is only one
of several devices that protest poets use as a means of demarcating
between 'the fighting men' and the civilian population of the country.
The same function is served when they counter the highmindedness
of civilians by claiming for combatants alone such principles as 'gentle-
ness' and love for one's fellow men, or when they explicitly reject the
predominantly civilian precepts of patriotic heroism. Portraying civil-
ians as manipulators and combatants as victims reinforces the division.
The physical distance between the Front and home is demonstrated in
poems that describe the terrible reality of the other world, and it is
echoed in the mental distance that the soldiers of the protest poetry
perceive between themselves and those who have not shared their
experience. Georges Chennevière insists in 'L'Étranger' (The stranger)

that the two worlds are totally irreconcilable; a man who has travelled in the land of red suffering can never forget that other existence, and he belongs no more in the country of home:

> Je reviens du pays de la souffrance rouge
> Et de la reine mort.
> Je ne l'ai pas quitté, puisqu'il me suit toujours
> Et m'attend à la porte.
>
> Je ne suis plus d'ici; je suis un étranger
> Qui ne s'arrête pas.[3]

(I have returned from the land of red suffering, whose queen is death. I have not left it, since it follows me everywhere and is waiting for me outside the door. I belong here no more; I am a stranger who can never stay anywhere.)

In its ultimate form the combatant–civilian division is described in terms of a complete realignment of loyalties – an international version of the familiar 'two nations' concept that became popular through retrospective writings about the war. Boundaries between nations are replaced by a new 'Partage de l'humanité par la guerre' (dividing-up of humanity by the war), as Pierre Drieu la Rochelle calls it, with all the combatants, regardless of official nationality, as a single international community, in opposition to all the people not on active service – 'les combattants et les non-combattants'.[4] The basis of the new allegiance, to which (amongst many other poems) Gerrit Engelke's 'An die Soldaten des großen Krieges' attests, is the awareness of shared suffering:

> Lagst du bei Ypern, dem zertrümmerten? Auch ich lag dort.
> Bei Mihiel, dem verkümmertern? Ich war an diesem Ort.
>   [. . .]
> Mit dir im Schnee vor Düneburg, frierend, immer trüber,
> An der leichenfressenden Somme lag ich dir gegenüber.[5]

(Were you at Ypres, that shattered city? I lay there, too. And at ruined Mihiel? I was also there. I was with you in the snow before Dunaburg, freezing, more and more gloomy; I lay opposite you by the corpse-devouring Somme.)

In this new alignment, animosity amongst the soldiers has been replaced by a sense of brotherhood, and hatred of the country's enemies is confined to civilians. Opponents have become paradoxical 'mein Bruder Feind' (my foe, my brother) and 'the enemy you killed, my friend', while the new enemy is the civilian population of the country in question – or of all countries, since the 'partage de l'humanité par la guerre' is total.[6]

So convincingly is the realignment of loyalties presented that one is tempted to accept these poems as a reflection of the actual situation: to believe, for instance, that the troops *en masse* regarded home as an alien place, or that they were on the point of laying down their weapons to fraternise with the enemy. In reality, however, like many other facets of the collective memory of the war, these perceptions became more distinct with hindsight. Admittedly it is not unusual to find in combatant writings from the war years an expression of sympathy for the enemy, especially in conjunction with the recognition that the men on the opposing side are ordinary people, with homes and families. And some letters and journals reiterate the sense of estrangement that Chennevière captures in 'L'Étranger', in particular an awareness of the incredible mental distance between home and the 'pays de la souffrance rouge'. Nevertheless, for most writers leave is something to be savoured and treasured, with a new appreciation for the pleasures of home, and with only a passing thought for the companionship of the Front. (It is worth noting that in Drieu la Rochelle's 'partage de l'humanité', soldiers on leave are placed on the side of 'les non-combattants'.) Furthermore, so long as political decision-makers allowed the war to continue, the new international brotherhood of the trenches could be nothing more than a dream – as many poets acknowledged. Despite their mutual sympathy, the fraternal enemies continued to fire on each other, and two talented combatant poets from opposing sides who gave voice to the dream were killed in the same region of northern France within the last month of the war. Gerrit Engelke died on 13 October 1918, in an English field-hospital at Cambrai, of a wound received the previous day, and Wilfred Owen was killed on November 4, as the men in his charge were attempting to cross the Sambre canal.

Not only was the exclusive kinship amongst combatants, whether national or international, less pervasive than the mythology of the war suggests, but in other respects, too, the gap between combatant and civilian attitudes was narrower than many of the protest poems pretend, or than the after-the-event promoters of the 'two nations' concept maintain. The accepted picture contrasts civilian ignorance with combatant knowledge, and continuing bellicosity at home with the combatants' growing pacifism. While one cannot doubt that the soldiers' experience at the Front was far beyond the comprehension of most people who had not seen action, civilians were by no means uninformed about the reality of the war – as, indeed, one sees from poems like Helen Hamilton's 'The Romancing Poet'. News reports certainly veiled the facts, but casualty lists gave an indication of the massive scale of the destruction, and the large number of severely wounded and handicapped men returning from the Front bore witness to the devastating effects of modern weapons. Meanwhile, civilian protest in all three countries – and not only in poetry – was quite as extensive as that amongst combatants (apart from the short-lived French army mutiny of 1917). Yet the image of the wartime situation that some of the combatant protest poetry offers – an image that has survived in popular memory – makes no allowance for any deviation from the two extreme positions.

As far as the English collective memory of the war is concerned, one of the most influential figures in establishing the generally-accepted 'binary' model is Siegfried Sassoon, whose two series of retrospective autobiographical writings reinforce what his poems demonstrate – a totality of opposition between combatant and civilian attitudes. Sassoon's wartime letters and diaries, however, present a considerably more moderate picture, since these contemporary responses make it very clear that the author's protest, though it was aroused by his combatant experience, matured in the company of civilians, and with their encouragement and support. A letter that Sassoon wrote in early October 1917 to his friend Robbie Ross (himself a civilian) reveals quite distinctly the difference between the actual situation and the image that the poet wishes to promote. Sassoon reports that he has written 'a *very good* sonnet', which he has sent to Harold Massingham, the editor of *The Nation*: 'It is called "Glory of Women" – and gives them beans.'[7] Until Catherine Reilly's anthology helped finally to dispel the myth about women's attitudes in the war (at least as far as war-poetry criticism is concerned), the poem served for several decades not only to exemplify the animosity of combatants towards women, but also to sustain the prevalent belief that women were unanimous and ardent flag-wavers. Yet in the same letter in which he rejoices in his condemnation of women in general, Sassoon tells of an invitation to lunch with Margaret Sackville, whom he describes as 'a rival to Lady Ottoline; and quite ten years younger' – Lady Ottoline Morrell being, like Sackville, a leading pacifist organiser. Although the letter gives evidence of his acquaintance with two women deeply involved in the anti-war movement – and he certainly knew others through his contact with Morrell's circle – Sassoon chooses in the poem to ignore the truth as he knows it, and to pretend that all women refuse to acknowledge the reality of the war. For his poetic purpose, total opposition between combatants and others is necessary, and in this case the chosen opponents are women. (One wonders whether Massingham found the attack too extreme, for the poem first appeared, not in *The Nation*, but in the *Cambridge Magazine* in December.) To the extent that 'Glory of Women' has been regarded as a model of the true situation during the war, Sassoon might be considered guilty of 'misrepresentation'. One must remember, however, that his poem is intentional propaganda, and that propagandists cannot afford to be afraid of overstating their case. Rather, the accusation of misrepresenting the facts must be directed at those readers who, taking the protest poets at their word in their claim to 'tell the truth', have used poems like 'Glory of Women' as historical evidence of civilian ignorance.

For a variety of possible reasons – because propaganda literature in the present century has been stigmatised for its service to totalitarian regimes, or because modern poetry criticism regards the didactic element as inimical to the aesthetic ideal and the favoured concept of the 'autonomous text', or even because one tends to take as fact, rather than propaganda, those statements of opinion with which one agrees – the propagandist aspect of the protest verse has been minimised in the English war poetry studies. A simple explanation is offered for the working of the poetry as propaganda: the writer, inspired by his recognition of the immense destructiveness of modern warfare, seeks to inform the civilian world of the facts. Otherwise the propagandist function receives little attention, nor is there any attempt to explain a major discrepancy between this description, with its emphasis on the poet's intention to inform, and the evidence of the poetry itself. To inform implies a desire to narrow the gap between the ignorance of one party and the knowledge of the other – in the present case, to bring civilian readers nearer to the poet's own understanding of what the combatants are suffering. Yet Sassoon's letter about 'Glory of Women' suggests a different purpose; the poem is designed, it seems, not to enlighten women by informing them of the truth, but to 'give them beans' – to berate or reprimand them. Its primary effect is to draw attention to the distance between combatant and civilian attitudes – between the soldiers who know that 'British troops retire', for instance, and the women who refuse to believe such sacrilege. And because the potential audience is also the butt of disapprobation and ridicule, there is little reason to hope that the poem will bring the two sides closer together.

When Joseph Cohen writes of Sassoon that 'his rash attacks alienated many whom he might otherwise have induced to accept his point of view', he implies that Sassoon thoughtlessly allowed his anger to interfere with the effectiveness of his poetry, which accordingly failed to fulfill its propagandist purpose.[8] Both Cohen's remark and its implication are applicable to the protest verse in general, for there can be no doubt about the poets' anger, nor about the alienating effect of their poetry upon potential civilian readers. Yet it appears highly improbable that so many capable poets, in circumstances that precluded or minimised the possibility of international influence, should have made precisely the same error of judgement, in failing to recognise the inadequacy of their persuasive method. Moreover, Sassoon himself, on the evidence of his self-congratulation about his *'very good* sonnet', is far from sharing the critic's view that his propaganda is destined to failure; his intention is to 'give them beans', and he unquestionably succeeds. The discrepancy between the accepted view of the poets' purpose – to win the support of the population at large by telling them the truth about the war – and the intention that is evident in their poetry – to condemn rather than to convince – leads one to wonder whether the functioning of this propaganda of protest is really so straightforward as critics have tended to assume. Fortunately, an alternative explanation, which takes full account of the poets' apparent wish to alienate the civilian reading public, is not hard to find, and it indicates that, far from making an error of judgement, writers like Sassoon and Martinet, Becher and Arcos, were well aware of their propagandist goal, and understood fully how it was to be realised.

While almost any poem that is consensually recognised as a work of protest would be suitable to demonstrate the propagandist process (including many of Sassoon's), 'Recruiting', by E.A. Mackintosh, is particularly useful because it exemplifies many of the features I have identified in the previous two chapters. Mackintosh, according to Brian Gardner's biographical note, left Oxford to join the Seaforth Highlanders, and was killed in 1917, when he was twenty-four. Other poems by this author explore, usually with a tone of pity rather than of explicit protest, the feeling of community amongst combatants. In 'Before the Somme', for example, the speaker envisions the 'broken regiments' that will return after the battle, and he hopes that he, too, will be 'lying there in wind and mud and rain' instead of surviving when his friends are dead. And 'In Memoriam' merges compassion for the father of one of the privates in the speaker's company – the work on the hill-farm left undone 'Because of an old man weeping' for an only son who will not return – with his own lament for his 'fifty sons', the young men who called to him, their officer, for help and pity, 'That could not help at all'.[9] In 'Recruiting', however, good comradeship is placed in direct opposition to the cowardice and dishonesty of civilians.[10] The poem is divided, appropriately enough, into two sections, of which the first deals largely with civilians and the second with combatants:

'Lads, you're wanted, go and help,'
On the railway carriage wall
Stuck the poster, and I thought
Of the hands that penned the call.

Fat civilians wishing they
'Could go and fight the Hun.'
Can't you see them thanking God
That they're over forty-one?

Girls with feathers, vulgar songs –
Washy verse on England's need –
God – and don't we damned well know
How the message ought to read.

'Lads, you're wanted!' Over there
Shiver in the morning dew,
More poor devils like yourselves
Waiting to be killed by you.

Go and help to swell the names
In the casualty lists.
Help to make a column's stuff
For the blasted journalists.

Help to keep them nice and safe
From the wicked German foe.
Don't let him come over here!
'Lads, you're wanted – out you go.'

Mackintosh makes it clear that, although the poster's message comes
in anonymous form, the people responsible for it can and should be
identified. His list offers several civilian 'stock types' that recur in the
protest poetry – 'fat' men (whether physically or financially), 'jingo-
women', and journalists – and he reiterates some popular objections,
including the complaint that such people deliberately pervert the
meaning of words in order to manipulate others. He accuses them of
cowardice, hypocrisy, and selfishness, and he dismisses their heroes
as 'poor devils' simply waiting to be killed. Mackintosh's view of
combatants and their way of life, however, is no less standardised:

There's a better word than that,
Lads, and can't you hear it come
From a million men that call
You to share their martyrdom?

Leave the harlots still to sing
Comic songs about the Hun,
Leave the fat old men to say
Now *we've* got them on the run.

Better twenty honest years
Than their dull three score and ten.
Lads, you're wanted. Come and learn
To live and die with honest men.

You shall learn what man can do
If you will but pay the price,
Learn the gaiety and strength
In the gallant sacrifice.

Take your risk of life and death
Underneath the open sky.
Live clean or go out quick –
Lads, you're wanted. Come and die.

The two groups represent polarities quite as extreme as any in patriotic verse, with 'strength', 'gaiety', 'the open sky', 'risk', 'Live clean' and, above all, 'honest', on the one hand, in opposition to 'fat', 'dull', indoors (implied in the music hall reference, for instance), 'safe', 'harlots', 'vulgar' and hypocrisy on the other. So intent is Mackintosh on emphasising the difference that his representation of the soldiers' life comes full circle, back to the myth itself – the image of the soldiers as, without exception, fine upstanding young men participating in 'the gallant sacrifice'.

Even so, the line that separates 'us' from 'them' is thickly drawn. Mackintosh's tone in general is deliberately offensive, as he belittles the civilians in many ways, dismisses their poetry as 'washy verse', and accuses them of dishonestly claiming a share in the soldiers' success. When he says 'God – and don't we damned well know' he employs language which one must assume he knows to be unacceptable to a large number of potential readers. Nor is he averse to using sarcasm against them, urging the 'lads' to volunteer so that they can help to keep the despised civilians 'nice and safe / From the wicked German foe'. One is reminded very forcefully of the many patriotic poems that speak of the enemy in the same tone, with invective and insult, sarcasm, and a totality of biased words that allow for only a black-and-white viewpoint. While the war poems of William Watson and those of Wilfred Owen are not usually discussed on the basis of similarities (since the writers appear to represent opposing sides in all the major dichotomies), poetry like theirs definitely invites comparison as two kinds of propaganda. Fussell maintains rightly that 'civilised ambiguity' is one of the first victims of war, and certainly it has no part in the battle that the propagandist poets wage, whether in the primary campaign on behalf of their country, or in this

secondary conflict against the people who use the war and the com-
batants for their own ends.

The analogy between poetry and warfare, however, is not entirely
appropriate, because, as I suggested earlier in connection with patriotic
verse, the shafts that propaganda poets aim at their enemy in these
verbal battles are not, apparently, designed to reach as far as the
enemy's lines. The use of sarcasm is a case in point. Like other forms
of irony, sarcasm involves a distinction between knowing and lack of
knowledge, in that the words may, in theory at least, be taken at their
face value by the unknowing, but the *cognoscenti* appreciate the author's
intended meaning. The inference is that the poet is writing for an
implied reader who shares his or her knowledge and outlook, and
that there is no desire to be conciliatory towards the victims of the
attack. Invective, too, suggests divisiveness rather than persuasion,
and that effect is enhanced if the poet uses a language that the enemy
does not understand. When 'Caliban' writes sarcastically of 'Tommy
Atkins' as 'feinste Kultur unter Lack' (highly cultured – under the
varnish), or when William Watson makes his superbly vituperative
comments about the Kaiser ('Thou sceptred Smear / Across the Day'),
these poets clearly have no intention of trying to convert the opposing
side to their way of thinking, nor, because of the language barrier, do
they more than pretend that the enemy will read their poems. While
they may hope ultimately to annihilate the enemy's position, the
immediate function of their writing is to reinforce the feeling of
animosity in their compatriots – that is, in people who are already
sympathetic to the cause. This intended audience is represented in the
text by the implied reader, an imaginary figure who shares the poet's
knowledge and taste. But because animosity is the original reason for
the poem's existence, authors like Watson and 'Caliban' write with a
close eye upon the opposition – the enemy whom, for the fulfilling of
their purpose of unifying their compatriots, they must appear to wish
to offend. This enemy is obviously not to be equated with the poet's
sympathetic implied reader; on the contrary, it seems that these
poems posit also an 'implied non-reader', an entity deliberately and
thoroughly excluded from the circle of the poet's intended audience.

In that 'Recruiting' employs many of the same devices as patriotic
verse – sarcasm, invective, the elimination of ambiguity, amongst
others – its position with regard to reader and 'non-reader' must be
seen in the same light. The implied reader (perhaps to be identified
with 'you' in the first section of the poem), like the 'we' audience of
patriotic verse, is sympathetic to the poet's viewpoint and able to
appreciate the deliberately provocative nature of his approach. This
poem, too, posits excluded non-readers: not the official enemy, but
the civilian manipulators, the supporters of the myth and preservers

of the social status quo, whom the poet designs to shock or anger, by attacking the very precepts that they hold most dear. The easy assumption that protest poets were intent on conveying their knowledge of the war to the civilian world at large does not accord well with the extreme animosity in their poetry, yet their goal was certainly to spread their message, and to draw others to their way of thinking. And since their purpose was clearly not to convince the people whom they viewed with so much animosity, their intended audience must be the real-life counterpart of their sympathetic 'implied reader'. The alienation that Cohen regrets in Sassoon's writing is not an unfortunate accident, but a vital factor in the poet's propagandist technique. His poetry, after the manner of patriotic verse – or after the manner of a politician's speech to a crowd of his supporters – works by reinforcing the attitude of the like-minded, rather than by attempting to convert the enemy, and it depends on animosity to help establish the identity of both the included and the excluded group. The 'many' whom (according to Cohen) Sassoon failed to convince – such people as Owen's 'dullards whom no cannon stuns', Martinet's often-maligned 'civils', and 'die fetten Eunuchen des Himmelspalastes' (the fat eunuchs of the heavenly palace) who have banished 'den bärtigen Jesu Christ' (the bearded Jesus Christ) in Hans Koch's 'Karfreitag 1915' (Good Friday, 1915) – are in fact quite as much outside the realm of persuasion as the 'non-readers' of Watson's 'To the German Emperor' or Lissauer's 'Haßgesang gegen England.'[11]

Accordingly, one must reconsider the question of the intended audience of protest poetry. J.H. Johnston is representative of the generally-accepted view, when he writes that 'the poet who had some prospect of publishing his verse' regarded his mission as being 'to communicate his sense of the reality of war to the millions at home who could not or would not appreciate the magnitude of the experiences and sacrifices of the common soldier'.[12] Since Johnston is obviously concerned here, not with the literary theorist's implied reader, but with the practicalities of 'some prospect' of publication and a 'ready public outlet' (a phrase he uses in the same connection), one is justified in asking to what extent this assessment of the poets' goal may be taken as valid. It seems improbable that writers whose 'ready public outlet' was *The New Statesman* or *The Workers' Dreadnought* imagined they were communicating with millions of readers, just as it is doubtful whether any soldier-poet submitting his work to *Die Aktion* expected that a vast number would read that 'by-subscription-only' magazine. Nor can one unhesitatingly assume that, given the choice, the poets would have preferred to publish in a large-circulation journal like the *Daily Express* or *Der Tag*. Bertolt Brecht, concerned under much more difficult circumstances with propagating unacceptable material (in Germany during the Nazi regime) listed

five problems associated with the writing of the truth ('Fünf Schwierig-
keiten beim Schreiben der Wahrheit') and amongst them was the
requirement that the writer must have 'the judgement to select the
people in whose hands the truth will be effective'.[13] Although the
protest poets of the Great War were far less restricted by censorship
and the threat of imprisonment than Brecht's fellow-subversives in
1935, their propaganda was nevertheless designed to subvert the
official and widely-accepted viewpoint. And as the poets recognised,
such truth would be effective only within a relatively limited circle.
Publications catering to 'the millions' during the war were unlikely to
print poems like Sassoon's 'Great Men' and Kanehl's 'Soldatenmiß-
handlung', but the failure to reach a mass audience was no handicap
to the poets. Their work was designed (both as text and as commodity)
to appeal to a small and sympathetic group of readers, and 'the truth'
would be spread as the circle expanded gradually through personal
or semi-personal contact.

For poets such as Watson and Lissauer the use of their mother-
tongue, serving, as language does, to exclude as well as to unite,
immediately makes clear the identity of their intended audience and
of the excluded group of 'non-readers'. (Hence the fact that the
various terms for *patria* are rarely ambiguous, even when the country
is not named.) Since this convenient device is not available when the
two sides share the same language, the protest poets must rely on
animosity itself to set up a comparable barrier between those who
sympathise with their cause and those who oppose it. Many of them
evidently feel that insult, sarcasm, and a direct rebuttal of the
opponent's ethic are not enough, and they often turn to deliberately
non-poetic language to help establish the divergence of their poetry
from the norms of the other society. When Mackintosh overtly rejects
euphemism and hypocrisy, he chooses a conversational tone and
down-to-earth vocabulary – not inherently shocking, but likely to
have an alienating effect upon readers attuned to poetry in the high-
sounding manner of William Watson and Albrecht Schaeffer. (Even a
sympathetic contemporary critic, Sturge Moore, found Sorley's lan-
guage 'poor and thin'.[14]) And it is not uncommon to observe protest
poets resorting, as Mackintosh does, to mild profanity in their deter-
mination to make their poetry as foreign as possible to devotees of
patriotic verse. Welland traces the evolution of the last line of Owen's
'The Chances' in the manuscript, from 'The old, old lot' via 'The
ruddy lot' to 'The bloody lot'; the ultimate 'solitary epithet', Welland
says, 'intensifies the protest'.[15]

The result in general is a tone of irreverence, strongly reminiscent
of folksongs of social or political protest, where a 'thumb-to-nose'
attitude towards the established order, in addition to being a part of

the doctrine of the cause, helps to unite the audience in a mood of defiance. Particularly relevant examples are to be found amongst Irish rebel songs from the time of the 1916 Dublin uprising. 'The Recruiting Sergeant', for instance, is the tale of a man whose task is made impossible, when the young Irishmen he approaches declare,

> We're not going out to Flanders, o!
> There's fighting in Dublin to be done;
> Let your sergeants and commanders go.
>
> Let Englishmen for England fight,
> 'Tis just about time they started, o!

Dominic Behan reports that 'In 1917, 14 young men were sentenced to terms of from six to twelve months for singing this ' "seditious" ballad' – another indication (if one is needed) that such an approach is divisive rather than persuasive.[16] There is also an obvious parallel between protest poetry and the tradition that soldiers' songs, of the Great War and others, are often profane and disrespectful; they, too, work to unify and encourage one group, while excluding others, but they differ from both patriotic verse and protest poetry in that they maintain simultaneously two distinct enmities, the official enemy and the 'powers-that-be', with the implication that the ordinary soldier is caught in the middle. That the songs persist in spite of the soldier's powerlessness to alter his circumstances is perhaps an indication that the value of derogatory poetry and song lies to a large extent in the palliative effect of name-calling.

Not all the protest poems owe their provocative tone to a folksong manner, however. The idea of disturbing the *Bürger* or 'Philistines' was also an inheritance from immediately pre-war avant garde artistic circles, and from various nineteenth-century predecessors, so that, for instance, simply to write in free verse instead of adhering to a recognisable metric pattern was on the whole to place oneself on the side of the dissenters. In German poetry the effect of being a rebel was increased both before and during the war by the Expressionists' preference for Roman instead of Gothic print, to the extent that a mere glance at the printed page usually gives an indication of the poet's attitude towards the war and the established order. The context of publication also has its effect in making a work seem seditious. Even in a peacetime situation certain journals were proud to be regarded as provocative – *Blast*, for instance, or the American poetry magazine *Others*. Ortheil quotes from a mocking newspaper review of a June 1914 poetry-reading in which Wilhelm Klemm took part. The reviewer notes the harmless-looking surroundings – 'it doesn't *look* so very revolutionary' – but reminds his readers that the organisers of the event are Franz Pfemfert and his associates in *Die Aktion*, and, he continues, 'for that reason, we can expect terrible things to happen'.[17] (The mild-looking and bespectacled Klemm is the first of the 'furchtbar wilden Dichter', the fearfully wild writers, to be called upon to read.) That particular authors allowed themselves to be identified with magazines like *Die Aktion* during the war was certainly enough to give an aura of rebelliousness to work that was perhaps not intrinsically protest writing.

A relevant footnote to the discussion about readers and 'non-readers' is the case of the Munich magazine *Simplicissimus*, noted before the war for its satirical attacks upon the Establishment. When war was declared the staff of the journal, which was edited by Ludwig Thoma, agreed that this would be no time to continue promoting divisiveness, and they assumed that the magazine would voluntarily cease publication. The director, however, offered an alternative – that the journal should continue as before, but that the writers and cartoonists should redirect their satire towards the country's enemies. Unfortunately, with regard to poetry at least, the move was not entirely successful; presumably because the writers (including Peter Scher, to whom Lichtenstein's 'Abschied' was dedicated) were accustomed to taking an anti-Establishment stance, and to writing provocatively about 'non-readers' close at hand, they had difficulty in finding a technique appropriate for their new situation, in which they were spokesmen for the majority against an enemy from whom they were in no danger of retribution. Lacking the bombastic and grandiloquent rhetoric that characterises the most successful invective against the official enemy, their attacks sound petty and unconvincing, and their pre-war satire gives place to sarcasm. Although *Simplicissimus* continued to publish and even gained new popularity in some quarters, it lost many former readers in the process, as well as much of the respect in which it had been held in the literary community before the war.[18]

Like sarcasm and profanity, the realism of the protest poetry may be regarded as an alienating device. In part, its value as a divisive element lay in its necessary rejection of the restrictive conventions of poetic language, but equally important was the poets' apparent urge to shock by telling the truth. Looking back upon the period, and on his own and Owen's writing, Sassoon observed,

Let it be remembered that, when this [Owen's 'The Show'] was written, all truthful reportings of experience were regarded as unpatriotic and subversive to the War Effort. Officialdom suppressed, and the great majority of non-combatants shunned and resented, such revelations. Sensitive people couldn't bear to be told the facts.[19]

Though the ignorance of civilians was probably less total than Sassoon's recollection suggests, his assessment of Owen's motive is undoubtedly accurate: to report the facts was deliberately to offend those imagined representatives of the 'other side'. The single feature that characterises most of the poems in Franz Pfemfert's 1914–1916 anthology is their factual picture of the war. Although Pfemfert does not state explicitly that he regards the poems as works of protest, he describes his book in his brief 'Afterword' as the 'refuge of an idea that nowadays is homeless' – presumably referring to his commitment to the cause of humanity that was driven from the pages of *Die Aktion* by the threat of censorship.[20] If realism was indeed Pfemfert's primary criterion for selecting poems for the anthology, one must conclude that he equates it with protest. Patrick Bridgwater makes the same equation, when he writes, 'The typical front-line poet of the First World War portrays the suffering and tragedy around him as an implicit, or – if he is a satirist – explicit protest against the war in which he is involved.'[21] In criticism of the English poetry, too, the prevalence of realistic description as a protest device has been emphasised. What Bergonzi says of Sassoon – that his main concern was 'to use poetry as a means of forcibly impressing on the civilian world some notion of the realities of front-line life' – is representative of the accepted view concerning the war poets in general, to the extent that realism has come to be regarded as the hallmark of protest. Yet although Sassoon's observation is at least partially valid, the claim of many commentators that realistic description of 'front-line life' was the main concern of the protest poets must be challenged, since it neither accounts for all the protest nor explains all the realism.

The term 'realism' in the English criticism appears to have two possible meanings. In its wider sense, which would encompass all of the protest poetry, it implies a readiness to view the war realistically: that is, without the idealisation inherent in the patriotic-heroic myth. J.M. Gregson uses the word in that way in his chapter-title 'Charles Sorley and the First Hints of Realism'. Its second and more common meaning refers to the attempt of poets 'to represent or to imitate observable realities' (to borrow a phrase from Michael Hamburger and Christopher Middleton); that is, to what Welland calls the poets' 'graphic fidelity', A.E. Lane the 'experiential actuality' of their writing, and Johnston their 'savage' or 'crude' or 'photographic' realism and 'their obsessive emphasis on isolated and irrelevant sensory detail'.[22] The consensus is that, as Lane phrases it, the poets wish to 'communicate a felt reality to those who, by accident or by choice, are cut off from this reality'.[23] The reality most of the critics refer to is that of life at the Front, but it is worth noting that some combatant poets apply the same 'graphic fidelity' to situations that civilians could easily observe for themselves. Sassoon's 'Does it Matter?' Owen's 'Disabled', and Piscator's 'Der Mutter zweier Söhne', for example, all deal with a reality that was actually less accessible to combatants than to civilians. Furthermore, as I have already argued, by no means all civilians are blind to such 'observable realities', especially with regard to the wounded and maimed. Apparently it is a mental attitude as much as the physical situation that cuts people off from these aspects of the 'felt reality' of the war.

While there is no doubt that realism in the war poetry is more common in the work of combatants than civilians, and that it is concerned primarily with details, frequently unpleasant, of life at the Front, a troubling inconsistency remains between the evidence of the realistic poetry and the insistence that it is designed above all to communicate the horrible truth to civilian readers. Johnston, who finds the First World War poetry insufficiently heroic, condemns it for its 'compulsive focus on the obscene details of crude animal needs and reactions, on wounds, death and decomposition'.[24] His comment, however, would apply much more accurately to prose writing about the war. The 'photographic realism' with which the poets apparently choose to introduce their readers and non-readers to the truth of the situation at the Front is decidedly less crude than that in many novels and memoirs of the war, or even in diaries and letters. Their preoccupation with sensory detail leads the poets only infrequently to deal at any length with unpleasant or sordid effects, almost as if a standard of acceptable conduct for poetry had been applied. Certainly Wilhelm Klemm's 'Lazarett' stands apart from most protest poems in any of the languages as an example of 'truthful reporting'. It describes the scene in a military hospital, where 'Jeden Morgen ist wieder Krieg' – every morning there is another battle – as the wounded are brought in:

Die Skala der Gerüche:
Die großen Eimer voll Eiter, Watte, Blut, amputierten
    Gliedern,
Die Verbände voll Maden. Die Wunden voll Knochen
    und Stroh.
. . .
Ein Darm hängt heraus. Aus einem zerrissenen Rücken
quoll die Milz und der Magen. Ein Kreuzbein klafft
    um ein Astloch,
Am Amputationsstumpf brandet das Fleisch in die Höhe.

Pilzartig wuchernd Ströme von hellgrünem Eiter
fließen; über das Fleisch herausragend
pulsiert der unterbundene Arterienstamm.[25]

(The scale of odours: the large pails full of pus, wadding, blood, amputated limbs. The bandages full of maggots. The wounds full of bone and straw. [. . .] A bowel is hanging out. From a torn back the spleen and stomach have spilled. A sacrum gapes around an arse-hole; on an amputated stump the gangrenous flesh swells up. Spreading like a fungus, streams of bright green pus flow; projecting beyond the flesh, the ligatured artery-stem pulsates.)

The use of objective medical terms increases the horror rather than reducing it, presumably because the diction is so convincingly that of a well-informed and truthful observer. By comparison with this horrifying picture, some of the most 'shocking' descriptions in the English poetry – Robert Graves' 'certain cure for boodlust', a 'dead Boche', who 'scowled and stunk / With clothes and face a sodden green', the 'naked sodden buttocks, mats of hair, / Bulged, clotted heads' of the corpses in Sassoon's 'Counter-Attack', or even an 'archipelago / Of corrupt fragments' through which the men must crawl in A.G. West's 'Night Patrol' – are quite bearable. The sensory detail of Owen's 'Dulce et Decorum est', another of the apparently more truthful poems in English, owes less to photographic realism than to the quest for poetic effect. The most shockingly realistic lines in that account of a soldier's death by gas tell how his blood comes

> gargling from the froth-corrupted lungs,
> Obscene as cancer, bitter as the cud
> Of vile, incurable sores on innocent tongues.

Neither the obscene cancer nor the vile sores belong to the scene, for the similes in which they occur are related only loosely to the visual or aural facts (and are incidentally, as Welland points out, a late amendment to Owen's manuscript).[26] The value of the second simile lies in part in providing a connotative link between the man's suffering and the vulnerability of the innocent 'children ardent for some desperate glory', thus emphasising the urgency of discrediting 'the old Lie'. Jon Silkin writes of Sassoon that 'The gap between the accepted or acceptable poetic norm and the facts themselves provides the energy with which his satire operates.'[27] A similar gap generates the power for Owen's protest, and for that of many other poets who appear to be chiefly concerned with 'the facts themselves'. In their writing the 'truth' *per se* is less important than the way it is used in juxtaposition with the 'poetic norm' of the myth. Accordingly, Ivor Gurney in 'To his Love' needs to resort to no more gory description than the words 'red wet / Thing' to produce a sense of horror, when he places this object that used to be a man in a pastoral and elegiac context, alongside 'memoried flowers' and the idea of noble death. Klemm's poem, on the other hand, lacks such juxtaposition of truth against myth, and as a result, it seems, must find the 'energy' for its protest in a more shocking kind of realism.

Yet oddly enough, apart from the presumably deliberate shock effects of its horrifying details, 'Lazarett' does not leave the impression of being a work of propaganda. It lacks the characteristic delineation between victims and manipulators, and it posits no excluded 'non-reader'. Nor has the persona anything in common with the impassioned speech-maker and spokesman who addresses the 'smug-faced crowds' in Sassoon's 'Suicide in Trenches', who speaks to and for the combatants in Mackintosh's 'Recruiting', or who pleads with the workers of Europe in Martinet's 'Tu vas te battre'. Klemm's persona is an impartial observer; although he is not totally outside the picture at which the simile in the second line of the poem hints ('Nackte Verwundete, wie auf alten Gemälden' – naked wounded, as in old paintings) – a doctor, perhaps, surveying the wounded and their surroundings, avoiding 'Die Fetzen geronnenen Blutes, auf denen man ausgleitet' (the patches of wet blood, on which one slips) – he refrains from partisan involvement in the suffering of individual patients. Further, unlike the similarly (though less starkly) realistic poems of Sassoon and Owen, 'Lazarett' does not measure the reality directly against the myth, or make any accusation of deceit. On the contrary, Klemm uses patriotic-heroic terms quite without irony, when he describes the sounds of dying:

und das Geheul, das Wimmern und Schrein, das
    Jammern und Flehen,
Das schweigende Heldentum und rührende: 'fürs
    Vaterland'.

(And the howling, the whimpering and shouting, the moaning and pleading, the silent heroism and the touching, 'For the Fatherland'.)

This ambivalence leads one to wonder whether shocking others into condemnation of the war was in fact the author's main intention. One encounters a similar problem with Isaac Rosenberg's poetry. 'Dead Man's Dump', for example, is to a considerable extent 'shockingly' realistic, with lines like 'The wheels lurched over sprawled dead' or 'a man's brains splattered on / A stretcher-bearer's face', but the realism is not turned into a comment on the patriotic–heroic myth.[28] There is certainly more compassion throughout this poem than in Klemm's, yet, as Silkin observes, there is no indication that Rosenberg considers himself to be a spokesman addressing a particular audience on behalf of other people, nor, one might add, is his poetry directed against a 'non-reader'.[29] Wandrey raises similar doubts about the intention of most of the realistic war poems in *Die Aktion* for, unlike other scholars whom he cites, he does not find this verse 'kriegskritisch' (critical of the war).[30] The difficulty is not entirely a matter of how an individual reader perceives the poems. In Klemm's case, for instance, the writer's personal attitude towards the war was ambivalent. While publishing in the radical *Aktion* as that journal's most prolific soldier-poet and the author of its first 'Verse vom Schlachtfeld' column, Klemm maintained contact with the magazine *Simplicissimus*, which had chosen not to take a stand against the war. His 1915 collection *Gloria! Kriegsgedichte aus dem Feld*, was published not by Pfemfert but by the firm of Albert Langen (the founder of *Simplicissimus*), whose poets were on the whole more conservative. (The book is printed in Gothic type.) Ortheil, in his monograph on Klemm, publishes for the first time a letter from Pfemfert to Klemm's wife where the editor reiterates his disagreement with the poet on the latter's refusal to condemn the country's participation in the war, but acknowledges that he still values Klemm 'as a poet and a private individual'.[31] Unlike Klemm, Isaac Rosenberg had no enthusiasm for the war, whether early or late. He volunteered out of poverty, with no hopeful ideals, and he found the situation at the Front to be even worse than he expected. Yet his letters echo the position implicit in his poetry. He is clearly suffering all the discomfort of training camp and the trenches, but his complaints are personal, and contain no hint of practical protest – the suggestion that something could be done, or that he might initiate some action. This is not, of course, intended as a criticism of Rosenberg, whose attitude is quite understandable in view of the problems he encountered – not least, that of persuading the army to pay the maintenance allowance it owed to his mother. Nevertheless, the absence of explicit propagandist intent, in both the poetry and the extra-literary attitude of two important writers who use realistic description, suggests that the equating of realism with protest should perhaps not be automatic.

To claim that Klemm and Rosenberg, who clearly have no illusions about the war, are not protest poets invites the question of what one means by 'protest' and, more basically, by 'propagandist intent'. The problem of distinguishing between propagandist and non-propagandist writing is raised by both C.M. Bowra and Michael Hamburger in studies that treat the First World War poetry in an international context. Although the two scholars use the term 'public' rather than 'propagandist', the question they address is the same as mine, and both place writing of this kind, as I do, in opposition to that which is 'personal' or 'private'. The co-existence of the two kinds is the major theme of *The Truth of Poetry*, where Hamburger argues that twentieth-century verse reflects two almost incompatible conceptions of poetry, both of them inherited from Baudelaire – the conviction, on the one hand, that 'the writing of poetry is an auto-nomous and autotelic activity', and, on the other, the concern with 'the public function of the arts as much as with their inner laws'.[32] Tracing the development of the two parallel streams, Hamburger suggests that 'The distinction between public and private poetry is valid if we apply it not so much to subjects or themes as to the relationship between poet and reader posited by the very structure and texture of poems on any subject whatsoever.'[33] Although he does not explain the terms 'structure' and 'texture', or indicate how they are special in 'public' poems, an inference may be drawn from his suggestion that English political poetry of the 1930s was 'hortatory or descriptive' rather than 'exploratory'. Unfortunately, however, Hamburger's discussion of the work of individual poets does not lead, on the whole, to generalisations that might be applicable to traditional as well as modern verse.

By contrast, a survey of features of traditional 'public' poetry is the starting-point for Bowra's *Poetry and Politics*, a study of some of the developments in political verse of the present century. Unlike Ham-burger, Bowra considers the poet's choice of subject-matter to be the primary criterion by which one may judge a poem to be 'public' or 'personal'. Poetry of the former kind 'deals with events which concern a large number of people, and can be grasped, not as immediate, personal experience, but as matters known largely from hearsay and presented in simplified and often abstract forms'.[34] It is, Bowra says, 'the antithesis of all poetry which deals with the special individual activity of the self', and he draws a contrast between 'conscious majesty and a cosmic outlook' on the one hand, and 'the careful presentation of private sensations and states of mind' on the other.[35] Bowra's 'public' category is certainly valid for the patriotic poetry of the war, where the 'we' persona precludes any explicit concern with 'the self', and it is applicable also to some works of protest, such as Kanehl's 'Krieg' or the poems of 'A.E.', which undoubtedly evince what Bowra terms 'wider vision' and 'public themes'. On the other hand, for many protest poems Bowra's thematic distinction is inappro-priate, since their focus is often deliberately narrow and tied to individual experience, yet the ultimate concern is not personal but public. Owen's 'Dulce et Decorum Est' is a case in point, for it relates an incident that is posited as a personal narrative and it tells of the consequences for the individuals involved, but it uses this personal account to validate a propagandist statement. Hamburger's distinc-tion on the basis of 'the relationship between poet and reader' has potentially a wider applicability, if one can describe in more specific terms the kind of relationship that is involved.

A useful starting point is to be found in Hamburger's discussion of the theory of poetry propounded by Gottfried Benn. Benn, as Hamburger points out, takes the extreme anti-propagandist view of the function of poetry. He insists that poets are not in a position to alter the world, nor should they attempt to do so. His ideal is the 'absolute' poem – 'the poem without belief, the poem without hope, the poem addressed to no-one, a poem made of words that you arrange in a fascinating manner' and he sees art as 'purely a phenomenon, with no historical effect, no practical consequences'.[36] The intent of propagandist poetry may be expressed in terms directly antithetical to Benn's quintessential 'art for art's sake' doctrine: propagandist poetry is closely linked with what one can assume to be the poet's hopes and beliefs; words are used to formulate a message, not purely for the pleasure of 'arranging' them; and the poem is directed specifically towards one or many readers. The poet strives, moreover, for the maximum in practical consequences and historical effectiveness, to the extent that the ultimate aim – to affect the reader's course of action – is entirely outside literature.

With regard to the war poetry, the poems that one unhesitatingly identifies as propagandist, whether for or against the country's involvement, leave one in no doubt about the author's beliefs and expectations. The immediate message is similarly clear, for the most obviously propagandist poems avoid what Hamburger calls an 'exploratory' approach, the arranging of words in a way that might impede comprehension. Most important, the 'relationship between poet and reader' implicit here is easy to perceive and describe, for it rests in the shared sense of animosity towards an alien group. The recognition that some people are excluded immediately determines the identity of the included group, while placing the limit of the intended audience. Meanwhile, the devices that underline this opposition, such as the 'we' persona of patriotic poetry and the deliberately provocative and alienating tone in much of the protest writing, serve to confirm that the speaker's hopes and beliefs are held in common with his or her community of readers. As the person responsible for reinforcing the distinction between opposing groups, the speaker becomes a spokesman, whether on behalf of compatriots in the patriotic writing, or on behalf of the victims in the poetry of protest. And because the voice speaks both to and for others, the tone is often (though not invariably) 'hortatory'. Between the extremes of Benn's anti-propagandist 'absolute' poem and the most rampantly propagandist war poetry, such as Lissauer's 'Haßgesang' or Martinet's attacks on civilians, lies an entire scale of possibilities, where poets use none, some, or all of the propagandist techniques. Although this description of the functioning of propaganda poetry in the war is oversimplified, it offers a possible measure of 'propagandist intent' and 'protest'. Propaganda is ultimately a matter of individual perception, but the presence (or absence) of identifiable textual elements helps to explain why some poems are perceived as propagandist by many readers, and why realism alone is a questionable propaganda device. The propagandist intention of poets who try to exclude their 'non-readers' solely through unpleasant description, without reinforcing their purpose by means of other protest techniques, is clearly not to be equated with that of, say, Martinet or Sassoon at their most bitter.

The weight that the English criticism has placed on realism as a protest device has led to the neglect of protest poems that do not present the 'observable realities' of the Front. The focus on excellence may indeed lead to a concentration on realistic verse, but there is reason to feel indignant that the substantially larger amount of non-realistic protest poetry in English has not been granted even the courtesy of a dismissal: it is simply ignored as if it did not exist. Yet in Bertram Lloyd's two protest anthologies, realists are decidedly in the minority. Of the more than fifty poems in each volume, only a quarter could be regarded as an attempt to familiarise readers with some aspect of the reality of life at the Front, and in each case, several of those are from one author, Sassoon. Amongst the remaining poems in the anthologies, there is a preponderance of what Hamburger, with reference to Trakl, calls 'archetypal rather than phenomenal' imagery.[37] Some of it is apocalyptic, depicting monstrous or demonic beings, biblical and classical prototypes of evil, war and death, or pageant-like scenes reminiscent of Brueghel or Bosch. These images are supplemented with a sprinkling of more commonplace representative figures such as mothers, soldiers, peasants and exploiters, and in general the poetry is highly allegorical. Instead of constructing a verbal world akin to the reality of the Front, and measuring it against some aspect of the patriotic-heroic myth, these visionary writers create a metaphor or allegory that reveals the accepted attitude towards war, or the war's effect on humanity, in its true light. T.W. Earp, for example, demonstrates the pointlessness and irrelevance of the conflict by ascribing its origin to three ancient kings, Arthur, Charlemagne and Barbarossa, playing a game of dice.[38] Margaret Sackville's 'pageant of triumphant War' is an endless procession led by the magnificent but masked figure of War, followed by his emissaries and the 'pitiful, bright army of the dead', down a startlingly white road, made from the dust of trampled bones.[39] Images of this kind are prevalent also in the protest poetry of the other two languages: Georg Trakl's 'Grodek', Kolbenheyer's 'Chronica II 1915', Hugo Ball's 'Totentanz' (Dance of Death); and many of the poems in the anthology *Les Poètes contre la guerre*, for instance, are in the same visionary mode. So widespread is allegorical or archetypal imagery that the technique which dominates Lloyd's anthologies clearly represents one of the main currents of the protest poetry, not the remote backwater to which English critical bias has condemned it by neglect.

While realistic poems sometimes seek to discredit nationalistic idealism by emphasising the war's devastating effect on individuals, allegorical or visionary writers tend to move in the opposite direction, and place the conflict between nations in a cosmic perspective. The war is located as an element in the total history of human development, usually in order either to emphasise its futility – the fact that 'in a thousand years / It will be all the same', in the words of the 'old proverb' that Dora Sigerson quotes – or to deplore the recurrence of what Laurence Housman calls 'the old Coercion Act'.[40] The cosmic perspective that characterises poems like these applies to spatial as well as temporal vision. A remote viewpoint can serve to make human activity seem insignificant; in Maurice Pottecher's 'Le Point de vue des corbeaux' (Crow's-eye-view), for example, three crows discuss what they see of Europe, and the bird's-eye perspective not only reveals the full extent of the destruction but also implies both its pointlessness and the superior intelligence of the birds (since their race, unlike that of the humans, is unified):

> Le second dit: 'Je viens de l'Est, où le soleil
> Fait chaque soir fumer la plaine:
> Et la terre est rougeâtre, et le fleuve, vermeil,
> Et mon peuple jamais n'a fait festin pareil
> Tant y pourrait de chair humaine'[41]

> (The second says, 'I come from the east, where every evening the sun turns the plain to smoke: and the land is reddish, and the river, vermillion, and my people have never had such a feast, so much human flesh is rotting there'.)

This wide vision makes a striking contrast with the restricted, ground-level perspective of many realistic poems – most notably Plagge's 'Die Schlacht', where part of the reported action is observed through a 'Schiesßloch', a firing-hole.[42] In his study No Man's Land, an exploration of the psychological consequences of war experience, E.J. Leed explains that the adoption of a distant perspective by combatants in their retrospective writings is related to what Freud observed of dreams about death, where the dreamer, experiencing a split of consciousness, 'witnessed his own death as a spectacle, while surviving as an observer'.[43] Leed also offers a psychological explanation for the popularity of Leviathan-like figures, which, he suggests, were a means of projecting one's identity as powerless combatant in a meaningless war onto 'a creature of will and purpose', whose 'godlike eye' replaced one's own 'constricted vision'. Nevertheless caution is needed in applying either of these interpretations in the poetry, since apocalyptic metaphors (including monsters) and a remote viewpoint are at least as popular amongst non-combatant as amongst combatant writers.

In accordance with the conventions of allegory, the persona in the non-realistic poems is an individual possessed of special insight, sometimes (especially, it seems, in English) attributed explicitly to a dream or vision. In 'Strange Meeting' and 'The Show' Owen's 'voice' speaks as if from the afterlife; the persona of Isaac Rosenberg's 'Daughters of War' 'saw in prophetic gleams / These mighty daughters' luring men to war; the narrator in Israel Zangwill's 'The War of the World' journeys Dante-like from the Witches' Sabbath of war to a mad-house, 'the place of peace'.[44] Even when the persona is not explicitly a visionary or prophet, the language often has a biblical ring. Albert Ehrenstein's description of the aftermath of a battle, 'Walstatt', borrows the repetitive sentence structure that one finds in the more poetic sections of the Old Testament (such as the Book of Psalms and the Song of Solomon):

> Weiß weint der Schnee auf den Äckern,
> Bitterlich schwarz sind die Witwen,
> Grün warst du, Wiese des Frühlings,
> Gelb verkrümmt sich das Herbstlaub,
> Grauer Soldat im Feld,
> Rot sinkst du hinab zur hündischen Erde
> Unter des Himmels unverfrorenem Blau.[45]

> (White weeps the snow on the fields; the widows are a bitter black; you were once green, springtime meadow; the autumn foliage is bent yellow; grey soldier in the field, you sink down red to the cynical earth, under the imperturbable blue of the heavens.)

René Arcos also assumes the voice of an Old Testament narrator, when he depicts the war, and the hatred that accompanies it, as a plague, spreading everywhere, until it overcomes even the last islands of resistance:

> Alors la guerre fut partout:
> Dans les vallées et sur les monts,
> À tous les étages de l'air
> Et dans la profondeur des mers.

> Alors la haine fut partout:
> Dans la gueule des canons,
> Dans les strophes des poètes
> Et les oraisons des prêtres.[46]

(Then the war was everywhere: in the valleys, on the mountains, at all the stages of the heavens, and in the depths of the oceans. Then hatred was everywhere: in the mouth of cannons, in the verses of poets, in the prayers of priests.)

Owen's 'Parable of the Old Man and the Young' echoes the account in Genesis of Abraham's preparations for the sacrificial slaughter of his son Isaac (a sacrifice demanded by God as a test of faith):

Then Abram bound the youth with belts and straps
And builded parapets and trenches there,
And stretchèd forth the knife to slay his son.[47]

Owen revises the ending – this 'Abram', unlike his biblical prototype, refuses to abandon at God's request his plan to sacrifice his son, persisting until 'all the youth of Europe' has been killed – and the poet's protest is underlined by the parodic effect of the language, which reiterates many phrases from the King James version. For Yvan Goll the biblical tone is not parody but a necessary component in creating the apocalyptic vision of a land red with blood:

Rot waren die Hügel des Frühlings. Im Winter fiel roter Schnee.
Blut sprang aus den Bergen in Strom und See.
Blutheiße Strahlen die Landstraßen und Boulevards.[48]

(In springtime the hills were red. In the winter red snow fell. Blood flowed from springs in the mountains into river and lake. The streets and highways were beams hot with blood)

D.S.R. Welland uses the term 'bardic' to describe the tone of the poetry that welcomed the war; yet it is hard to imagine that patriotic verse could be more bardic than this allegorical or apocalyptic protest writing. The term characterises precisely the language of poems like Visiak's 'The Pacifist' – 'Thy words / Are desolate winds and jagged spurs of rock' – Werfel's 'Krieg' – 'Höhnisch, erbarmungslos, / Gnadenlos starren die Wände der Welt' (Scornfully, without pity, without mercy, the walls of the world stare forth) – or 'A.E.' 's 'Statesmen' – 'The foe ye meet is still yourselves, the blade ye forged the sword that kills'.[49] Clearly the poet's commitment for or against war cannot be tied to this particular kind of language.

While the purpose of many protest poets is served by a single dominant image, whether realistic or allegorical, for others imagery is a secondary concern, a device to reinforce the strength of a case presented chiefly through direct argument. Here, instead of a visionary or an on-the-spot observer, the persona is a public speaker taking part in a debate, though the role of speechmaker may incorporate those of both prophet and spokesman. Occasionally one finds a poem of this kind where the argument is presented calmly and rationally – H.F. Constantine's 'The Use of War' for instance, which assesses from the viewpoint of November 1918 the accuracy of the prediction that 'from this evil / Good would come'.[50] The speaker admits that men have learnt of the bondage of fear, that 'the brave have been brave, / The pure have been pure, and the generous have laid down their lives'. But as for the others, he says, no-one can tell whether people in general have been improved by the war – 'Not you, nor I, nor all the busy scribes of England'. In contrast with Constantine's calm reasoning, most of the poets whose case relies on argument seek to convince through emotion rather than rationality, and their poems frequently take on the haranguing tone of political or religious oratory. Karl Otten's

> Es ist Zeit, mein Bruder, alles zu verlassen, hin-
> zuwerfen Zweifel auf Eid, Lust auf Begierde,
> Klugheit auf Witz

> (It is time, brother, to leave everything behind, to cast away doubts and oaths, lust and desire, cleverness and wit),

calls for the pious (or pietistic) voice of a preacher, while René Arcos'

> Je vous accuse nommément:
> Politiques et diplomates,
> Bonneteurs jouant à la passe,
> Le sort des peuples sous la toile

> (I accuse you by name: politicians and diplomats, card-sharpers playing with the fate of peoples)

must surely be accompanied by a politician's finger-pointing or fist-waving.[51] Almost all the protest writing has something of the quality of public address, but only the debate poems boast a plethora of commands, exclamations, repetition, parallelism, pleas and rhetorical questions – as if the excessive rhetoric itself were a protest device. Even when a calmer, more meditative tone prevails – as in Pioch's 'Dédicace à la pitié' or Owen's 'Insensibility' – the rhetorical manner is close at hand, and one finds many lines like 'But cursed are dullards whom no cannon stuns', from 'Insensibility', which are declamatory enough for any public orator. And, as befits their role as speechmaker, many of the protest poets who rely on direct argument advocate a political solution to humanity's problems, for this mode is favoured by writers (especially in French and German) with a definite commitment to socialism.

In the functioning of the verse that expresses patriotic loyalty the persona plays a special role, and the same is true in the other kind of propagandist writing, the protest poetry. As a means of emphasising the gap between readers and 'non-readers', a first person plural persona ('we') is an obvious choice. For Oskar Kanehl in 'Soldaten-mißhandlung', for example, 'wir' serves to underline the difference between the situation of the soldiers compelled to attend a 'Gottes-dienst' – a service of God – in church, and the 'Bürger' comfortably at home in bed, performing a service for his wife. In Toller's 'Marschlied' 'wir' introduces more than half of the poem's twelve lines, and the repetition enhances the theme – the total isolation from the rest of society of the men marching to the sacrifice:

Wir Tränen der Frauen,
Wir lichtloser Nacht,
Wir Weisen der Erde
Ziehn stumm in die Schlacht.[52]

(We, the tears of women; we, of the night without light; orphaned by the world, we go in silence to the slaughter.)

A.P. Herbert in 'After the Battle' uses 'we' and 'you' with explicitly divisive intent, as the soldiers address the 'beaming General' who will speak at 'the usual Thanks Parade':

We who must mourn those spaces in the mess,
And somehow fill those hollows in the heart,
We do not want your Sermon on Success,
Your greasy benisons on Being Smart.[53]

The deliberate 'we'-'you' alternation, maintained throughout the poem, helps to underline the totality of opposition inherent in phrases like 'greasy benisons' and the capitalised 'Sermon on Success' (which, since it has a fixed title, presumably never varies), and in the recognition that one side receives the reward ('A K.C.B. perhaps, perhaps a Corps') for the suffering that is borne by the other.

Yet the use of the 'we' voice as a divisive mechanism is less common in the protest poetry than one would expect, for the poets frequently choose instead to speak as 'I' or, as Sassoon often does, to use a hidden persona (which is 'I' by implication). To a large degree the reason for this preference is functional. Allegories, where the speaker's insights are presented as the consequence of a visionary experience, are often first person narratives, and the tradition is followed here. The 'I' voice is important, too, in the poetry that relies on direct argument, since the orator persuades by the depth and sincerity of his or her personal conviction. And for poets whose protest is based on war experience, the singular persona is especially valuable. If their propaganda is to be effective, and particularly if they wish to arouse compassion for the men's suffering, the truth that they juxtapose against the myth must appear to exist in the empirical world, not merely in the poetic world of the text. The use of an 'I' voice (whether explicit or implied) that is likely to be equated with the poet's self is a potential link between the two worlds. Most readers make such an identification of persona and poet very readily, to the extent that, as Joseph Cohen has pointed out, some criticism is more concerned with the poets' heroism than with their poetry.[54] Even so, imagination can substitute in large measure for experience; for instance, it would be difficult to say, strictly on the evidence of the poem, that Winifred Letts' 'The Deserter', which I discussed earlier, is not a first-person observation. Karl Stamm's 'Soldat vor dem Ge-kreuzigten' (Soldier before the crucified Christ) is even more fully convincing, yet this first-person account of a soldier's struggle with his conscience after killing an enemy was written by a Swiss soldier whose closest encounter with combat was in a border patrol (where no enemy was sighted).[55] Nevertheless, the same principle applies, since the 'I' persona adds to the credibility of the account.

To a large extent, then, protest poets speak as 'I', and their choice of persona is intentional. In the war years, people who voiced in poetry their antagonism to the myth and its upholders established through their verse a public and personal identity, just as their patriotic counterparts had done. If they were pacifists, their poetry represented a contribution to their cause as well as a validation of their non-combatant status (especially amongst the men of combatant age). For the soldier-poets their public declaration of opposition may have served to appease a conscience troubled by killing, or, since many of the combatant protest writers were officers, to counter the knowledge that they were contributing, however reluctantly, to the suffering of the men under their command. Civilians or combatants, however, the internationalism that they promoted, together with their rejection of the patriotic–heroic myth, ensured that they were, if not quite outside the law, at least beyond the bounds of general acceptance. Their stand placed them in an isolated and vulnerable position, like that in Richard Fischer's image of the only true hero – a man willing to stand upright and alone on the battlefield, crying out to both sides, 'Lüge, Lüge, Lüge!' (Lies).[56] In the poetry the protesting voice, whether of prophet, observer-spokesman or public orator, comes from a person possessed of special knowledge or insight which it is his or her responsibility to spread, and that persona is an echo of the dissenter's actual position *vis à vis* society in general. Those – 'a few alone amid the mass of men' – who tried to uncover the deception and the suffering perpetrated in the name of the nation did indeed run the risk of being branded as 'liars and iniquitous / At best as fibreless fools'.

Nevertheless, although the individuality of the persona is important in establishing the poet's deliberate separation from an unthinking commitment to the tenets of nationalistic patriotism, the isolation implicit in this 'I' voice may exist more truly within the poem than outside it. In actuality, most of the poets had contact with people who shared their views about the war. Letters and memoirs, names that recur frequently in a particular magazine or newspaper, dedications, and sometimes even the poems themselves (such as Piscator's lament for his fellow-contributor to *Die Aktion*, Kurd Adler), all attest to a sense of community amongst the writers. This feeling of connectedness owed much to prewar literary contacts, for in English and German in particular, the years from about 1910 to 1914 had witnessed a major revival of interest in poetry. In various centres throughout the German-speaking countries, including Berlin, Munich, Leipzig and Vienna, groups of writers who became known as Expressionists had started magazines and initiated other publishing ventures. With the coming of war, publishers associated with Expressionism, especially Kurt Wolff in Leipzig and the press of *Die Aktion* in Berlin, were responsible for disseminating most of the German protest poetry. Some of the Expressionist magazines continued to appear – *Die Fackel*, *Die weißen Blätter* (in Zurich from 1916), and most notably from the point of view of poetry, *Die Aktion*. The editor of the latter, Franz Pfemfert, seems to have been delighted to publish as many dissenting poems as possible, and the awareness of Pfemfert's anti-chauvinist stand attracted new contributors with an inclination towards scepticism, Piscator amongst them. Most of the writers, whether old or new, make several appearances, and Pfemfert passes on to his readers the news he has received in letters and postcards from regular contributors, especially those on active service, as well as any information he has gleaned about interesting poets in other countries. When, not infrequently, he announces or confirms the news of the death of one of his 'Mitarbeiter' (collaborators), one can imagine even after seventy years the sense of loss in this community of poets.

The same feeling of belonging is evident amongst English protest writers. Although the relationship between the English protest and pre-war poetic radicalism is less direct than in the case of *Die Aktion*, and although one of the major figures of the poetry revival, Edward Marsh, is usually associated with Brooke and accordingly with a so-called 'pro-war' attitude, the Georgian and Imagiste connections amongst the poets were important in the development of the protest poetry. Many of the writers were acquainted with each other – Sassoon and Graves, for instance, and the Oxford group with which Osbert Sitwell was associated – or knew of each other through mutual acquaintances or through publication in the same anthologies or magazines. (Sorley was granted posthumous membership in the fraternity, when Graves published a poem about him.) Marsh, as editor of the *Georgian Poetry* anthologies, and Harold Monro, whose Poetry Bookshop in London provided a meeting-place and accommodation for poets, were important figures in this chain of connections, as was Sassoon's friend Robert Ross. Though not necessarily involved directly in the protest (Monro voiced opposition to the war, but Marsh remained committed to the national cause), these men served as catalysts by helping to establish the kind of contact on which protest poetry seems to have flourished. In addition to the literary circles, in all of which the original incentive had been the desire to create a new kind of poetry, there were also groups whose shared conviction was ethical or political, such as the pacifists and the writers who published in *The Herald*. But whatever their motivation, the protest poets found the support of a publisher and a sympathetic audience, to lend them both courage and encouragement. It is worth noting that Owen did not begin to write protest poetry when he was exposed to the devastating effects of the war, or even when he returned to Britain, but when he met another protest poet, Sassoon. Although the influence of Sassoon's poetry on some of Owen's is evident, the difference between the two poets is sufficiently large to make it clear that Sassoon's main value, for Owen, was less as a model than as sympathetic and supportive reader (as, indeed, their letters and Sassoon's memoirs indicate). A.G. West's anti-war sentiments crystallised when he was in the company of some friends of similar inclination, and at least one historian has argued that Sassoon's own protest was given the focus it otherwise lacked by his encounter with the pacifist group around Ottoline Morrell.[57] Fischer's isolated and vulnerable hero, shouting out his solitary protest on the battlefield, makes an impressive image, but the reality demands that one recognise the supreme importance of mutual support amongst the 'few alone' who protested against the war. Without such a sense of belonging to a minority group there would have been little poetry of uncompromising protest.

In France, too, one finds evidence of a feeling of community amongst protest poets. Several of the more prominent anti-war writers had belonged before the war to a group known as 'unanimiste', promoting (amongst other things) the cause of pan-Europeanism. The central figure of the group was Jules Romains, and his associates included Georges Chennevière, Georges Duhamel (the editor of *La Nouvelle Revue Franìaise* at the beginning of the war), René Arcos, Pierre-Jean Jouve and Charles Vildrac. That there was less protest poetry in French than in the other two languages was undoubtedly in part a consequence of the ban on publication of magazines (such as *La Nouvelle Revue Franìaise*) which might otherwise have printed dissenting verse, but it also reflects the fact that the prewar poetic revival in France was less immediate and intense than in the other languages. The avant garde group around Apollinaire had been active but small, and otherwise the movements that brought about the change from traditional to modern poetry in France – dating from as early as the 1870s – were no longer new and lively, ready to serve as catalysts in the generating of protest verse. Accordingly, the network of connections amongst dissenting poets, though strong, was not so wide as in the other countries, and fewer protest poems were written or published. Nevertheless, writers with anti-war leanings usually found support – often, it seems, by way of Geneva and Romain Rolland. Rolland made himself very unpopular in France by publicly deploring the blind enthusiasm for war and the commitment to hatred of many French intellectuals. (That he also recognised the justice of the French cause and condemned the German invasion tended to be overlooked.) As a renowned writer who had taken a stand against nationalistic propaganda, he served as a focal point for the protest amongst the French. In his introduction to the 1920 anthology *Les Poètes contre la guerre*, Rolland tells of the sense of fraternity amongst the protest poets in Geneva, most of whom, he observes, were his personal friends. His wartime journal reveals an amazing web of connections by correspondence. It includes not only the relatively well-known protest writers such as Arcos and Vildrac, but also obscure figures like Marc Larreguy de Civrieux, whose father wrote to Rolland after Marc's death, reporting his son's admiration for the author of *Jean Christoph*, and expressing his own dedication to the cause of peace.[58]

Rolland's network of contacts, however, is not confined to France; he tells for instance of having heard through a mutual friend that the German poet Heinrich Lersch, who was formerly intensely patriotic, now considers himself (in 1917) 'tout à fait européen' (totally European); he is well-informed about the author of the new anti-war novel *Menschen im Krieg*, published anonymously in Zurich (a Hungarian lieutenant called Latzko, injured and now convalescent in Davos); he is in contact with pacifists in England, including the art critic Roger Fry, who translated some of Jouve's poetry into English.[59] As one looks back from an age where, even in peacetime, boundaries between nations may take on the look of war frontiers, the readiness with which literary works and information about authors passed from one side to another during the war is astonishing. The French women in Martinet's 'Femmes' are familiar with the work of Latzko, who wrote in German, and Henri Barbusse's *Le Feu* was available in English and German not long after its initial publication. Switzerland, of course, proved to be a useful literary go-between, as well as harbouring anti-war writers from both France and Germany, including Yvan Goll, who wrote and published in both languages. Bertram Lloyd's first anthology, which appeared in the early autumn of 1918, includes translations of German, French and Russian poems of protest, and Martinet's 'Poètes d'Allemagne, ô frères inconnus' elicited a reply in Die Aktion (by Karl Otten) long before the end of the war. The pan-European concepts of Unanimism, the ideals of international socialism (revived considerably by the Russian uprising of 1917) and the sense of brotherhood amongst combatants are thus all echoed in the feeling of community amongst protest writers of different nations.

While one finds occasional references to censorship, the censors appear to have interfered little with the distribution of protest poetry. (Such a statement can only be tentative, of course, since it is impossible to know how many poems were refused publication, and whether the refusal came from publishers or from the censor.) Government inter-ference seems to have had most effect on the French writing – that is, of the languages under consideration – though the initial impetus was partly economic. In August 1914 all French magazines were forbidden to publish because of the national emergency. The ban was total for only a few months, and most of the larger-circulation journals returned gradually as the war progressed. Many of the small magazines, how-ever, simply did not come back into publication; apart from other problems, editors as well as writers (being predominantly young men) were likely to be on military service. This was not officially censorship, but it had a similar effect. When censorship was enforced, it seems to have been rather arbitrary, for Pierre-Jean Jouve and Jules Romains both published without objection collections that included protest poems (in 1915 and 1916 respectively), while Maurice Pot-techer's relatively mild 'Le Point de vue des corbeaux' was removed from Les Chants de la tourmente (1916) at the request – and not the command, according to the author – of the censors.[60] An anecdote in Rolland's journal shows similar arbitrariness in German censorship procedures. Rolland reports having heard from René Schickele that the Munich censor has attempted to persuade his counterpart in Leipzig to ban Schickele's magazine Die weißen Blätter, but, Rolland observes, 'It happens that the Leipzig censor prides himself on his literary taste, and so he lets it pass.'[61] Nevertheless, Die weißen Blätter moved to Switzerland in 1916 because of problems with censorship, and another Expressionist magazine, Neue Jugend, was closed down completely.

Yet one has the impression that the effect of censorship was not entirely for the worst. Johannes Becher's 'An Deutschland', as it appears in the postwar anthology Kameraden der Menschheit, is prefaced with the words 'Written in 1915 and suppressed by the censor', while Richard Fischer announces in the foreword to his collection *Schrei in die Welt,* that 'the censor of 1917 and 18 throttled the cry' of his poems 'from the murder-fields of Rumania, Flanders and France'.[62] These poets, however, wear censorship with pride, like a military medal, as proof that during the war they fought well for the right cause. The threat of censorship that was imposed on *Die Aktion* in August 1914, after Pfemfert's editorial condemning chauvinism, appears to have reinforced the commitment of the editor, his collaborators, and their circle of readers, rather than impeding it. Even more important, because Pfemfert was ordered to refrain from further political comment of the same kind, he resorted to publishing short literary works which, in his opinion, accomplished the same purpose by different means. In this respect, censorship worked decidedly to the benefit of German protest poetry, since it opened up the pages of *Die Aktion* to many poets – to the extent that, in 1919, Pfemfert was praised as being single-handedly responsible for bringing the poetry of 'Menschlichkeit' safely through the war.[63]

Despite these examples, and although the possibility of irritating the censors may have inspired some protest poets (just as annoying the Philistines was important to the Aesthetes of an earlier generation), one is led to conclude that censorship boards on the whole were little concerned with poetry. Uwe Wandrey observes, in connection with Expressionist verse, that even the strengthening of censorship measures in 1917 appears to have affected neither the type of poetry nor the output.[64] In England, too, poetry seems to have passed the censors unscathed. Conceivably the readiness to allow soldier-poets to publish, despite their occasional animosity towards the upholders of the myth, owed something to their role as the nation's heroes, but more probably it arose because poetry was simply not viewed as a hazard. There is evidence to support both these possibilities in the anthology *Soldier Poets: Songs of the Fighting Men*, published in 1916 by Erskine Macdonald. Galloway Kyle writes in the preface,

> The soldier-poets leave the maudlin and the mock-heroic, the gruesome and fearful handling of Death and his allies to the neurotic civilian who stayed behind to gloat on imagined horrors and inconveniences and to anticipate the uncomfortable demise of friends.

Yet a glance at the book shows that many of the soldier-poets were well aware of the 'horrors and inconveniences', whether in describing the ruins of a village, where 'in greening slime / The bloated body of a puny kitten / Floats, decayed and foul', or in assessing the probable outcome of an attack as nothing more than 'To tend the wounded, for the dead to weep'.[65] Since Kyle, the editor of *Poetry Review* and therefore a habitual reader of verse, saw in this only 'a unity of spirit, of exultant sincerity and unconquerable idealism', it is hardly surprising that the censors apparently paid little heed to what the poetry of combatants actually said. The work of civilians, however, seems to have provoked no stronger objection. Although *The Nation* was forbidden to distribute overseas, there is no indication that its poetry contributed to the decision. Indeed, the question of the censorship of opinion in the press seems to have been handled very pragmatically by the British Prime Minister, David Lloyd George, who is quoted (by Stephen Koss in *The Rise and Fall of the Political Press in Britain*) as having remarked retrospectively, 'Nobody cared what the *Daily News* and the *Nation* said because they made it their business to find fault.'[66] Similarly, when some members of his Cabinet, at a meeting in January 1918, called for the suppression of *The Herald*, Lloyd George suggested that the evening papers, with their 'sensational headlines' and large sales, 'did more damage to the morale of the nation than did the *Herald*, with its limited circulation of 40,000 to 50,000'.[67] The protest poetry, it seems, fared no worse when it appeared in a political than in a literary publication, as far as censorship is concerned.

One must emphasise, however, that with only very rare exceptions, such as some of the work of 'A.E.', which appeared in *The Times*, the protest poems reached only a limited audience. It was, moreover, an audience predisposed, by the very fact of being readers of the particular limited-circulation journal or newspaper, to listen sympathetically, and to share in the poet's animosity towards the alien 'them'. Since the reading of seditious material is in itself construed as an act of sedition, an unusually strong bond existed between the writers and their audience; they, too, were a 'band of brothers'. This feeling of mutual belonging was as important to the protest poets, and to their poetry, as the sense of nationhood that determined the functioning of patriotic verse. It gave the writers courage to make public their views about the war (and for combatants in particular that step was potentially hazardous), and it provided them with the physical means to do so. Meanwhile, both the sense of community and the publication of the poems helped reinforce the commitment of readers, not only inspiring some of them to write, but also, more important, encouraging them to spread the message of protest within a gradually widening circle. And the manner in which the poetry functioned in society is echoed in the nature of the texts, for the various alienating devices reflect the desire to appeal to a specific and limited audience, by means of the exclusion of the alien majority from the circle of sympathetic readers.

If the patriotic poetry of the war in each country may be regarded as a special system of communication working in unison with the nation as a whole – in tune with its official policies, its unofficial attitudes, and its various mechanisms for reaching the general reading public – the protest poetry forms a similar system, though contrary and in miniature. In some respects the two systems are widely different. The former functions because of and by means of its mass appeal, while the latter owes its existence to its exclusiveness. And while the one, where the poet speaks as 'we', is intent on proving its uniqueness as the expression of a single nation, the other, where the poet's voice is individual, strives for international connection. Yet the two systems function together, in that the smaller operates within the larger in each country, and readers, writers and publishers are at liberty to belong to both, if they choose. By the time of the Second World War, the power of propaganda in the modern age was more fully appreciated, at least in dictatorships, whether of the left or the right, and access to the media of propagation was strictly controlled in much of Continental Europe. Accordingly, during the 1939–45 war the protest system in both German and French was almost completely separate from the contemporary literature of the nation as a whole; in occupied France, poetry of the Resistance was printed clandestinely, while German protest poetry came almost entirely from poets in exile who were able to publish abroad. By comparison, the simultaneous and collocative existence of the two propagandist systems, the poetry of patriotism and that of protest, in the First World War seems remarkably civilised.

7

Men would gather sense
Non-propagandist poetry of combatants

What did they expect of our toil and extreme
Hunger – the perfect drawing of a heart's dream?
Did they look for a book of wrought art's perfection,
Who promised no reading, nor praise, nor publication?
Out of the heart's sickness the spirit wrote,
For delight, or to escape hunger, or of war's worst anger,
When the guns died to silence, and men would gather sense
Somehow together, and find this was life indeed.

Ivor Gurney, 'War Books'.[1]

A *Punch* cartoon from a few years ago shows a soldier in the trenches explaining desperately to a companion, 'I shouldn't really be here, you know. I've never written a poem in my life.' And another has the caption, 'Things are serious. We're running out of poets.' In the popular image, First World War poetry is inseparable from the concept of the soldier-poet, but as the cartoonists hint, one must retain a sense of proportion. The four hundred combatants whose names appear in Catherine Reilly's war-poetry bibliography comprise only a minute fraction of the almost nine-million-strong military force that the British Empire mustered, and even amongst the war poets those four hundred are outnumbered four to one by civilians. Yet the soldier-poet phenomenon has consistently been both a striking and an appealing aspect of the war and its poetry, no less to modern readers than to contemporaries. Over the years the image of the typical First World War combatant-poet has changed, together with the significance of the concept, but one interesting facet has remained constant: ever since the existence of soldier-poets was recognised in late 1914 or early 1915, their dual role has made them a useful tool for the promotion of causes. Unfortunately, however, the tendency to use them in this way has led to a biased picture of their poetry, since that which does not serve to reinforce the desired image has usually been either ignored or misrepresented.

The initial value of the soldier-poet phenomenon undoubtedly lay in its contribution to the picture of the ideal national hero. That the young men of the countries in question should be ready to risk their lives for the nation was taken for granted in 1914, but that some of them might also write poetry was apparently an unexpected bonus for observers concerned with national image. The new hero, they discovered, was not only willing and brave; he was also sensitive and articulate. If the term 'poet' had attracted some derision from the populace at large as a consequence of the homoerotic tendencies of nineteenth-century Aestheticism and Decadence, the merging of 'poet' with 'soldier' restored the title to manly respectability. Furthermore, the combination of man of action and man of letters located the nation's new heroes within a traditional ideal, that of the well-rounded 'Renaissance man'; hence, for instance, the title for E.B. Osborn's 1919 biographical study of some of the English poets, 'The New Elizabethans'. The propaganda value of the soldier-poet image was well recognised, not least by the Dean of St Paul's, who read Rupert Brooke's 'The Soldier' from the pulpit, and by the German Chancellor Bethmann-Hollweg, who quoted from Karl Bröger's 'Bekenntnis' as evidence of the loyalty of the German working classes. Galloway Kyle, the editor of the two 'Soldier Poets' anthologies, summarises both the ideal and its propagandist effect, when he writes about the reception accorded in the United States to the first volume, published when the debate about American involvement was still in process: 'It is well said that "Soldier Poets" was of greater service to the Allied cause in America than many Blue Books and specially prepared statements; it showed the high clean spirit of ardent, generous youth engaged in a new Crusade.'[2]

The ideal that Kyle identifies here existed almost without regard to the type of verse the combatants produced. Charles Péguy, who exemplified the soldier-poet concept for the French, was killed on 5 September 1914, and wrote no war poems. That Charles Sorley sometimes explicitly rejected the patriotic norm seems to have been overlooked, except by people who sympathised with his view, when a selection of his poems was published shortly after his death in 1915. Amongst combatant poets the predominant mood is not 'rhetorical welcoming' of the war but 'passive resignation' (to use D.S.R. Welland's terms), and even in anthologies that contributed most to the image, like those of Kyle and Bab, some of their verse approaches the border with protest – H. Smalley Sarson's 'The Village, 1915', for instance, with its examples of the 'sovereign cruelty' and pointlessness of war, or Lersch's 'Ein Kamerad', which tells of a man mentally destroyed by his experience.[3] Realism like this was apparently easily forgiven in its context. Even so, contrary to the impression that the English

criticism may have conveyed, relatively little of the poetry of com-
batants can be classified as protest propaganda, whether anti-war or
anti-myth. Although writers acknowledge the unpleasantness of war
and its terrible consequences, their perspective is largely personal,
and such realism as one encounters usually leads, not to 'ardent
rejection' (as Welland calls his third category), but to a longing for
peace. Alfred Richard Meyer's 'An meine Erde' (To my earth), an
example chosen almost at random from amongst the poems identified
by Bab as the work of combatants, opens with a theme that occurs
widely in the literature of the war – the combatants' feeling that the
conflict is destined to last for ever:

Bisweilen ist es mir, als könne dieser Krieg niemals
                    ein Ende haben,
Als müsse ich bis in ein fernes Greisentum hinein nur
                    Schützengräben graben.[4]

(Sometimes it seems to me as if this war might never come to an
end, as if I might have to dig trenches, and only that, far into my
old age.)

But instead of pursuing this complaint, and perhaps developing it
into a condemnation of the war, Meyer turns aside to take up a
different theme – his love for the soil he is digging, which will help
protect his fellow-soldiers, and his wish that it might once again be
lying 'in der Ebene eines Frühlings' (in the smoothness of a spring-
time). Because poems of this kind voiced no explicit rejection of the
war or the heroic ethic, and might be used as evidence of the men's
noble acceptance of their suffering, they could contribute without
difficulty to the soldier-poet ideal. But even when there was more
direct protest it seems to have been overlooked, unless extra-textual
factors, such as publication in *Die Aktion*, helped to make the poet's
intention unavoidably clear.

The image of the soldier-poet as ideal hero was also fed more
directly by combatant verse that subscribed explicitly to the patriotic
or heroic ethic. 'The spirit of a high resolve' (as a reviewer quoted in
Soldier Poets phrases it) is evident in the numerous departure poems
where the speaker declares that, although leaving is difficult, the
cause is worthwhile, and in German 'oath' poems in which the com-
batant merges his individual pledge of allegiance with that of the
nation. While much of the idealistic verse appears from both internal
and extra-textual evidence to have been a product of the early stages
of the war, there are exceptions. Private Wilfrid Halliday's 'Today',
which includes the lines,

>Shall blood of slaughtered sons buy grace?
>Then, England, let it flow!

appeared for the first time in the 1916 *Soldier Poets* anthology; one can only hope that it was written before the poet had witnessed any incident that might promise to fulfill his terrible prayer.[5] W.N. Hodgson's idealistic 'Before Action' ('Help me to die, o Lord') was also first published in 1916, and reputedly written shortly before the Somme offensive – although, as Hibberd and Onions point out, the date of writing is actually uncertain. Maurice Bouignol's 'Douaumont', on the other hand, is definitely from 1916. This battle narrative tells of an incident where a whole unit ('escouade') is buried in a trench when a shell drops nearby:

>Ce qui fut un fossé n'est plus qu'un noir chaos
>De mottes, de cailloux, de corps meutris, qui saigne,
>Où l'homme avec le sol cruellement s'étreignent.[6]

(What was a ditch is now nothing but a black, bloody chaos of clods of earth, pebbles, murdered bodies, where man and soil are joined in a cruel embrace.)

Although this description may seem like material for a poem of protest, Bouignol continues instead by telling of the bravery of the rescue squad that immediately moves into action, and then goes on to pledge eternal remembrance and honour to the men who were killed. A junior officer like several of the English protest poets, Bouignol regarded himself as a spokesman for the men in his charge in much the same way as, for example, Owen and Mackintosh; his purpose, however, was not to voice protest but to ensure that the effort and sacrifice of the *poilus*, these 'pauvres bougres héroïques' whom he describes with both realism and compassion, was properly appreciated.[7] Ultimately, after Bouignol had been on active service for three years, his idealism seems to have given way almost totally to the kind of compassionate identification one finds in Herbert Read's 'My Company', which excludes *de facto* the myth and the people who promote it, but even then he did not turn to bitter protest. One wonders whether, if Bouignol had come upon a circle of combatant protest poets like that around Sassoon in England, his attitude would have changed. (He was killed early in 1918.)

While both Halliday and Bouignol speak on behalf of others, though in radically different ways, most of the soldier-poets with idealistic inclinations are spokesmen only for themselves, using their poetry as a means of examining the nature of their personal commitment. A well-known example in English is Julian Grenfell's 'Into Battle', which, though it speaks of 'the fighting man' in the third person, as if impersonally, analyses a personal response to the demands of heroism and the possibility of dying:

> And when the burning moment breaks,
>   And all things else are out of mind,
> And only Joy of Battle takes
>   Him by the throat, and makes him blind,
> Through joy and blindness he shall know,
>   Nor caring much to know, that still
> Nor lead nor steel shall reach him, so
>   That it be not the Destined Will.[8]

By no means everyone is so confident as Grenfell about the ability to greet the 'burning moment' with joy and courage, and one finds many poems dealing with the problem of conquering fear – or, indeed, of being conquered by it. That possibility is raised by Karl von Eisenstein, a professional soldier like Grenfell, who claims that the worst days for a soldier are not those of battle but those of waiting, when fear lurks like a thief 'in einem Winkel deiner Seele' (in a corner of your soul) ready to attack.[9] Nor do all the poets share Grenfell's almost careless attitude towards death – the implication that, since Destiny is in charge, there is no purpose in worrying. On the contrary, it is obvious that for most of these young men the thought of death is often close at hand. E. F. Wilkinson, one of Kyle's soldier-poets, has no doubt that to die for one's country is a privilege, and that, if there is any existence after death, he will return home, his spirit merged with 'the voice of birds, the scent of flowers'.[10] Patrick Shaw-Stewart, on the other hand, is not convinced that to die as a hero is consolation enough for what one loses. 'Was it so hard, Achilles, / So very hard to die?' he asks, retracing, as he returns to Gallipoli from leave in Greece, Achilles' journey to Troy; 'Thou knowest and I know not – / So much the happier am I.'[11]

One might be tempted to dismiss as mere weak imitations the innumerable variants, in the English poetry, of Rupert Brooke's famous 'If I should die' – such openings as 'If I should chance to fall', 'If I should die while I am yet in France', 'If I should fall, grieve not that one so weak' – except that one comes repeatedly upon similar opening lines in French: 'Si je meurs', 'Si je ne reviens pas', 'Si, loin de toi, ton frère meurt', to quote only a few examples.[12] 'What if I die?' is clearly an important question for the combatants. Individual speculation about death varies widely. Charles Sorley anticipates – if not with joy, at least with curiosity and acceptance – the prospect of exploring a wild and unknown land; like Wilkinson, Clifford Druce looks forward to returning in spirit to scenes of former happiness; Gerhard

Moerner, plucking the petals from a daisy to determine whether death or life loves him more, concludes that the question is unimportant, since to be buried in the 'Blütenboden', the blossoming earth, would be no hardship; and Anton Schnack considers some traditional images of the afterlife before offering his own interpretation of what death will be like – familiar and happy memories, then a process of increasing estrangement – 'eine Dunkelheit, ein Rätsel, ein Geheimnis, eine Finsternis' (a dimness, a puzzle, a secret, a darkness) – culminating in nothingness.[13] It is remarkable how many of these young poets accept the prospect of dying, as if through the act of writing they had resolved a worrying problem; Schnack's title 'In Bereitschaft' (In readiness, in preparation) is singularly appropriate. And while by no means all the poems about death are concerned with patriotic or heroic ideals, one cannot doubt that, for many soldier-poets, the resolution was made easier by the belief that the cause for which they were fighting would give value to their sacrifice.

In the most explicitly patriotic variation on the 'If I should die' theme amongst the poems I cited, the speaker urges his mother to take consolation in her pride at her son's death:

> Then thou canst say – 'I too had a son;
> He died for England's sake!'

The writer is Rifleman S. Donald Cox of the London Rifle Brigade. Since the title, 'To my Mother, 1916', suggests that the poem is intended to be read as autobiographical, one is at least cautiously justified in regarding the sentiment Cox expresses as evidence of the effectiveness of nationalistic education. This 'other ranks' poet appears to view death in the nation's cause as a route to social acceptability. Cox is one of several privates and non-commissioned officers represented in *Soldier Poets* and *More Songs of the Fighting Men* – a reminder that, for some contemporary observers at least, a particularly appealing aspect of the soldier-poet phenomenon was its lack of class-consciousness. An editorial in the *Daily Telegraph* in June of 1917, on the subject of how 'Poetry was reborn in the throes of war', makes it clear that all ranks were considered to have been equally affected when 'Mars once more claimed kinship with Apollo and the Muses': 'Guardsmen wrote sonnets; privates composed odes; corporals and sergeants – so unlike the non-commissioned officers of the past – relaxed their stern and practical souls in "soldier songs".'[14] (Although the tone here may sound mocking, the article as a whole suggests that the author was not so much amused as impressed by the phenomenon he or she was describing.) Edmund Blunden reinforces the 'regardless of rank' image in his foreword to Brian Gardner's 1964 anthology, when he tells how, 'one quiet afternoon after a hideous and killing night' in 1916, he came upon 'a cheerful soldier from the East End of London, a private', sitting on an ammunition box in a trench, writing a poem to send home to his wife.

Yet interestingly enough, with regard to the English poetry at least, the impression that the soldier-poet phenomenon applied to all ranks (and thus, by implication, to all classes) has not survived. Gardner himself, for instance, observes that 'working-class writers like Rosenberg were very much the exception', and indicates that most of the combatant poetry came from young officers (which means, in effect, at least the lower middle class). While I confess to a leaning towards Gardner's view, I recognise a possibility of reconciling these conflicting impressions. Undoubtedly Gardner's evidence, like my own, comes mainly from the many books of individual verse that have survived – that is, from published collections – while for contemporaries the soldier-poet concept was almost certainly fed by a variety of additional sources. Evidence may have existed not only in short-lived printed materials such as local newspapers and combatants' magazines, but also in letters, oral accounts, and personal encounters like that reported by Blunden, most of which have left no lasting trace. Although combatants of all ranks had potentially equal access to the privilege of writing poetry, they certainly did not have equal access to publication, and therefore to permanence. The poems of Blunden's 'cheerful soldier' were intended for the writer's wife, who, even if she considered having them published, is unlikely to have been audacious enough to send them to a large-circulation newspaper like the *Times*, as Lord Desborough did when he received 'Into Battle' from his son. Similarly, although a few of Rifleman Cox's poems appeared in print during the war, they were ultimately collected only in typescript form, not in a published volume that would have helped to perpetuate the author's name and rank. The system to which A.G. West refers in his diatribe against 'pious' soldier-poets, with 'mothers, local vicars, college deans' nurturing the verse of those 'young cheerful men' through to publication after their death, was not available to writers from the working class. Instead of being able to rely on knowledgeable friends and relations, possibly with connections in the publishing industry, they had to depend almost entirely on the kindness and encouragement of a single editor; and if they were killed in the war, their work was easily forgotten, unless, like Isaac Rosenberg's, their talent was clearly above the ordinary. (Here, surely, the soldier-poets offer grist for the mill of yet another cause.)

To the extent that the 'all ranks' image of the soldier-poet prevailed in England for at least a short time, it owed much to the efforts of Galloway Kyle, who was editor of *Poetry Review*, the journal of the Poetry Society, and managing director of the publishing firm Erskine

Macdonald. The journal made a point of accepting combatants' verse from early in the war and, in addition to the two anthologies, *Soldier Poets* and *More Songs of the Fighting Men*, Kyle, with the assistance of S. Gertrude Ford, was responsible for publishing many collections of the work of individual soldier-poets, regardless of rank. Amongst those Kyle encouraged was John William Streets, a miner from Derbyshire, who had published in *Poetry Review* before the war. One of Streets' poems appeared in the *Times* in April 1915, and provided the original inspiration for the first 'Soldier Poets' anthology. For Kyle he seems to have exemplified all that was best in the soldier-poet concept, not least because of his persistent idealism, so it is hardly surprising that a 'memorial volume' of Sergeant Streets' work, *The Undying Splendour*, was published by Erskine Macdonald shortly after the poet's death at the Somme. In general, however, little of the English poetry that has survived in individual collections came from the working class.   As for the 'all ranks' image of the soldier-poet in the other countries, the *poilu* as poet was not, so far as I have discovered, an important part of the French heroic ideal (although the *poilu* was endowed with a surprising number of virtues otherwise). Occasionally, however, one finds poems and even collections that are identified as the work of a *poilu* – Gilles Normand's *La Voix de la Fournaise*, for example, and some of the contributions to trench magazines in *Tous les journaux du Front*, while a poem by Henri Céard praises the skill of *poilus* as letter-writers.[15] In Germany, on the other hand, the terms 'soldier-poet' and 'worker-poet' are almost synonymous, for although the worker-poet movement had begun before the war, it attained popular recognition only when the patriotic declarations of Lersch and Bröger reached a wide audience. Almost all the better-known worker-poets were on active service, with the exception of Alfons Petzold, who suffered from tuberculosis, and the steelworker Christoph Wieprecht, ineligible by both age and occupation. (Bruno Schönlank, unlike most of his confrères, was in the army only under protest, conscripted after being arrested during a workers' peace demonstration that he helped organise in Berlin in 1915.) Although the later war poetry of the combatant worker-poets expresses doubts about the value of the war, and at least one member of the group, Max Barthel, voices fervent (poetic) support for the Russian Revolution, the impression that has persisted is definitely of their loyal dedication to the nation, and much of their poetry was appropriated by National Socialism in the 1930s.

Apart from his role as a working-class poet, the soldier in Blunden's narrative represents another valuable facet of the image, and one that has proved to be both more durable and more universal – the writer at work in the unprepossessing conditions of the trenches. This characteristic is so well established that one sometimes finds the term 'trench poet' used interchangeably with 'soldier-poet', while the fact that a substantial part of the combatant war poetry was not produced in the trenches, or even immediately behind the front lines, tends to be ignored – in the case of Wilfred Owen, Siegfried Sassoon and Edmund Blunden, for example. Nevertheless, there is evidence that many poems were indeed written at the Front (or 'im Feld' or 'dans les tranchées'), and under conditions that were far from ideal. One of J. W. Streets' contributions to *Soldier Poets* is prefaced with an explication that begins, 'These verses were inspired while I was in the trenches, where I have been so busy that I have had little time to polish them.'[16] Charles Sorley refers to the same difficulty in a letter that accompanied some poems he sent home from France:

> 'You will notice that most of what I have written is as hurried and angular as the handwriting: written out at different times and dirty with my pocket: but I have had no time for the final touch nor seem likely to for some time.'[17]

René Hughes offers his *apologia* in verse:

> Apollon-roi, si ne te plaisent mes sonnets
> Qu'en spontanéité tristement relative,
> Excuse: l'heure était incontemplative.[18]

> (Apollo, King, if my sonnets please you only in their sadly relative spontaneity, forgive me: the time was not suitable for contemplation.)

The problem that troubles all these writers, however – the lack of time for contemplation or revision – is intimately related to the very factors that account for the appeal of poetry as an artistic medium in circumstances like these: the immediacy of the response to experience, and the 'relative spontaneity' that allows one to produce a reasonably well-finished work in a short time, with the minimum of equipment. Louis de Gonzague Frick, addressing the poems that have been developing in his head all day, describes the 'complète du poète en campagne', the poet's war-outfit, and the word 'complète' conveys the appropriate impression that, however far from ideal, this 'outfit' is at least minimally satisfactory:

> Je ne possède en guerre pour vous transcrire qu'un bien
>   pèle crayon
> Et qu'un mince cahier couleur cendre,
> Déjà plein de macules et tout recroquevillé.[19]

> (Here in the war I have nothing to transcribe you with but a very pale pencil and a thin notebook the colour of ashes, already full of stains and all curled up.)

It is interesting to note how often a distinction is made between composing and writing the poems; something like Gonzague Frick's 'transcrire' is implied, for instance, in Streets' 'inspired' and Sorley's 'written out', and in Julius Bab's comment that Gerhard Moerner's 'Liebt mich – liebt mich nicht' (Loves me, loves me not) was 'written down' ('niedergeschrieben') an hour before the poet was killed.[20] Presumably mental composition was another major advantage of poetry as far as the combatant poets were concerned. Similarly widely-shared is Gonzague Frick's difficulty with writing-paper – he wishes he had a 'digne parchemin' (worthy parchment) instead of his grey exercise-book. Solutions to the problem vary: Brian Gardner writes that many of the poems in his anthology 'were jotted on to the backs of envelopes and messages'; Franz Pfemfert occasionally notes that contributions to *Die Aktion* have arrived on 'Feldpostkarten' – military post-cards; and Galloway Kyle reports that Streets' poems were 'written in pencil on scraps of paper stained with mud and sent off unpolished, lest the death that lurked by day and night should suddenly strike.'[21] Fortunately, the challenges of the situation did not completely stifle creativity.

It is apparent from these examples, however, that the appeal of spontaneity and immediacy was not exclusively to poets; editors, too, seem to have appreciated the idea that poems could be written in a hurry, almost carelessly, under adverse conditions and with death 'lurking' nearby. One obvious advantage, from the editorial point of view, is to explain away unevenness in quality, by offering a hint that, in such circumstances, one should not expect what Gurney terms 'wrought art's perfection'. Yet that facet appears to have been relatively unimportant, in comparison with the enormous value of 'written in the trenches' in establishing the role of the soldier-poet according to a particular image. For Galloway Kyle and other commentators similarly concerned with promoting a national ideal, the picture of poets writing from the Front, with no time for revision or reflection, suggests that they are first and foremost soldiers, for whom poetry comes second to patriotic commitment. In this respect, therefore, (according to Kyle, at least) they stand in proud contrast to another type of soldier-poet, who is definitely not worthy of the name – 'the conscript poetasters who have found a new stimulant to jaded literary exercises' in the war.[22] Rupert Brooke, in his sonnet 'Now, God be thanked Who has matched us with his hour', juxtaposed the joy and 'cleanness' of the combatants' future against an old world that included, amongst other things, 'half-men, and their dirty songs and dreary'. Kyle takes up Brooke's words as a counterpart to his own phrase 'conscript poetasters', and suggests that such people (who joined the army only when they were conscripted, instead of volunteering) 'whimpered in safety with none to heed them' at the beginning of the war, while 'the braver spirits were shocked into poetry'.[23] According to the *Telegraph* leading article I cited earlier, the poems of the combatants, these young men inspired by 'chivalry and hardihood and moral fervour', 'come hot from excited brains' so it is safe to assume that their work has little in common with the 'jaded literary exercises' of the 'half-men'. One is not surprised therefore when the article ends by suggesting that the soldier-poets and their poetry give evidence of the 'virile qualities' of the English race. Kyle's contrasting of the 'pessimism and decadence' in the verse of 'conscript poetasters' with the vitality and ardour in the work of his real soldier-poets – a view shared implicitly by the editorial writer – is undoubtedly an inheritance from the nineteenth-century battle between Aesthetes and Philistines. But in linking that old antipathy to the image of the ideal national hero (almost to the extent, one feels, of wishing to banish the writers of 'jaded literary exercises' from the nation's army) Kyle moves to a position many paces closer to the attitude evinced in the banning of 'entartete Kunst' – degenerate art – (meaning any that was not representational and easily understood) 'in the national interest' in Germany in 1937, and the consequent persecution of the artists.

By 1937 most of the German protest poets who had survived the war and its aftermath were already in exile, their wartime opposition to the chauvinistic Establishment reinforced by practices carried out in the name of National Socialism. As Pfemfert (exiled in 1933) recognised when he inaugurated his column of 'Verse vom Schlachtfeld' in 1914, poems by combatants about their experience at the Front could provide an effective antidote to the lies or half-truths with which, in his opinion, the national cause was promoted. For Pfemfert, 'vom Schlachtfeld' implied, above all, the kind of knowledge that only first-hand experience could provide. The dual role of the soldier-poets, as perceived not only by Pfemfert but also by most of the modern editors and critics, placed them in the unique position of having both access to the truth about the war, as eye-witnesses to its horror, and the skill to communicate the facts to an audience (in such a way, moreover, as to avoid the censorship that stifled ordinary news-reports). While Pfemfert was primarily interested in what Sassoon calls 'truthful reportings', English critics have added a strong element of compassion to the image: the soldier-poets were not merely objective reporters, but spokesmen on behalf of the men who were suffering. In both cases, however, the importance of the poets' experience as combatants is recognised as being crucial, not only because it inspired the protest but also because it validated the propagandist message; and 'from the trenches' or 'vom Schlachtfeld' is assumed to ensure both its honesty and its immediacy.

For modern readers, the appeal of the combatant protest-poet image lies in part in the recognition that, while speaking out fervently in the cause of peace, the poets continued to share the hardships of the men around them, including the possibility of being killed. This image is no less heroic, in its own way, than the concept of the ideal national hero, but it also serves an anti-war purpose, as evidence that modern warfare destroys without discrimination. In this respect, then, the poets themselves (apart from their work) offer a lesson against war, as one mourns the talent that was lost with the death of Rosenberg, for example, or commiserates with Gurney in his terrible survival. (He died in 1937, having spent many years in mental asylums.) And their poetry, too, continues to be used as a tool for anti-war propaganda, whether explicitly, in anthologies like *Ohne Haß und Fahne* and *Poems of War Resistance*, or in veiled form, as in most of the modern English criticism (including conceivably the present study), which posits in its readers an anti-war stance. For this reason the image of the combatant poet as an anti-war propagandist is now so widely and firmly established as to be taken as a *donnée*. Its validity is supported by the evidence of a substantial body of verse, much of it from writers of some repute (though not necessarily on account of their war poetry) – Sassoon, Owen, Osbert Sitwell, Charles Vildrac, Georges Chennevière, Ernst Toller, Erwin Piscator, and Johannes Becher, amongst others. Admittedly not all the war poetry of these writers was composed in the trenches (as the ideal would require) but the immediacy that enhances their propaganda value for others is far less important, in spreading their own propagandist message, than their skill in converting their combatant experience into a convincing poem that conveys the impression of immediacy and spontaneity. (One might even argue that, since the anger of the poets was exacerbated by the apparent indifference of many civilians, protest poems are far more likely to have been written at home than at the Front.) Yet the protest image is no more universally applicable than that of the soldier-poet as exemplary national hero, for neither takes account of the majority of poems. Moreover, in both cases the predominance of the image has led to assumptions about the intentions of some poets that are not justified by the evidence of their poems, including, as I suggested in an earlier chapter, Klemm and Rosenberg. By avoiding these images – which, like most propagandist devices, lack subtlety – one can perhaps come a little closer to understanding what the writing of poetry meant to the soldier-poets, to discovering why, 'when the guns died to silence' and at many other times, combatants took to their pencil and frequently unworthy parchment, and composed (or at least 'wrote down') a few lines of verse.

In discussing a corpus of poetry which includes that of First World

War combatants, C.M. Bowra, D.S.R. Welland and Michael Hamburger
have all used the terms 'personal' or 'private' to categorise some of the
writing. Although the three concepts of 'personal' differ slightly, they
are by no means incompatible, and a merging of them allows one to
identify a series of tendencies in this highly diverse body of poetry. I
suggested earlier that the war poetry might be perceived as arrayed
between two extremes determined by authorial intention (as it is
revealed in the poem), and that the poetry which is immediately and
consensually recognisable as propagandist has several distinctive
features: it reflects in an obvious way the poet's commitment to a
cause; there is an easily identifiable audience, of which the boundaries
are often established by the exclusion of 'non-readers'; and the voice
speaks not only for itself but also on behalf of others. As one moves to
the other extreme, cause and commitment are lacking, the speaker no
longer assumes the role of spokesman, the intended audience is less
obviously designated, and the poet's primary concern, it appears, is
something other than to convey a message that might ultimately
influence the actions of the person who reads the poem. Michael
Hamburger's distinction between 'public' and 'private' relies on a
similar intentional dichotomy, but with particular emphasis on two
features. First, the term 'private' refers to a tendency towards objectivity
and lack of involvement, as distinct from the deep commitment of
'public' writing. And second, it has stylistic implications that reflect a
conception of poetry as an 'autonomous and autotelic activity'. Most
notably, then, Hamburger's 'private' or 'exploratory' writing is objec-
tive, esoteric and technically experimental, much concerned with
form for its own sake, in contrast to 'public' poetry's essential
communicativeness and involvement.

C.M. Bowra's 'public' and 'personal' categories involve a different
set of oppositions, based on the writer's choice of a public or a private
theme, and on his or her preference for a 'wider vision' on the one
hand or 'the special individual activity of the self' on the other.
Personal poetry of this kind, of which the subject is often, in Bowra's
words, 'the careful presentation of private sensations and states of
mind' is in the 'confessional' tradition inherited from Romanticism,
where the poet and his or her 'I' persona are usually assumed to be
the same.[24] In this respect, however, its opposite is not only 'public'
poetry (moving away from the personal towards the general) but also
the experimental modern verse that Hamburger designates as 'private',
which opposes the personal or subjective with the impersonal. One of
the major aims of early Modernist poets was to free themselves from
the 'lyric I' of Romanticism; their techniques included adopting a
variety of other personae and deliberately striving for objectivity and
apparent non-commitment, as in Benn's 'absolute' ideal.

In one sense at least, therefore, Hamburger's and Bowra's 'private' kinds, both of them forming a contrast with 'public' or propagandist writing, are complementary: non-propagandist poetry may tend either towards objectivity and impersonality or towards the subjectivity of confessional verse. (Or, since one is concerned with tendencies, not distinct categories, it may lean instead towards the 'public' position of compassionate involvement with other people.) But the two kinds of personal writing are also complementary from the stylistic view-point. Because the confessional mode follows an established tradition, the poetry of self-expression (as evinced in the work of combatants, at least) is usually traditional in form and easily understood, as opposed to the primarily experimental and deliberately esoteric style that frequently coincides with the objective approach. It appears, there-fore, that personal poems (as distinct from propagandist or 'audience-centred' work) may be regarded as lying between two extremes: 'poet-centred' writing on the one hand – traditional in form, readily comprehensible, subjective in manner and apparently intended primari-ly to give expression to the poet's thoughts and feelings; and that which is 'poem-centred' on the other, characterised by an objective stance, an esoteric approach, experimental technique, and an obviously conscious concern with the functioning of the medium as a form of art. Furthermore, these two versions of non-propagandist poetry, as they are manifested in the work of combatants, are also 'personal' in the sense of Welland's use of the term: that is to say, the poets' attitude towards the war is neither 'rhetorical welcoming' nor 'ardent rejection' but mere 'passive resignation', an acceptance (with varying degrees of willingness and reluctance) of their combatant involvement and experience.

Ivor Gurney implies in 'War Books' that 'wrought art's perfection' is beyond the capability of combatant poets writing under difficult conditions, yet it is precisely the task of attempting to create a work of 'perfect' and purposeless art, or indulging in mental exercises with words for the sake only of the exercise, that appeals to many poets. Jean Cocteau calls poetry his 'jeu d'échecs', his game of chess, to which he turns for companionship and comfort; Richard Aldington tells of composing little poems for himself, poems which 'fly away like white-winged doves'; and Georges Sabiron puts the same game into practice in his 'Haï-Kaï' about a starfish of corpses.[25] It is the work of Guillaume Apollinaire, however, that offers the most obvious examples of combatant poetry written primarily for what Benn calls the fascination of setting up words – and especially his concrete poems. In part of 'La Petite Auto' for instance the printed words form a picture of a car, while one stanza of 'Paris' – a statement of patriotic determination – is arranged in the form of the Eiffel Tower. No doubt

Galloway Kyle would castigate this as a 'literary exercise', and although it seems unlikely that even he could apply the term 'jaded' to Apollinaire's lively collection of 'Calligrammes', this writer certainly belongs to the class of poets to which Kyle refers, the inheritors of nineteenth-century Aestheticism. One might expect that these aesthetically-inclined poets, who before the war saw themselves as opponents of the literary Establishment, would have converted that opposition into a protest against the Establishment's promotion of the patriotic–heroic myth. But instead most of them continued to devote themselves to experimental verse, as if they found the rejection of traditional technique to be protest enough. In its most extreme form, such 'aesthetic' poetry might seem almost callous in its disregard of the destruction and suffering that roused many other writers to protest: Sabiron's 'Haï-Kaï', for instance, evinces no sympathy at all for the five men whose bodies form the 'lugubre étoile de mer'. Nevertheless, the technically experimental verse is rarely so devoid of compassion and involvement as the ideal of the 'absolute poem' would require; Apollinaire's 'Calligrammes' are both human and humane, and even when its style is as difficult as August Stramm's or Georg Trakl's, the 'exploratory' poetry almost always provides evidence of the poet's awareness of what Owen calls 'the pity of war'.

In comparison with Stramm's 'Schlachtfeld' and Trakl's 'Grodek', Ivor Gurney's 'To his Love' (which I discussed earlier in the context of poems dealing with insanity) sounds traditional and confessional, especially in its peaceful opening:

> He's gone, and all our plans
>   Are useless indeed.
> We'll walk no more on Cotswold
>   Where the sheep feed
>   Quietly and take no heed.

Yet, as one reads and re-reads the poem, it becomes obvious that here too, despite Gurney's disclaimer, is a work of 'wrought art's perfection'. At the start of successive stanzas the speaker warns with increasing urgency that the man is not merely dead but horribly destroyed – 'He's gone'. . . 'His body that was so quick / Is not as you / Knew it'. . . 'You would not know him now' . . .'Cover him, cover him soon.' At the end he admits that his friend is no longer a human being but a 'red wet / Thing', the memory of which, he implies, threatens to obliterate not only his recollections of those earlier times, but also his sanity. The artistry of the poem rests in many details in addition to the precise stanza-structure. It lies, for instance, in the technique of introducing line-breaks in mid-phrase ('feed / Quietly', 'you / Knew', 'wet / Thing') thus not only ensuring that the two words are equally stressed, but also creating a sense of unease in the reader, a hint that the poem may be less straightforward than the opening lines suggest. Gurney's artistic skill is evident, too, in the subtle change of pronouns, from 'he'-'we' at the beginning (contrasting, as elegies often do, the dead and the living) to 'he'-'you'-'I' at the end, to emphasise the point that there are two distinct groups amongst the survivors: those who have witnessed the terrible destruction of the war, and those whose memories remain untroubled. While this distinguishing between combatants and civilians hints at a propagandist intent, 'To his Love' is also, and perhaps more obviously, a personal poem. Yet the careful attention to detail, the very perfection of the work, makes one suspect that the value for Gurney in the writing of this poem lay, not in any 'confessional' benefit – and indeed, there is no extra-textual evidence that the poem was autobiographical – but in creating a polished work of art that explores the possible effect of war experience on the individual.

As this example makes clear, one cannot assume that poems which seem to be primarily self-expression are indeed so, nor that traditional poets must be less concerned with form than their experimental counterparts; and similarly one must not infer from the objectivity of the experimental verse a lack of sensitivity. Who knows what nightmare lay behind Sabiron's starfish of corpses, or what extremity led Wilhelm Klemm to describe with almost scientific precision and seeming detachment the ultimate awfulness of a field hospital? Although the dichotomy 'poet-centred' and 'poem-centred' is useful in helping one to distinguish features in the poetry, it is not necessarily valid as an indicator of the poet's reasons for writing. Rather, one is led to conclude that poems of both tendencies reflect a similar purpose: the use of poetry on the one hand as a way of exploring the situation and its implications, and on the other as a mental challenge that offers not only a sense of escape and accomplishment, but also a means of controlling one's reaction. Poets undertook this challenge and carried out this process of exploration in diverse ways – with traditional or innovative style, with intellectual detachment or emotional subjectivity, with humour, compassion, apparent self-centredness. But whatever their approach, there is little doubt that poetry served an important function in their existence as combatants, or, for some of those who survived and continued to write about the war, in their postwar experience of re-living the past.

The 'exploratory' poetry of combatants (and Hamburger's term may be extended beyond the stylistically experimental, to encompass all the personal poems) reveals a wide variety of recurrent themes, most of which cross international boundaries. Amongst many others one finds, for instance, a reassessment of the meaning of love or friendship, or of the significance of home and family; the recollection of a past that now seems impossibly remote, or the longing for future peace; a coming-to-terms with the prospect of death; the concern for one's sanity in the continuing noise of a bombardment; the love for the earth which offers protection – and which, for French poets, is also the sacred soil of the homeland; the problem of the de-humanisation of men in battle, or of a conscience troubled by killing (both of which can be raised without questioning the need for war); accounts of acts of heroism or the excitement of aerial battles; deprecation of one of the various anathemas of the soldier's life – rats, rain, mud, lice, and, in poems from the Middle East, flies – or a celebration of the return of hope with the coming of spring and sunshine. One of the high points of all the French war poetry is Léon Chancerel's *La Chanson des sept jours*, a series of short poems in which the author seeks to capture ('mettre en cage') the bliss of a week's leave, his 'Bel Oiseau Bleu' (beautiful bluebird); though even as he tells of his exquisite pleasure in rediscovering all the little things that, before the war, counted for nothing – the swan-like taps in the bathroom, the woman's perfume, a visit to the cinema – one senses 'Le Spectre du Départ qui ricane dans l'ombre' (the Spectre of Departure grinning in the shadows), for this is, in the line from Baudelaire that is quoted at the end, 'Une splendeur triste, la volupté du regret' (a sad splendour, the voluptuousness of regret).[26]

Much of the combatant verse that has received wide critical attention depicts realistically the scene and the way of life at the Front, and the common assumption is that its purpose was to inform the civilian world about the facts. Undoubtedly some of the writers intended that their poems should serve as a statement of protest, even in the absence of obvious propagandist devices, but there is little justification for attributing such a propagandist design to all of them. Isaac Rosenberg, for instance, makes a declaration that sounds remarkably like Aestheticism – the very antithesis of a propagandist intent – when he writes in a letter, 'I will not leave a corner of my consciousness covered up, but saturate myself with the strange and extraordinary new conditions of this life, and it will all refine itself into poetry later on.'[27] The propagandist hypothesis about realistic poetry – that the poet's purpose is to impress upon the civilian world 'the realities of front-line life' – implies that the poet is mainly an intermediary between 'things as they are' and his civilian readers, at the mercy of his subject (which he must convey truthfully) and his audience. In Rosenberg's picture, on the other hand, the poet is in complete command, able to decide whether to 'cover up' his consciousness or to absorb everything possible, and if he chooses the latter course, it is purely for the sake of writing good poems. Yet the evidence of the combatant poetry as a whole indicates that neither view is the norm. The persona that predominates is neither a news reporter with an anti-war bias, nor a disengaged exponent of 'pure art', but someone faced with a bewildering and disturbing world that forces itself upon his attention – and, if the poet survives the war, often refuses to be forgotten. It is a world in which, as T. E. Hulme observes, 'nothing suggests itself', and in the poems that serve as a means of exploring this reality, one finds that questions sometimes outnumber statements of fact.[28]

In noting the unusual aesthetic detachment that Rosenberg displays in his remark about exposing his consciousness, one can easily overlook a possibly more important point, his comment about the 'strange and extraordinary new conditions' of life at the Front. In *No Man's Land*, a study of combatants' recollections of the war, E.J. Leed claims that the enduring psychological effect of the conflict on soldiers who survived came mainly from their awareness of having existed in two 'incommensurable' societies, their prewar life on the one hand and life at the Front on the other, with a resultant feeling of 'psychic and social estrangement', of 'radical discontinuity' and with the loss of a sense of identity.[29] In attempting to specify how the new reality was, to borrow Rosenberg's term, 'strange and extraordinary', Leed suggests that the strangeness arose from the breakdown of what in normal circumstances are considered mutually exclusive categories. He continues:

> But war experience is nothing if not a transgression of categories. In providing bridges across the boundaries between the visible and the invisible, the known and the unknown, the human and the inhuman, war offered numerous occasions for the shattering of distinctions that were central to orderly thought, communicable experience, and normal human relations. Much of the bewilderment, stupefaction, or sense of growing strangeness to which combatants testified can be attributed to those realities of war that broke down [. . .] 'our cherished classifications'.[30]

Surprisingly often, the realism of the combatant poets focuses upon such 'bridges', though the categories are perhaps even more basic than those that Leed mentions here. Unlike his 'visible and invisible' or 'known and unknown', they are absolutes, the fundamental oppositions of alive and dead, human and animal, animate and inanimate – categories between which there is no possibility of middle ground. The invisible may become visible as the perceiver's situation changes, but only if the laws of nature are broken can the dead return to life, or the living associate with those who have died. As structuralist anthropology has shown, throughout human culture the perception of the supernatural has rested in the rupturing of borders between absolute categories like these. In the war, however, (according to Leed's argument) such borders were constantly threatened or 'bridged'. Because wars represent a disruption of many normal social practices, not least by granting the sanction to kill one's fellow-humans, they have probably always had a similarly troubling effect, but the situation of the First World War, and especially the circumstances of trench warfare, magnified the problem. The fact that this war brought to the Front an unusually large number of men with 'sensibilities essentially civilian' need not be particularly significant, since the majority of wars have involved civilians as victims – and, in the case of civil war, as combatants – and military forces have not uncommonly been augmented from within the population at large. What made the First World War different, in addition to the extent of literacy amongst the combatants (though even this, as Van Wyk Smith has shown, was not entirely new) was the simultaneous and interrelated invention of mass armies and industrialised weaponry, which, together with an effective but limited transportation system and a particular concept of how wars should be fought, produced a war of stagnation, long duration, and appalling destructiveness. The result, for the soldiers in the trenches, was a sense of entrapment, of being inescapably confined to a severely abnormal situation, where they were compelled to observe, but could not alter, the many strange and sometimes horrifying instances of the bridging of categories.

A recurring motif in the combatant poetry is the circumstance of dwelling in the ground like an animal, rather than on its surface, exposed to the elements instead of with the customary 'roof over one's head'. In Rosenberg's 'Break of Day in the Trenches', the fact that the soldiers are underground while the 'queer sardonic rat' runs on the surface is only one of several reversals of role: unlike the humans, the rat has 'cosmopolitan sympathies' and the freedom to come and go; this short-lived creature will almost certainly outlast the 'haughty athletes' who share its home; and the speaker wonders what fear it sees in the eyes of the men cowering in the trench during a bombardment – the men who have become proverbial cornered rats.[31] Like Rosenberg, Edmund Blunden in 'Third Ypres' implies that animals are better adapted than humans to the devastation that man has brought about, when he compares his own conduct during a bombardment ('I squeak and gibber') to the unperturbed behaviour of a family of field-mice.[32] Watching these animals brings him back from the edge of 'the abyss of madness', in much the same way that the speaker in Hermann Sendelbach's 'Trommelfeuer' (Barrage) saves his mind by observing the activities of a beetle trying to climb the side of the shell hole in which the soldier is sheltering.[33] One half-expects a moral lesson after the manner of the story of Robert the Bruce and the spider, but instead Sendelbach's theme is the abnormality of the situation – the speaker's amazement that he could spend three hours so concentratedly watching a 'blöden Käfer' – a stupid beetle – a creature to which, however, he acknowledges that he owes his sanity. Blunden's 'Third Ypres' serves also to demonstrate how 'bridging' may be almost unnoticeable, though it is none the less effective. When the soldiers think they are to be relieved and imagine their escape –

> The sweet relief, the straggling out of hell
> Into whatever burrows may be given
> For life's recall –

the word 'burrows' creates subtleties of meaning that no 'human' term, such as 'refuge' or 'shelter', could possibly supply.

The bridging of the animal and human categories is of course only one of several possibilities. A major concern is the need to accustom oneself to the fact that human 'flesh, and blood, and brains', which, to borrow R.D. Laing's term, belong 'inside', have become a part of the 'outside' world, where, in a long tradition, they have always been objects of revulsion. Klemm's 'Lazarett' was possibly inspired, not by a desire to shock the reader, but by the writer's need to communicate – to put into words – some of the horrifying abnormalities that this terrible war effected on the human body. The extraordinary situation of living amongst the dead is explored in numerous poems. The topic is treated with detachment, almost humour, by Wilhelm Stolzenberg in 'Gefallene', where the corpses of 'the Fallen' are given the attributes of the living ('Manche sind verwundert, daß sie fielen, / Solch ein Staunen ist in ihren Mienen' – Many seem amazed that they fell, such astonishment is in their eyes), and with irony by Edgell Rickword in 'Trench Poets', which tells of the speaker's difficulty in finding the appropriate poem to read to the rotting corpse on the wire near his trench.[34] For Wilfred Owen in 'Futility' and Siegfried Sassoon in 'I Stood with the Dead', corpses serve as a reminder of how thin, yet how absolute, is the borderline between life and death. One especially unpleasant aspect of trench living, according to combatants' reports (including poems), was the omnipresent smell of the dead ('a vile, sickly smell of rottenness', in A.G. West's words). Measures for avoiding this particular bridging of categories have played an important part in burial customs throughout the history of human society, so in this respect the war set aside almost the whole of human culture.

'In the literature of war,' Leed maintains, 'one can see clearly those patterns used to shape the disorder of the environment, patterns which allow the participant to determine exactly what is anomalous, uncanny, or ironical about the juxtapositions of men and things that he finds.'[35] The most widely recurring pattern, for poets who write of 'the realities of front-line life', is a binary approach, the juxtaposing of incongruities, the contrasting of the normal and the abnormal. Although Fussell explains the 'remorselessly binary' attitude in the writings he studied as largely the consequence of the 'total opposition' situation of trench warfare, and although some of the most aggressively protesting poetry seems to have taken the border-drawing of nationalism as its model, the tendency to dichotomise may also lie, as Leed's hypothesis suggests, at a deeper level of consciousness, in 'the shattering of distinctions that were central to orderly thought'. And the exploration of anomalies is undertaken less for the sake of the reader than for the poet's own benefit, a means to 'gather sense / Somehow together' and to 'impose meaning, pattern and significance' on a world of disorder.

Silkin finds Edmund Blunden's war poetry 'hard to characterise'.[36] The poems of Kurd Adler may leave one with a similar sense of unease, especially if one assumes that the purpose of realistic poetry is to generate anti-war sentiment, or at the very least to make a statement of 'the truth'. On the other hand, if one approaches the work of these two poets with the assumption that their purpose is exploratory, and that one of their main concerns is to pinpoint the abnormalities of their situation as a means of 'ordering' or making sense of their world, then their poetry is less problematic. A recurring motif in Adler's verse is a feeling of amazement that two wholly disparate realities can co-exist. The speaker of 'Ausblick' (Lookout) serves as a pivotal point between the normality of 'hinter uns' (behind us), where there are women, animals, railways, and 'keine Grenze' (no boundary), and the 'Von Grauen durchklungene Nacht' (the night full of the noise of dread) that lies 'vor uns' (before us). In 'In der Beobachtung' (From the observation-post), the traditional and fitting serenity of a rural summer evening is shattered by a bomb attack, and the speaker's parenthesised comment epitomises a common feeling of incredulity at the impropriety of such instants of encounter between 'incommensurable' facts:

(Am Abend noch – am weichen, lauen Abend –
lagen sechs Mützen voll Blut und Schmutz am
    Gassenrand.)[37]

(On that same evening – that soft, mild evening – seven caps lay beside the lane, full of blood and dirt.)

'Sehr dunkel nur' (Only very dimly) explains that the past and present in personal lives, which should be a continuum, have been severed:

Fast ist es seltsam, daß wir Menschen waren
denen das Leben wie Gebete schien.

(It's almost strange that we were people, to whom life seemed like prayers.)

And in 'Wiederkehr' (Return) the soldier home on leave observes how strange it is that his war experience has already sunk away into an abyss, and how a narrow bridge, little more than a rope, reaches tenuously across the dividing days to his earlier existence.

Adler's technique is to separate the two sides of the dichotomy, thus emphasising the point of their meeting. Blunden, on the other hand, prefers to undertake his exploration of the 'strange and extra-ordinary' environment by a complete intermingling of categories, so that the one is always at hand as a point of reference for a comment (usually ironic) on the other. In addition to bearing witness to the breakdown of the more basic oppositions such as animal and human or living and dead, Blunden confronts reality with the traditions of art, literature, and rural culture, and finds that those old perceptions do not adequately accommodate the 'new conditions' of life at the Front. In 'The Zonnebeke Road', morning is no longer the literary or mythical 'merry flame / Which the young day was wont to fling through space', but a 'late withered light'; in 'Come on, My Lucky Lads' the speaker describes in effusively poetic terms the red dawn painted by 'the artist of creation' – 'O celestial work of wonder – / A million mornings in one bloom' – but in the end he sees instead the red (and non-poetic) blood of 'poor Jock with a gash in the poll'; and in 'Preparations for Victory' 'the soul', urged to take comfort in the sight of 'mossed boughs' (a hint of Keats' 'moss'd cottage trees') and 'the tokens of dear homes', replies, 'I'll do my best [. . .] And yet I see them not as I would see.'[38]

'Vlamertinghe: Passing the Chateau, July, 1917' raises the possibility of many transgressions of categories – the sacrifice of men instead of an animal, the experience of living amongst the dead, funereal flowers, which would normally indicate respect for the dead, joined with the colloquial 'not yet gone West', 'brute guns', and even the juxtaposing of the two sides of human achievement in the linking of those guns with the 'proud mansion'.[39] The octet of this sonnet is a play on a line from Keats' 'Ode on a Grecian Urn', 'And all her silken flanks in garlands drest', but the reference is specifically to the fact that Keats' persona, too, is an observer looking at a picture of a sacrificial proces-sion. As its title promises, Blunden's poem describes the setting of a painting or photograph, but the speaker and his companions bridge categories by being simultaneously spectators and participants in this scene before the flower-filled gardens of the Château. Critics who have discussed Blunden's war poems have often focused on the consolatory or 'sanative' effect of nature in them, but the poet makes it clear time after time that the traditional calming effect of nature, whether literary or actual, is often only transitory and false in the war. The soul in 'Preparations for Victory' knows that, behind those 'mossy boughs' and 'tokens of dear homes', 'a ghostly enemy' is hiding (hence the speaker's inability to see things as he would like to); the quietness of the village in 'Gouzeaucourt: The Deceitful Calm' is, as the title suggests, a 'false mildness', for which the soldiers 'soon paid'; while the theme of 'La Quinque Rue' is not the peacefulness of the natural scene – the moonlight in which the observer can almost imagine hearing flutes or fiddles played in 'scarless houses' – but its deceptiveness, the dangers and desecrations that the moonlight veils.[40] Similarly, in 'Vlamertinghe' the observers of the scene admire the 'queenly face' of the mansion and the profusion of flowers around it, as if they had forgotten – until a colloquial voice interrupts the poetic description to protest that the red of the flowers is 'scarcely right' for blood – that, as participants, they are on their way to be sacrificed.

If one believes that realism is designed as a protest against the war, and especially if one looks for either compassion or irony as its invariable accompaniment, Arnold Ulitz's 'Gasangriff' (Gas Attack) is likely to be disappointing.[41] If, however, one reads the poem as exploratory, as the author's attempt to specify what is strange and anomalous, one can appreciate much more fully the significance of the event and the importance of the final question, which anticipates one of the twentieth century's major concerns. The poem tells how the attackers, of which the speaker is one, let loose the 'Gasraubtier' (the predatory animal, gas) from its cage, and how it creeps animal-like over the ground towards the woods held by the Russians; the attackers follow, coming first upon some dead soldiers, their human eyes ('Menschenaugen') wide open and pleading behind the 'Froschaugen' (frog eyes) of their gas-masks. The account continues:

> Vor den toten Menschen sind wir nicht erschrocken,
> Toten Menschen sahn wir zu oft ins Gesicht.
> Aber siehe, siehe! Allerorten
> Fallen tote Vögel von den Bäumen, die verdorrten,
> Fallen fruchtschwer ins ergraute Moos.
> Und wir horchen, wie sie fallen, und wir reden nicht.
>
> Und wir hören auch die toten Blätter fallen,
> Knisternd, wie verbrannt, auf kleine Nachtigallen.

(At the sight of the dead men we're not frightened – we have stared dead men in the face too often. But look, look! All around, dead birds are falling from the dried-up trees, falling like heavy fruit onto the greying moss. And we listen to them falling, and we don't speak. And we hear, too, the dead leaves falling onto the little nightingales, crackling as though they were burnt.)

The speaker's acknowledgment that dead men are commonplace, while the death of birds is disturbing, is in itself a comment on the abnormality of this war, but what is particularly frightening for the attackers is the recognition of the capability of their weapon – its capacity to disrupt the most fundamental pattern, the progression of the seasons:

Vor den toten Menschen sind wir nicht erschrocken,
Vor den toten Vögeln wissen wir mit einem Male:
Wo wir gehn, da ist bald Herbst geworden,
Gottes Zeitenfolge müssen wir ermorden.

(The dead men don't frighten us, but with the dead birds we suddenly know: Wherever we go, it soon becomes autumn; we are required to murder the cycle of God's seasons.)

It is this recognition which leads to the ultimate fearful questioning, not of the necessity for war, but of the possibility that this war is unleashing a kind of destruction from which there may be no recovery:

Seht, das Raubtier weidet schon im Tale.
Wird noch einmal Frühling werden, Brüder,
Glaubt ihr noch?

(Look, the predator is already grazing in the valley. Will there be another Spring, brothers, do you still believe?)

In most of Wilfred Owen's war poems there is no doubt about the author's propagandist intent, for they typically present evidence of the devastating physical or mental effect of the war on individual soldiers, with comments by the observer persona to underline the message. 'Exposure' is atypical in the absence of the author's usual explicit protest, and, indeed, in the acknowledgment that the war may have a valid purpose.[42] The soldiers in this poem feel remote from their former life, but there is no indication of enmity towards civilians, and they are 'not loath' to be fighting to maintain the 'kind fires' of home. The suffering is not imputed to a third person, with the speaker as observer, but is shared by the whole group, and is of such a kind that 'Exposure' might easily have served as a model for Leed's claim that it was not 'specific, terrifying or horrifying war experiences' that most impressed the combatants, but 'the sense of difference and strangeness'.[43] The worrying, uncanny silence, the enforced exposure to the 'merciless iced east winds', and the inability to re-establish, even through 'forgotten dreams', their contact with the world of home and their personal past, all work to convince the speaker that he and his companions exist in a state between life and death. This is not the kind of realism that can readily be used to arouse sympathy and protest, and it is probable that Owen in this case was more concerned with trying to 'gather sense' for himself than with conveying a propagandist message to his readers. According to Sassoon, the first draft of this poem was written six months before he and Owen met, while Owen, 'after enduring the arctic weather of January, 1917', was away from the Front for a few weeks.[44] If this recollection is accurate, it certainly helps to explain the anomaly, since all Owen's explicitly protesting poems postdate their meeting (though 'Futility', which is definitely a later poem, is also more exploratory than propagandist).

Pfemfert's *1914–1916* anthology is dominated by a technique similar to Owen's in 'Exposure', where the poet, speaking in a first person plural voice, and using a disjointed present tense rather than the continuous narrative of the past, presents a series of realistic impressions of his surroundings. This manner of writing seems to bear out Johnston's contention that Great War poetry is characterised by a 'fragmentation of reality' and 'an obsessive emphasis on isolated and irrelevant sensory detail'.[45] Several of Klemm's poems in the anthology are a compilation of seemingly fortuitous impressions, so loosely bound together that individual lines might almost have been extracted from separate poems. The first stanza of 'An der Front' is typical:

Das Land ist öde. Die Felder sind wie verweint.
Auf böser Straße fährt ein grauer Wagen.
Von einem Haus ist das Dach herabgerutscht.
Tote Pferde verfaulen in Lachen.[46]

(The countryside is desolate. The fields look worn out with crying. On a bad road a grey wagon drives by. From one house the roof has slid off. Dead horses putrify in pools of water.)

Hermann Plagge's technique in 'Die Schlacht' (The Battle) differs only in having slightly longer sentences and more similes (and, in comparison with this example from Klemm, more closely-related details):

Irgendwo im Graben schreit man kläglich nach Sanitätern.
Ein Toter wird über die Brustwehr geworfen wie Ballast
    aus einem Schiff.
Kommandos würgen sich durch den Schlund und ersticken.
Ein Telefon tutet angstvoll in einem Erdloch.
Bajonette werden von zittrigen Händen aufgepflanzt.[47]

(Somewhere in the trench someone calls plaintively for stretcher-bearers. A dead men is thrown over the parapet like ballast from a ship. Commands struggle through the throat and suffocate. A telephone hoots anxiously in a dugout. Bayonets are fixed with trembling hands.)

Most of the action here is carried out anonymously, as if the battle were happening without the volition of the participants, while the seemingly arbitrary arrangement of facts, emphasised by the list-like repetition of the sentence structure, gives the impression that the poem, too, happened unintentionally. Oskar Kanehl in 'Vormarsch im Winter' (Advance in Winter) is decidedly less objective and detached, and he makes much wider use of metaphor, but he employs the same underlying technique of juxtaposing facts. The poem begins, like 'Exposure', with icy winds, though without any hint of a possible escape into 'forgotten dreams':

Bespannt von grauem Leichentuche ist der Himmel.
Das Land schneeüberweht,
Eiswind peitscht splittriges Glas in unser Fleisch.[48]

(The sky is spread with a gray shroud. The countryside is covered with blown snow, an icy wind whips splinters of glass into our flesh.)

'Vormarsch', which exemplifies the technique at its most effective, continues with a series of sensory impressions, disconnected and momentary, but each contributing, after the manner of *pointillisme*, to the total impression of a march to death through the relentless cold of a dead landscape:

Auf gefrorenem Boden hallt unser Schritt hohl
als gingen wir auf Sargdeckeln riesiger Massengräber.
Einzeln stoßen Strauchstrunke durch den Schnee
wie Hände eines der noch leben wollte.
Vielleicht eines meiner getöteten Freunde.
Bleibt wach! Ihr werdet alle mit uns auferstehen!
Baumkronen hängen als groteske Fesselballons über der Erde.
Wegweiser zeigen mit schwarzer Hand
in unbekannte Tode.

(On the frozen ground our steps sound hollow, as though we were walking on the coffin lids of immense mass-graves. Isolated trunks of bushes push through the snow, like the hands of someone who wishes he were still alive. Perhaps they belong to one of my dead friends. Keep watch! you'll all arise with us! The crowns of trees hang like grotesque barrage-balloons above the earth. Signposts point with a black hand towards unknown deaths.)

Patrick Bridgwater maintains that 'it is the "modern attitude" of "compassionate realism"[. . .] that comes closest to conveying a true and truly tragic conception of war', though he adds that the compassion and realism must be combined with 'as much of objectivity as possible'.[49] Jon Silkin might well disagree, since he finds that compassion 'works best' when merged with anger; but Silkin's concern is with the effect of the poem in generating anti-war sentiment, while Bridgwater is looking for a 'true' conception of war.[50] In the *1914–1916* anthology, however, it is objectivity rather than compassion that predominates. In the majority of poems the speaker is one of the sufferers, so that although he is perhaps not unsympathetic towards his fellows, his compassion is less obvious than if the focus were on the misfortune of a third person, 'him' or 'them' (as it is in many poems by Owen, Sassoon, Piscator and Vildrac, for instance). Most of the description is impersonal and objective, and observations of human suffering are intermingled with other effects as though all were of equal value. Rather than speaking as a compassionate observer committed to revealing the suffering of others the persona here, in taking up this non-judgemental attitude, often seems to be intent on distancing himself from the events around him. Although the use of the present tense is obviously only a literary device and not a reflection of the author's actual situation, it nevertheless reinforces the impression of the poet as a detached observer – in Plagge's poem, for example – by suggesting a bystander so far removed from the activity around him that he is able to record it contemporaneously.

It is possible that the *Aktion* poets who used the technique of compiling 'isolated and irrelevant sensory detail' intended that their fragmented description should work as implicit protest – as, indeed, the context of publication suggests. Certainly it helps to underline the contrast between, on the one hand, the combatants' perception of war as governed by chance rather than by purpose, and, on the other, the intensity of meaning placed upon it by the tenets of patriotic heroism. Other factors, however, are probably more important in dictating the style that these writers developed. Their technique differs little from that used in some prewar Expressionist poems, which similarly list apparently random observations of a scene – Georg Trakl's 'Im Winter', for instance:

Der Acker leuchtet weiß und kalt.
Der Himmel ist einsam und ungeheuer.
Dohlen kreisen über dem Weiher
Und Jäger steigen nieder vom Wald,[51]

(The field glows white and cold. The sky is lonely and vast. Jackdaws circle above the pond and hunters are coming down from the woods.)

or Ernst Stadler's 'Judenviertel in London' (Jewish Quarter in London):

> Gestank von faulem Fleisch und Fischen klebt an Wänden.
> Süßlicher Brodem tränkt die Luft, die leise nachtet.
> Ein altes Weib scharrt Abfall ein mit gierigen Händen.[52]

(The stench of rotten meat and fish clings to walls. Sweetish steam impregnates the air, which is quietly turning to night. An old woman scrapes through rubbish with greedy hands.)

Poems like Stadler's had already proved the effectiveness of the *pointilliste* technique in describing modern reality. By following such examples, German combatant-poets of an Expressionist bent were able, right from the beginning of the war, to embark on the process of examining through poetry the nature of the 'strange and extra-ordinary' reality around them. Their verse was not necessarily 'anti-Krieg', as Pfemfert designated it, and as critics have usually assumed. Nor is it simply that their anger against the war 'is sublimated into sad and resigned pessimism', as Wandrey suggests.[53] Rather, the process of recording, in the form of a list of facts, their reactions to the 'disorder' around them, its anomalies, its surprises ('Man weiß plötzlich nicht, warum das Korn hier nicht geschnitten ist und die Kartoffeln faulen' (One suddenly doesn't know why the corn here hasn't been cut and why the potatoes are rotting), Plagge observes in 'Die Schlacht'), its unpleasantness and, occasionally, its horrors, is an echo of the ancient process of naming ('And God called the light Day, and the darkness he called Night'): a way to impose meaning, to give 'pattern and significance' to a world of chaos, to 'gather' or make sense through the use of language, and thus to re-establish human value amidst the massive inhumaneness of war.

8

Relics for the present
Poems and history

The historian is both discoverer and creator. To the uniqueness of his role we have a clue in the very word 'history', which means both the course of the past and the legible account of the past. [. . .] Historians can rediscover the past only by the relics it has left for the present. They try to convince us that the relics they have examined and interpreted in their narrative are a reliable sample of the experiences people really had.

Daniel J. Boorstin, 'The Historian: "A Wrestler with the Angel" '

In comparison with the extraordinary existence at the Front, the way of life at home in the war years must have seemed almost idyllically normal. Nevertheless, non-propagandist war poems by civilians serve as a reminder that the accepted image of a world untouched by the conflict has derived largely from the observation of people who were in a position to make the comparison, and whose purpose, at times, was best served by emphasising the difference. To many of the civilians themselves life appeared to be (and indeed was) far from normal, and the war formed a constant background to all other activities. Some of the preoccupations evident in the exploratory writing of combatants are revealed also in the personal poetry of civilians, especially the incredible gap between 'a year ago' and the present, and the seemingly impossible fact that the cycle of nature is unaffected by the terrible suffering and slaughter. Here, too, death is a major concern, as poets record the attempt to come to terms with worry and grief. The death of a son destroys the anticipated progression of generations as well as bringing an end to companionship and hope; but the 'bright sharp pain of anguish' may perhaps be eased, as Irene McLeod implies in *One Mother*, by offering forgiveness – and pre-sumably, if the poem is autobiographical, by the effort of converting the anguish into words.[1] Lesbia Thanet in 'In Time of War' and Klara Blüthgen in 'Vermißt' (Missing) both confront the dread under which many civilians lived for months or even years – the fear that the men they cared about would not return. The speaker in Blüthgen's poem observes how, on the surface, home life seems to be the same as ever, yet the word of doubt, the word with no response, gnaws constantly at the heart.[2] Thanet admits that the heroic ethic is ineffectual when one is faced with reality. The speaker in her poem recalls her romantic dreams of sending a lover off to war with the words, 'Go forth: do gloriously for my dear sake'; now, however, when her dream lover has been replaced by an actual person, 'so commonplace, so dear', she finds she can only say, 'God bring you back – God bring you back!'[3] Thanet's juxtaposition of words against words – the plain against the *précieux* – is as effective as any in the protest poetry, though there is no other obvious indication of a propagandist intent in this rejection of the myth.

A considerable amount of civilian poetry about the war was the work of women. The examples I have cited here may seem to bear out the claim made by Sassoon in 'Their Frailty', that women are concerned only with the safety of their particular 'hero'. But by no means all their poetry takes such a personal approach, and propaganda poems by women, whether promoting or rejecting the patriotic–heroic myth, are largely indistinguishable from those of men. One must also remember that apparently 'confessional' poems may reflect a compassionate imagination rather than an actual experience, and compassion certainly has an important place in the poetry of women. Sometimes it borders on protest; Margaret Postgate's 'The Veteran', for instance, tells of a blind and seemingly old man giving advice to some young soldiers, and commenting to the bystanders, 'Poor chaps, how'd they know what it's like?'[4] This blind veteran sitting in the sun, whom an age of experience separates from the other men, then reveals that he is just nineteen. Although there is no explicit protest, the narrative itself serves to negate the glory that the heroic ethic promotes. Often, however, especially in poems by nurses, the compassion merges with a sense of respect that approaches implicit acceptance of the patriotic–heroic ethic, as if the nurses, no less than the men they are pledged to help, need the comfort of believing that the suffering has value and the destruction a purpose. Whether one should consider the poetry of nurses in military hospitals as the work of civilians is open to debate; Catherine Reilly includes them in her tally of uniformed personnel, and medical staff who happen to be male are usually considered to have been on active service – Klemm, Trakl, Georges Duhamel, e.e. cummings, and John McCrae, amongst them – but the nurses themselves make a clear distinction between their own role and that of the combatants, and like other women in the poetry, they apparently consider their own function in the war to be decidedly secondary.

The part played by compassion or pity in the war poetry has

received almost as much attention from English critics as realism. Discussion focuses on a sentence from Owen's draft for a preface to a collection of his verse – 'The Poetry is in the pity' – and it is generally taken for granted that pity is linked with protest. Although the terms 'pity' and 'compassion' are often interchanged, in Owen's usage pity is less an emotion experienced by the poet or reader than an impersonal and abstract quality, a 'fact' to which the poet's expression gives permanence. One sees this meaning particularly clearly in 'Strange Meeting' where one of the speakers laments that, because he has died, his knowledge of 'the pity of war' must go unrecorded:

> For of my glee might many men have laughed,
> And of my weeping something have been left
> Which must die now. I mean the truth untold,
> The pity of war, the pity war distilled. [5]

Georges Duhamel expresses a concern for precisely the same kind of truth – and the same fear that it may be remain 'untold' – when he writes in *Vie des martyrs*, 'I wish to ensure that all the suffering is not merely lost in the abyss. And that is why I give an exact account of it.'[6] This factual 'pity', of which compassion is only the original inspiration (as in the phrase 'What a pity!'), infuses some of the most impressive poetry of the war. Duhamel's 'Ballade de Florentin Prunier' tells, totally without sentimentality, of the slow death of a wounded man, while his mother sits patiently by his side willing him to live.[7] The poem conveys the author's profound respect for those who suffer, and his awareness of the importance of such small measures, however futile, as ordinary people can take in the face of the massive destruction brought about by war. Pity, in Owen's sense, is evident also in Trakl's 'Grodek', in the recognition of a 'schwarzerer Trauer', a darker sorrow than the immediate deaths – that of 'die ungeborenen Enkel' (the unborn descendants), the consequences of the war for the future. In August Stramm's 'Schlachtfeld', the lines 'Mordesmorde / blinzen / Kinderblicken' (murder upon murder blink the glances of children) convey a double measure of pity: not only are the soldiers, hardly older than children, compelled to witness so many murders, but murder lies also in their own eyes.

The recognition of 'the pity war distilled' permeates Isaac Rosenberg's 'Dead Man's Dump', which, like many other poems by combatants, examines the significance of death. Its main theme is the brevity of the moment between being alive and being dead, and the absoluteness of the change which that moment effects (the subject also of Owen's 'Futility'). As Rosenberg explores different ways of describing what happens in the instant of death – when the essence that makes one alive departs from the physical entity called the body –

he evokes both compassion for the men who have died (and whose corpses are now being crushed by wagons) and the pity of the loss of their young lives:

> None saw their spirits' shadows shake the grass,
> Or stood aside for the half used life to pass
> Out of those doomed nostrils and the doomed mouth,
> When the swift iron burning bee
> Drained the wild honey of their youth.[8]

Karl von Eisensteins's 'Tod' focuses on a single death, and the opening echoes not only Rosenberg's description of the moment when the 'half used life' escapes the body, but also his awareness of the pity of that loss:

> Er ist tot.
> Alle seine tausend Hoffnungen
> Sind in den kalten harten Wintermorgen
> Hinausgeflattert
> An dem er fiel.
> In alle Winde hinaus.
> Keiner fängt sie mehr ein. [9]

> (He is dead. All his thousand hopes fluttered away into the cold, hard winter morning on which he died, scattered to the four winds. No-one will ever recapture them.)

'The pity of war' lies in the significance of the loss of life, not just for the individual, but for all of humanity, as the hopes of thousands of 'half used lives' are scattered to the four winds.

Even so, neither compassion nor the more abstract quality, pity, is a protest device *per se*, for, as Jon Silkin has pointed out, compassion 'can tend to self-indulgence' and may be 'manipulated by warmongers'.[10] Certainly one finds both compassion and pity in patriotic poems – exemplified, like so many other aspects of the patriotic–heroic myth, in Binyon's 'For the Fallen', in such lines as

> They mingle not with their laughing comrades again,
> They sit no more at the familiar tables of home.

Compassion here is easily outweighed by the consolation inherent in the myth – Binyon's 'music in the midst of desolation' – but even the combination of pity and anger that both Silkin and Hamburger identify in the poetry that 'works best' (the phrase is Silkin's) is not confined to protest writing. Some of Jean Aicard's poems describe incidents involving brave French civilians ill-treated by the Germans, such as the fourteen-year old hero, Émile Desjardins. Atypically for patriotic verse, Aicard focuses in these poems on the suffering of one individual, and like Owen in 'Dulce et Decorum Est', he uses a narrative to validate a propagandist message. But while Owen's purpose in arousing compassion is to generate anger against his unfeeling compatriots, Aicard's target is the official enemy. The same technique as Owen's – a narrative focusing on individual suffering – is used to great effect by the Belgian poet A. Marcel in 'La Dentellière', the story of the old lacemaker fleeing from the Germans, but here, too, pity and anger support a declaration of patriotic loyalty.

Interestingly enough, although English poets not uncommonly lend support to their protest by telling of the war's effect on an individual, this device seems to have appealed far less to protest writers in the other two languages. With only a few exceptions – Duhamel's 'Ballade de Florentin Prunier', Piscator's 'Der Mutter zweier Söhne, welche fielen', and Vildrac's 'Élégie villageoise' (the story of a farmer, Jean Ruet) come first to mind – the preference is definitely for plural forms and generalisations, as if a single example were insufficiently convincing. The trend of most of the French and German protest poetry is towards direct argument instead of narrative, and towards a declaration of protest rather than a demonstration of its cause. Marcel Martinet's 'Celui-là' is one of that prolific poet's few attempts to arouse compassion and anger through an account of the suffering of one person. The speaker tells of the bravery and agony of a friend who has died of gangrene after his leg was amputated, but Martinet has so little confidence in the power of his narrative to convince that he intercedes with a direct attack upon his 'non-readers':

Et la plaie s'envenimait toujours.
Il a fallu couper une seconde fois, plus haut,
Dans cette chair encore vivante –
La chair, vous savez, comme la vôtre,
Comme la vôtre, guerriers des journaux, vous sentez?[11]

(And the wound continued to putrify. They had to cut a second time, higher up, into his still-living flesh – flesh like yours, you know, like yours, newspaper warriors – can you feel it?)

Even the title ('That one', rather than a name) suggests that Martinet is reluctant to commit his argument to a specific case and, as his other poems demonstrate, he is obviously more comfortable making his point with the help of invective, rhetoric and multiple examples, instead of depending on a closely-focused picture of individual suffering.

A partial explanation for this international difference in approach undoubtedly lies in the fact that the protest of such French or German writers as Martinet, Yvan Goll, Karl Otten and René Arcos originated in an intellectual premise – the belief, whether politically or ethically grounded, that the country's participation in the war was wrong. For most of the better-known English war poets, on the other hand, including Owen and Sassoon, the protest evolved as a consequence of war experience. It may be significant that Duhamel, whose 'Florentin Prunier' differs from the poems of most of his French confrères, refused to subscribe to Romain Rolland's initial protest.[12] His own objection to the war arose from his direct awareness of its terrible effects, and his collection of prose vignettes, *Vie des martyrs*, like the non-protesting poetry of Maurice Bouignol, was designed to honour the *poilus* by showing truthfully what they had to endure. At the same time, Duhamel's intention was to forge a permanent memory of the suffering, to make sure that it was not 'lost in the abyss', in much the same way as the Belgian patriotic poets sought to ensure the survival of their threatened culture. And like the Belgian writers, Duhamel found that concrete imagery and precise focus – 'la littérature du témoignage' (the literature of witness), to use his own phrase – served his purpose better than abstract argument.

In an essay published in 1931, a French scholar, Floris Delattre, complains that the English poetry of the war lacks both a vision of beauty and a revealing moral concept.[13] The reason for this failing, he implies, is the English preference for realism, at the expense of the kind of intellectual discussion that delights the French:

> The Englishman is not, generally speaking, an intellectual. Faced with abstract ideas, he remains a little naive, a little gauche, and, as it turns out, rather distrustful. His mind, which plunges deep roots into the real and the concrete, [. . .] is less lively than our own, which resembles [. . .] a silky fabric, so supply shimmering and floating. Logic, in which we take such pleasure, and general concepts, where we are past masters, scarcely hold his attention.[14]

Because of this limitation, Delattre claims, the English poetry fails to arouse in the reader's mind any thrill of discovery, despite its intensity and truthfulness.[15] Yet in view of the continuing popularity of some of the realistic poems, and not only amongst English readers, it is clear that this critical taste is not shared universally. On the contrary, the practice of creating a single concrete image, and especially one which shows how the war affects individuals, appears to be a very valuable manipulative device, whether the image is followed by a patriotic declaration (as in Marcel's 'La Dentellière'), merged with rejection of the patriotic–heroic ethic (in poems by Owen and Piscator, for instance), or, as in Duhamel's 'Ballade de Florentin Prunier' and Margaret Postgate's 'The Veteran' allowed to stand alone to exemplify 'the pity war distilled'. There is certainly no lack of compassion behind Yvan Goll's *Requiem für die Gefallenen von Europa*, but the soldiers whom the speaker addresses in the first 'Rezitativ' are very closely related to the idealised heroes of patriotic verse, and they remain, like those others, an abstraction:

O ihr hymnischen Menschen, Jünglinge meiner Zeit,
Warum beräubt ihr die Erde von euerer Herrlichkeit?.[16]

(O men worthy of hymns, the youth of my generation, why do you rob the earth of your splendour?)

By contrast, when the speaker in Sassoon's 'Twelve Months After' reminisces about 'Young Gibson, with his grin; and Morgan, tired and white', one is able to visualise clearly two living and ordinary soldiers, who would probably feel quite out of place amongst 'hymnischen Menschen' and 'Herrlichkeit'.[17] The confidence with which the speaker names them is evidence of both his reliability as a witness and his compassionate observation, and the briefly-drawn picture proves that, for all its massive scale, the war happens, not to abstract 'heroes' but to real people – 'des hommes comme nous' – who have names, and who participate and suffer as individuals.

While the perception of the war poetry as a single literary phenomenon reveals many international similarities, it also accentuates a number of national preferences like this predominantly English inclination to focus on individuals. Long political arguments (or harangues) in free verse, such as Martinet's 'Tu vas te battre' and Otten's 'Für Martinet', are common in German and French but apparently non-existent in English, where similar themes are treated only in shorter poems, traditional in style. On the other hand, fully-developed allegorical images like Sackville's 'The Pageant of War', Ewer's 'Three Gods' and 'A.E.' 's 'Chivalry', though by no means rare in the other languages, are especially popular as a protest device in English. Battle narratives in the heroic manner seem to be confined mainly to German, where they occur not uncommonly in the patriotic verse of the early months of the war, to the extent that Bab is able to devote an entire anthology to such 'Balladen'. That most of them deal with sea battles may explain why they are less prevalent in French (the war at sea having been fought mainly between Britain and Germany), but not their absence from the poetry of the English literary Establishment. One can appreciate the appeal of naval battles as a heroic subject in this war, since they are easy to imagine (being in essence no different from others over the centuries, despite the advent of new warships and underwater vessels), and success or failure can readily be measured. It is interesting, therefore, that few English poets seem to have seized this opportunity to celebrate the success of their heroes, preferring instead to write of them in elegaic terms like those of 'For the Fallen', which is similarly a product of the early war.

In addition to these 'set piece' narratives, which appear to have been largely the work of civilians, there are also stories of battle told from the combatant viewpoint. In his study of the Boer War poetry, M. Van Wyk Smith reports on the many examples of ballad-like narratives that imitate the manner of Victorian parlour verse, designed for recitation rather than private reading. By the time of the First World War, although one finds occasional examples published through the normal distribution system, this particular form seems to have survived chiefly in the music hall. It is possible that the chaos of the First World War battlefields discouraged such a straightforward and simple narrative approach in general – a possibility supported by the fact that most of the examples of ballad-like tales deal with aerial warfare, which offered a much clearer picture of winners and losers; on the other hand, the genre may merely have been regarded as old-fashioned, suitable for mock-heroic tales like the never-ending battle against lice, but not for serious use. Many of the individual collections of poems by combatants include at least one description of a battle incident, but although some are tales of successful ventures and heroic deeds, a sense of loss tends to predominate, as if to hint that success was perhaps too dearly bought. Even so, the ironic tone, tending towards protest, of such well-known English battle poems as Blunden's 'Third Ypres' and Sassoon's 'Counter-Attack', or of Anton Schnack's Verdun poems, is unusual; the intention of most of the poets is apparently to place their own experience, and more particularly that of their friends, in the heroic tradition, rather than to imply (as these better-known works do) the purposelessness of the war.

A narrative format that seems to have appealed particularly to French poets, not all of them combatants, is a collection of long poems systematically tracing the combatant experience – the departure from home, the journey to the Front, an account of a battle, home leave, the death of a comrade – so that the cumulative effect is of a single tale divided into episodes. Maurice Bouignol's *Sans gestes*, Franìois Porché's *Images de guerre* and *Le Poème de la Tranchée*, Marc Leclerc's *La Passion de notre frère le poilu* and Henri Dérieux's *En ces jours déchirants*, amongst others, all follow such an epic-like pattern. Apart from Anton Schnack's *Tier rang gewaltig gegen Tier*, a volume of free-verse sonnets which, as Patrick Bridgwater points out, have the quality and the appearance of epic verse, the closest counterparts I have found to these collections are some English works published in the 1930s – Leonard Barnes' *Youth at Arms*, David Jones' *In Parenthesis*, where the individual poems actually merge to form an epic, and, though told from a different perspective, Herbert Read's *The End of a War*.[18] Unlike the English examples, however, the French works I named were published in the war years, from as early as 1916. Why this epic-like format should have appealed so widely to French poets during the war, but to English writers only in retrospect, is hard to imagine. Possibly the decimation of the French army in August and September 1914 allowed the French to perceive the conflict as a journey from 'la gloire' to 'le deuil et la boue' (mourning and mud) at a very early stage, and to view the individual combatant's experience as a similar journey, but this explanation in isolation is not convincing. Like other national tendencies in the poetry, this predominantly French response is easy to identify but difficult to explain.

Early critics liked to attribute distinctive features in the war poetry of different countries to what might be termed national character. H.C. Grumbine, in his introduction to *Humanity or Hate – Which?*, attempts to establish motives for the war on the basis of the different conceptions of God which are evident in the French and German poetry, and which reflect social attitudes of the two nations. Ronald Peacock implies that the patriotic love expressed in the German verse is unique, for it is 'profoundly German in its aspirations, tenderness, and child-like simplicity';[19] and Delattre's discussion of the English poetry is biased by his belief in the superiority of the French mind, with its preference for the abstract over the concrete. Such general-isations, however, are difficult to uphold. Grumbine conveniently ignores the powerful theme of hatred in the French poetry; and most of Peacock's observations are equally applicable to the English patriotic verse, which was largely out of fashion in academic circles – and presumably, therefore, out of sight – by the time the critic was writing in 1934. Delattre's assertion is contradicted by many examples, whether the substantial amount of realistic poetry by French combatants, or the patriotic verse of civilians, which is equally abstract in the two languages. Other factors are obviously at work, in addition to – or perhaps instead of – the underlying national attitudes that these critics detect.

The absence of long free-verse diatribes in the English protest poetry may seem to bear out Delattre's assertion about the English fear of abstract ideas and logical reasoning, but the 'general concept' of pacifism had as much support in England as in France, and evidence of socialist opposition to the war is not hard to find. Yet while the French and German poets who promoted those causes preferred an experimental verse form, pacifist and socialist poems in English are traditional in style. The most obvious explanation for this difference in taste is the relative stage of development towards poetic

Modernism in the three languages. By 1914, *vers libre* was still confined to a very small group of English poets, mainly the Imagistes and their friends, while it had achieved much greater currency in the other countries. Further, the context of publication of the protest poems encouraged this greater English tendency to adhere to the traditional. The major outlets for protest poetry on the Continent were journals and publishers for whom literature was of major interest – *Die Aktion*, for instance, and the publishing houses of Kurt Wolff in Leipzig and *La Nouvelle Revue Franìaise* in Paris. The English protest verse, on the other hand, first appeared in political rather than literary publications, most notably *The Herald* and *The Nation*. Conceivably the literary editors of journals like these – and the writers themselves – assumed that readers would not appreciate long experimental poems, at a time when the public taste in poetry was largely traditional, and especially when space was limited by the high cost of newsprint.

Another significant contributing factor was almost certainly the relative neglect of the poetry of Walt Whitman by the English literary Establishment before the war. In studies of the French and German literature of the prewar years, and in literary magazines from that time, Whitman's name occurs with great regularity; he was obviously very highly regarded, both by writers who shared his humanitarian and democratic standards (including the German worker-poets) and by those who admired his *vers libre* technique. (The Unanimistes, amongst others, appreciated him on both counts.) In England, on the other hand, his work seems to have attracted little attention in the prewar period except amongst experimental poets. Consequently, while his influence on the war poetry of France and Germany is obvious and wide-spread, affecting some patriotic poems as well as many works of protest, on the English it appears to have left very little trace, even amongst the socialist and pacifist writers who might have found in his verse a particularly useful model. The result, however, is not necessarily for the worse, for instead of direct argument and diatribe, most of these poets presented their case equally effectively through allegory – a traditional tool for political comment amongst writers and artists of all three cultures in the past, and destined to assume a central role as a protest device in literature under oppressive governments later in the century. (Like sarcasm, allegory offers a hidden as well as an overt message, so that a text which a 'non-reader' may perceive as innocuous has different significance for the intended audience.)

Provided one does not venture into the more complex question of why Whitman was largely neglected by the English literary community immediately before the war, or why English poets and readers adhered more firmly to tradition, the absence of free-verse political diatribes in that language is relatively easy to understand. In general, however, there is no such simple explanation for national tendencies in the poetry; immediate and more remote literary tradition, local influence (amongst friends, for instance), the cultural past, the demands of the context of publication, and the historical situation of the war, must all have played their part, no doubt with the help of other factors. To explore the differing tendencies individually would require a close examination not only of the poems within each group, the circumstances that inspired them, the date of writing and the form of their initial publication, but also of the culture and the specific literary tradition from which they emanated, all blended with a substantial amount of speculation. And ultimately one might conclude, as most comparatists do, that differences are less significant than similarities in the discussion of international literary relationships.

There is no doubt that the international approach to First World War poetry as a whole has given emphasis to many features that are less obvious in the product of a single language. Critics of the English poetry have easily dismissed patriotic verse as the last flourish of an old tradition, but as an international phenomenon it clearly demands much more than passing attention, if only because of its scale and homogeneity. Although the hindsight provided by the knowledge of events leading up to the Second World War tends to colour one's perception, it is difficult to subscribe to Ronald Peacock's belief that the German attitude towards the homeland was unique. The evidence of the patriotic poetry suggests, on the contrary, that at the time of the First World War the inhabitants of Great Britain, France and Germany all held a very similar concept of what it means to belong to a nation. Some of the accoutrements of nationalism differ from country to country: the 'play the game' philosophy of the Victorian public school is merged with patriotic commitment by some of the English poets (though perhaps less markedly than in the Boer War), but it has no part in the verse of the other two languages; physical destruction as a symbol for the attack upon the nation as a whole is (not surprisingly) confined largely to French poetry; and the German version of medievalism in the war leans towards specifically Germanic sources, rather than the Arthurian mythology common to all three cultures in the Middle Ages. But beneath these superficial and understandable differences lies a shared perception of the homeland as the centre of one's existence and one's identity. Binyon's words in 'For the Fallen', 'Flesh of her flesh they were, spirit of her spirit', with their 'bardic' phrasing, their personification of the homeland as a god-like being, and their sense of intense mutual belonging between the individual and the nation, could equally well have come from a French or German poet. While the Germans are apparently more willing to voice directly their devotion to the new god, a similar attitude of absolute loyalty and quasi-religious worship is implied in, and no less central to, the English and French patriotic verse. Unlike France and Germany, Britons could not justifiably claim to be fighting to defend the physical terrain of their homeland; yet the sense of a threat to the nation's sovereignty is quite as prevalent in the English poetry as in that of the other two languages. To defend the nation, it is clear, means not only to protect the land, but also to fight for the country's prestige. (Appeals to American patriotism during the Vietnam War often took a similar form.) For all the belligerent countries the major weapon in the war was not guns or shells but people, and the availability of that weapon depended on the readiness of individuals to sacrifice their lives, or to condone the death of hundreds and thousands of compatriots, in the nation's cause. The patriotic and heroic poetry helped to further the acceptance of the creed of 'the supreme sacrifice', but at the same time the existence of the poetry, coming from a diverse group of writers within the population at large, and published very widely in accordance with what one must assume to be the taste of the reading public, serves as a reminder that the belief was already firmly implanted.

Considered collectively, and especially in light of the readiness with which it was accepted for publication, the patriotic poetry conveys the impression that an excuse for an outburst of loyal fervour had been eagerly awaited. The nations involved in the war were not necessarily especially bellicose before August 1914, but there is no doubt that citizens as individuals seized with enthusiasm the opportunity to give full voice to the response for which their upbringing had prepared them – hence the feeling of gratitude at having lived to experience the 'supreme moment' or 'His hour'. Since Prussia and France had had state systems of education for over a century, and since both France and Germany had subjected a large number of young men to military training, it is perhaps not surprising that the outcome in these cases was a similar sense of commitment to the nation's cause. Britain had neither a long history of systematic national schooling nor any compulsory military training, but the evolution of the three societies was roughly parallel in other respects, especially in the spread of education and the enfranchisement of an increasing proportion of the population, and by 1914 the same concept of the nation prevailed. The evidence of the war poetry suggests that in this concept the homogeneity of the people was taken for granted, for although traces of Social Darwinism remain, and of condescension towards the working class, these remnants are limited. Dialect poems, which emphasise differences within the nation by imputing to specific classes and regions a distinctive manner of speaking and writing, and which had been very popular in the second half of the nineteenth century (they were a major feature of Boer War poetry, for instance), are relatively uncommon in the widely-circulated Great War anthologies. The examples that occur come almost exclusively from middle-class writers; one senses that working-class poets were anxious to prove their ability to write their language correctly, in keeping with their serious subject, rather than drawing attention to their own peculiarities of speech. Although dialect poems are more common in German than in English or French (apart from those performed in the English music hall), for the most part it is taken for granted in all three languages that readers and writers from all classes are familiar with the same vocabulary, the same patriotic clichés and allusions, and the same verse patterns. Furthermore, individuality is minimised throughout the poetry: description is general, heroes are celebrated *en masse* and anonymously, and even the traditional 'lyric I' is replaced by a collective 'we'. The poetry is thus entirely in keeping with its position as a reflection of the kind of society that produced both mass literacy and mass armies.

While one might be tempted to dismiss as a poetic device the assumption that all members of the nation were fully committed to the national cause, the evidence of social history suggests that the enthusiasm for war and the readiness to fight were indeed shared by all classes (though not necessarily by all individuals). Poems that can justifiably be attributed to writers from the working class tended to voice strong patriotic dedication, while protest verse concerning the exploitation of the workers came mainly from people who were not amongst the exploited. Although poetry in itself cannot safely be considered as direct evidence of popular opinion, since poets are always a minority, and since one must also allow for the factors that control publication (especially when a challenge to the literary or political Establishment is involved), in this case there is no reason to doubt that general education had produced mass loyalty to the nation. Nevertheless, just as the homogeneity within the poetry was an involuntary consequence of the ethic that inspired the writers, rather than a deliberate choice, so the equalising effect of nationalism upon society in general was largely unintentional. Indeed, the 'invention', in the last three decades of the old century, of traditions designed to promote national unity was contemporaneous with the introduction of others whose effect – whether intentional or otherwise – was to establish or maintain class distinction.[20] *Studentenkorps* in German universities (introduced, like fraternities in American colleges, when these institutions began to attract substantially larger numbers of students in the 1860s), public schools and Old Boys' dinners in Britain, and élite club sports such as golf and tennis ('invented' around 1870) all served to exclude the lower-middle and working classes and thus keep them 'in their place'. So while the workers themselves saw schooling as a vital first step towards social and financial equality, the political implementation of general education was not viewed by the majority of its promoters as a means of obliterating existing social divisions; it was intended, rather, to preserve the new industrial and bourgeois status quo. And similarly, the significance of patriotic commitment in the war was perceived in different ways according to the perceiver's social status. Despite the nationalistic edict that all citizens were children of the same mother or sons of the same father, the upper classes had apparently not anticipated that the lower orders would share their own intense patriotic dedication when war broke out. The workers, on the other hand, had taken that edict to heart, assuming that the verbal expression of loyalty meant also a claim to equality, and that the willingness to risk one's life on behalf of the nation was the ultimate form of both loyalty and equality. This class-related disparity in expectations – the members of the one group taking it for granted, because of their loyal dedication, that postwar society would be egalitarian, and the other side seeing no reason why it should be so – affected the future of Europe ineradicably, most notably through the part it played in the progress of Nazism and communism.

Like the patriotic verse of the war, the protest poetry assumes a different appearance when it is viewed internationally. The aphorism 'They use propaganda; we just tell the truth' treats lightheartedly the serious fact that one tends to overlook the propagandist function of statements with which one agrees. Since the predominant attitude towards war in literary–critical circles in the last few decades has been anti-militaristic, criticism of the well-known English protest poetry has focused on truth rather than propaganda – and the more so, since to designate a literary work as propagandist is often considered an insult. But if poems like those of Sassoon and Owen are placed against the background of protest verse from other languages, their propagandist intention is brought to the fore, and the poetry's functioning is seen in a clearer light. It becomes evident that the protest was not primarily a response to the terrible reality of the Front, but an attempt to counter the outpouring of chauvinistic rhetoric that the war generated – a battle of words against words; and the juxtaposing of the language of the patriotic-heroic creed against the reality of the soldiers' experience was only one of several possible means of attack. Viewing the texts as an international corpus, one perceives very readily that the accepted account of the war poetry in terms of historical progression from pro-war to anti-war attitudes distorts the picture as a whole, robbing some well-known poems of contextual features that might contribute to a more complete understanding of the poet's intention, and denying others their proper role in the history of the period. The protest of Owen and Sassoon was not, as some critics have implied, an expression of personal disillusionment (though in retrospect it may have seemed so) and it was not a reaction against the hope and idealism of 1914; rather, it was a reflection of the circumstances at the time the poems were written – a response to the fact that in 1917 and 1918 the glory of sacrificial death *pro patria* was still being preached, while official policy maintained that victory was the only possible resolution of the war, regardless of the cost. The international perspective also shows that most of the work of combatant protesters is not significantly different from that of civilians, since the realistic description that most readily distinguishes between the two proves, in terms of quantity, to have played a relatively minor role (though qualitatively an impressive one) in the protest. Otherwise, similar imagery, the same tone of animosity or provocation, and the same overriding concern with 'truth' are found on both sides of the supposed 'two nations' divide. The recognition that the poets' protest is a response less to the horror of war than to the words and wordmakers of nationalistic chauvinism resolves two troubling problems. One can reconcile the supposedly anti-war attitude of combatant protest poets with their willingness to continue fighting, and one can understand why some of the poets were prepared to countenance another war, presumably destined to be no less bloody and destructive than the last, only twenty years later, when circumstances had changed and an evil of a different kind had to be fought.

In Marcel Martinet's 'Poètes d'Allemagne, ô frères inconnus', the famous and established poets of the two countries seek to validate their position as spokesmen for the public by pointing out that they are successful authors, whose books sell. Speaking on behalf of their opponents, the 'unknown' combatant writers, Osbert Sitwell in 'Rhapsode' sets out what might be termed the manifesto of these international 'frères inconnus': 'But we are poets, and shall tell the truth.' The juxtaposing of truth against lies is the single most persistent motif in the protest poetry. It is significant, however, that 'Rhapsode' was first published under the pseudonym 'Miles' ('a soldier'), for it is Sitwell's role as observer-participant, rather than as poet, that guarantees his truthfulness. As both Sitwell and Martinet recognise, factors outside the text itself affect credibility. And just as an established literary reputation undoubtedly helped already famous writers like Paul Claudel and Thomas Hardy to be believed when they spoke out on the subject of national commitment, so the dual role of Sitwell and his cohorts has proved to be a highly convincing propagandist device, by upholding the validity of their account of the soldiers' experience.

Sitwell's particular objection in 'Rhapsode' is to the way people have accepted as empirical truth the propaganda of patriotic heroism, and have applied this literary or mythical standard to the conduct of men in the world of reality. It is ironic, therefore, that many readers of verse like his have made precisely the same error, in accepting at face value the protest poets' representation of 'the facts themselves', and assuming without question that the poems reflect the actual situation in all respects. Heroism is a case in point. Many protest poems by combatants, especially in English, convey the impression that mechanised warfare allowed no opportunity for the kind of action that, in the past, would have been designated as heroic. Yet outside the protest poetry there is ample evidence of individual acts of outstanding courage, including many tales of men who risked their lives to help the wounded comrades. (It is worth recalling that the heroes of the past were always a small minority, otherwise their story would not be considered worth telling; Grace Darling and Florence Nightingale were no ordinary women.) To the retrospective observer, incidents of heroism in the war are likely to appear insignificant against the background of the chaos of the battlefields and the massive slaughter, but the poets themselves must surely have been aware of some of them; indeed, both Owen and Sassoon were awarded the Military Cross for bravery, and they presumably did not consider themselves unique. The picture of war that they draw in their poetry, however, makes no allowance for heroism.

Instead of being persuaded by the combatant poets' dual role to believe that the persona's observations may be taken as a reflection of 'the whole truth' (rather than just a part of it), one should enquire more closely about their propagandist intent. Although there is no doubt that their poems served as a much-needed antidote to the patriotic–heroic creed, their primary aim was not so much to replace that 'romancing' with an objective and unbiased picture as to discredit the beliefs of their opponents. Such a hostile position could not permit the 'civilised ambiguity' of acknowledging, for example, that some soldiers actually did 'die a hero's death', that some women campaigned fiercely against the war, or that combatants in real life did not all feel alienated from the world of home. While the poets' protest was certainly not frivolous, nor their concern for the suffering insincere, there is occasionally a hint of game-playing in their apparent aim of alienating their 'non-readers', and the tone of some of the poems suggests that they were written, not out of 'shared distress', as Jon Silkin phrases it, but out of a shared pleasure in appearing to provoke the opposition.[21] Yet for the poets this, too, was a means of accommodating the reality of the war – as one sees in the willingness with which Owen, a year after he was sent home suffering from shell-shock, chose to return to France, where he not only continued his fight on behalf of the men, but also proved himself to his own satisfaction as a soldier.

Because the tendency of war poetry criticism has been to locate the poems mainly in the context of the writer's personal experience, one has an impression of the well-known poets as more or less isolated individuals each producing a unique response to an unusual situation – a situation that threatens to overwhelm him. To view them instead as members of small political groups (to use the term 'political' in its wider sense), writing for each other and for a limited but sympathetic audience, and intent on alienating rather than persuading the mass of readers, is to place their poetry in a well-established tradition. The use of literature as a tool of resistance to an oppressive political regime has been a particularly marked characteristic of twentieth century social life in many European countries – Germany in the 1930s, France during the Occupation, Czechoslovakia, Poland and the Soviet Union, amongst others. Although the protest poets of the war had easy access to publication in comparison with their successors, and relatively little interference from the powers-that-be, most of the propaganda devices they chose to use reflect their awareness that their cause was unacceptable to the authorities, and potentially (if not actually) subject to suppression. While their work is generally in keeping with the old traditions of minority resistance, especially as these are evinced in folksongs of social protest, in one major respect it belongs firmly to the twentieth century: in the poets' recognition of the power of mass propaganda to create a climate in which the official creed is widely accepted and protest easily suppressed. The prediction of one of the speakers in Owen's 'Strange Meeting' – that 'None shall break rank, though nations trek from progress' – has come near to fulfilment many times. For the few individuals with the courage and the strength to resist persuasion and intimidation, to be isolated almost certainly means to abandon hope, and only through their association with like-minded people – whether in the immediate contact of a circle of companions, or through the more remote connection between writer and reader – can their resistance remain alive. The protest poetry of the war demonstrates very clearly how such minority propaganda reaches out to its designated audience, and its therapeutic value in helping writers and readers face an otherwise intolerable situation.

If one defines the protest poetry as that in which the writer posits an excluded non-reader and attacks the upholders of the patriotic–heroic myth (or the myth itself), it may seem tautological to argue that combatant verse which lacks these elements, however much it may be concerned with the reality of war, is not propagandist. Even so, other critics have also raised doubts about the protest function of poems by Rosenberg, Blunden and Gurney – amongst them, Desmond Graham in *The Truth of War* (1984) and Richard Hoffpauir in 'The War Poetry of Edmund Blunden and Ivor Gurney' (1985). Possibly, therefore, the definition merely offers a theoretical basis for a *de facto* and increasingly recognised distinction between propagandist and non-propagandist writing by combatants. The distinction can never be absolute because propaganda is ultimately in the eye of the beholder, and because the same 'strange and extraordinary' world confronted all the combatant poets, so that even the most obviously propagandist poems are also a personal means of mastering the horror of the war. Nevertheless, when writers like Rosenberg, Blunden and Klemm are considered primarily as exponents of personal or exploratory verse, rather than in the role of protester *manqué* that was assigned to them in some earlier criticism (including, with regard to Blunden at least, Jon Silkin's *Out of Battle*), one is in a position to appreciate much more fully the richness and significance of their work.

Graham argues that Rosenberg's poetry reveals, more accurately than that of the protest writers, 'the truth of war as the soldier experienced it'.[22] This assessment is valid in the sense that, instead of offering a picture of unremitting hardship (as the protest poets do), Rosenberg seizes also upon moments of pleasure – the antics of the men in 'Louse Hunting', for instance, or in 'Returning, we hear larks' the strange beauty of the birds' song in the darkness, as the men who have escaped death return to 'a little safe sleep'. On the other hand, Rosenberg's poetic account of his war experience is always fully controlled – there is little indication of any extreme emotion, or of the threat of madness that is hinted at in poems by Aldington and Lersch, amongst many others. As a reflection of 'the truth of war', poetry has the advantage of being able to intensify the experience, to represent it in a concentrated form; but this special perception implies the ability to distance oneself from the event, so that, to the ordinary participant, only in retrospect does the experience match the poem. The war poetry that has survived as literature (rather than merely as artifacts on library shelves) evinces to an extraordinary degree this ability to give focus and meaning which were probably not obvious in the original experience. One might expect, therefore, that the less able poetry of combatants – the kind written, perhaps, by Blunden's 'cheerful soldier from the East End' – would be more likely to reflect the experience of ordinary soldiers. In actuality, however, that is rarely the case, since in most of their work the demands of rhyme and metre, and the reluctance to break the conventions of what is considered poetic, tend to take precedence over the representation of reality, and the devices that usually contribute to the effectiveness of poetry as a medium of perception and communication serve instead as an impediment. (Their prose accounts, whether letters or memoirs, tend to be much more colourful.) Yet the poetry of ordinary soldiers, no less than the work of gifted poets, is a product of the war, and the fact that the writing of verse was important to them despite their difficulties with the medium is significant. Every poem, whatever its literary merit, reflects some aspect of the reality of the war, and although each in isolation may contribute little, together they form a mosaic, a composite picture that perhaps comes close to the 'truth' of the experience.[23]

So far as most people are concerned, history is a fixed chronology of events – the account of 'what actually happened' – and the past is assumed to be ultimately knowable, in the same sense as, say, the flora of a remote and rarely-visited part of the world; all one needs is the complete and unbiased evidence. Historians, however, are likely to hold a different view. J.G. Droysen, one of the nineteenth-century founders of historiography, persistently returns to a fundamental principle: that the past has gone, and that the basis of historical study is not the past but those remnants of the past that exist in the present, in the 'here and now'.[24] Daniel Boorstin, the former Librarian of Congress and a social historian, shares the same awareness that the past is accessible only through the 'relics' that, by chance, it has left behind.[25] Boorstin observes that the historian's role is both to discover and to create the past, and this duality, he says, is implicit in the very word 'history', which means both the course of events and the written account of them. The second meaning is emphasised even further in some modern philosophy of history, where the story of the past is perceived as a narrative like any other. The implication is that, just as there is no one correct analysis of a poem, and no single definitive performance of a piano concerto, but a balance between the text or musical score – the *donnée* or 'relics' – and the individual's interpretation, so there is no definitive version of the past. The 'best' history is in theory that which accounts most fully for what still exists in the 'here and now', though in practice an artistic narrative may be more convincing and more highly appreciated than a scientific re-examination of the relics.

The particular story that is told, however, depends on the selection of evidence. As Boorstin describes the process, historians examine the objects the past has left behind, and then 'try to convince us that the relics they have examined and interpreted in their narrative are a reliable sample of the experience people really had'. Unfortunately, he maintains, their account is necessarily biased by the accidents of survival – the tendency of things that are expensive or rarely used, for example, to outlast the commonplace objects that have a prominent part in the daily life of a community – with the result that the relics most readily available to the historian are not necessarily valuable as a reflection of ordinary experience. One can see a similar pattern in the war poetry, since the poems on which previous histories of the genre have been based are those that appeal to a modern audience, rather than those that were popular in their day. Their survival, however, reverses the process that determines the continuing existence of other kinds of relics: they have survived, not because of their uselessness, but because they have filled a need for modern critics and readers. Amongst the remains of the past that are to be found in the 'here and now', Droysen distinguishes between 'Erinnerungen' (recollections) – verbal responses that record how an event or situation was perceived or remembered – and 'überreste' (remnants), artifacts that have survived in something like their original form from one 'present' into another.[26] All the war poems clearly belong to both categories, but literary historians have viewed the majority only as 'überreste', material objects that happen to be preserved in museums or libraries, but that otherwise are unworthy of attention. The few that have been used as 'Erinnerungen' – that is, as a source of evidence about contemporary response – have also been circulated and analysed as current works of literature; and as a consequence of the merging of these two functions, the 'excellent' poems that recur in the modern anthologies and criticism have become an integral part of the present perception of the war, providing a direct link with the past as if in a living chain of memory. ('The poet is always our contemporary.') In the process, however, they appear to have lost some of their original force; the picture of war that was intended to shock is now simply taken for granted as 'the truth', and the poets' protest against militarism is assumed (quite inappropriately) to have been victorious. Critics and anthologists – and sometimes the poets themselves, in memoirs or autobiographies – have written their history of the war too convincingly, and readers, as Desmond Graham observes, are now inclined to 'absorb both [the] poetry and the war itself back into clichés of attitude'.[27]

If the clichés are indeed a serious threat to modern appreciation of the poems, and consequently to their future accessibility, the solution may be to separate the two functions. Owen and Rosenberg are poets as well as 'First World War poets'; the tragedy of the 'half used lives' of young men, the 'old Lie' that the cause makes dying in battle 'dulce et decorum', are almost as old, and certainly as modern, as war itself, and the poems need no validation from specific historical reference or biographical context. If the historical bonds were loosened, it is possible that, whether as observations about the sadly persistent social phenomenon called war, or as comments on the human condition in general, the poems would reach some of those readers whom the 'clichés of attitude' about the Great War have made (in Owen's own words) 'immune / To pity'. Alternatively, however, one might set aside temporarily their function as literary texts, and concentrate instead on their role as historical relics. Placed against the background of a wide range of similar 'recollections', including some from other countries, familiar poems reveal unexpected facets. Furthermore, the awareness that these remnants of the past are artifacts as well as texts serves as a reminder that, to have influenced the minds of people in another age, the poems must have passed through their hands, and that a publisher must have recognised each work's potential appeal to a specific group of readers. The writer's position *vis à vis* his or her anticipated audience (whether implied or actual) assumes new importance, and consequently the propagandist role of the poetry – or, in the case of many combatant poets, its non-propagandist intention – becomes more distinct. Meanwhile, as anthologists like Reilly and Hibberd and Onions have already shown, the neglected verse offers ample evidence of the inaccuracy of many long-standing assumptions. As the clichés dissipate before the broader selection of relics, a significantly different account of the poetry as a whole emerges, more complex than the old one, and capable of explaining factual details that the other could not begin to accommodate.

Not only is the past no longer accessible, but its shadow, history, is constantly shifting, reshaped by each generation to meet the needs of a changing present. The image of the First World War as a sudden and radical change of direction for modern civilisation is now challenged by many historians. It has survived longer in literary–critical circles, especially in association with the supposed shift from pro-war to anti-war attitudes, but the process of rewriting the history of the war poetry is under way. In the old version nationalism played little part, since it was equated with chauvinism and dismissed as irrelevant to 'the truth of war' and the work of the major poets. The new history, with its concern for a wider range of texts and a more complete picture of the contemporary scene, cannot ignore the principle of nationhood that lies behind both the poetry and the social structure. Before August 1914 the power of modern nations to inspire the unquestioning loyalty of all their members was largely untested, but in that 'supreme moment' at the start of the first total war, when the eagerness of citizens to prove their dedication was at last fully matched by the country's need, nationalism came to fruition. Nor did it decline as a result of the war. Nations – cohesive, distinct, autonomous and at least nominally democratic societies – are still accepted as the norm; national governments have assumed responsibility for the well-being of citizens in areas far beyond the schooling with which the welfare state began; and the sanctity of the homeland continues to be taken for granted, so that chauvinism re-appears with surprising strength, even amongst sophisticated people, whenever national sovereignty or prestige is threatened. Nevertheless, this no longer new 'form of social organisation' finds itself challenged on many fronts, and under the combined pressure of world-wide environmental concerns, international trade and finance, the 'new regional nationalisms', and a movement away from the national institutions and services that help maintain popular commitment, it is apparently destined for change or extinction. Internationalism, where the future seems to lie, offers many potential benefits, but at the same time the loss of national identity (one's 'insurance' and 'security', according to Gellner) may produce a sense of disorientation and considerable social disintegration. There is no doubt, however, that this new international society will be strongly affected by the nationalistic social structure that it must inherit and supersede, nor that internationalism, with its potential advantages and drawbacks, becomes easier to assess if one understands what nationhood and nationalism have meant in the life of individuals. First World War poetry, whether it celebrates national identity, pleads for the humane standards endangered by total commitment to the nation, or reflects unprotesting compliance with the demand for sacrifice, is a comprehensive verbal response to the war in which nationalism came into its own, and it can certainly contribute to that understanding.

Notes

1 They All Write Poetry

1 Charles Sorley, *The Letters of Charles Sorley, with a Chapter of Biography* (Cambridge: University Press, 1919), p. 183.
2 Michael Hamburger, *The Truth of Poetry: Tensions in Modern Poetry from Baudelaire to the 1960s* (Harmondsworth: Penguin, 1969), p. 164.
3 'Aufschriften an Eisenbahn-wagen, Unterständen u. dergleichen.' *Deutsches Bücherverzeichnis*, vol. VI (1915–20), p. 1855.
4 *Das literarische Echo*, 1 October 1914, p. 5.
5 '. . . als relativ harmloser Herausgeber einer Anthologie von Kriegsgedichten.' *Das literarische Echo*, 15 December 1914, p. 342.
6 '1 500 000', in Julius Bab (ed.), *1914: Der deutsche Krieg im deutschen Gedicht* (12 vols, Berlin: Morawe und Scheffelt, 1914–19), vol. VII, p. 46.
7 August Stramm, 'Haidekampf', *Tropfblut: Gedichte* (Berlin: Der Sturm, 1915), p. 33.
8 Georges Sabiron, 'Haï-Kaï', in Association des Écrivains Combattants, *Anthologie des écrivains morts à la guerre, 1914–1918* (5 vols, Amiens: E. Malfère, 1924–6), vol. I, p. 619.
9 'La plupart des écrivains que ces jeunes gens admiraient dans leur adolescence avaient plus ou moins mis leur plume au service de "l'effort de guerre".' . . . 'Les futurs surréalistes ne songeaient pas à prolonger un mouvement dont les représentants les plus en vue s'étaient si gravement compromis avec la débilité martiale.' Philippe Audoin, *Les Surréalistes* (Paris: Seuil, 1973), pp. 10, 14.
10 Joy Cave, *What Became of Corporal Pittman?* (Portugal Cove, Newfoundland: Breakwater Books, 1976), p. 151.
11 Jon Silkin, *Out of Battle: The Poetry of the Great War* (Oxford: Oxford University Press, 1972), p. 1.
12 Letter to Lady Hylton, quoted by John Press, *A Map of Modern English Verse*, (London: Oxford University Press, 1969), p. 147.
13 'Der Chauvinismus ist die ständige Lebensgefahr der Menschheit.' Franz Pfemfert, 'Die Besessenen', *Die Aktion*, 1 August 1914, p. 672; Wilfred Owen, 'Insensibility', *Complete Poems and Fragments*, ed. Jon Stallworthy (London: Chatto and Windus, 1983), vol. I, p. 145.
14 Reilly, Gardner and Hibberd and Onions all offer very useful biographical notes on the poets they have selected.
15 For example, Michel Décaudin, 'Études sur la poésie française contemporaine, IV: Destin de l'unanimisme', *L'Information littéraire* 19 (1967),

pp. 156–65; B. F. Stoltzfus, 'Unanimism Revisited', *Modern Language Quarterly* 21 (1960), pp. 239–45.

16 Volkmann writes in his introduction, 'Der Vorstand der Gesellschaft "Deutsche Literatur" war sich mit den Herausgebern und dem Bearbeiter darin einig, daß es heute nicht angebracht wäre, auch die Gruppe "Dichtung der Kriegsgegner" in dieser Sammlung neuerlich zu Wort kommen zu lassen.' *Deutsche Dichtung im Weltkrieg (1914–1918)* (Leipzig: Reclam, 1934), p. 48.

17 The year of Georg Heym's death is given as 1913 instead of 1912 (p. 4), F.T. Marinetti is supplied with the wrong forename (p. 13), and, more seriously, the words 'in Schilf' in Heym's poem 'Der Krieg' are mistranslated as 'on the shelves' instead of 'amongst reeds' (p. 5), and the mistranslation used as a basis for interpretation.

18 Robert de Sousa, 'L'Heure nous tient', in Robert de la Vaissière (ed.), *Anthologie poétique du XXe siècle* (Paris: Crès, 1923), vol. II, p. 155.

19 *The Nation*, 5 December 1914, p. 308.

20 'Die politische Bedeutung der *Aktion*', in Paul Raabe, *Expressionismus: Aufzeichnungen und Erinnerungen der Zeitgenossen* (Olten: Walter, 1965), p. 194.

21 Dominic Hibberd and John Onions (eds), *Poetry of the Great War: An Anthology* (Basingstoke: Macmillan, 1986), p. 4.

22 Brian Gardner (ed.), *Up the Line to Death: The War Poets 1914–1918* (London: Eyre Methuen, 1976), p. xxii.

23 [George Willis], 'Any Soldier to His Son', *The Nation*, 23 November 1918, p. 221.

24 Patrick Bridgwater, *The German Poets of the First World War* (London: Croom Helm, 1985), p. 1. Fortunately this perception is not central to Bridgwater's argument, and does not affect the value of his comments on individual poets.

25 See Eric Hobsbawm and Terence Ranger (eds), *The Invention of Tradition: Europe, 1870–1914* (Cambridge: Cambridge University Press, 1983).

26 William Ray, *Literary Meaning: From Phenomenology to Deconstruction* (Oxford: Blackwell, 1984), p.12.

27 *Poetics*, trans. Gerald F. Else (Ann Arbor: University of Michigan Press, 1967), p. 33.

28 Bernard Bergonzi, *Heroes' Twilight: A Study of the Literature of the Great War*, 2nd edition (London: Macmillan, 1980), p. 10.

29 Paul Fussell, *The Great War and Modern Memory* (New York: Oxford University Press, 1975), p. ix.

30 ibid., p. 247.

31 Hugh Kenner, *The Pound Era* (Berkeley and Los Angeles: University of California Press, 1971), p. 201; Gaudier-Brzeska letter quoted in Noel Stock, *The Life of Ezra Pound* (London: Routledge and Kegan Paul, 1970), p. 172.

2 Heilig Vaterland

1 'Holy Fatherland, at this moment raise thy head boldly and gaze around. See us all aflame, son standing by sons: We shall pass away but thou, land, shalt remain.' Rudolf Alexander Schröder, 'Heilig Vaterland', *Heilig Vaterland* (Leipzig: Insel, 1914), p. 9. The poem also appears under the title 'Deutscher Schwur'.

2 Basil H. Liddell Hart, *The War in Outline 1914–1918* (New York: The Modern Library, 1936), p. 19.
3 A.J.P. Taylor, *The First World War: An Illustrated History* (Harmondsworth: Penguin, 1966).
4 Tony Ashworth, *Trench Warfare 1914–1918: The Live and Let Live System* (London: Macmillan, 1980).
5 Liddell Hart, *The War in Outline*, p. 19.
6 Laurence Lafore, *The Long Fuse: An Interpretation of the Origins of World War One* (Philadelphia: Lippencott, 1965), p. 17.
7 Barry Hunt and Adrian Preston (eds), *War Aims and Strategic Policy in the Great War* (London: Croom Helm, 1977), p. 10.
8 Betty T. Bennett (ed.), *British War Poetry in the Age of Romanticism* (New York: Garland, 1976), p. 245. Southey tells of the consequences of a battle that was fought in 1704, but as Bennett recognises, the poem, first published in 1800, is actually a comment on the current war against France.
9 Gerhart Hauptmann, 'O mein Vaterland', in Bab (ed.), *1914: Der deutsche Krieg im deutschen Gedicht*, vol. II, p. 4; Heinrich Lersch, 'Soldaten-Abschied', ibid., vol. I, p. 6; Fritz von Unruh, 'Reiterlied', ibid., vol. I, p. 16; Theodore Botrel, 'Hardi, les gâs', *Les Chants du bivouac: 1er août—31 décembre, 1914* (Paris: Payot, 1915), p. 17; Paul Claudel, 'Tant que vous voudrez, mon général', *Poèmes de guerre* (Paris: La Nouvelle Revue Française, 1922), p. 13; Raymond de la Tailhède, *Hymne pour la France* (Paris: Émile-Paul, 1917), p. 7; John Freeman, 'Happy is England Now', in Edward Marsh (ed.) *Georgian Poetry 1916–1917* (London: Poetry Bookshop, 1917), p. 138; Laurence Binyon, 'For the Fallen', *The Four Years* (London: Elkin Mathews, 1919), p. 42; Rudyard Kipling, 'For All We Have and Are', in *Songs and Sonnets for England in War Time* (London: Bodley Head, 1914), p. 94.
10 Ronald Peacock, 'The Great War in German Lyrical Poetry', *Proceedings of the Leeds Philosophical and Literary Society 3* (1934), p. 194.
11 Rudolf Herzog, 'Zwei Worte', *Ritter, Tod und Teufel: Kriegsgedichte* (Leipzig: Quelle und Meyer, 1915), p. 19.
12 Ernest Gellner, *Nations and Nationalism* (Oxford: Blackwell, 1983), p. 48.
13 Ernest Gellner, *Culture, Identity and Politics* (Cambridge: Cambridge University Press), p. 114.
14 Gellner, *Nations*, p. 22.
15 ibid., p. 10.
16 ibid., p. 57.
17 Gellner, *Culture*, p. 15, p. 17.
18 Gellner, *Nations*, p. 55.
19 Lersch, 'Bekenntnis', *Deutschland! Lieder und Gesänge von Volk und Vaterland* (Jena: Diederichs, 1918), p. 28; Auguste Prieur, 'Accalmie', in Georges Turpin (ed.), *Les Poètes de la guerre* (Paris: Fischbacher, 1917), vol. I, p. 159.
20 Carlton J.H. Hayes, *Nationalism: A Religion* (New York: Macmillan, 1960). The title is unfortunate, since the parallel to nationalism is not a single religion but religion in general. 'A religion', in nationalistic terms, would be the worship of a specific nation. Nevertheless, Hayes' book offers many interesting insights.
21 Cited in J.M. Golby and A.W. Purdue, *The Civilisation of the Crowd: Popular Culture in England, 1750–1900* (London: Batsford, 1984), p. 138.
22 Quoted in Valerie Chancellor, *History for their Masters: Opinion in the English History Textbook, 1800–1914* (Bath: Adams and Dart, 1970), title page.

23 Gordon C. Craig, *Germany, 1866–1945* (New York: Oxford University Press, 1978).
24 Golby and Purdue, *The Civilisation of the Crowd*, pp. 24, 30, 34.
25 'Mass-Producing Traditions: Europe, 1870–1914', in Eric Hobsbawm and Terence Ranger (eds), *The Invention of Tradition* (Cambridge: Cambridge University Press, 1983), pp. 263–307.
26 'The British Monarchy, c. 1820–1977', in Hobsbawm and Ranger (eds), *Invention of Tradition*, pp. 101–64.
27 Craig, *Germany*, p. 189.
28 '. . .da diesselben in den meisten Lesebüchern enthalten sind.' L.E. Seidel (ed.), *Das fünfte Schuljahr* (Langensalza: Greßler Schulbuchhandlung, 1902), p. 190.
29 From elementary history textbooks of 1890 quoted by Chancellor, *History for their Masters*, p. 130.
30 Wilfred Campbell (ed.), *Poems of Loyalty by British and Canadian Authors* (London: Nelson, n.d. [1912]), p. v.
31 Mona Ozouf, *L'École, l'Église et la République, 1871–1914* (Paris: Armand Colin, 1963), pp. 112, 114, 123.
32 '. . . le livre par excellence des Français de 1880 à 1914.' Jean Lestocquoy, *Histoire du patriotisme en France des origines à nos jours* (Paris: Albin Michel, 1968), p. 149.
33 'Tout le monde y parle un français grammatical, pur comme l'eau minérale.' ibid., p. 150.
34 Charles Tilly *et al.*, *The Rebellious Century, 1830–1930* (London: Dent, 1975), pp. 19, 199.
35 Hobsbawm and Ranger (eds), *Invention of Tradition*, p. 268.
36 Craig, *Germany*, p. 189.
37 Hobsbawm and Ranger (eds), *Invention of Tradition*, p. 263.
38 Benedict Anderson, *Imagined Communities: Reflections on the Origin and Spread of Nationalism* (London: Verso Editions and N.L.B., 1983), p. 31.
39 ibid., pp. 38–40.
40 Hamburger, *Truth of Poetry*, p. 164.
41 Nicolas Beauduin, 'Collecte', *L'Offrande héroïque: Poèmes* (Neuilly-Paris: La Vie des Lettres, [1916]), p. 56.
42 Victorin Baret, 'La Guerre', in Turpin (ed.), *Poètes de la guerre*, vol. I, p. 15; Pierre Nebout, *France et Belgique: À-propos dramatique en vers* (Paris: E. de Boccard, 1916), p. 6.
43 La Tailhède, *Hymne pour la France*, p. 13.
44 Adolphe Aderer, 'Reims', *Les Heures de la guerre* (Paris: Calmann-Lévy, 1918), p. 37.
45 Émile Verhaeren, 'Reims', *Les Ailes rouges de la guerre: Poèmes* (Paris: Mercure de France, 1919), p. 37.
46 Lersch, 'Soldaten-Abschied', in Bab (ed.) *1914*, vol. I, p. 6.
47 Karl Bröger, 'Bekenntnis', *Kamerad, als wir marschiert: Kriegsgedichte* (Jena: Diederichs, 1917), p. 3.
48 Cäsar Flaischlen, 'Deutscher Weltkrieg', in *Neue Kriegslieder* (Berlin-Charlottenburg: Axel Juncker, n.d.), p. 72.
49 Bab, 'Die Kriegslyrik von heute', *Das literarische Echo*, 15 December 1914, p. 344; Hauptman, 'Reiterlied', in Bab (ed.) *1914*, vol. I, p. 17; 'O Nikolaus', ibid., p. 21. In the original edition the author is not named, but in the article noted here Bab identifies him as Wilhelm Platz.
50 Kipling, 'For All We Have and Are', in *Songs and Sonnets*, p. 92.
51 Coulson Kernahan, 'To "Little" Belgium', ibid., p. 21.

52 Owen Seaman, 'The Avengers', in H.B. Elliott (ed.), *Lest We Forget: A War Anthology* (London: Jarrold, 1915), p. 56; James Silvester, 'Sound the Alarm', in Charles F. Forshaw (ed.), *One Hundred of the Best Poems of the European War by Poets of the Empire* (London: Elliott Stock, 1915), vol. I, p. 164; Charles William Brodribb, 'Expeditional', in G.H. Clarke (ed.), *A Treasury of War Poetry* (London: Hodder and Stoughton, [1919]), p. 45; R.Gorell Barnes, 'To the British Army', in *Songs and Sonnets*, p. 79.

53 Ian Colvin, 'The Answer', in *Songs and Sonnets*, p. 15.

54 James Lill, 'The Issues', in Forshaw (ed.), *One Hundred Best Poems*, vol. I, p. 121.

55 Fabre des Essarts, 'Joffre', in Turpin (ed.), *Poètes de la guerre*, vol. I, p. 80; Jeanne-Benita Azaïs, 'Ode aux soldats de France', ibid., vol. II, p. 21.

56 Richard Nordhausen, 'Die faule Grete (42 cm. Mörser)', in Bab (ed.), *1914*, vol. I, p. 38; Joseph von Lauff, 'Die fleißige Berta', *Singendes Schwert: Lieder aus großer Zeit* (Berlin: August Scherl, [1915]), p. 32.

57 Joseph Win[c]kler, 'Den Meistern und Arbeitern von Krupp gewidmet', in Bab (ed.), *1914*, vol. X, p. 29; Franz Langheinrich, 'Im Schmelzbau Krupp', in *Neue Kriegslieder*, p. 54; K. H. Strobl, 'Die Heizer', in Bab (ed.), *1914*, vol. III, p. 29.

58 Günter Heintz (ed.), *Deutsche Arbeiterdichtung 1910–1933* (Stuttgart: Reclam, 1974), p. 379. Heintz's anthology offers a useful biography and bibliography for each of the poets.

59 Gellner, *Nations*, p. 56.

60 Seaman, 'Pro Patria', in *Songs and Sonnets*, p. 26; Colvin 'The Answer', ibid., p. 15; R.G. Barnes, 'To the British Army', ibid., p. 79.

61 Paul Warncke, 'Vaterlandslied', *Sturm: Kriegsgedichte* (Berlin: A. Hofmann, 1915), p. 84.

62 Hauptmann, 'Reiterlied', in Bab (ed.), *1914*, vol. I, p. 17.

63 Gabriel Mourey, 'Le Salut aux Alliés', *Le Chant du Renouveau: Poèmes de guerre* (Paris/Nancy: Librairie Militaire Berger-Levrault, 1916), p. 13; Fabre des Essarts, 'Quatre sonnets', in Turpin (ed.), *Poètes de la guerre*, vol. I, p. 79.

64 R.M. Freeman, 'The War Cry', in *Songs and Sonnets*, p. 28.

65 William Watson, 'The Fourth of August', *The Man Who Saw and Other Poems* (London: John Murray, 1917), p. 25.

66 Hanns Johst, 'Der Sturm bricht los!' in Volkmann (ed.), *Deutsche Dichtung*, p. 55; Karl Hackenschmidt, 'An die Hetzer', ibid., p. 82; Schröder, 'Heilig Vaterland'.

67 John Drinkwater, 'We Willed it Not', in Clarke (ed.), *Treasury*, p. 146; Thomas Hardy, 'The Pity of It', *Satires of Circumstance: Lyrics and Reveries: Moments of Vision and Miscellaneous Verses* (London: Macmillan, 1919), p. 389.

68 Schröder, 'Zum 1. August 1914', *Heilig Vaterland*, p. 7; Kipling, 'For All We Have and Are', in *Songs and Sonnets*, p. 92; Gabriele d'Annunzio, 'A la France', in Turpin (ed.), *Poètes de la guerre*, vol. II, p. 17; Beauduin, 'Crédo', *L'Offrande héroïque*, p. 30.

69 Victorin Baret 'La Guerre', in Turpin (ed.), *Poètes de la guerre*, vol. I, p. 15.

70 Baret, 'Désirs de paix', ibid., p. 17.

71 Lienhard, 'Deutsche Sendung', *Heldentum und Liebe: Kriegsgedichte* (Stuttgart: Greiner und Pfeiffer, 1915), p. 33; 'Heerschau', ibid., p. 36.

72 Lienhard, 'Den Gästen von Bayreuth', ibid., p. 31.

73 John R. Palmer, 'Pro Patria', in Forshaw (ed.), *One Hundred Best Poems*, vol. I, p. 149.

74 Gilbert Cannan, 'The Spirit of England', in *Songs and Sonnets*, p. 50;

George Edward Woodberry, 'Sonnets Written in the Autumn of 1914, II', in Clarke (ed.), *Treasury*, p. 143.

75 Heinrich Keinzl, 'Der nationale Gott', in Bab (ed.), *1914*, vol. IV, p. 7.

76 H.A.F. Tech, 'Das auserwählte Volk', *Kampfreime eines Friedfertigen aus dem Kriegsjahre 1914* (Wüsterhause: Selbstverlag des Verfassers, 1915), p. 30.

77 J.J. Brown, 'War and Christ', in Forshaw (ed.), *One Hundred Best Poems*, vol. I, p. 41.

78 W. Vesper, 'Liebe oder Haß?' in Bab (ed.), *1914*, vol. IV, p. 6; H. Schmidt-Kestner, 'Gebet des deutschen Wehrmanns', in Bab (ed.), *1914*, vol. I, p. 19.

79 Maurice Allou, 'Leur image', *Strophes d'acier (1914–1916)* (Paris/Nancy: Librairie Militaire Berger-Levrault, 1919), p. 21; William Archer, 'Louvain', in Elliott (ed.), *Lest We Forget*, p. 69.

80 Benjamin Buisson, 'Emmanuel Kant', *Teutoniana* (Paris: Alphonse Lemerre, 1917), p. 33.

81 Kathleen Knox, 'A Lost Land', in Clarke (ed.), *Treasury*, p. 159.

82 Richard Schaukal, 'An England', *1914: Eherne Sonette* (München: Georg Müller, 1914), p. 19.

83 Herzog, 'Jeanne d'Arc', *Ritter, Tod und Teufel*, p. 129.

84 Mourey, 'Le Salut aux Alliés', *Chant du Renouveau*, p. 13.

85 Karl Strecker, 'Die Kriegeserklärung Englands', in Bab (ed.), *1914*, vol. I, p. 9; Ludwig Ganghofer, 'Wilhelm der Große', *Eiserne Zitter: Kriegslieder* (Stuttgart: Adolf Bonz, 1914), p. 69; Seaman, 'Dies Irae', in Elliott (ed.), *Lest We Forget*, p. 53; Watson, 'To the Troubler of the World', in *Songs and Sonnets*, p. 1.

86 Adolf Ey, 'Der deutsche Michel und John Bull', in Bab (ed.), *1914*, vol. II, p. 35.

87 'Caliban', 'The Hun is at the gate', in Karl Quenzel (ed.), *Des Vaterlandes Hochgesang: Eine Auslese deutscher Kriegs- und Siegeslieder* (Leipzig: Hesse und Becker, 1915), p. 142; 'Caliban', 'Der Nothelfer', ibid., p. 143.

88 Schaukal, 'An Japan', *1914*, p. 30; Edgar Steiger, 'Tsingtau', in Alfred Biese (ed.), *Poesie des Krieges*, p. 54.

89 Émile Bergerat, 'Jusqu'au bout', *Les Poètes de la guerre: Recueil de poésies parues depuis le 1er août 1914* (Paris/Nancy: Librairie Militaire Berger-Levrault, 1915), p. 12; Madeleine Regnault, 'Turcs, Allemands, Bulgares', in Turpin (ed.), *Poètes de la guerre*, vol. II, p. 148.

90 H.H. Ewers, 'Wir und die Welt', *Deutsche Kriegslieder* (New York: The Fatherland, 1915), p. 8. Ewers' collection has as an appendix a group of pro-German poems translated into German, under the heading 'Deutsch-freundliche Stimmen in Amerika–Kriegslieder amerikanischer, jüdischer und irischer Dichter'; Ernst Lissauer, 'Haßgesang gegen England', in Volkmann (ed.), *Deutsche Dichtung*, p. 92.

91 '. . .vielleicht das volkstümlichste Gedicht der neuen Zeit.' *Kölnische Zeitung*, quoted by Volkmann, ibid., p. 296.

92 The Imperial War Museum has two versions printed on single sheets–'The German Hymn of Hate' (Central Committee for National Patriotic Organisations), and Lina Blémont's translation 'Un Chant de haine contre l'Angleterre', reprinted from *La Revue historique. Das literarische Echo* of 15 December 1914 also printed an English version.

93 '. . . die unerwartete, als unfair [sic] empfundene Kriegserklärung Englands.' Volkmann (ed.), *Deutsche Dichtung*, p. 46.

94 '. . . ein leiser, von Achtung durchklungener Ton des Bedauerns.' ibid., pp. 43–4.

95 Edward Thomas, 'This is no Case of Petty Right or Wrong', *Collected Poems* (London: Selwyn and Blount, 1920), p. 168.

96 Schröder, 'An die deutschen Krieger', in Volkmann (ed.), *Deutsche Dichtung*, p. 57; Laurence Gomme, 'The Call', in Elliott (ed.), *Lest We Forget*, p. 48.

97 Henri de Regnier, 'Le Serment', *1914–1916* (Paris: Mercure de France, 1918), p. 19; Gabriel Mourey, 'Le vin de la haine', *Chant du Renouveau*, p. 10; Jean Bertot, 'Les Ruines de Reims', in Turpin (ed.), *Poètes de la guerre*, vol. I, p. 34.

98 Buisson, 'Emmanuel Kant', *Teutoniana*, p. 33.

99 Warncke, 'Ostpreußen', *Sturm*, p. 46; Schröder, 'Zum 1. August, 1914', *Heilig Vaterland*, p. 7.

100 'Caliban', 'The Hun is at the gate', in Quenzel (ed.), *Des Vaterlandes Hochgesang*, p. 142.

101 Barry Pain, 'The Kaiser and God', in *Songs and Sonnets*, p. 83.

102 Marcel Martinet, 'Droit de gens', *Les Temps maudits: Poèmes 1914–1916* (Paris: Union Générale d'Éditions, 1975), p. 116.

103 Jean Aicard, 'Le Jeune héros de quatorze ans, Émile Desjardins', in Turpin (ed.), *Poètes de la guerre*, vol. I, p. 6.

104 Paul Fournier, 'Émile Desprès', ibid., p. 86.

105 Victor d'Auriac, 'Qu'il vive', *Le Vieux dieu* (Paris: Alphonse Lemerre, 1916), p. 8; Fleming Tuckerman, 'Le Boy Scout', *War Poems in French and English* (New York: Brentanos, 1917), p. 15. Cate Haste in *Keep the Home Fires Burning: Propaganda in the First World War* (London: Allen Lane, 1977) refers to a story about a boy with a wooden gun in the Franco-Prussian War.

106 'Les soldats du Kronprinz ont envoyé comme cadeau de naissance à la petite-fille du Kaiser un berceau teinté de sang français. Les journaux.' Germaine Abadie-Sem-Boucherie, 'Le Berceau rouge', in Turpin (ed.), *Poètes de la guerre*, vol. II, p. 12.

107 Lienhard, 'Münstergespräch', *Heldentum*, p. 45. Louis is accused of having stolen Alsace from the Germans.

108 C. Donner, 'Kaiser Wilhelm the Sower', in Forshaw (ed.), *One Hundred Best Poems*, vol. I, p. 59; H.H. Chamberlin, 'To Wilhelm II', in Donald Tulloch (ed.), *Songs and Poems of the Great War* (Worcester, Mass.: Davis Press, 1915), p. 253; Watson, 'To the Troubler of the World', in *Songs and Sonnets*, p. 1; Beauduin, 'Dyptique–L'Empereur fourbe', *L'Offrande héroïque*, p. 14; Prieur, 'Guillaume veut la paix', in Turpin (ed.), *Poètes de la guerre*, vol. I, p. 166; G.H. Wilson, 'The Mad Kaiser's Folly', in Forshaw (ed.), *One Hundred Best Poems*, vol. I, p. 189.

109 Abel Aaronson, 'To the Kaiser', in Forshaw (ed.), *One Hundred Best Poems*, vol. I, p. 11.

110 Watson, 'To the German Emperor, after the Sack of Louvain', *The Man Who Saw*, p. 27.

111 See Cate Haste, *Keep the Home Fires Burning*.

112 M.L. Sanders and Philip M. Taylor, *British Propaganda in the First World War, 1914–18* (London and Basingstoke: Macmillan, 1982), p. 23.

3 We serve you best

1 Owen Seaman, 'Pro Patria', in *Songs and Sonnets*, p. 26.

2 August Dorchaine, *Hymne aux cloches de Pâques* (Paris: Alphonse Lemerre,

1915); August van der Verren, *Neutres! À la Belgique martyre* (Paris: Imprimerie Populaire, 1916).

3 Kurt Münzer, 'Vaterland', *Taten und Kränze: Lieder zum Kriege 1914* (Berlin: Alex Juncker, [1914]), p. 26.

4 Rudolf Herzog, 'Der Deutschen Kriegslied 1914', *Ritter, Tod und Teufel*, p. 14.

5 Henry Allsopp, 'Here and There', in Mabel Edwards and Mary Booth (eds), *The Fiery Cross: An Anthology* (London: Grant Richards, 1915), p. 44.

6 Gabrielle Moyse, 'Aux Fils de France', in Turpin (ed.), *Poètes de la guerre*, vol. I, p. 149.

7 Anon., 'Meine Jungen', in Bab (ed.), *1914*, vol. II, p. 10.

8 Rilke, 'Fünf Gesänge, August 1914', *Sämtliche Werke*, vol. II (Wiesbaden: Insel, 1956), p. 86.

9 Bruno Frank, 'Stolze Zeit', in Bab (ed.), *1914*, vol. VI, p. 5; Hans Krailsheimer, 'Unser ist die Glut!', ibid., vol. VI, p. 4; Friedrich Freksa, 'Kriegsfahrt des Automobilisten', ibid., vol. I, p. 27.

10 Apollinaire, 'La Petite Auto', *Calligrammes: Poèmes de la paix et de la guerre, 1913–1916* (Paris: Gallimard, 1925), p. 61.

11 René Hughes, 'Le Poilu', *Dans la Guerre: Sonnets* (Paris: Sansot, [1918]), p. 7.

12 Lienhard, 'Soldatenauszug aus Erfurt', *Heldentum und Liebe*, p. 38.

13 Binyon, 'For the Fallen', *The Four Years*, p. 42.

14 Victor Compas, 'Les Poilus', in Turpin (ed.), *Poètes de la guerre*, vol. I, p. 62.

15 Ernst Preczang, 'Gefallen, ein Mann', in Bab (ed.), *1914*, vol. II, p. 14.

16 Georges Pioch, 'Pour les gens simples', in Turpin (ed.), *Poètes de la guerre*, vol. II, p. 137.

17 E. Angereau, 'L'Ame des drapeaux', in Turpin (ed.), *Poètes de la guerre*, vol. I, p. 13.

18 B.R.M. Hetherington, 'The Patriot', in Gertrude S. Ford and Erskine Macdonald (eds), *A Crown of Amaranth: A Collection of Poems to the Memory of the Brave and Gallant Gentlemen Who Have Given their Lives for Great and Greater Britain, MCMIV–MCMXVII* (London: Erskine Macdonald, 1917), p. 56.

19 A.L. J., 'Happy Warriors', *Westminster Gazette*, 10 February 1916.

20 Eden Phillpotts, 'To a Mother', *Westminster Gazette*, 2 February 1916; Will Vesper, 'Aufruf an Deutschland: 6. August 1914', in Volkmann (ed.), *Deutsche Dichtung*, p. 70.

21 W.N. Ewer, 'Three Gods', in Bertram Lloyd (ed.), *Poems Written during the Great War, 1914–1918: An Anthology* (London: Allen and Unwin, 1918), p. 40.

22 Alice Meynell, 'Summer in England, 1914', Ford and Macdonald (eds), *Crown of Amaranth*, p. 25.

23 Klabund, 'Kriegsfreiwillige', in *Neue Kriegslieder*, p. 19.

24 Herbert Eulenberg, 'Für die Gefallenen', in *Neue Kriegslieder*, p. 20; Louis Texier, *Aux Morts pour la Patrie* (Paris: Albert Messein, 1914), p. 5.

25 Francis Trochu, 'O Souffrance', *Poèmes de la guerre 1914–1915* (Paris: Jouve [1915]), p. 47.

26 Victor Snell, 'Les Croix', in Turpin (ed.), *Poètes de la guerre*, vol. I, p. 172; Henri de Regnier, 'Le Père', ibid., p. 167; Victor Compas, 'La Cueillette tragique', ibid., p. 65.

27 Harvey C. Grumbine, *Humanity or Hate: Which?* (Boston: Cornhill, 1918), p. 8.

28 J.A. Brooke, 'For England', in Ford and Macdonald (eds), *Crown of Amaranth*, p. 14; Binyon, 'For the Fallen', *Four Years*, p. 42.

29 Dyneley Hussey, 'Ode to a Young Man Killed in Flanders', in Ford and Macdonald (eds), *Crown of Amaranth*, p. 47; Katharine Tynan, 'Flower of Youth', ibid., p. 23; Beatrice A. Lees, 'The Front', ibid., p. 33.

30 See M. Van Wyk Smith, *Drummer Hodge: The Poetry of the Anglo-Boer War, 1899–1902* (Oxford: Clarendon Press, 1978).

31 Clément Chanteloube, 'Deux ans après', in Turpin (ed.), *Poètes de la guerre*, vol. I, p. 51.

32 Henry-Jacques, 'Le Charnier', *Nous . . . de la guerre* (Paris: Fernand Sorlot, 1940), p. 92; Maurice Pottecher, 'Le Point de vue des corbeaux', in *Les Poètes contre la guerre: Anthologie de la poésie française, 1914–1919* (Genève: Le Sablier, 1920), p.108.

33 G.A. Fauré, 'La Guerre', *Mes Impressions sur la guerre, 1914–15–16* (printed Nevers, 1916), p. 7; 'La Mère', ibid., p. 16.

34 Julius Bab, *Die deutsche Kriegslyrik, 1914–1918: Eine kritische Bibliographie* (Stettin: Norddeutsche Verlag für Literatur und Kunst, 1920), p. 115.

35 The cards by Clay and a copy of Chappell's broadsheet are to be found in Vol. I of the Birmingham Public Libraries' *War Poetry Scrap Book: A Collection of Broadsides, Leaflets, Newspaper Cuttings, etc.* (1914–1921).

36 Vol. IV, *War Poetry Scrap Book*.

37 Quoted with permission of Birmingham Public Libraries.

38 Karl Strecker, 'Die Kriegserklärung Englands', in Bab (ed.), *1914*, vol. II, p. 9; Binyon, 'Fourth of August', *Four Years*, p. 23.

39 Gardner (ed.), *Up the Line to Death*, p. xxii.

40 J.A. Brooke, 'What Will You Say?' in Forshaw (ed.), *One Hundred Best Poems*, vol. I, p. 10.

41 Walter Sichel, 'What are you Waiting For? To the Slackers: A Recruiting Song', *Evening News*, 2 June, 1915. (*War Poetry Scrap Book*, vol. IV.)

42 Louisa Prior, 'To a Hesitant Briton', in Forshaw (ed.), *One Hundred Best Poems*, vol. II, p. 126; Marjorie Pratt, 'To a Shirker', ibid., p. 124.

43 Charles Preston Stevenson, 'Queen of Night: A Mother's Reverie', in Forshaw (ed.), *One Hundred Best Poems*, vol. I, p. 166.

44 'War Poetry', *Poetry and Drama* 8 (December 1914), p. 344.

45 Economou and Ferrante, *In Pursuit of Perfection: Courtly Love in Medieval Literature* (Port Washington, N.Y.: Kennikat Press, 1975), p. 53.

46 Walter Flex, 'Preußischer Fahneneid', *Sonne und Schild* (Braunschweig: Georg Westermann, 1915), p. 3.

47 Nicolas Beauduin, 'À la France', *L'Offrande héroïque*, p. 7; 'Acte de foi', ibid., p. 27; 'L'Offrande héroïque', ibid., p. 47.

48 F.W. Harvey, 'The Soldier Speaks', *A Gloucestershire Lad at Home and Abroad* (London: Sidgwick and Jackson, 1916), p. 23.

49 Rupert Brooke, 'The Soldier', *1914 and Other Poems* (London: Sidgwick and Jackson, 1915), p. 15.

50 Edward Thomas, 'This is No Case of Petty Right or Wrong', *Collected Poems*, p. 168.

51 Silkin, *Out of Battle*, p. 88.

52 Arnold Ulitz, 'Belagerung', in Volkmann (ed.), *Deutsche Dichtung*, p. 103.

53 Silkin, *Out of Battle*, pp. 87–8; E.D. Blodgett, 'A Mouthful of Earth: A Word for Edward Thomas', *Modern Poetry Studies* 3 (1972), p. 159.

54 'Poems in Wartime', Birmingham Public Libraries, *Press Poems of the Great War 1914–1919* (E. Lawrence Levy Collection), vol. I, p. 271. The source is not indicated.

55 Marcel Wyseur, 'Les Mortes', *La Flandre rouge: Poèmes* (Paris: Perrin, 1916), p. 152.

56 Alfred Droin, 'Le Carnage', *Le Crêpe étoilé: 1914–1917* (Paris: Charpentier, 1917), p. 13.

57 A. Marcel, 'Mai 1915', in Gaston Bernard et Victor Buissonville (eds), *Poètes-soldats: Recueil de poèmes du front Belge* (Paris: Jouve, 1917), p. 162.

58 Wyseur, 'La Tour des Templiers', *La Flandre rouge*, p. 130.

59 Fussell, *The Great War and Modern Memory*, p. 21.

60 Marcel, 'La Dentellière', in Bernard et Buissonville (eds), *Poètes-soldats*, p. 155.

4 Cruel thy sword

1 E.H. Visiak, 'The Pacifist', in Bertram Lloyd (ed.), *Poems Written during the Great War*, p. 106.

2 D.S.R. Welland, *Wilfred Owen: A Critical Study*, 2nd edition (London: Chatto and Windus, 1978), p. 23.

3 E. Hilton Young, 'Air Service', *The Nation*, 19 May 1917, p. 170; Siegfried Sassoon, 'Died of Wounds', *The Nation*, 3 March 1917, p. 735.

4 Franz Werfel, 'Die Wortemacher des Krieges', *Einander: Oden, Lieder, Gestalten* (Leipzig: Kurt Wolff, 1917), p. 50; [George Willis], 'Any Soldier to his Son', *The Nation*, 23 November 1918, p. 221; E.G. Kolbenheyer, 'Chronica II, 1915', *Lyrisches Brevier* (München: Georg Müller, 1929), p. 132; Marcel Martinet, 'Civils', *Les Temps maudits*, p. 123.

5 Owen, *Collected Letters*, ed. Harold Owen and John Bell (London: Oxford University Press, 1967), p. 461.

6 Sorley, *Letters*, p. 241.

7 Owen, 'Dulce et Decorum Est', *Complete Poems*, p. 140.

8 Quoted by Hibberd, *Poetry of the First World War*, p. 72.

9 Werfel, 'Krieg', *Einander*, p. 47.

10 Werfel, 'Die Wortemacher des Krieges', *Einander*, p. 50.

11 Anon., 'Soldier M.P.', *The Nation*, 20 January 1917.

12 Kolbenheyer, 'Chronica II, 1915'. The poem is stylistically atypical of Kolbenheyer's work, and the attitude unexpected. Volkmann, who prints an abbreviated version under the title 'Leviathan', quotes the poet as observing (in 1934), 'Ich habe mich mit Bewußtsein von dieser Gilde [der 'Kriegslyriker'] zurückgehalten, die während des Krieges am patriotischen Lärm nicht genug tun konnte und nach dem Kriege und Umsturz fast alle in das pazifistische Lager übergegangen sind.' (p. 307.) Volkmann's version of the poem appears far less 'pazifistisch' than the original.

13 Osbert Sitwell, 'Sheep-Song', in Bertram Lloyd (ed.), *The Paths of Glory: A Collection of Poems Written during the War 1914–1919* (London: Allen and Unwin, 1919), p. 108.

14 A.O. Weber, 'Der Verteidigungskrieg', *Wenn Mars regiert* (Berlin: Bachmair, 1917), p. 7.

15 Weber, 'Berliner Theaterkunst im Kriege', ibid., p. 51; 'Das Café Grössenwahn zur Zivildienstfrage', ibid., p. 7.

16 J.C. Squire, 'The Entente', *The Survival of the Fittest* (London: Allen and Unwin, 1919), p. 59. Squire refers to the Turkish genocide of the Armenians and the German destruction of Belgian towns.

17 Squire, 'The Dilemma', *Survival*, p. 57.

18 Lois Cendré, 'Reproche aux poètes', in *Les Poètes contre la guerre*, p. 44.

19 Hibberd and Onions (eds), *Poetry of the Great War*, p. 204.
20 Arthur Graeme West, 'God! How I hate you, you young cheerful men', *The Diary of a Dead Officer: Being the Posthumous Papers of A. G. West* (London: Allen and Unwin, [1918]), p. 79.
21 H. Reginald Freston, 'O Fortunati', in John Hardie (ed.), *Verse of Valour: An Anthology of Shorter War Poems of Sea, Land, Air* (Glasgow: Art and Educational Publishers, 1943), p. 79. Another of Freston's poems cited by West begins, 'I know that God will never let me die.'
22 Helen Hamilton, 'The Romancing Poet', in Catherine Reilly (ed.), *Scars upon my Heart: Women's Poetry and Verse of the First World War* (London: Virago, 1981), p. 49.
23 Alfred Lichtenstein, 'Abschied', *Gedichte und Geschichten*, ed. Kurt Labasch (München: Georg Müller, 1919), vol. I, p. 103. The word 'mit' at the end of line 4 in this edition is a misprint for 'nit'.
24 Bridgwater, *German Poets*, p. 67.
25 W.N. Hodgson, 'Before Action', in Gardner (ed.), *Up the Line to Death*, p. 29.
26 Lichtenstein, 'Gebet vor der Schlacht', *Gedichte und Geschichten*, p. 106.
27 Martinet, 'Poètes d'Allemagne', *Temps Maudits*, p. 72.
28 Martinet, 'Civils', ibid., p. 123.
29 Sassoon, 'Great Men', in Lloyd (ed.), *Paths*, p. 93.
30 Sassoon, 'They', *War Poems* (London: Heinemann, 1919), p. 47.
31 Bruno Schönlank, 'Europa', in Heintz (ed.), *Deutsche Arbeiterdichtung*, p. 97; Oskar Kanehl, 'Soldatenmißhandlung', *Die Schande: Gedichte eines dienstpflichtigen Soldaten aus der Mordsaison 1914–18* (Berlin-Wilmersdorf: Die Aktion, 1922), p. 8.
32 W.N. Ewer, 'Five Souls', reprinted in Lloyd (ed.), *Poems*, p. 30.
33 Charles Vildrac, 'Élégie à Henri Doucet', *Les Chants du désespéré (1914–1920)* (Paris: La Nouvelle Revue Française, 1920), p. 39.
34 'Miles', 'The Modern Abraham', in Lloyd (ed.), *Poems*, p. 74.
35 Squire, 'Lord Molasses', *Survival*, p. 58.
36 Sassoon, 'The General', *War Poems*, p. 50.
37 Georges Chennevière, 'Ravitaillement', in *Poètes contre*, p. 48.
38 Walter Hasenclever, 'Die Mörder sitzen in der Oper', in Ludwig Rubiner (ed.), *Kameraden der Menschheit: Dichtungen zur Weltrevolution* (Potsdam: Kiepenheuer, 1919), p. 76.
39 André Spire, 'Petits Gens', *Le Secrèt* (Paris: La Nouvelle Revue Française, 1919), p. 95.
40 Owen, 'Insensibility', *Complete Poems*, p. 145.
41 Martinet, 'Droit de gens', *Temps maudits*, p. 118; Rose Macaulay, 'Picnic', in Reilly (ed.) *Scars*, p.122.
42 Eliot Crawshay-Williams, 'Sonnet of a Son', *The Gutter and the Stars* (London: Erskine Macdonald, 1918), p. 29.
43 F. S. Flint, 'Lament', *Otherworld. Cadences* (London: Poetry Bookshop, 1920), p.49.
44 Sitwell, 'Armchair', in Lloyd (ed.), *Poems*, p. 94
45 Karl Otten 'Für Martinet', *Die Thronerhebung des Herzens* (Berlin-Wilmersdorf: Die Aktion, 1918), p. 11.
46 Alec Waugh, 'Joy Bells', in Lloyd (ed.), *Paths*, p. 115.
47 Sassoon, 'Glory of Women', *War Poems*, p. 57.
48 Sassoon, 'Their Frailty', ibid., p. 58.
49 Marinet, 'Elles Disent. . . ' *Temps maudits*, p. 122.
50 Laurence Housman, 'Caesar's Image', in Lloyd (ed.), *Poems*, p. 60.

51 Hamilton, 'The Jingo-Woman', in Reilly (ed.), *Scars*, p. 47.
52 Pauline Barrington, 'Education', in Lloyd (ed.), *Poems*, p. 22.
53 Cécile Périn, 'Les Femmes de tous les pays', in *Poètes contre*, p. 96.
54 Margaret Sackville, 'Nostra Culpa', *The Pageant of War* (London: Simpkin Marshall, [1916]), p. 36.
55 Ivan Goll, 'Klage der Braut', *Requiem: Für die Gefallenen von Europa* (Zürich: Rascher, 1917), p. 24; Waugh, 'The Other Side', in Lloyd (ed.), *Paths*, p. 114.
56 Squire, 'Christmas Hymn for Lambeth', in Lloyd (ed.), *Poems*, p. 99.
57 Erwin Piscator, 'Der Mutter zweier Söhne, welche fielen', in Franz Pfemfert (ed.), *1914–1916: Eine Anthologie* (Berlin-Wilmersdorf: Die Aktion, 1916), p. 92.
58 Deutsche Akademie der Künste zu Berlin, *Erwin Piscator*, p. 74.
59 Piscator, *Das politische Theater* (Hamburg: Rowohlt, 1963).
60 Kanehl, 'Krieg', *Schande*, p. 6.
61 Ewer, '1814–1914: On Reading *The Dynasts*', *The Herald*, 20 March 1915.
62 Introduction to Henry Dérieux, *En ces jours déchirants* (Paris: Payot, 1916), p. 13.
63 Martinet, 'Tu vas te battre', *Temps maudits*, p. 55; Kanehl, 'Krieg', *Schande*, p. 6.
64 Sackville, 'A Song of War', in Lloyd (ed.), *Paths*, p. 80.
65 Quoted in Heintz (ed.), *Deutsche Arbeiterdichtung*, p. 27.
66 Jacques Ellul, *Propaganda: The Formation of Men's Attitudes* (New York: Knopf, 1965), p. 108.

5 Laissez-les donc dormir

1 'Let them rest in peace, these dead! After all, what harm have they done you, that you pursue them even into their dark refuge?' Marc Larreguy de Civrieux, 'Debout les morts', in *Poètes contre*, p. 83.
2 Friedrich Lienhard, 'Soldatenauszug aus Erfurt', *Heldentum*, p. 38.
3 Charles Sorley, 'All the hills and vales along', *Marlborough and Other Poems* (Cambridge: Cambridge University Press, 1919), p. 71.
4 H. d'A. B., 'The March', in *Soldier Poets: Songs of the Fighting Men* (London: Erskine Macdonald, 1916), p. 15; Ernst Toller, 'Marschlied', *Vormorgen* (Potsdam: Kiepenheuer, 1924), p. 10.
5 Kanehl, 'Auf dem Marsch', *Schande*, p. 16.
6 Owen, 'The Send-Off', *Complete Poems*, p. 172.
7 'Altgraf Erich', 'Neujahrsbrief', *Kriegsgedichte: Sarajevo, 1914–1915* (Sarajevo: Selbstverlag des Verfassers, n.d.), p. 26.
8 Th. Mary, 'Aux aveugles de la guerre', *À nos chers Blessés; Poésies patriotiques* (Paris: Sirey, 1915), p. 27.
9 Joseph Bayer, 'La Manche vide', in Turpin (ed.), *Poètes de la guerre*, vol. II, p. 32.
10 Owen, 'Disabled', *Complete Poems*, p. 175.
11 Georges Pioch, 'Épitaphe', *Les Victimes* (Paris: Ollendorff, [1917]), p. 1.
12 Pioch, 'Mutilés', ibid., p. 9.
13 Tech, 'Der Krüppel in der Siegesallee', *Kampfreime*, p. 35.
14 Owen, 'Mental Cases', *Complete Poems*, p. 169.
15 Toller, 'Gang zur Ruhestellung', *Vormorgen*, p. 14.
16 Ivor Gurney, 'To his Love', *Collected Poems*, ed. P.J. Kavanagh (Oxford: Oxford University Press, 1982), p. 41.
17 Richard Aldington, 'Soliloquy I', *Images of War* (Boston: Four Seas, 1921),

p. 39; Richard Fischer, 'O diese Zeit der Fäulnis!', *Schrei in die Welt* (Dresden: Dresdner Verlag von 1917, 1919), p. 21.

18 Hermann Plagge, 'Nacht im Granatenfeuer', in Pfemfert (ed.), *1914–1916*, p. 96.

19 Herbert Read, 'The Happy Warrior', in Lloyd (ed.), *Poems*, p. 80.

20 Read, 'The Execution of Cornelius Vane', in Lloyd (ed.), *Paths*, p. 81.

21 Winifred Letts, 'The Deserter', in Reilly (ed.), *Scars*, p. 61.

22 Owen, 'S.I.W.', *Complete Poems*, p. 160.

23 Sassoon, 'How to Die', *War Poems*, p. 51.

24 'Miles', 'Rhapsode', in Lloyd (ed.), *Poems*, p. 70.

25 J.R. A., 'The Everlasting Terror', Imperial War Museum.

26 Robert Graves, 'The Leveller', *Country Sentiment* (London: Martin Secker, 1920), p. 76.

27 Piscator, 'Denk an seine Bleisoldaten', in Pfemfert (ed.), *1914–1916*, p. 90.

28 M. Hall, 'After the Battle', in Forshaw (ed.), *One Hundred Best Poems*, vol. II, p. 72; Katherine Hale, 'Grey Knitting', *Grey Knitting and Other Poems* (Toronto: William Briggs, 1914), p. 3. A.E. Lane quotes this stanza, but in a slightly different version, in *An Adequate Response: The War Poetry of Siegfried Sassoon and Wilfred Owen* (Detroit: Wayne State University Press, 1972).

29 Max Plowman, 'Going into the Line', in Gardner (ed.), *Up the Line to Death*, p. 102.

30 Joseph Billiet, 'Terre', in *Poètes contre*, p. 39.

31 Plowman, 'The Dead Soldiers', in Gardner (ed.), *Up the Line to Death*, p. 103.

32 Henry-Jacques, 'Les Martyrs', *Nous . . . de la Guerre*, p. 83.

33 H.F. Constantine, 'The Glory of War', in Lloyd (ed.), *Paths*, p. 38.

34 A.G. West, 'The Night Patrol', *Diary*, p. 82.

35 Plagge, 'Die Schlacht', in Pfemfert (ed.), *1914–1916*, p. 97.

36 Toller, 'Leichen im Priesterwald', *Vormorgen*, p. 17.

37 René Arcos, 'Les Morts', *Le Sang des autres: Poèmes, 1914–1917* (Genève: Le Sablier, 1919), p. 26.

38 Laurence Housman, 'Armageddon – and after', in Lloyd (ed.), *Paths*, p. 67.

39 Pierre-Jean Jouve, 'Les Voix d'Europe', *Vous êtes les hommes* (Paris: Nouvelle Revue Française, 1915), p. 8.

40 Martinet, 'Tu vas te battre', *Temps maudits*, p. 59.

41 Sassoon, 'Remorse', *War Poems*, p. 44.

42 Edlef Köppen, 'Loretto', in Pfemfert (ed.), *1914–1916*, p. 81.

43 Karl Stamm, 'Soldat vor dem Gekreuzigten', *Der Aufbruch des Herzens* (Zürich: Rascher, 1920), p. 40.

44 Kanehl, 'Unterwegs', *Schande*, p. 14.

45 Paul Bewsher, 'Nox Mortis', in Gardner (ed.), *Up the Line to Death*, p. 55.

46 Marc Larreguy de Civrieux, 'Debout les Morts!' in *Poètes contre*, p. 83.

47 Sorley, 'Such, such is Death', *Marlborough*, p. 77; 'Saints have adored the lofty soul of you', ibid., p. 76.

48 Bergonzi, *Heroes' Twilight*, p. 57.

49 Sorley, 'When you see millions of the mouthless dead', *Marlborough*, p. 78.

50 Fussell, *The Great War and Modern Memory*, p. 57.

51 Bertolt Brecht, 'Legende vom toten Soldaten', *Hauspostille: Mit Anleitungen, Gesangsnoten und einem Anhang* (Berlin: Propyläen-Verlag, 1927), p. 125.

52 Helen Hamilton, 'Ghouls', in Reilly (ed.), *Scars*, p. 47.

6 A few alone

1 Anon., 'Stone-axe and club', from 'Europe – 1916', in Bertram Lloyd (ed.), *Poems Written during the Great War*, p. 15.
2 Graves, 'Two Fusiliers', in Gardner (ed.), *Up the Line to Death*, p. 148.
3 Georges Chennevière, 'L'Étranger', in *Les Poètes contre la guerre*, p. 51.
4 Pierre Drieu la Rochelle, 'Plainte des soldats européens', *Intérrogations: Poèmes* (Paris: La Nouvelle Revue Française, 1917), p. 27.
5 Gerrit Engelke, 'An die Soldaten des großen Krieges', *Rhythmus des neuen Europa: Gedichte* (Jena: Diederichs, 1923), p. 106.
6 W.G. Hartmann, 'Mein Bruder Feind', *Wir Menschen: Gedichte* (München: Kurt Wolff, 1920), p. 10; Owen, 'Strange Meeting', *Complete Poems*, p. 148.
7 Letter to Robbie Ross, 3 October 1917, *Diaries 1915–1918*, ed. Rupert Hart-Davis (London: Faber & Faber, 1983), p. 106.
8 Joseph Cohen, 'The Three Roles of Siegfried Sassoon', *Tulane Studies of English* 7 (1957), p. 175.
9 E.A. Mackintosh, 'Before the Somme', in Gardner (ed.), *Up the Line to Death*, p. 33; 'In Memoriam', ibid., p. 94.
10 Mackintosh, 'Recruiting', ibid., p. 111.
11 Owen, 'Insensibility', *Collected Poems*, p. 38; Hans Koch, 'Karfreitag 1915', in Pfemfert (ed.), *1914–1916*, p. 74.
12 J.H. Johnston, *English Poetry of the First World War: A Study of the Evolution of Lyric and Narrative Form* (Princeton: Princeton University Press, 1964), p. 12.
13 '[. . .] das Urteil, jene auszuwählen, in deren Händen sie [die Wahrheit] wirksam wird'. Quoted in Wolfgang Brekle, *Schriftsteller im antifaschistischen Widerstand 1933–1945 in Deutschland* (Berlin und Weimar: Aufbau, 1985). Brecht himself was already abroad by this time.
14 Sturge Moore, *Some Soldier Poets* (London: Grant Richards, 1919), p. 55.
15 Welland, *Wilfred Owen*, p. 69.
16 Dominic Behan, *Songs of the Irish Republican Army*, Riverside Records, RLP 12–820, 1957.
17 'Es sieht gar nicht so revolutionär aus. [. . .] Schreckliche Dinge sind darum zu erwarten.' Hanns-Josef Ortheil, *Wilhelm Klemm: Ein Lyriker der 'Menschheitsdammerung'* (Stuttgart: Kroner, 1979), p. 26.
18 Introduction to Christian Schütze (ed.), *Das Beste aus dem Simplicissimus* (München, 1975), p. 15.
19 B.B.C. talk, August 22, 1948, reprinted in T.J. Walsh (ed.), *A Tribute to Wilfred Owen* (Birkenhead, n.d.), p. 38.
20 'Asil einer heute obdachlosen Idee.' Pfemfert, *1914–1916*, p. 118.
21 Bridgwater, 'German Poetry and the First World War', *European Studies Review* 1 (1971), p. 163.
22 Michael Hamburger and Christopher Middleton, *Modern German Poetry, 1910 to 1960: An Anthology with Verse Translations* (New York: Grove Press, 1962), p. xxi; Welland, *Wilfred Owen*, p. 29; Lane, *Adequate Response*, p. 21; Johnston, *English Poetry*, p. 13.
23 Lane, *Adequate Response*, p. 24.
24 Johnston, *English Poetry*, p. 13.
25 Klemm, 'Lazarett', in Pfemfert (ed.), *1914–1916*, p. 71.
26 Welland, *Wilfred Owen*, p. 50.
27 Silkin, *Out of Battle*, pp. 154–5.
28 Isaac Rosenberg, 'Dead Man's Dump', *The Collected Works: Poetry, Prose,*

Letters, Paintings and Drawings, ed. Ian Parsons (London: Chatto and Windus, 1979), p. 110.

29 Jon Silkin, *The Penguin Book of First World War Poetry*, 2nd edition (Harmondsworth: Penguin, 1981), p. 31.

30 Uwe Wandrey, *Das Motiv des Krieges in der expressionistischen Lyrik* (Hamburg: Hartmut Ludke, 1973), p. 225.

31 '. . . als Dichter und als Privatmenschen', Ortheil, *Wilhelm Klemm*, p. 51.

32 Hamburger, *Truth of Poetry*, pp. 4, 6, 7.

33 ibid., p. 201.

34 C.M. Bowra, *Poetry and Politics, 1900–1960* (Cambridge: University Press, 1966), p. 2.

35 ibid., pp. 2, 4.

36 '. . . das Gedicht ohne Glauben, das Gedicht ohne Hoffnung, das Gedicht an niemanden gerichtet, ein Gedicht aus Worten, die Sie faszinierend montieren.' 'Soll die Dichtung das Leben bessern?' Benn, *Gesammelte Werke* (Wiesbaden: Limes, 1968), vol. IV, p. 1156; '. . . phänomenal, historisch unwirksam, praktisch folgenlos.' 'Können die Dichter die Welt ändern?' ibid., vol. VII, p. 1671.

37 Hamburger, *Truth of Poetry*, p. 172.

38 T.W. Earp, 'Arthur, Charlemagne and Barbarossa', in Lloyd (ed.), *The Paths of Glory*, p. 51.

39 Sackville, 'The Pageant of War', *Pageant of War*, p. 9.

40 Dora Sigerson, 'An Old Proverb', in Lloyd (ed.), *Paths*, p. 104; Laurence Housman, 'The Brand of Cain', in Lloyd (ed.), *Poems*, p. 56.

41 Pottecher, 'Le Point de vue des corbeaux', in *Poètes contre*, p. 108.

42 Plagge, 'Die Schlacht', in Pfemfert (ed.), *1914–1916*, p. 97.

43 E.J. Leed, *No Man's Land: Combat and Identity in World War I* (Cambridge: University Press, 1979), p. 137.

44 Israel Zangwill, 'The Place of Peace', in Lloyd (ed.), *Poems*, p. 107.

45 Alfred Ehrenstein, 'Walstatt', *Der Mensch schreit: Gedichte 1914–1915* (Leipzig, 1916), p. 42.

46 Arcos, 'La Guerre', *Sang des autres*, p. 14.

47 Owen, 'The Parable of the Old Men and the Young', *Complete Poems*, p. 174.

48 Goll, 'Rezitativ', *Requiem*, p. 28.

49 Visiak, 'The Pacifist', in Lloyd (ed.), *Poems*, p. 106; Werfel, 'Der Krieg', *Einander*, p. 47; 'A.E.', 'Statesmen', in Lloyd (ed.), *Paths*, p. 20.

50 Constantine, 'The Use of War', in Lloyd (ed.), *Paths*, p. 37.

51 Otten, 'Für Martinet', *Thronerhebung*, p. 17; Arcos, 'À la mémoire d'un ami', *Sang des autres*, p. 76.

52 Toller, 'Marschlied', *Vormorgen*, p. 10.

53 A.P. Herbert, 'After the Battle', *The Bomber Gipsy and Other Poems* (London: Methuen, 1918), p. 21.

54 Joseph Cohen, 'The War Poet as Archetypal Spokesman', *Stand* 4, no. 3 (1960), p. 23.

55 Karl Stamm, 'Soldat vor dem Gekreuzigten', *Aufbruch des Herzens*, p. 33. Biographical information from *Die Dichtungen* (Zürich: Rascher, 1920), vol. II, pp. 184–5.

56 Richard Fischer, 'Feld der Ehre', *Schrei*, p. 11.

57 Martin Ceadal, *Pacifism in Britain 1914–1945: The Defining of a Faith* (Oxford: Clarendon Press, 1980), pp. 56–7.

58 'La plupart me sont des amis personels.' Rolland, introduction to *Poètes contre; Journal des années de guerre, 1914–1919*, p. 1452.

59 ibid., p. 1339, p. 539.
60 '. . . et non interdiction', Pottecher, *Les Chants de la tourmente* (Paris: Ollendorff, 1916), prefatory note.
61 '. . . il se trouve que le censeur de Leipzig se pique de littérature, et il laisse tout passer.' Rolland, *Journal*, p. 563.
62 Becher, 'Geschrieben 1915 und von der Zensur unterdrückt', in Rubiner, *Kameraden der Menschheit*, p. 58; Fischer, 'Gegen den Krieg, für die Menschheit schrein diese Gedichte aus den Mordfeldern Rumäniens, Flanderns und Frankreichs in die Welt. Sie wollten in die Welt schrein – aber die Zensur von 1917 und 18 drosselte den Schrei.' *Schrei*, p. 5.
63 '. . . der einzige Schriftsteller, Herausgeber und Verleger in der Öffentlichkeit Deutschlands, der durch Veröffentlichung die Dichter der Menschlichkeit über den Krieg hinüber rettete.' Rubiner, *Kameraden der Menschheit*, p. 170.
64 Wandrey, *Motif des Krieges*, p. 245.
65 H. Smalley Sarson, 'The Village, 1915', in *Soldier Poets*, p. 85; Sydney Oswald, 'The Attack', ibid., p. 70.
66 Stephen Koss, *The Rise and Fall of the Political Press in Britain*, vol. II (London: Hamish Hamilton, 1984), p. 312.
67 ibid., p. 328.

7 Men would gather sense

1 Gurney, 'War Books', *Collected Poems*, p. 196.
2 *More Songs of the Fighting Men*, Soldier Poets, Second Series (London: Erskine Macdonald, 1917), p. 8.
3 H. Smalley Sarson, 'The Village, 1915', in *Soldier Poets*, p. 83; Heinrich Lersch, 'Ein Kamerad', in Bab (ed.), *1914*, vol. VIII, p. 12.
4 Alfred Richard Meyer, 'An meine Erde', in Bab (ed.), *1914*, vol. XI, p. 22.
5 Wilfrid J. Halliday, 'Today', in *Soldier Poets*, p. 39.
6 Maurice Bouignol, 'Douaumont', *Sans gestes: Poèmes héroïques* (Paris: Charpentier, 1918), p. 7.
7 Bouignol, 'À la louange des poilus', ibid., p. 15.
8 Julian Grenfell, 'Into Battle', in *Soldier Poets*, p. 27.
9 Karl von Eisenstein, 'Das sind die Schlimmsten deiner Tage nicht', in Bab (ed.), *1914*, vol. X, p. 14.
10 E.F. Wilkinson, 'To 'My People', before the 'Great Offensive''', in *Soldier Poets*, p.104.
11 Patrick Shaw-Stewart, 'I saw a man this morning', in Gardner (ed.), *Up the Line to Death*, p. 59.
12 Clifford J. Druce, 'Forecast', in *More Songs*, p. 58; Carroll Carstairs, 'Death in France', ibid., p. 19; S. Donald Cox, 'To my Mother – 1916', in *Soldier Poets*, p.22; Sylvain Royé, 'Stances', *Le Livre de l'holocauste (1914–1916)* (Paris: Garnier, [1937]), p. 115; Royé, 'Si je ne reviens pas', ibid., p.43; Marc Larreguy de Civrieux, 'À celle qui oubliera', in *Les Poètes contre la guerre*, p. 81.
13 Sorley, 'Saints have adored the lofty soul of you', *Marlborough*, p. 76; Clifford Druce, 'Forecast', in *More Songs*, p. 58; Gerhard Moerner, 'Liebt mich, liebt mich nicht', in Bab (ed.), *1914*, vol. XII, p. 12; Anton Schnack, 'In Bereitschaft', quoted in Bridgwater, *German Poets*, p. 116.
14 Quoted in *More Songs*, p. 145.

15 Henri Céard, 'Lettres du Front', *Sonnets de guerre, 1914–1918* (Paris: Librairie Française, 1919), p. 19.
16 J.W. Streets, 'Youth's Consecration', in *Soldier Poets*, p. 95.
17 Sorley, *Letters*, p. 308.
18 René Hughes, 'Apollon-roi, si ne te plaisent', *Dans la guerre*, p. 13.
19 Louis de Gonzague Frick, 'Complète du poète en campagne', in *Poètes contre*, p. 73.
20 Editor's note, Bab, *1914*, vol. XII, p. 12.
21 Gardner (ed.), *Up the Line to Death*, p. xxiii; Kyle, preface to J. W. Streets, *The Undying Splendour* (London: Erskine Macdonald, 1917).
22 Kyle, preface to *Soldier Poets*, p. 8.
23 ibid., p. 9.
24 C.M. Bowra, *Poetry and Politics*, p. 4.
25 Jean Cocteau, 'Prologue', *Le Cap de Bonne Espérance, suivi de Le Discours du grand sommeil* (Paris: Gallimard, 1967), p. 145; Richard Aldington, 'Insouciance', *Images of War*, p. 20.
26 Léon Chancerel, 'Le Spectre du Depart', *La Chanson des sept jours* (Paris: La Renaissance du Livre, 1916), p. 24.
27 Letter to Laurence Binyon, in Rosenberg, *Collected Works*, p. 248.
28 T.E. Hulme, 'Trenches: St Eloi', in Silkin, *Penguin*, p. 149.
29 E.J. Leed, *No Man's Land*, p. 3.
30 ibid., p. 21.
31 Rosenberg, 'Break of Day in the Trenches', *Collected Works*, p. 103.
32 Edmund Blunden, 'Third Ypres', *Undertones of War* (London: Cobden-Sanderson, 1929), p. 288.
33 Hermann Sendelbach, 'Trommelfeuer', in Bab (ed.), *1914*, vol. XII, p. 30.
34 Wilhelm Stolzenberg, 'Gefallene', in Pfemfert (ed.), *1914–1916*, p. 108; Edgell Rickword, 'Trench Poets', *Behind the Eyes* (London: Sidgwick and Jackson, 1921), p. 44.
35 Leed, *No Man's Land*, p. 12.
36 Silkin, *Out of Battle*, p. 102.
37 Kurd Adler, 'Ausblick', in Pfemfert (ed.), *1914–1916*, p. 14; 'In der Beobachtung', ibid., p. 8; 'Sehr dunkel nur', ibid., p. 16; 'Wiederkehr (Juni 1916)', ibid., p. 18.
38 Edmund Blunden, 'The Zonnebeke Road', *Undertones*, p. 277; 'Come On, My Lucky Lads', ibid., p. 275; 'Preparations for Victory', ibid., p. 274.
39 Blunden, 'Vlamertinghe: Passing the Château, July, 1917', ibid., p. 287.
40 Blunden, 'Gouzeaucourt: The Deceitful Calm', ibid., p.295; 'La Quinque Rue', ibid., p. 300.
41 Arnold Ulitz, 'Gasangriff', in Volkmann (ed.), *Deutsche Dichtung*, p. 238.
42 Owen, 'Exposure', *Complete Poems*, p. 48.
43 Leed, *No Man's Land*, pp. 4–5.
44 Sassoon, B.B.C. talk, 22 August 1948. Printed in Walsh (ed.), *A Tribute to Wilfred Owen*, p. 37.
45 Johnston, *English Poetry*, p. 13.
46 Klemm, 'An der Front', in Pfemfert (ed.), *1914–1916*, p. 64.
47 Plagge, 'Die Schlacht', ibid., p. 97.
48 Kanehl, 'Vormarsch im Winter', ibid., p. 47.
49 Bridgwater, *German Poets*, p. 165.
50 Silkin, *Penguin*, p. 28.
51 Georg Trakl, 'Im Winter', *Die Dichtungen* (Salzburg: Otto Müller, 1938), p. 34.

52 Ernst Stadler, 'Judenviertel in London', *Der Aufbruch* (Leipzig: Verlag der Weißen Bücher, 1914), p. 67.
53 '. . . sublimiert in traurigem und resignierenden Pessimismus.' Wandrey, *Motif des Krieges*, p. 244.

8 Relics for the present

1 Irene Rutherford McLeod, *One Mother* (London: Chatto and Windus, 1916), p. 4.
2 Klara Blüthgen, 'Vermißt', in Bab (ed.), *1914*, vol. V, p. 12.
3 Lesbia Thanet, 'In Time of War', in Reilly (ed.), *Scars upon my Heart*, p. 112.
4 Margaret Postgate[Cole], 'The Veteran', in Frederick Brereton (ed.), *An Anthology of War Poems* (London: Collins, 1930), p. 121.
5 Wilfred Owen, 'Strange Meeting', *Collected Poems*, p. 148.
6 Je ne veux pas que toute la souffrance se perde dans l'abîme. Et c'est pourquoi je la raconte très exactement.' *Vie des martyrs*. Quoted in John Cruickshank, *Variations on Catastrophe: Some French Responses to the Great War* (Oxford: Clarendon Press, 1982), p.86.
7 Georges Duhamel, 'Ballade de Florentin Prunier', *Élégies* (Paris: Mercure de France, 1920), p. 75.
8 Isaac Rosenberg, 'Dead Man's Dump', *Collected Works*, p. 109.
9 Karl von Eisenstein, 'Tod', *Lieder im Kampf* (Berlin: A. Collignon, 1916), p. 34.
10 Silkin, *Penguin*, p. 29.
11 Martinet, 'Celui-là', *Temps maudits*, p. 81.
12 Rolland, *Journal*, p. 479.
13 Floris Delattre, 'Les Poètes anglais et la Guerre', *Deux essaies sur la psychologie sociale de l'Angleterre* (Paris: Gamber, 1931), p. 13.
14 'L'Anglais n'est pas, généralement parlant, un intellectuel. Il demeure, en face des idées abstraites, un peu naïf, un peu gauche, et, comme il arrive, plutôt méfiant. Son esprit, qui plonge des racines profondes dans le réel et le concret [. . .] est moins vif que le nôtre, qui ressemblerait plutôt à une étoffe soyeuse, si souplement chatoyante et flottante. La logique, où nous prenons tant de plaisir, les notions générales, où nous sommes passés maîtres, ne retiennent guère son attention.' 'Les Poètes anglais', p. 55.
15 'Aucune oeuvre ne nous apporte soit une vision de beauté, soit une conception morale révélatrice, et, par son intensité et sa vérité tout ensemble, ne traverse notre esprit d'un frisson nouveau.' ibid., p. 13.
16 Goll, 'Rezitativ', *Requiem*, p. 5.
17 Sassoon, 'Twelve Months After', *War Poems*, p. 72.
18 Since I was unable to examine a copy of Schnack's volume, I rely on Bridgwater's comment that the book offers a systematic account of the poet's war experience.
19 Ronald Peacock, 'The Great War in German Lyrical Poetry', p. 195.
20 See Eric Hobsbawm, 'Mass-Producing Traditions', in Hobsbawm and Ranger (eds), *The Invention of Tradition*, pp. 263–307.
21 Preface to 1987 edition Silkin, *Out of Battle*, p. xviii.
22 Desmond Graham, *The Truth of War: Owen, Blunden, Rosenberg* (Manchester: Carcanet Press, 1984), p. 137.
23 F.-J. Brüggemeier uses a similar mosaic analogy in the essay 'Sounds of Silents: History, Narrative and Life Recollections.' (*Poetics* 15 (1986), pp. 5–24), to argue for the value of oral accounts as historical evidence.

24 For example, 'Das Gegebene für die historische Erfahrung und Forschung ist nicht die Vergangenheit – sie ist eben vergangen – sondern das von den Vergangenheiten in dem Jetzt und Hier noch Unvergangene.' *Historik: Historisch-kritische Ausgabe*, ed. Peter Leyh (Stuttgart: Frommann-Holzboog, 1977), p. 397.

25 Daniel J. Boorstin, 'The Historian: "A Wrestler with the Angel", '*New York Times Review of Books*, 20 September 1987, p. 1.

26 Droysen, *Historik*, p. 70.

27 Graham, *The Truth of War*, p. 24.

Bibliography

N.B. Because of the constraints of space, this list is confined to works cited.

PRIMARY SOURCES: FIRST WORLD WAR POETRY

a) International

Deppe, Wolfgang G., Christopher Middleton and Herbert Schönherr (eds) (1959) *Ohne Haß und Fahne. No Hatred and No Flag. Sans haine et sans drapeau: War Poems of the Twentieth Century*, Hamburg: Rowohlt.

Grumbine, Harvey Carson (ed.) (1918) *Humanity or Hate: Which?*, Boston: Cornhill.

Hartmann, Wolf Justin (ed.) (1939) *Sie alle fielen: Gedichte europäischer Soldaten*, München: Oldenbourg.

Silkin, Jon (ed.) (1981) *The Penguin Book of First World War Poetry*, 2nd edition, Harmondsworth: Penguin.

Tuckermann, Fleming (1917) *War Poems in French and English*, New York: Brentanos (For the Author).

b) English

'A.E.' (pseud. of George William Russell) (1915) *Gods of War with Other Poems*. 'Printed for private circulation', Dublin.

A., J.R. (1916) 'The Everlasting Terror.' Printed on reverse of a concert programme, London: Imperial War Museum.

Adams, Arthur A. [1915] *My Friend, Remember! Lines Written on Reading. Lissauer's Chant of Hate*, Sydney: Angus & Robertson.

Aldington, Richard (1921) *Images of War*, Boston: Four Seas.

Bewsher, Paul [1917] *The Dawn Patrol and Other Poems of an Aviator*, London: Erskine Macdonald.

Binyon, Laurence (1919) *The Four Years*, London: Elkin Mathews.

Birmingham Public Libraries, *Press Poems of the Great War 1914–1919*, 2 vols. (Edward Lawrence Levy collection).

—— (1914–21) *War Poetry Scrap Book: A Collection of Broadsides, Leaflets, Newspaper Cuttings, etc.*, 4 vols.

Blunden, Edmund C. (1929) *Undertones of War*, London: Cobden-Sanderson.

Bereton, Frederick (pseud. of Frederick Thompson Smith), (ed.) (1930) *An*

Anthology of War Poems, London: Collins.

Brittain, Vera M. (1918) *Verses of a V.A.D.*, London: Erskine Macdonald.

Brooke, Rupert (1915) *1914 and Other Poems*, London: Sidgwick & Jackson.

Cinquante-Quatre: France 1917, 54th Squadron, Air Force Corps, Printed Cambridge, 1917.

Clarke, George Herbert (ed.) [1919] *A Treasury of War Poetry: British and American Poems of the World War, 1914–1919*, London: Hodder and Stoughton.

Cox, S. Donald *Selected Poems*, bound typescript, London: Imperial War Museum.

Crawshay-Williams, Eliot (1918) *The Gutter and the Stars*, London: Erskine Macdonald.

Edwards, Mabel C. and Mary Booth (eds) (1915) *The Fiery Cross: An Anthology*, London: Grant Richards.

Elliott, H.B. (ed.) (1915) *Lest We Forget: A War Anthology*, London: Jarrold.

Ewer, W.N. [1917] *Five Souls and Other War-Time Verses*, London: The Herald.

Fiske, Isabelle Howe (n.d.) *Sonnets of Protest*, [USA] n.p., Imperial War Museum.

Flint, F.S. (1920) *Otherworld. Cadences*, London: Poetry Bookshop.

Ford, Gertrude S. and Erskine Macdonald (eds) (1917) *A Crown of Amaranth: A Collection of Poems to the Memory of the Brave and Gallant Gentlemen Who Have Given their Lives for Great and Greater Britain. MCMIV – MCMXVII*, London: Erskine Macdonald.

Forshaw, Charles F. (ed.) (1915) *One Hundred of the Best Poems of the European War by Poets of the Empire*, vol. I, London: Elliott Stock.

—— (1916) *One Hundred Best Poems of the European War by Women Poets of the Empire*, vol.II, London: Elliot Stock.

Gardner, Brian (ed.) (1976) *Up the Line to Death: The War Poets, 1914–1918*, London: Eyre Methuen.

Graves, Robert (1917) *Fairies and Fusiliers*, London: Heinemann.

—— (1920) *Country Sentiment*, London: Martin Secker.

Gurney, Ivor (1982) *Collected Poems of Ivor Gurney*, ed. P.J. Kavanagh, Oxford: Oxford University Press.

Hale, Katherine (pseud. of Amelia Beers Garvin) (1914) *Grey Knitting and Other Poems*, Toronto: William Briggs.

Halliday, Wilfrid J. (1917) *Refining Fires*, London: Erskine Macdonald.

Hardie, John L. (ed.) (1943) *Verse of Valour: An Anthology of Shorter War Poems of Sea, Land, Air*, Glasgow: Art and Educational Publishers.

Hardy, Thomas (1919) *Satires of Circumstance: Lyrics and Reveries: Moments of Vision and Miscellaneous Verses*, London: Macmillan.

Harvey, Frederick William (1916) *A Gloucestershire Lad at Home and Abroad*, London: Sidgwick & Jackson.

Herbert, Alan. P. (1918) *The Bomber Gipsy and Other Poems*, London: Methuen.

Hibberd, Dominic and John Onions (eds) (1986) *Poetry of the Great War: An Anthology*, Basingstoke: Macmillan.

Hodgson, William Noel (1916) *Verse and Prose in Peace and War*, London: Smith, Elder.

Housman, Laurence (1918) *The Heart of Peace and other Poems*, London: Heinemann.

Kipling, Rudyard (1940) *Verse: Definitive Edition*, London: Hodder and Stoughton.

Lloyd, Bertram (ed.) (1918) *Poems Written during the Great War, 1914–1918: An Anthology*, London: Allen & Unwin.

—— (1919) *The Paths of Glory: A Collection of Poems Written during the War*

1914–1919, London: Allen & Unwin.

Mackintosh, Ewart A. (1917) *A Highland Regiment*, London: John Lane.

McLeod, Irene Rutherford (1916) *One Mother*, London: Chatto & Windus.

Marsh, Edward (ed.) (1917) *Georgian Poetry, 1916–1917*, London: Poetry Bookshop.

More Songs of the Fighting Men (1917) Soldier Poets, Second Series, London: Erskine Macdonald.

Owen, Wilfred (1983) *The Complete Poems and Fragments*, ed. Jon Stallworthy, London: Chatto & Windus.

Parsons, Ian M. (ed.) (1966) *Men Who March Away: Poems of the First World War*, Toronto: Clarke, Irwin.

Plowman, Max (1920) *Shoots in the Stubble*, London: C.W. Daniel.

Pound, Ezra (1920) *Cathay*, London: The Ovid Press.

Read, Herbert (1919) *Naked Warriors*, London: Art and Letters.

—— (1935) *Poems 1914–1934*, London: Faber & Faber.

Reilly, Catherine W. (ed.) (1981) *Scars upon my Heart: Women's Poetry and Verse of the First World War*, London: Virago.

Rickword, Edgell (1921) *Behind the Eyes*, London: Sidgwick & Jackson.

Rosenberg, Isaac (1979) *The Collected Works: Poetry, Prose, Letters, Paintings and Drawings*, ed. Ian Parsons, London: Chatto & Windus.

Sackville, Margaret [1916] *The Pageant of War*, London: Simpkin Marshall.

Sassoon, Siegfried (1919) *The War Poems*, London: Heinemann.

Silkin, Jon (ed.) (1979, 1981) *The Penguin Book of First World War Poetry*, London: Allen Lane.

Soldier Poets: Songs of the Fighting Men (1916) London: Erskine Macdonald.

Sorley, Charles H. (1919) *Marlborough and Other Poems*, Cambridge: Cambridge University Press.

Songs and Sonnets for England in War Time (1914) London: Bodley Head.

Squire, J.C. (1919) *The Survival of the Fittest*, London: Allen & Unwin.

Streets, John William (1917) *The Undying Splendour*, London: Erskine Macdonald.

Thomas, Edward (1920) *Collected Poems*, London: Selwyn & Blount.

Tulloch, Donald (ed.) (1915) *Songs and Poems of the Great World War*, Worcester, Mass.: Davis Press.

Watson, William (1917) *The Man Who Saw and Other Poems*, London: John Murray.

West, Arthur Graeme (1918) *The Diary of a Dead Officer: Being the Posthumous Papers of A.G. West*, London: Allen & Unwin.

Willis, George (1919) *Any Soldier to his Son*, London: Allen & Unwin.

Wisby, R. *The Mother's Son*, typed sheet, Imperial War Museum.

Ziv, Frederic W. (ed.) (1936) *The Valiant Muse: An Anthology of Poems by Poets Killed in the World War*, New York: Putnam.

c) French

Aderer, Adolphe (1918) *Les Heures de la guerre*, Paris: Calmann-Lévy.

Aicard, Jean (1917) *Le Sang du sacrifice*, Paris: Flammarion.

Allou, Maurice (1919) *Strophes d'acier (1914–1916)*, Paris / Nancy: Librairie Militaire Berger-Levrault.

Apollinaire, Guillaume (1925) *Calligrammes: Poèmes de la paix et de la guerre 1913–1916*, Paris: Gallimard.

Arcangues, Pierre d' (1916) *Les Lauriers sur les tombes*, Paris: Pierre Lafitte.

Arcos, René (1919) *Le Sang des autres: Poèmes, 1914–1917*, Genève: Le Sablier.

Association des Écrivains Combattants (1924–6) *Anthologie des écrivains morts à la guerre, 1914–1918*, 5 vols. Amiens: E. Malfère.

Auriac, Victor d' (1916) *Le Vieux Dieu*, Paris: Alphonse Lemerre.

Beauduin, Nicolas [1916] *L'Offrande héroïque: Poèmes*, Neuilly–Paris: La Vie des Lettres.

Bernard, Gaston et Victor Buissonville (eds) (1917) *Poètes-Soldats: Recueil de poèmes du front Belge*, Paris: Jouve.

Botrel, Théodore (1915) *Les Chants du bivouac: 1er août–31 décembre, 1914*, Paris: Payot.

Bouignol, Maurice (1918) *Sans gestes: Poèmes héroïques*, Paris: Charpentier.

Bourgeois, Gaston (1919) *Rouge, jaune et noir: Poèmes*, Bruxelles: Larcie.

Buisson, Benjamin (pseud. of Ben Adam) (1917) *Teutoniana*, Paris: Alphonse Lemerre.

Cammaerts, Émile (1915) *Belgian Poems: Chants patriotiques et autres poèmes*, London: John Lane.

Céard, Henri (1919) *Sonnets de guerre, 1914–1918*, Paris: Librairie Française.

Chancerel, Léon (1916) *La Chanson des sept jours*, Paris: La Renaissance du Livre.

Claudel, Paul (1922) *Poèmes de guerre*, Paris: La Nouvelle Revue Française.

Cocteau, Jean (1967) *Le Cap de Bonne Espérance suivi de Le Discours du grand sommeil*, Paris: Gallimard.

Dérieux, Henry (1916) *En ces jours déchirants*, Paris: Payot.

Dorchaine, Auguste (1915) *Hymne aux cloches de Pâques*, Paris: Alphonse Lemerre.

Drieu la Rochelle, Pierre (1917) *Interrogations: Poèmes*, Paris: La Nouvelle Revue Française.

Droin, Alfred (1917) *Le Crêpe étoilé: 1914–1917*, Paris: Charpentier.

Duhamel, Georges (1920) *Élégies*, Paris: Mercure de France.

Fauré, G.A. (1916) *Mes Impressions sur la guerre, 1914–15–16*, printed Nevers.

Fort, Paul (1917) *Ballades françaises: Que j'ai le plaisir d'être français! suivi de Temps de guerre*, Paris: Charpentier.

Hardt, Ernst (ed.) (1939) 'Gedichte von gefallenen Franzosen aus dem Weltkrieg: Deutsche Nachdichtungen.' *Neue Rundschau*, 50, No. 1 (1939), pp. 116–23.

Henry-Jacques (pseud. of Henry Jacques) (1940) *Nous...de la guerre*, Paris: Fernand Sorlot.

Hugues, René [1918] *Dans la guerre: Sonnets*, Paris: Sansot.

Jouve, Pierre-Jean (1915) *Vous êtes les hommes*, Paris: Nouvelle Revue Française.

La Tailhède, Raymond de (1917) *Hymne pour la France*, Paris: Émile-Paul.

Larronde, Carlos (ed.) (1916) *Anthologie des écrivains français morts pour la patrie*, Paris: Larousse.

La Vaissière, Robert de (ed.) (1923) *Anthologie poétique du XXe siècle*, 2 vols, Paris: Crès.

LeClerc, Marc (1916) *La Passion de notre frère le poilu*, Paris: Crès.

Les Poètes contre la guerre: Anthologie de la poésie française, 1914–1919 (1920) Genève: Le Sablier.

Les Poètes de la guerre: Recueil de poésies parues depuis le 1er août 1914 (1915) Pages d'histoire, 1914–1915, Paris / Nancy: Librairie Militaire Berger-Levrault.

Martel, André (1916) *Poèmes d'un Poilu 1914–15*, Reims: Jules Matol.

Martinet, Marcel (1975) *Le Temps maudits: Poèmes 1914–1916*, Paris: Union Générale d'Editions.

Mary, Th. (1915) *A nos chers blessés: Poésies patriotiques*, Paris: Sirey.

Mourey, Gabriel (1916) *Le Chant du Renouveau: Poèmes de guerre*, Paris / Nancy: Librairie Militaire Berger-Levrault.

Nebout, Pierre (1916) *France et Belgique: A-Propos dramatique en vers*, Paris: E. de Boccard.

Normand, Gilles (1916) *Les Voix de la fournaise: Poèmes d'un poilu*, Paris: Perrin.

Pioch, Georges [1917] *Les Victimes*, Paris: Ollendorff.

Porché, François (1919) *Le Poème de la délivrance: précédé des images de guerre*, Paris: Émile-Paul.

—— (1916) *Le Poème de la tranchée*, Paris: La Nouvelle Revue Française.

Pottecher, Maurice (1916) *Les Chants de la tourmente*, Paris: Ollendorff.

Regnier, Henri de (1918) *1914–1916: Poésies*, Paris: Mercure de France.

Romains, Jules (1960) *Europe: Poèmes*, Paris: Gallimard.

Royé, Sylvain (1937) *Le Livre de l'holocauste (1914–1916): Poèmes*, Paris: Garnier.

Spire, André (1919) *Le Secret*, Paris: La Nouvelle Revue Française.

Texier, Louis (1914) *Aux morts pour la patrie*, Paris: Albert Messein.

Trochu, Francis [1915] *Poèmes de la guerre 1914–1915*, Paris: Jouve

Turpin, Georges (ed.) (1917) *Les Poètes de la guerre*, 2 vols, Paris: Fischbacher.

Van der Verren, August (1916) *Neutres! A la Belgique martyre*, Paris: Imprimerie Populaire.

Verhaeren, Émile (1919) *Les Ailes rouges de la guerre: Poèmes*, Paris: Mercure de France.

Vildrac, Charles (1920) *Chants du désespéré (1914–1920)*, Paris: La Nouvelle Revue Française.

Wyseur, Marcel (1916) *La Flandre rouge: Poèmes*, Paris: Perrin.

d) German

Adler, Kurd (1918) *Wiederkehr*, Der rote Hahn 27–8, Berlin-Wilmersdorf: Die Aktion.

Altgraf Erich (pseud. of Erich Maria J.H.E., Altgraf zu Salm-Reifferschied) (n.d.) *Kriegsgedichte: Sarajevo. 1914–1915*. Sarajevo: Selbstverlag des Verfassers.

Anz, Thomas and Thomas Vogl (eds) (1982) *Die Dichter und der Krieg: Deutsche Lyrik, 1914–1918*, München: C. Hanser.

Bab, Julius (ed.) (1914–19) *1914: Der deutsche Krieg im deutschen Gedicht*. 12 vols, Berlin: Morawe und Scheffelt.

Barthel, Max (1917) *Freiheit: Neue Gedichte aus dem Kriege*, Jena: Diederichs.

Becher, Johannes R. (1916) *An Europa: Neue Gedichte*, Leipzig: Kurt Wolff.

Bern, Maximilian (ed.) (1916) *Deutschland, Deutschland über alles: Ein vaterländisches Hausbuch für jung und alt zur Verherrlichung deutscher Heldenkraft und Herzensgüte, deutscher Kultur und Wesensart*, Berlin: Elsner.

Biese, Alfred (ed.) (1915) *Poesie des Krieges*, Neue Folge, Berlin: Grote.

Binding, Rudolf G. (1923) *Stolz und Trauer*, Frankfurt a. M.: Rütten und Loening.

Braun, Reinhold (ed.) (1917) *Heil Kaiser Dir!* Hamburg: Agentur des Rauhen Hauses Biedermann.

Brecht, Bertolt (1927) *Bertolt Brechts Hauspostille: Mit Anleitungen. Gesangsnoten und einem Anhang*, Berlin: Propyläen-Verlag.

Bröger, Karl (1917) *Kamerad, als wir marschiert: Kriegsgedichte*, Jena: Diederichs.

Das zweite Jahr: Kriegsgedichte der Täglichen Rundschau (1915) Berlin: Tägliche Rundschau.

Deutsche Vaterlandslieder (n.d.) Insel-Bücherei 154, Leipzig: Insel.

Ehrenstein, Albert (1916) *Der Mensch schreit: Gedichte 1914–1915*, Leipzig; rpt.. Nendeln: Kraus.

Eisenstein, Karl von (1916) *Lieder im Kampf*, Berlin: A. Collignon.

Engelke, Gerrit (1923) *Rhythmus des neuen Europa: Gedichte*, Jena: Diederichs.

Eulenberg, Herbert (1925) *Lyrische und Dramatische Dichtungen*, Stuttgart: Engelhorn.

Ewers, Hanns Heinz (1915) *Deutsche Kriegslieder*, 6th edition, New York: The Fatherland.

Fischer, Richard (1919) *Schrei in die Welt*, Das neuste Gedicht 20, Dresden: Dresdner Verlag von 1917.

Flex, Walter (1915) *Sonne und Schild*, Braunschweig: Georg Westermann.

Ganghofer, Ludwig, G. Hochstetter, M.G. Conrad, Heinrich Vierordt (1914) *Deutsches Flugblatt: Weihnachtsmappe*, München: Goltz.

—— (1914) 'Wilhelm der Große' *Eiserne Zitter: Kriegslieder*, Stuttgart: Adolf Bonz.

Goll, Ivan (1917) *Requiem: Für die Gefallenen von Europa*, Zürich: Rascher.

Hartmann, Walther G. (1920) *Wir Menschen: Gedichte*, Der Jüngste Tag 79, München: Kurt Wolff.

Herzog, Rudolf (1915) *Ritter, Tod und Teufel: Kriegsgedichte*, Leipzig: Quelle und Meyer.

Kanehl, Oskar (1922) *Die Schande: Gedichte eines dienstpflichtigen Soldaten aus der Mordsaison 1914–18*, Die Aktionslyrik 7, Berlin-Wilmersdorf: Die Aktion.

Klabund (pseud. of Alfred Henschke) (n.d.) *Die Himmelsleiter: Neue Gedichte*, Berlin: Ernst Reiss.

Klemm, Wilhelm (1915) *Gloria! Kriegsgedichte aus dem Feld*, München: A. Langen.

—— *Aufforderung: Gesammelte Verse*, (1917) Die Aktionslyrik 4, Berlin-Wilmersdorf: Die Aktion.

Kolbenheyer, Erwin G. (1929) *Lyrisches Brevier*, München: Georg Müller.

Kriegsflugblätter der Simplicissimus (1914–15) München.

Lauff, Joseph von [1915] *Singendes Schwert: Lieder aus großer Zeit*, Berlin: August Scherl.

Lersch, Heinrich (1918) *Deutschland! Lieder und Gesänge von Volk und Vaterland*, Jena: Diederichs.

Lichtenstein, Alfred (1919) *Gedichte und Geschichten*, ed. Kurt Labasch, München: Georg Müller.

Lienhard, Friedrich (1915) *Heldentum und Liebe: Kriegsgedichte*, Stuttgart: Greiner und Pfeiffer.

Münzer, Kurt (pseud. of Georg Fink) (1914) *Taten und Kränze: Lieder zum Kriege 1914*, Orplidbücher 13, Berlin: Alex Juncker.

Neue Kriegslieder (n.d.) Orplidbücher 12, Berlin-Charlottenburg: Axel Juncker.

Otten, Karl (1918) *Die Thronerhebung des Herzens*, Der rote Hahn 4, Berlin-Wilmersdorf: Die Aktion.

Petzold, Alfons (1915) *Volk, mein Volk: Gedichte der Kriegszeit*, Jena: Diederichs.

Pfemfert, Franz (ed.) (1916) *1914–1916: Eine Anthologie*, Die Aktionslyrik 1, Berlin-Wilmersdorf: Die Aktion.

Pinthus, Kurt (ed.) (1920) *Menschheitsdämmerung: Symphonie jüngster Dichtung*, Berlin: Rowohlt.

Quenzel, Karl (ed.) (1915) *Des Vaterlandes Hochgesang: Eine Auslese deutscher Kriegs- und Siegeslieder*, Leipzig: Hesse und Becker.
Rilke, Rainer Maria (1956) 'Fünf Gesänge: August 1914' *Sämtliche Werke*, vol. II, Wiesbaden: Insel.
Rubiner, Ludwig (ed.) (1919) *Kameraden der Menschheit: Dichtungen zur Weltrevolution*, Potsdam: Kiepenheuer.
Schaeffer, Albrecht (1915) *Des Michael Schwertlos vaterländische Gedichte*, Leipzig: Insel.
Schaukal, Richard (1914) *1914: Eherne Sonnete*, München: Georg Müller.
Schröder, Rudolf Alexander (1914) *Heilig Vaterland: Kriegsgedichte*, Leipzig: Insel.
Stamm, Karl (1920) *Der Aufbruch des Herzens*, Zürich: Rascher.
—— (1920) *Die Dichtungen*, Zürich: Rascher.
Stramm, August (1915) *Tropfblut: Gedichte*, Berlin: Der Sturm.
Tech, H.A.F. (1915) *Kampfreime eines Friedfertigen aus dem Kriegsjahre 1914*, Wüsterhause (Kreis Neustettin): Selbstverlag des Verfassers.
Toller, Ernst (1924) *Vormorgen*, Potsdam: Kiepenheuer.
Trakl, Georg (1938) *Die Dichtungen*, Salzburg: Otto Müller.
Volkmann, Ernst (ed.) (1934) *Deutsche Dichtung im Weltkrieg (1914–1918)*, Deutsche Literatur: Sammlung literarischer Kunst- und Kulturdenkmäler in Entwicklungsreihen, Reihe Politische Dichtung 8, Leipzig: Reclam.
Warncke, Paul (1915) *Sturm: Kriegsgedichte*, Berlin: A. Holfmann.
Weber, A.O. (1917) *Wenn Mars regiert*, Berlin: Bachmair.
Werfel, Franz (1917) *Einander: Oden. Lieder. Gestalten*, Leipzig: Kurt Wolff.
Wieprecht, Christoph (1918) *Hammer und Schwert: Gedichte der Arbeit*, Mönchen-Gladbach: Volksverein-Verlag.
Winckler, Josef (1919) *Mitten im Weltkrieg*, Nyland-Werke 2, Jena: Diederichs.

SECONDARY SOURCES

Anderson, Benedict (1983) *Imagined Communities: Reflections on the Origin and Spread of Nationalism*, London: Verso Editions and N.L.B.
Ashworth, Tony (1980) *Trench Warfare 1914–1918: The Live and Let Live System*, London: Macmillan.
Aristotle (1967) *Poetics*, trans. Gerald F. Else, Ann Arbor: University of Michigan Press.
Audoin, Philippe (1973) *Les Surréalistes*, Paris: Seuil.
Bab, Julius (1914) 'Die Kriegslyrik von heute.' *Das literarische Echo*, 1 Oktober, pp. 5–8.
—— (1914) 'Die Kriegslyrik von heute, II.' *Das literarische Echo*, 15 Dezember, pp. 342–48.
—— (1920) *Die deutsche Kriegslyrik, 1914–1918: Eine kritische Bibliographie*, Stettin: Norddeutsche Verlag für Literatur und Kunst.
—— (1930) *Arbeiterdichtung*, Berlin: Volksbühnen-Verlag.
Bates, Scott (ed.) (1969) *Poems of War Resistance*, New York: Grossmann.
Benn, Gottfried (1968) 'Können Dichter die Welt ändern?' *Gesammelte Werke 7*, Wiesbaden: Limes, pp. 1669–78.
—— 'Soll die Dichtung das Leben bessern?' *Gesammelte Werke 4*, Wiesbaden: Limes, pp. 1147–57.
Bennett, Betty T. (ed.) (1976) *British War Poetry in the Age of Romanticism*, New York: Garland.

Bergonzi, Bernard (1980) *Heroes' Twilight: A Study of the Literature of the Great War*, 2nd edition London: Macmillan.

Birmingham Public Libraries (1921) *A Catalogue of the War Poetry Collection*, Birmingham Printers.

Blodgett, E.D. (1972) 'Mouthful of Earth: A Word for Edward Thomas.' *Modern Poetry Studies* 3, pp. 145–60

Blunden, Edmund (1958) *War Poets, 1914–1918*, London: Longmans, Green (for the British Book Council).

Boorstin, Daniel J. (1987) 'The historian: "A wrestler with the angel".' *New York Times Review of Books*, 20 September.

Bowra, C.M. (1966) *Poetry and Politics, 1900–1960*, Cambridge: Cambridge University Press.

—— (1961) *Poetry and the First World War* (The Taylorian Lecture, 1961) Oxford: Clarendon Press.

Brekle, Wolfgang (1985) *Schriftsteller in der antifaschistischen Widerstand 1933–1945 in Deutschland*, Berlin und Weimar: Aufbau.

Bridgwater, Patrick (1971) 'German Poetry and the First World War.' *European Studies Review* 1, pp. 147–86.

—— (1985) *The German Poets of the First World War*, London: Croom Helm.

Brüggemeier, F.-J. (1986) 'Sounds of silents: History, narrative and life recollections.' *Poetics*, 15, pp. 5–24.

Campbell, Wilfred (ed.) [1912] *Poems of Loyalty by British and Canadian Authors*, Short Studies in English Literature 21, London: Nelson.

Cave, Joy B. (1976) *What Became of Corporal Pittman?*, Portugal Cove, Newfoundland: Breakwater Books.

Ceadel, Martin (1980) *Pacifism in Britain 1914–1945: The Defining of a Faith*, Oxford: Clarendon Press.

Chancellor, Valerie (1970) *History for their Masters: Opinion in the English History Textbook, 1800–1914*, Bath: Adams and Dart.

Cohen Joseph (1957) 'The Three Roles of Siegfried Sassoon.' *Tulane Studies of English* 7, pp. 169–85.

—— (1960) 'The War Poet as Archetypal Spokesman.' *Stand* 4, No. 3, pp. 23–7.

Craig, Gordon A. (1978) *Germany, 1866–1945*, New York: Oxford University Press.

Cruickshank, John (1982) *Variations on Catastrophe: Some French Responses to the Great War*, Oxford: Clarendon Press.

Cysarz, Herbert (1931) *Zur Geistesgeschichte des Weltkrieges: Die dichterischen Wandlungen des deutschen Kriegsbilds, 1910–1930*, Halle: Max Niemeyer.

Michael Décaudin (1967) 'Etudes sur la poésie française contemporaine, IV: Destin de l'unanimisme.' *L'Information littéraire* 19 (1967), pp. 156–65.

Delattre, Floris (1931) *Deux essais sur la psychologie sociale de l'Angleterre*, Paris: Gamber.

Deutsche Akademie der Künste zu Berlin, *Erwin Piscator*. Catalogue of exhibition, *Erwin Piscator: Political Theatre, 1920–1966.*

Deutsches Bücherverzeichnis, vol. III (1911–14), pt. 2, pp. 1787–9.

—— vol. VI (1915–20), pt. 2, pp. 1828–40.

Droysen, Johann Gustav (1977) *Historik: Historisch-kritische Ausgabe*, ed. Peter Leyh, Stuttgart: Frommann-Holzboog.

Economou, George D. and Joan M. Ferrante (eds) (1975) *In Pursuit of Perfection: Courtly Love in Medieval Literature*, Port Washington, N.Y.: Kennikat Press.

Ellul, Jacques (1965) *Propaganda: The Formation of Men's Attitudes*, trans. Konrad Keller and Jean Lerner, New York: Knopf.

Fussell, Paul (1975) *The Great War and Modern Memory*, New York: Oxford University Press.

Gellner, Ernest (1983) *Nations and Nationalism*, Oxford: Blackwell.

—— (1987) *Culture, Identity and Politics*, Cambridge: Cambridge University Press.

Girouard, Mark (1981) *The Return to Camelot: Chivalry and the English Gentleman*, New Haven: Yale University Press.

Gleim, J.L.W. (1906) *Preußische Kriegslieder in den Feldzügen 1756 and 1757 von einem Grenadier*, Leipzig: Poeschel und Treple.

Golby, J.M. and A.W. Purdue (1984) *The Civilisation of the Crowd: Popular Culture in England, 1750–1900*, London: Batsford.

Goodchild, George (1914) *England my England: A War Anthology*, London: Jarrold.

Graham, Desmond (1984) *The Truth of War: Owen, Blunden, Rosenberg*, Manchester: Carcanet Press.

Gregson, J.M. (1976) *Poetry of the First World War*, London: Edward Arnold.

Grumbine, Harvey C. (1918) *Humanity or Hate: Which?* Boston: Cornhill.

Hamburger, Michael and Christopher Middleton (1962) Introduction to *Modern German Poetry, 1910 to 1960: An Anthology with Verse Translations*, New York: Grove Press.

Hamburger, Michael (1969) *The Truth of Poetry: Tensions in Modern Poetry from Baudelaire to the 1960s*, Harmondsworth: Penguin.

Haste, Cate (1977) *Keep the Home Fires Burning: Propaganda in the First World War*, London: Allen Lane.

Hayes, Carlton J.H. (1960) *Nationalism: A Religion*, New York: Macmillan.

Heintz, Günter (ed.) (1974) *Deutsche Arbeiterdichtung 1910–1933*, Stuttgart: Reclam.

Hibberd, Dominic (ed.) (1981) *Poetry of the First World War*, Casebook Series, London: Macmillan.

Hobsbawm, Eric and Terence Ranger (eds) (1983) *The Invention of Tradition: Europe, 1870–1914*, Cambridge: Cambridge University Press.

Hoffpauir, Richard (1985) 'The War Poetry of Edmund Blunden and Ivor Gurney.' *PN Review* 45, pp. 46–51.

Hunt, Barry and Adrian Preston (eds) (1977) *War Aims and Strategic Policy in the Great War 1914–1918*, London: Croom Helm.

Johnston, John H. (1964) *English Poetry of the First World War: A Study of the Evolution of Lyric and Narrative Form*, Princeton: Princeton University Press.

Kenner, Hugh (1971) *The Pound Era*, Berkeley and Los Angeles: University of California Press.

Korte, Hermann (1981) *Der Krieg in der Lyrik des Expressionismus: Studien zur Evolution eines literarischen Themas*, Bonn: Bouvier.

Koss, Stephen (1984) *The Rise and Fall of the Political Press in Britain*, vol.II, London: Hamish Hamilton.

Lafore, Laurence (1965) *The Long Fuse: An Interpretation of the Origins of World War One*, Philadelphia: Lippencott.

Lane, Arthur E. (1972) *An Adequate Response: The War Poetry of Siegfried Sassoon and Wilfred Owen*, Detroit: Wayne State University Press.

Leed, Eric J. (1979) *No Man's Land: Combat and Identity in World War I*, Cambridge: Cambridge University Press.

Lestocquoy, Jean (1968) *Histoire du patriotisme en France des origines à nos jours*, Paris: Albin Michel.

Liddell Hart, Basil H. (1936) *The War in Outline, 1914–1916*, New York: The Modern Library.

Moore, Sturge (1919) *Some Soldier Poets*, London: Grant Richards.

Newman, Gerald (1987) *The Rise of English Nationalism: A Cultural History, 1740–1830*, New York: St Martin's Press.

Ortheil, Hanns-Josef (1979) *Wilhelm Klemm: Ein Lyriker der 'Menschheitsdämmerung'*, Stuttgart: Kroner.

Osborn, E.B. (1919) *The New Elizabethans: A First Selection of the Lives of Young Men Who Have Fallen in the Great War*, London: John Lane.

Owen, Wilfred (1967) *Collected Letters*, ed. Harold Owen and John Bell, London: Oxford University Press.

Ozouf, Mona (1963) *L'École, l'Église et la République 1871–1914*, Paris: Armand Colin.

Peacock, Ronald (1934) 'The Great War in German Lyrical Poetry.' *Proceedings of the Leeds Philosophical and Literary Society*, 3, pp. 189–243.

Pfemfert, Franz (1914) 'Die Besessenen.' *Die Aktion*, 1 August, pp. 671–2.

Piscator, Erwin (1963) *Das politische Theater*, Hamburg: Rowohlt.

Press, John (1969) *A Map of Modern English Verse*, London: Oxford University Press.

Raabe, Paul (1965) *Expressionismus: Aufzeichnungen und Erinnerungen der Zeitgenossen*, Olten: Walter.

Ray, William (1984) *Literary Meaning: From Phenomenology to Deconstruction*, Oxford: Blackwell.

Reilly, Catherine W. (1978) *English Poetry of the First World War: A Bibliography*, London: George Prior, 1978.

Rolland, Romain (1952) *Journal des années de guerre 1914–1919*, Paris: Albin Michel.

Roscher, Archim (1965) *Tränen und Rosen: Krieg und Frieden in Gedichten aus fünf Jahrtausenden*, Berlin: Verlag der Nation.

Sanders, M.L. and Philip M. Taylor (1982) *British Propaganda during the First World War, 1914–18*, London and Basingstoke: Macmillan.

Sassoon, Siegfried (1983) *Diaries 1915–1918*, ed. Rupert Hart-Davis, London: Faber & Faber.

Schütze, Christian (ed.) (1975) *Das Beste aus dem Simplicissimus*, München.

Seidel, L.E. (1902) *Das fünfte Schuljahr: Theoretisch-praktische Anweisung für Lehrer und Lehrerinnen zur Erteilung eines erfolgreichen Unterrichts in Volksschulen nebst vollständig ausgeführten Präparationen*, vol. V, Langensalza: Greßler Schulbuchhandlung.

Silkin, Jon (1972) *Out of Battle: The Poetry of the Great War*, Oxford: Oxford University Press.

Sorley, Charles Hamilton (1919) *The Letters of Charles Sorley, with a Chapter of Biography*, Cambridge: Cambridge University Press.

Stadler, Ernst (1914) *Der Aufbruch*, Leipzig: Verlag der Weißen Bücher.

Stead, C.K. (1967) *The New Poetic: Yeats to Eliot*, Harmondsworth: Penguin.

Stock, Noel (1970) *The Life of Ezra Pound*, London: Routledge & Kegan Paul.

Stoltzfus, Ben F. (1960) 'Unanimism Revisited.' *Modern Languages Quarterly*, 21, 239–45.

Taylor, A.J.P. (1966) *The First World War: An Illustrated History*, Harmondsworth: Penguin.

Thomas, Edward (1914) 'War Poetry.' *Poetry and Drama*, 8, pp. 341–5.

Tilly Charles, Louis E. Tilly and Richard Tilly (1975) *The Rebellious Century, 1830–1930*, London: Dent.

Van Wyk Smith, M. (1978) *Drummer Hodge: The Poetry of the Anglo-Boer War, 1899–1902*, Oxford: Clarendon Press.

Vic, Jean (1923) *La Littérature de guerre: Manuel méthodique et critique des publications de langue française*, 5 vols, Paris: Les Presses Françaises.

Walsh, T.J. (ed.) (n.d.) *A Tribute to Wilfred Owen*, Birkenhead.

Wandrey, Uwe (1973) *Das Motiv des Krieges in der expressionistischen Lyrik*, Hamburg: Hartmut Ludke.

Welland, Dennis S.R. (1978) *Wilfred Owen: A Critical Study*, 2nd edition, London: Chatto and Windus.

White, Gertrude M. (1969) *Wilfred Owen*, New York: Twayne.

General index

Page references for individual poems are excluded; see Index of Poems

Adler, Kurd 211
'A.E.' 175, 189
aestheticism 192, 201, 205, 207
Aicard, Jean 223
Aldington, Richard 4, 236
allegory 177–9, 180, 182, 225, 228
Altgraf Erich 91
Anderson, Benedict 44, 54
Anz, Thomas 9, 13
Apollinaire, Guillaume 4, 9, 11, 71, 144, 186, 205
Arbeiterdichtung 53, 198, 228
Arcangues, Pierre d' 29
Arcos, René 8, 11, 128, 162, 185–6, 224
Aristotle 24
Ashworth, Tony 33
atrocity stories 65–6
audience 4, 24, 44, 92, 161, 165–7, 175–6, 189, 203–4, 228, 239
Audoin, Philippe 6

Bab, Julius 2, 11–12, 49, 50, 53, 87, 192–3, 200, 225
Barbusse, Henri 186
Barnes, Leonard 226
Barthel, Max 198
Bates, Scott 6, 107
battle narratives 81, 225–7
Baudelaire, Charles 175
Beauduin, Nicolas 97
Becher, Johannes 162, 202
Behan, Dominic 168
Belgian poetry 3, 30, 99, 100–1, 103, 138, 223–4

Benn, Gottfried 176, 203
Bennett, Betty T. 35, 55, 106
Bergonzi, Bernard 10, 25–6, 28, 153, 170
Bethmann-Hollweg, Theobald v. 54, 192
Bismarck, Otto v. 60
Blake, William 51
Blodgett, E.D. 99
Blunden, Edmund 10, 14, 102, 196–9, 211–13, 236
Boer War 107, 130, 209: poetry 52, 72, 79, 85–6, 94, 107, 226, 229, 231
book illustrations 7, 84
Boorstin, Daniel 219, 237
Bouignol, Maurice 194, 224, 226
Bowra, C.M. 13, 174, 175, 203–4
Brekle, Wolfgang 167
Brereton, Frederick 10
Bridgwater, Patrick 12, 13, 14, 19, 20, 116, 170, 196, 217, 226
Brittain, Vera 7
broadside ballads 89
Brooke, Rupert 14, 21, 93, 184
Bröger, Karl 13, 53
Bund der Werkleute auf Haus Nyland 53

Cammaerts, Émile 100
Campbell, Wilfred 42
Cannadine, David 42
Carroll, Lewis 25
Cave, Joy 7
Cavell, Edith 4, 66

Ceadal, Martin 185
censorship 6, 167, 170, 187–9,
    201, 235
Chancellor, Valerie 40, 42–3
Chappell, Henry 91
Chennevière, Georges 11, 185,
    202
Chesterton, G.K. 107
chivalry 19, 74, 83–4
Claudel, Paul 9, 71, 233
Clay, Marie E. 90
Cohen, Joseph 161, 166, 183
comradeship 156–8, 187, 189
courtly love lyric 95
Cox, S. Donald 197
Craig, Gordon A. 40, 42–3
cummings, e.e. 220
Cysarz, Herbert 12

Defence of the Realm Act 69
Delattre, Floris 224, 227
Décaudin, Michel 11
Dérieux, Henri 226
dialect poems 230–1
Droin, Alfred 8
Droysen, J.G. 237–8
Duhamel, Georges 11, 185, 220–
    1, 224
Durkheim, Émile 54

Eliot, T.S. 9, 29
Engelke, Gerrit 53, 131, 159
Ewer, W.N. 18
Ewers, H.H. 87
Expressionism 4, 7, 12–13, 168,
    184, 187–8, 217–8

Farjeon, Eleanor 99
First World War: heroism 234;
    mass armies 34; outbreak 35;
    Somme offensive 17; warfare
    33–4
Fischer, Richard 188
Fiske, Isabelle Howe 30
Flint, F.S. 5
folksong 90, 106, 167
Ford, S. Gertrude 198
Fort, Paul 71
Franco-Prussian War 34, 40, 66,
    84, 130
Freud, Sigmund 178
Fry, Roger 15, 186

Fussell, Paul 10, 17, 26–8, 69, 72,
    86, 92, 101, 117, 153, 164, 211

Gardner, Brian 9–10, 17, 93, 162,
    196–7, 200
Gaudier-Brzeska, Henri 29
Gellner, Ernest 30, 37–9, 43, 45,
    54, 240
Girouard, Mark 56
Gladstone, William 40
Gleim, J.L.W. 70
Goethe, Johann Wolfgang v. 27,
    56, 58, 73
Golby, J.M. 40–1
Goldin, Frederick 95
Goll, Yvan 224
Goodman, Nelson 26
Graham, Desmond 28, 236, 238
Graves, Robert 14, 17, 184–5
Gregson, J.M. 170
Grenfell, Julian 195
Grimmelshausen, H.J.C. v. 80,
    116
Grumbine, Harvey C. 13, 63, 82,
    227
Gurney, Ivor 10, 14, 97, 202, 236

Hackenschmidt, Karl 63
Halliday, Wilfrid J. 194
Hamburger, Michael 1, 13, 15,
    45, 170, 174–7, 203–4, 206, 222
Hardt, Ernst 12
Hardy, Thomas 14, 20, 61, 86,
    233
Hartmann, W.J. 12
Haste, Cate 48, 66
Hayes, Carlton J.H. 39
Heintz, Günter 54
Henley, W.E. 52
Hibberd, Dominic 9, 11, 16, 194,
    239
Hobsbawm, Eric 42, 43, 44
Hoffpauir, Richard 236
homogeneity 1, 2, 22, 30, 38, 68,
    71, 77, 83, 94, 104, 229, 230–1
honour 20, 37, 42, 55–7, 63, 72,
    74, 85, 95, 134, 137–8, 153
Horace 80, 109
Hugo, Victor 56
Hulme, T.E. 4
Hunt, Barry 35

Imagistes 4, 5, 184
implied reader 24, 91–2, 165–6

International Workingmen's
Association 43
invention of tradition 21, 42–4,
71, 231
Irish independence movement
30, 68, 168

Johnston, John H. 10, 166, 170–1,
215
Jones, David 14, 226
Jouve, Jean-Pierre 11, 15, 185,
187

Kaiser Wilhelm II 42–3, 67
Kanehl, Oskar 128
Keats, John 146, 212
Kenner, Hugh 29
King Albert 67–8
King George V 68
Kipling, Rudyard 20, 65, 83
Klemm, Wilhelm 13, 168, 173–4,
202, 206, 220
Kneip, Jacob 53
Korte, Hermann 13
Koss, Stephen 189
Körner, Thomas 116
Kyle, Galloway 188, 192, 195,
197–8, 200–1, 205

Lafore, Laurence 35
Laing, R.D. 210
Lane, Arthur E. 170
Lansbury, George 18
Larreguy de Civrieux, Marc 186
Latzko 186
Leclerc, Marc 226
Leed, Eric. J. 178, 208–11, 214
Lersch, Heinrich 13, 53, 186, 236
Lestocquoy, Jean 43
Lichtenstein, Alfred 16
Liddell Hart, Basil H. 33, 35
Lienhard, Friedrich 63, 85
Liliencron, Detlev v. 27
Lissauer, Ernst 167
literary system 25, 90, 190
Lloyd, Bertram 9, 18, 108, 177–8,
187
Lloyd George, David 189

Mackintosh, E.A. 167, 194
Marsh, Edward 184, 185
Martinet, Marcel 15, 128, 162,
166, 176, 224

Masefield, John 143
Massingham, Harold 160
McCrae, John 220
medievalism 56, 74, 82–4, 229
Mewis, Elsie 90
Middleton, Christopher 170
'Miles' [Osbert Sitwell] 142, 233
Modernism 4, 71, 203, 228
Monro, Harold 185
Moore, Sturge 167
Morrell, Ottoline 160, 185
Morris, William 51
music hall 79, 164, 226, 231

Napoleon 60, 79
Napoleonic Wars 55, 56, 82, 106,
116, 130
national character 62, 227
national identity 30, 39, 41, 44,
54, 65, 132
national image 51, 52, 54, 60
National Socialism 12, 54, 127,
198, 201, 232
nationalism 21, 29, 30, 37, 41, 45,
69, 84, 92, 133, 229, 239
nationalism and: borders 39, 45–
6, 133; and education 38–40,
44, 46, 65, 77, 134, 230–1, 239;
and suffrage 40, 43, 230; and
history 42, 59; and industry 37,
41, 232; and mass armies
34, 65; and patriotic education
42; and race 61; and religion
39, 47, 59, 230; and the working
class 43, 78, 192, 231–2; and
total war 65, 88, 134, 239
Newbolt, Henry 8, 20
Newman, Gerald 41
newspapers 2, 44, 46, 68 89
newspapers and magazines:
Die Aktion 7, 9, 12, 16, 127, 166,
169, 170, 174, 184, 187–8, 193,
200, 217
Blast 168
Cambridge Magazine 160
Daily Express 166
Daily Mail 6
Daily News 189
Daily Telegraph 96, 201
Die Fackel 184
Frankfurter Zeitung 6
The Herald 18, 52, 126, 128, 185,
189, 228

Kölnische Zeitung 62
Das literarische Echo 11
The Nation 16, 19, 105, 119, 160, 189, 228
Neue Jugend 187
Neue Rundschau 12
New Statesman 18, 19, 166
La Nouvelle Revue Française 185, 186
Others 168
Ploughshare 19
Poetry Review 188, 197, 198
Punch 191
Simplicissimus 169, 174
Der Tag 166
Tägliche Rundschau 6
The Times 6, 19, 63, 126, 189, 197, 198
Tous les journaux du Front 198
Die weißen Blätter 12, 184, 187
Westminster Gazette 79
Workers' Dreadnought 19, 166
Nibelungenlied 79, 82
non-reader 165, 166, 167, 169, 173, 177, 182, 203, 228, 234
Normand, Gilles 198

oath poems 96, 97
Onions, John 11, 16, 194, 239
Ortheil, Hanns-Josef 13, 168, 174
Osborn, E.B. 192
Otten, Karl 128, 224
Owen, Wilfred 8, 10, 14, 21, 107, 159, 164, 169, 170, 172–3, 185, 194, 199, 202, 205, 214–5, 217, 221, 223–4, 232–4, 238–9
Ozouf, Mona 42

pacifists 15, 18, 109, 160, 183, 185–6, 227–8
Palgrave, F.T. 28
Parsons, Ian M. 10
Peacock, Ronald 12, 36, 37, 46, 55, 227, 229
persona 23, 87–8, 91–2, 96–9, 104, 115, 123, 173, 175–6, 179–84, 203, 208, 212, 217, 231, 234
Peterloo 130
Petzold, Alfons 53–4, 198
Péguy, Charles 192
Pfemfert, Franz 9, 12, 127–8, 169–70, 174, 184, 188, 200–1, 215, 218

Pioch, Georges 128
Piscator, Erwin 16, 184, 202, 217, 224
poems as artifacts 7, 238–9
poems as commodities 25
political poetry 3, 10, 12–13, 50, 128, 129
Pope, Jessie 113
Porché, François 226
Pound, Ezra 4, 5, 57
Press, John 8
Preston, Adrian 35
propaganda 16, 30, 43, 46, 48, 50–51, 63–9, 86, 92, 99, 108, 111, 126, 131–132, 137, 164, 167, 169, 182, 186, 190, 193, 202–4, 232, 235
propaganda poetry 4, 13, 24, 31, 94, 162, 165, 174–6, 182
propagandist intent 24, 31, 95, 154, 161, 166, 173–7, 207, 234, 239
Purdue, A.W. 40, 41

Racine, Jean 84
Ray, William 23
Read, H. 14
realism 109, 157, 169–74, 177, 192, 207–8, 213, 215, 218
recruiting poems 93–4
Regnier, Henri de 71, 101
Reilly, Catherine 2, 9, 11, 18, 191, 220, 239
Reims 47–8, 50, 64, 66, 100
Remarque, Erich 12
Rilke, Rainer Maria 9
Rolland, Romain 186–7, 224
Romains, Jules 11, 15, 185, 187
Roscher, Archim 107
Rosenberg, Isaac 8, 10, 14, 174, 197, 202, 207–8, 236, 238
Ross, Robert 160, 185
Rubiner, Ludwig 188
Russell, George 18, 19

Sabiron, Georges 206
Sackville, Margaret 18, 160
Sanders, M.L. 69
Sassoon, Siegfried 8, 14–15, 19, 27, 128, 160–2, 166, 169–73, 177, 182, 184–5, 194, 199, 201–2, 215, 217, 224, 232–4

Schaeffer, Albrecht 150, 167
Schaukal, Richard 30
Scher, Peter 169
Schickele, René 187
Schiller, Friedrich 56, 73
Schnack, Anton 226
Schönlank, Bruno 198
Scott, Walter 56
Seaman, Owen 93
Second World War 54, 66, 133, 134, 190: poetry 153
Shakespeare, William 70, 80, 83, 136, 139
Silkin, Jon 8–10, 14, 20, 97, 99, 172–3, 217, 222, 234, 236
Sitwell, Osbert 184, 202 see also 'Miles'
Social Darwinism 78, 94, 230
socialism 78, 121, 128, 130, 132–3, 187, 227
socialist poets 228
'soldier's mother' persona 76, 95
Sorley, Charles 1, 2, 10, 14, 86, 97, 107, 131, 167, 170, 185, 192, 199, 200
Southey, Robert 35
Squire, J.C. 18
Stadler, Ernst 218
Stallworthy, Jon 28
Stoltzfus, Ben 11
Stramm, August 4, 8, 205
Streets, John William 198, 199, 200
Surrealists 6

Taylor, A.J.P. 33, 76
Taylor, Philip M. 69
Tech, H.A.F. 29
Thirty Years' War, poetry 106
Thoma, Ludwig 169
Thomas, Edward 14, 95, 99–100
Tilly, Charles 43
Toller, Ernst 128, 202
Tour de la France par deux enfants 42, 46
Trakl, Georg 9, 177, 205, 217, 220
triple threat 49–50, 61
'two nations' concept 158–9

Unanimisme 11, 187, 228

Valéry, Paul 9, 29
Van Wyk Smith, M. 85, 94, 107, 209, 226
Verhaeren, Émile 100–1
vers libre 4, 71, 228
Vershofen, Wilhelm 53
Vic, Jean 2
Vietnam War 6, 45, 230
Vildrac, Charles 11, 185–6, 202
Virgil 106
Vogl, Thomas 9, 13
Volkmann, Ernst 12, 63

Wagner, Richard 56, 60, 80
Wandrey, Uwe 13, 173, 188, 218
war enthusiasm 15, 128–30, 132, 134, 138, 174, 186, 230–1
Warwickshire Poem Aid Society 90
Watson, William 107, 164, 167
Welland, D.S.R. 31, 105, 167, 170, 172, 192–3, 203–4
West, Arthur Graeme 185
Whitman, Walt 3, 71, 228
Wieprecht, Christoph 53, 198
Wilcox, Ella Wheeler 100
Willis, George 19
Winckler, Josef 53, 54
Wolfram von Eschenbach 106
women poets 11, 18, 113–14, 125
Woolf, Virginia 8
Wordsworth, William 23, 55, 80, 141
working-class poetry 53, 54, 197, 198, 231
Wyseur, Marcel 101

Yeats, W.B. 9, 18

Zech, Paul 53
Ziesel, Kurt 54
Ziv, Frederic W. 10

Index of poems

A., J.R.
'The Everlasting Terror' 143
Aaronson, A.
'To the Kaiser' 67
Abadie-Sem-Boucherie, G.
'Le Berceau rouge' 66
Adams, A.
My Friend, Remember! Lines
    Written on Reading Lissauer's
    Chant of Hate 7-8
Aderer, A.
'Reims' 48
Adler, K.
'Ausblick' 211
'In der Beobachtung' 211
'Sehr dunkel nur' 211
'Wiederkehr' 212
'A.E.' (George Russell)
'Chivalry' 225
'Statesmen' 111, 180
Aicard, J.
'Le Jeune héros de quatorze
    ans, Émile Desjardins' 66, 222
Aldington, R.
'In the Trenches' 139
'Insouciance' 204
'Soliloquy I' 140
Allou, M.
'Leur image' 60
Allsopp, H.
'Here and There' 75
Altgraf Erich
'Neujahrsbrief 1915' 136
Angerau, E.
'L'Ame des drapeaux' 78
Anon.
'Draw the sword, Britannia' 62

'Europe–1916' 156
'Meine Jungen' 75
'Soldier M.P.' 110
'The Recruiting Sergeant' 168
Apollinaire, G.
'La Petite Auto' 76, 204
'Paris' 204
Archer, W.
'Louvain' 60
Arcos, R.
'A la mémoire d'un ami' 181
'La Guerre' 179
'Les Morts' 149
Auriac, V. d'
'Qu'il vive' 66
Azaïs, J.-B.
'Ode aux soldats de France' 52
B., H. d'A.
'The March' 135
Ball, H.
'Totentanz' 177
Baret, V.
'Désirs de paix' 58
'La Guerre' 46, 58
Barnes, R.G.
'To the British Army' 50, 55
Barrington, P.
'Education' 125
Bayer, J.
'La Manche vide' 136, 137
Bäumer, L.
'Dämmerung im Graben' 9
Beauduin, N.
'A la France' 96
'Collecte' 46
'Crédo' 58
'Dyptique–L'Empereur fourbe'
    67

Becher, J.
  'An Deutschland' 187
Bergerat, É.
  'Jusqu'au bout' 61
Bertot, J.
  'Les Ruines de Reims' 63
Bewsher, P.
  'Nox Mortis' 151
Billiet, J.
  'Terre' 146
Binyon, L.
  'For the Fallen' 36, 77, 79, 83,
    121, 134, 140, 153, 222, 226, 229
  'Fourth of August' 92
Blunden, E.
  'Come on, My Lucky Lads' 212
  'Gouzeaucourt, The Deceitful
    Calm' 213
  'La Quinque Rue' 213
  'Preparations for Victory' 212,
    213
  'The Zonnebeke Road' 212
  'Third Ypres' 209, 210, 226
  'Vlamertinghe: Passing the
    Château, July 1917' 146, 212–3
Blüthgen, K.
  'Vermißt' 219, 220
Botrel, T.
  'Hardi, les gâs' 36
Bouignol, M.
  'A la louange des poilus' 194
  'Douaumont' 194
Brecht, B.
  'Legende vom toten Soldaten'
    154
Bridges, R.
  'England Stands for Honour'
    56
Brodribb, C.W.
  'Expeditional' 50
Brooke, J.A.
  'For England' 83
  'What Will you Say?' 93
Brooke, R.
  'Now, God be Thanked' 76,
    130, 200
  'The Soldier' 19, 97, 98, 143,
    192, 195
Brown, J.J.
  'War and Christ' 59
Bröger, K.
  'Bekenntnis' 49, 53, 192

Buisson, B.
  'Emmanuel Kant' 60, 64
'Caliban'
  'Der Nothelfer' 61
  'The Hun is at the gate' 61, 64,
    83, 165
Cannan, G.
  'The Spirit of England' 58
Carstairs, C.
  'Death in France' 195
Cendré, L.
  'Reproche aux poètes' 113
Céard, H.
  'Lettres du Front' 198
Chamberlin, H.H.
  'To Wilhelm II' 67
Chanteloube, C.
  'Deux ans après' 84
Chappell, H.
  'The Day' 90
Chennevière, G.
  'L'Étranger' 157, 159
  'Ravitaillement' 120
Claudel, P.
  'Tant que vous voudrez, mon
    général' 36
Cocteau, J.
  'Prologue au Discours du
    grand sommeil 204
Colvin, I.
  'The Answer' 50, 55
Compas, V.
  'La Cueillette tragique' 82
  'Les Poilus' 77
Constantine, H.F.
  'The Glory of War' 147
  'The Use of War' 181
Cox, S.D.
  'To my Mother, 1916' 195, 196
Crawshay-Williams, E.
  'Sonnet of a Son' 122
D'Annunzio, G.
  'A la France' 58
Donner, C.
  'Kaiser Wilhelm the Sower' 67
Drieu la Rochelle, P.
  'Plainte des soldats européens'
    158, 159
Drinkwater, J.
  'We Willed it Not' 57
Droin, A.
  'Le Carnage' 100
Druce, C.

'Forecast' 195
Duhamel, G.
  'Ballade de Florentin Prunier'
    221, 223, 224
Earp, T.W.
  'Arthur, Charlemagne and
    Barbarossa' 177
Ehrenstein, A.
  'Walstatt' 179
Eisenstein, K. v.
  'Das sind die Schlimmsten
    deiner Tage nicht' 195
  'Tod' 222
Engelke, G.
  'An die Soldaten des grossen
    Krieges' 158
Eulenberg, H.
  'Für die Gefallenen' 81
Ewer, W.N.
  '1814–1914: on Reading the
    Dynasts' 130, 132
  'Five Souls' 119
  'Three Gods' 80, 225
Ewers, H.H.
  'Wir und die Welt' 62
Ey, A.
  'Der deutsche Michel und
    John Bull' 61
Fabre des Essarts
  'Joffre' 52
  'Quatre sonnets de guerre' 57
Fauré, G.A.
  'La Guerre' 85
  'La Mère' 85
Fischer, R.
  'Feld der Ehre' 146, 183, 185
  'O diese Zeit der Fäulnis!' 140
Flaischlen, C.
  'Deutscher Weltkrieg' 49
Flecker, J.E.
  'God Save the King' 68
Flex, W.
  'Preußischer Fahneneid' 96
Flint, F.S.
  'Lament' 123
Fournier, P.
  'Émile Desprès' 66
Frank, B.
  'Stolze Zeit' 76
Freeman, J.
  'Happy is England Now' 36
Freeman, R.M.
  'The War Cry' 57

Freksa, F.
  'Kriegsfahrt des
    Automobilisten' 76
Freston, H.R.
  'O Fortunati' 114
G., J.
  'The Hero' 128
Ganghofer, L.
  'Wilhelm der Große' 61
Goll, Y.
  Requiem: Für die Gefallenen
    von Europa 125, 180, 225
Gomme, L.
  'The Call' 63
Gonzague Frick, L. de
  'Complète du poète en
    campagne' 199, 200
Graves, R.
  'A Dead Boche' 157, 172
  'The Leveller' 144, 157
  'Two Fusiliers' 156
Grenfell, J.
  'Into Battle' 194
Gurney, I.
  'To His Love' 140, 172, 205,
    206
  'War Books' 191, 200, 204
Hackenschmidt, K.
  'An die Hetzer' 57
Hale, K.
  'Grey Knitting' 145
Hall, M.
  'After the Battle' 145
Halliday, W.
  'Today' 193
Hamilton, H.
  'Ghouls' 154
  'The Jingo-Woman' 124
  'The Romancing Poet' 114, 159
Hardy, T.
  'In Time of "The Breaking of
    Nations"' 102
  'Men Who March Away' 19, 86
  'The Pity of It' 57
Hartmann, W.J.
  'Mein Bruder Feind' 158
Harvey, F.W.
  'The Soldier Speaks' 97
Hasenclever, W.
  'Die Mörder sitzen in der
    Oper' 121
Hauptmann, G.
  'O mein Vaterland' 36, 96

'Reiterlied' 50, 57
Henry-Jacques
  'Le Charnier' 84
  'Les Martyrs' 147
Herbert, A.P.
  'After the Battle' 182
Herzog, R.
  'Der Deutschen Kriegslied
    1914' 75
  'Jeanne d'Arc' 61
  'Zwei Worte' 37, 69
Hetherington, B.R.M.
  'The Patriot' 78
Hilton Young, E.
  'Air Service' 105
Hodgson, W.N.
  'Before Action' 116, 194
Housman, L.
  'Armageddon–and After' 149
  'Caesar's Image' 124
  'The Brand of Cain' 178
Hughes, R.
  'Apollon-roi, si ne te plaisent'
    199
Hulme, T.E.
  'Trenches, St. Eloi' 208
Hussey, D.
  'Ode to a Young Man Killed in
    Flanders' 83
J., A.L.
  'Happy Warriors' 79
Johst, H.
  'Der Sturm bricht los!' 57
Jouve, P.-J.
  'Les Voix d'Europe' 150
Kanehl, O.
  'Auf dem Marsch' 135
  'Krieg' 129, 131, 175
  'Soldatenmißhandlung' 119,
    167, 182
  'Unterwegs' 151
  'Vormarsch im Winter' 216
Keinzl, H.
  'Der nationale Gott' 59
Kernahan, C.
  To 'Little' Belgium' 50
Kipling, R.
  'For All We Have and Are' 36,
    50, 64
  'The Land' 102
Klabund
  'Kriegsfreiwillige' 81
Klemm, W.

'An der Front' 215
  'Lazarett' 171, 172, 173, 210
Knox, K.
  'A Lost Land' 60
Koch, H.
  'Karfreitag 1915' 166
Kolbenheyer, E.G.
  'Chronica II, 1915' 110, 177
Köppen, E.
  'Loretto' 150
Krailsheimer, H.
  'Unser ist die Glut!' 76
La Tailhède, R. de
  'Hymne pour la France' 36, 47
Langheinrich, F.
  'Im Schmelzbau Krupp' 53
Larreguy de Civrieux, M.
  'A celle qui oubliera' 195
  'Debout les Morts!' 9, 133, 151,
    153
Lauff, J.v.
  'Die fleißige Berta' 52
Lees, B.A.
  'The Front' 83
Lersch, H.
  'Bekenntnis' 39
  'Ein Kamerad' 192
  'Soldaten-Abschied' 36, 49, 96
Letts, W.
  'The Deserter' 141, 144, 183
Lichtenstein, A.
  'Abschied' 115, 169
  'Gebet vor der Schlacht' 116,
    136, 141, 157
Lienhard, F.
  'Den Gästen von Bayreuth' 58,
    60
  'Deutsche Sendung' 58
  'Heerschau' 58
  'Münstergespräch' 66, 85
  'Soldatenauszug aus Erfurt'
    77, 79, 85, 134
Lill, J.
  'The Issues' 51, 55
Limburger, H.
  'Frisch auf' 90
Lissauer, E.
  'Haßgesang gegen England' 7,
    62–3, 166, 176
Macaulay, R.
  'Picnic' 122
Mackintosh, E.A.
  'Before the Somme' 162

'In Memoriam' 162
'Recruiting' 162, 165, 167, 173
Marcel, A.
  'La Dentellière' 102, 223, 224
  'Mai 1915' 101
Martinet, M.
  'Celui-là' 223
  'Civils' 118
  'Droit de gens' 65, 122
  'Elles disent. . .' 124
  'Femmes' 186
  'Poètes d'Allemagne, ô frères
    inconnus' 117, 187, 233
  'Tu vas te battre' 15, 130, 150,
    173, 225
Mary, Th.
  'Aux Aveugles de la guerre'
    136
McCrae, J.
  'In Flanders Field' 30
McLeod, I.
  'One Mother' 219
Meyer, A.R.
  'An meine Erde' 193
Meynell, A.
  'Summer in England, 1914' 80
Miles
  'Rhapsode' 142
  'The Modern Abraham' 120
Moerner, G.
  'Liebt mich, liebt mich nicht'
    196, 200
Mourey, G.'
  'Le Salut aux Alliés' 57, 61
  'Le Vin de la haine' 63
Moyse, G.
  'Aux Fils de France' 75
Münzer, K.
  'Vaterland' 72, 96
Nebout, P.
  'France et Belgique' 46
Nordhausen, R.
  'Die faule Grete (42 cm.
    Mörser)' 52
Oswald, S.
  'The Attack' 188
Otten, K.
  'Für Martinet' 123, 181, 187,
    225
Owen, W.
  'Anthem for Doomed Youth'
    153
  'Disabled' 137, 171

'Dulce et Decorum Est' 108,
  138, 172, 175, 223
'Exposure' 214, 215, 216
'Futility' 210, 221
'Greater Love' 149
'Insensibility' 9, 122, 166, 181
'Mental Cases' 139
'Parable of the Old Man and
  the Young' 180
'S.I.W.' 142, 144
'Strange Meeting' 158, 179,
  221, 235
'The Chances' 167
'The Send-Off' 135
'The Show' 179
Pain, B.
  'The Kaiser and God' 65
Palmer, J.R.
  'Pro Patria' 58
Périn, C.
  'Les Femmes de tous les pays'
    125
Phillpotts, E.
  'To a Mother' 80
Pioch, G.
  'Dédicace à la pitié' 181
  'Mutilés' 138
  'Pour les gens simples' 78
Piscator, E.
  'Denk an seine Bleisoldaten'
    16, 128, 144, 147
  'Der Mutter zweier Söhne,
    welche fielen' 126, 171, 223
  'Einer ist tot' 128
  'Kurd Adler getötet' 184
Plagge, H.
  'Die Schlacht' 148, 178, 215,
    217, 218
  'Nacht im Granatenfeuer' 141
Platz, W.
  'O Nikolaus, O Nikolaus' 50
Plowman, M.
  'Going into the Line' 146
  'The Dead Soldiers' 147
Pope, J.
  'Lads of the Maple Leaf' 75
Postgate [Cole], M.
  'The Veteran' 220, 224
Pottecher, M.
  'Le Point de vue des corbeaux'
    84, 178, 187
Pound, E.

'Lament of the Frontier Guard'
29
'Song of the Bowmen of Shu'
29
Powell, M.E.
'The Reward' 126
Pratt, M.
'To a Shirker' 94
Preczang, E.
'Gefallen, ein Mann' 78
Prieur, A.
'Accalmie' 39
'Guillaume veut la paix' 67
Prior, L.
'To a Hesitant Briton' 94
Read, H.
'My Company' 194
'The Execution of Cornelius
Vane' 141
'The Happy Warrior' 141
Regnault, M.
'Turcs, Allemands, Bulgares'
61
Regnier, H. de
'Le Père' 82
'Le Serment' 63
Rice, C.Y.
'The Greater Crime' 18
Rickword, E.
'Trench Poets' 210
Rilke, R.M.
'Fünf Gesänge, August 1914' 9,
76
Rosenberg, I.
'Break of Day in the Trenches'
209
'Daughters of War' 179
'Dead Man's Dump' 173, 221,
222
'Louse Hunting' 236
'Returning, We Hear Larks'
236
Royé, S.
'Si je ne reviens pas' 195
'Stances' 195
S., G.E.D.
'The Kiddies He's Left Behind
Him' 126
Sabiron, G.
'Haï-Kaï' 5, 204, 205
Sackville, M.
'A Song of War' 131
'Nostra Culpa' 125

'Quo vaditis?' 9
'The Pageant of War' 177, 225
Sassoon, S.
'Counter-Attack' 172, 226
'Does it Matter?' 171
'Fight to a Finish' 118
'Glory of Women' 124, 160,
161
'Great Men' 118, 167
'How to Die' 142, 145
'I Stood with the Dead' 210
'Memorial Tablet' 118
'Remorse' 150
'Suicide in Trenches' 173
'The Effect' 118
'The General' 120
'Their Frailty' 124, 220
'They' 118
'Twelve Months After' 225
Schaukal, R.
'An England' 60
'An Japan' 61
Schmidt-Kestner, H.
'Gebet des deutschen
Wehrmanns' 59
Schnack, A.
'In Bereitschaft' 196
'Verdun' 226
Schönlank, B.
'Europa' 119
Schröder, R.A.
'An die deutschen Krieger' 63
'Heilig Vaterland' 33, 36, 57
'Zum 1. August 1914' 57, 64
Seaman, O.
'Dies Irae' 61
'Pro Patria' 55, 70, 75, 131
'The Avengers' 50
Sendelbach, H.
'Trommelfeuer' 209
Shaw-Stewart, P.
'I saw a man this morning' 195
Sichel, W.
'What are You Waiting For? To
the Slackers: A Recruiting
Song' 94
Sigerson, D.
'An Old Proverb' 178
Silvester, J.
'Sound the Alarm' 5
Sitwell, O.
'Armchair' 123
'Rhapsode' 142, 233, 234

'Sheep Song' 111
'The Modern Abraham' 120
Slocombe, G.E.
  'To the War Lords of Europe'
    129
Smalley Sarson, H.
  'The Village, 1915' 188, 192
Snell, V.
  'Les Croix' 82
Sorley, C.
  'All the hills and vales along'
    135
  'Saints have adored the lofty
    soul of you' 152, 195
  'Such, such is Death' 152
  'When you see millions of the
    mouthless dead' 153
Sousa, R. de
  'L'Heure nous tient' 15
Spire, A.
  'Petits Gens' 122
Squire, J.C.
  'Christmas Hymn for
    Lambeth' 112, 126
  'Lord Molasses' 120
  'The Dilemma' 112
  'The Entente' 112
  'The Survival of the Fittest'
    112
  'The Touch of Nature' 112
St. John Adcock, A.
  'The Way of Peace' 128, 132
Stamm, K.
  'Soldat vor dem Gekreuzigten'
    151, 183
Steiger, E.
  'Tsingtau' 61
Stevenson, C.P.
  'Queen of Night: A Mother's
    Reverie' 95
Stolzenberg, W.
  'Gefallene' 210
Stramm, A.
  'Haidekampf' 4, 5
  'Schlachtfeld' 205, 221
Strecker, K.
  'Die Kriegeserklärung
    Englands' 61, 92
Strobl, K.H.
  'Die Heizer' 53
Tech, H.A.F.
  'Das auserwählte Volk' 59
  'Der Krüppel in der

Siegesallee' 139
Texier, L.
  'Aux Morts pour la Patrie' 81
Thanet, L.
  'In Time of War' 219, 220
Thomas, E.
  'Lob' 102
  'This is No Case of Petty Right
    or Wrong' 63, 97
Toller, E.
  'Gang zur Ruhestellung' 139
  'Leichen im Priesterwald' 148
  'Marschlied' 135, 146, 182
Trakl, G.
  'Grodek' 16, 177, 205, 221
  'Im Osten' 16
  'Klage' 16
Trochu, F.
  'O Souffrance' 81
Tuckerman, F.
  'Le Boy Scout' 66
Tynan, K.
  'Flower of Youth' 83
Ulitz, A.
  'Belagerung' 98
  'Gasangriff' 9, 213–4
Unruh, F. v.
  'Reiterlied' 36
Verhaeren, É.
  'Reims' 48
Vesper, W.
  'Aufruf an Deutschland: 6.
    August 1914' 80
  'Liebe oder Haß?' 59
Vildrac, C.
  'Élégie à Henri Doucet' 120
  'Élégie villageoise' 223
Visiak, E.H.
  'The Pacifist' 104, 109, 180
Warncke, P.
  'Ostpreußen' 64
  'Vaterlandslied' 56
Watson, W.
  'The Fourth of August' 57
  'To the German Emperor, after
    the Sack of Louvain' 67, 165,
    167
  'To the Troubler of the World'
    61, 67
Waugh, A.
  'Joy Bells' 123
Weber, A.O.

'Berliner Theaterkunst im
    Kriege' 112
'Das Café Größenwahn zur
    Zivildienstfrage' 112
'Der Verteidigungskrieg' 111
Werfel, F.
  'Die Wortemacher des
    Krieges' 16, 107, 110
  'Krieg' 16, 110, 180
West, A.G.
  'God! How I hate you, you
    young cheerful men' 113, 197
  'The Night Patrol' 148, 172,
    210
Wilkinson, E.F.
  'To 'My People', before the
    'Great Offensive'' 195
Willis, G.

'Any Soldier to His Son' 19,
    107
Wilson, G.H.
  'The Mad Kaiser's Folly' 67
Win[c]kler, J.
  'Den Meistern und Arbeitern
    von Krupp gewidmet' 52
Wisby, R.
  'The Mother's Son' 8
Woodberry, G.E.
  'Sonnets Written in the
    Autumn of 1914, II' 58
Wyseur, M.
  'Les Mortes' 100
Yeats, W.B.
  'Easter 1916' 10
Zangwill, I.
  'The War of the World' 179